WORKING LIFE

WORKING LIFE

Luli Callinicos

Ravan Press  Johannesburg

A People's History of South Africa   Volume Two

1886-1940

Factories, Townships, and Popular Culture on the Rand

For my children
Helene, Thalia, Kimon and Alexia

Published by Ravan Press (Pty) Ltd
P O Box 31134, Braamfontein 2017
in association with the University
of the Witwatersrand History Workshop

First published 1987

ISBN 0 86975 278 2

Design: Ray Carpenter

Typeset by Opus 61 in 10 on 13pt English Times
and 10 on 13pt Stymie Light

Printed by Galvin and Sales Cape Town

Acknowledgements

Like most writers of books, especially history books, I
am indebted to many people. Firstly, I must thank my
colleagues in the History Workshop of the University
of the Witwatersrand for comments and constructive
criticisms of the manuscript. I should like especially to
thank Belinda Bozzoli for her warm encouragement
and interest in the progress of this book. Phil Bonner,
Tim Couzens, Peter Delius, Bernie Fanaroff, Doug
Hindson, Duncan Innes, Charles van Onselen and Eddie
Webster were very helpful with particular sections.
I should like to acknowledge, too, the generosity of
NOVIB and the University of the Witwatersrand's
Richard Ward Foundation, whose grants financed the
writing of this book. A number of departments of the
University were of great assistance to me, in particular
the School of Psychology, the Sociology Department,
Central Graphics, the Africana Library, Government
Publications, and the Church of the Province Library.
    Lastly, I want to thank the many working men and
women to whom I spoke while the book was taking
shape, in particular the Shop Steward Committee in
Katlehong, whose Thursday evening discussions on
workplace, transport and community issues brought
home to me, in a forceful and practical way, the strong
links between the past and present.

Contents

Introduction

'I talk about the past mainly because actually I am interested in the present' – Ngugi wa Thiong'o

In 1986, just a century after the discovery of gold on the Rand, the nature of South Africa's future is in the balance. But the future does not exist in a vacuum – it is being struggled over in the townships, the schools, the mines and factories, on the borders of our country and even beyond. The future therefore exists to a great extent in the present.

Today in South Africa, many groups are seeking to shape our future. These include business and national groupings, both black and white. But among these groups, it is the organised working class that holds the strategic advantage — every major political organisation working for social change, regardless of its strategies and policies, is seriously considering the role of the labour movement in its programme.

This working class did not suddenly appear. It has a history, and we can learn significant lessons from this history. We need to understand the forces that formed the working class through its struggles, its defeats and its victories.

Before the discovery of minerals in the 19th century, the vast majority of people in South Africa were dependent on the land for a living. The large industries of diamonds and gold changed the very nature of work. Today, nearly 10 million South Africans live in the townships, grouped like satellites around the segregated industrial cities. Millions more, living in the rural areas, depend on the wages of migrant workers to survive. Nearly half a million black workers are organised into trade unions.

The world that made the workers

What are the origins of South Africa's working people in the towns? What were the forces that led people to leave the land not so very long ago, and take the journey to the unknown life of wage labour in the towns? How did this steadily growing class of working people live? Through what struggles and processes did they pass to become the decisive human force they are today?

A People's History of South Africa tries to answer these questions. This book, *Working Life* – Volume 2 of the history – should be seen against the background of the mining revolution described in

Gold and Workers (Volume 1). That book showed how South
Africa's pattern of racial capitalism developed out of a mining
industry set in a colonial economy (in which white settlers were able
to seize most of the land and wealth of the country). It showed, too,
how South Africa's first working class was created:

- from deep-level mining on the Rand, which drew into existence a
  vast labour force based on a system of black migrant labour;
- from the pass, contract and compound systems which developed
  to control this labour and keep it cheap;
- as a racially divided working class because mining capitalism was
  able to benefit from South Africa's colonial background.

Volume 2 continues this story. In *Working Life*, we see that to a certain extent the forces that shaped the new industrial society in the
early mining days continued to influence working life in the towns,
attracting working people of all kinds — hawkers, traders, tailors,
market gardeners, flower sellers, washermen and women, brewers, as
well as rural newcomers from the *platteland*, peasants from Europe
and other parts of Africa.

A central theme of this volume is the development of a new form
of capitalism, the manufacturing industry, which began to grow up
alongside the mines and towns on the Rand. With the growth of
industry, the number of wage-earners – the people who work for
others to earn a living – was growing. In the factories, the most
powerful wage-earners in the early years were white skilled workers.
But in this book we begin to see how the nature and composition of
the workers began to change – from skilled to semi-skilled workers,
from men to women, from white to black. And we see, too, the
change in the nature of their organisations.

The World of Working People

Finally, we explore the new way of life which workers created in the
towns. Traditional knowledge gained from the old life in the country
before industrial times was married to the new skills people learned
in town. On this basis they were able to survive, to hope, to resist —
and to organise, in the search for a better life ●

Opposite: Organised workers today: National Union of
Mineworkers members demonstrate at the memorial service
for 177 workers killed in the Kinross mine disaster, September
1986. (Photo: Sandy Smit, Afrapix.)

How this book is written

Each chapter in this book is divided into two sections. The first part, the 'core' of each chapter, gives a general overview. The core section can be recognised by its appearance: it looks exactly the same as the print you are reading now.

The core is followed by a number of supplementary topics. These provide more specific or detailed information to illustrate the general argument of the core section. These supplementary sections can also be recognised by their appearance: they look exactly the same as the print you are reading now.

It is quite possible to read only the core section for a general discussion, or to read one of the 'topic' sections on its own for reference to a particular event. So the core sections and the topics can be used for different purposes. But they also reinforce one another by continual cross-reference throughout the book.

For instance, Chapter 1 makes the following general statement: that there were different reasons for people leaving the land to look for work, and that some left in spite of the opposition of chiefs, heads of households and the older generation. The full meaning of that statement depends on a reading of the topics – *Labour in Settler South Africa, How Mozane became Valentyn, Msilana Refuses, Mma-Pooe's Family: Sharecroppers, Two 'Bywoner' Families, A Message from the Queen of Mabudu,* and *Mduduma: A Migrant Worker's Story.* Furthermore, references to the change to wage labour occur later in the book – thousands of people, new to the towns, continued to arrive throughout the period we are looking at.

The reader should also be able to learn a great deal from the illustrations in this book. 'One picture: a thousand words' is an old Chinese proverb that is even more true in this age of advertisements and television. (Both these mediums have the power to influence us. And in South Africa, both are extensions of the state and capital.) This book includes photographs of ordinary people, which reveal the details and the 'feel' of everyday life – how people were dressed, the streets, the surroundings of their homes and workplaces. These illustrations give us a more vivid idea of working life in the past, and allow us to judge how much our lives have changed.

The structure of this book takes into account the fact that history is a *process* of trying to arrive at a pattern (the core sections try to suggest the pattern which I have found). Yet we must always allow ourselves to be open to the lessons of particular events (such as those found in the topics). And sometimes we must re-examine the pattern of the past that we have constructed. It is important to revise our ideas in the light of all the new or more detailed information, about the past and the present, which is constantly being revealed to us. For it is through this changing knowledge that we can try to gain a greater understanding of our lives, and perhaps even find the means of improving them.

Chapter 1
The Change to Wage Labour

Before 1870, most Africans in southern Africa lived in independent chiefdoms. These existed alongside some small Trekker or Boer Republics and the British colonies of the Cape and Natal.

Less than fifty years later, an industrial revolution had swept up all these little states and chiefdoms into one large state dominated by white capitalists. Few lives were left untouched. Nearly every family, even in the furthest corners of the country, had at least one member working for wages – on the mines, in the towns, or on commercial farms that were developed enough to employ wage labour.

This chapter examines the way most people lived before industrial times. It also contains a number of stories, taken from historical records, to show how in different parts of the country the change to wage labour came about in different ways and at different times.

Migrants at the diamond fields in the 1870s.

Jonas Podumo gets a gun

Jonas Podumo was born in 1830 in the north-eastern Transvaal, in what is now the Elandspruit area.[1] When Jonas was still a child, a major Swazi attack destroyed his parents' kraal. All their cattle were lost. For fear of further attacks, Jonas's parents made the first of many moves. They moved to the Crocodile River area, then to Mabhogo's people (near Roos-Senekal), to Boleu's chiefdom (near Middelburg), and finally to the Pretoria area.

Jonas learnt at an early age, therefore, that land could be taken from the weak by the strong. His contact with Boers in Pretoria taught him the value of firearms and he decided to get a gun of his own as a useful means of defence. When he was nineteen, he left home to find work in the Cape Colony to earn money for a gun.

Jonas found work in the Colesburg area, probably as a farm labourer, for after eight months' work he returned with his wages – three calves and six sheep. He sold one calf and with the money he bought an 'old English soldier's gun'.[2]

With his stock and his gun, Jonas then settled among the Pedi, in what was then one of the strongest chiefdoms in the Transvaal. He stayed there for more than ten years. Jonas's gun made him a useful member of Pedi society. In the 1820s, the Pedi had lost most of

A famous Pedi hunter, Jacob Makoetle.
He became a migrant worker in order to buy a gun.

their cattle during the raids of Zwide and others, and hunting had become very important for survival. In 1839, a visitor noted that the Pedi lived 'chiefly by the chase [hunting], on millet and beans'.[3]

Jonas made a second trip to earn money for a gun.

The journey was long and difficult – it took fifteen days of hard walking to reach the first kraals of Mshweshwe's kingdom, where travellers could fill up their travelling bags with cooked maize before continuing on their way. But on his way home, after many months' labour, Jonas was swindled of R6 (up to three months' wages in those days) in the Orange Free State when he tried to buy a gun from a Koranna.

Christian conversion

This was Podumo's last trip. But migrant labour had changed his life. For one thing his contact with the missionaries led to his conversion to Christianity. The same thing happened to many other Pedi who engaged in migrant labour.

For example, in 1857 two Pedi migrants, Masadi and Mantladi, found a Methodist missionary in Port Elizabeth who taught that:

> While other whites said that the black man was only suited to slave labour ... before God that black man was worth as much as the white, and that there was also a life after death for the black man and a land of joy and splendour.[4]

The two men were later converted. When they returned home to the Transvaal, they introduced Sunday as a day of prayer and religious discussion, and began to convert others to Christianity.

On their long journeys south, hundreds of Pedi migrants would stop at mission stations in Lesotho for food and shelter. Others encountered Christian missionaries at their places of work and even went to live with them. For example, a missionary visiting a mission station on Hospital Hill outside Port Elizabeth in 1895 noted in his diary:

> Kaffirs, Fingu, Basotho, [Pedi] and some Hottentots lived there, some of these lived in kaffir huts and others in small houses. The houses were small with one or two rooms with one window. The Sotho did not seek bigger or better as in the main they would only stay a few years until they had earned sufficient cash and a gun and then would return home.[5]

These positive encounters made many Pedi and other migrants sympathetic to Christianity, and when missionaries first entered the Pedi chiefdom about twenty years after the start of migrancy, they found a number of Pedi already practising Christianity.

For Jonas Podumo, 1861 was the year when his life changed completely. He became converted to the Christian church by German missionaries, who later wrote down his life story in their diaries. Jonas spent the rest of his life as a missionary, attending to the Christians, and so left the life of the chiefdom behind him.[6]

Different chiefdoms in the 1860s

Jonas Podumo is an example of an early migrant worker shortly before the discovery of diamonds and gold in South Africa. At that time, there were a number of chiefdoms in southern Africa. Some stronger, some weaker, they had all been affected by the great wars of the *Difaqane*. These wars scattered thousands of people. New chiefdoms were formed in new places. There was widespread upheaval, dispersal and change. Jonas Podumo's childhood is typical of the insecurity of the time.

The chiefdoms were all different. They differed according to their land and rainfall areas, which influenced whether their people were mainly farmers, hunters, or both. They had different records of victory and defeat in wars over land. They had fought these wars under different systems of military leadership and with different weapons. Some chiefdoms had special access to a skill (such as forging iron tools and weapons) or a commodity (such as ivory) that they could trade profitably. These and many other factors made each chiefdom a special case.

Martinus Sewushane, Chief Sekhukhune's gunsmith. He was converted to Christianity and became a missionary in the Pedi domain.

The chiefdoms also had different settlement patterns. Some, like the Tswana chiefdoms, consisted of towns. Family groups spanning four generations lived in large clusters of houses called wards, or *kgoro*. Close by would be other kgoro housing the generations of other family groups. This settlement pattern suited a dry climate. By living closely together people were able to conserve and organise resources, such as water supplies.

On the other hand, in the richer rainfall areas of the Nguni chiefdoms, families lived further apart in settlements called homesteads or *imizi*. In both homesteads and wards, each family cluster included a cattle kraal and a granary to store food.

An early Tswana town. The large clusters of homes are called *kgoro*.

It is important to note here that these general remarks cannot be true of all chiefdoms. They can only be a rough guide to how most people in chiefdoms lived.

Production

In all the chiefdoms men and women produced most of the things they needed (food, clothing, shelter and trade goods) from the land – through agriculture, stock-keeping or hunting and gathering. Although no one owned the land, each head controlled the portion allotted by the chief to the homestead or ward. The homesteads and the wards were therefore important units of production.

As with all societies before industrial times, more labour was needed because there were fewer tools. There was a sexual division of labour. For example, women's tasks included cultivating the crops, doing some of the home building and decorating, and making most of the household goods like pottery. Men did the heavier building and the clearing of the fields, supervised the care of cattle by young boys, hunted, and went on trading trips.

In the rich rainfall areas of the Nguni chiefdoms, families lived in more scattered homesteads, or *imizi*. Cattle were important to all the chiefdoms.

The importance of cattle

In the chiefdoms of southern Africa, cattle were very important. They produced milk and could provide skins and meat. But they were chiefly valued as a measure of wealth. Like money today, they were a means of exchange. For example, a person who was found guilty in court might have to pay a fine in cattle.

A marriage could not take place without the transfer of goods, often cattle. A young man's family would agree to offer a certain number of cattle to the family of the bride as compensation for losing their daughter – as a young woman, she was an important productive member of her homestead or ward. This transfer in marriage was called *lobola* or *bogadi*. After this was fully paid, the husband could claim the children of the marriage. The Sotho had a saying: 'The children belong to the cattle' – 'Ngoana ke oa likhomo'.

Cattle were therefore a measure of production. The son had worked for the homestead or ward, and often for the chief, too. When he was old enough to marry, he inherited cattle. His new wife was another productive member, and when and if she had children, they too became productive members of the family. Families with many cattle could afford to arrange more marriages – the more wives in a family, the more powerful, productive and wealthy that family could become.

Divisions

The chiefdoms were not without divisions and conflicts.

Firstly, there were differences between the royals (those who had close kinship with the chiefs) and the commoners – the chiefs often controlled the labour of young men, and could extract taxes from the commoners. The royals were wealthier and more powerful than the commoners, and in the Sotho chiefdom, for example, royals could demand high bogadi payments for their princesses. Most chiefs had the power to call up male labour for fighting and hunting, and to decide when a man could get married – the Zulu chief had the most power in this respect, as the story of *Msilana Refuses* on page 26 shows us. There was a certain amount of competition, therefore, over who controlled the labour of the young men – the homestead and ward heads, or the chiefs.

Then there was the power of the head of the homestead or ward, who controlled production of the family and decided what reward sons got for their labour – whether in cattle, sheep or goats. An unmarried man did not usually own valuable property, like cattle. The elders usually exercised strict discipline and control over the juniors – for example in marriage exchanges – and this sometimes resulted in tensions between the different generations.

There were also inequalities within the homesteads or wards between senior and junior sons – that is, children of senior and junior wives – and also between older and younger brothers. The older brothers and senior sons often inherited the wealth set aside in the households of their mothers (even though the mothers themselves did not usually own this wealth).

Conflict also arose between men and women. For example, in most chiefdoms, although women might trade some of their products like pottery for hoes or food, they were not allowed to own the most important means of exchange, cattle. Nor were they permitted to work iron or make iron tools. It was rarely that women became rich in their own right. All her life, a woman was under the official control of men, whether as an unmarried girl, a wife and mother, or an elderly widow.

These divisions influenced the different ways and times in which men and women left the land to seek jobs, and also to some extent what kind of work they did when they got to the industrial towns. An example of how tensions between elders and juniors, and royals and commoners, affected the movement of labour is shown amongst the Tsonga in *A Message from the Queen of Mabudu* on page 32.

Early migrant labour

As the story of Jonas Podumo has shown, migrant labour was already established in certain chiefdoms by the time diamonds and gold were discovered. The Pedi, the Tsonga and the southern Sotho were amongst those already engaged in migrant labour in the 1860s. In fact, the Pedi were already working as far afield as the Cape in the 1840s, and Natal in the 1850s.

Women transporting the harvest.

As Jonas's story shows, migrants were in constant danger of being attacked or robbed. For example, the Transvaal Boers jealously guarded their superiority in guns and horses by trying to prevent Africans from owning them. They would try to disarm groups of migrants passing through the Transvaal. There were many attacks, too, by the men of Chief Mabhogo, who often joined with the Boers of Lydenburg. The two groups would share the spoils.

It was safer, therefore, for migrants to travel in large parties which could repel these attacks. And when the migrants at last returned from their long absence, having survived the dangers of the journey home, the relief and rejoicing were great.

For example, late one evening in May, 1865, a German missionary in the Pedi domain was disturbed by the sounds of gunfire and shouting. The noise proved to be the celebrations of migrants glad to have reached the borders of their chiefdom. The missionary described these migrants in his diary:

> 'The returned migrants bearing themselves proudly passed the mission station; each was wrapped in a long sheepskin cloak which he had earned in the Cape Colony, and carried a gun and a small bag filled with goods. This was all the reward for one or more years' labour. They all wore various forms of headgear, some had red woollen tasselled caps, others felt and straw hats abundantly decorated with ostrich feathers.'[7]

Amongst the Pedi, a migrant labour system was organised by the chief, who sent young men off in regiments to obtain cattle and guns. When the new diamond fields of Kimberley called for more labour, offering higher wages than the settler farmers paid, it was the independent chiefdoms with established patterns of migrancy that sent their young men to become the first black miners.

Migrants returning from the diamond fields.

Colonial labour

But why did migrant labour exist before the discovery of diamonds? To answer this question one needs to understand the patterns of colonial labour in the settler-controlled parts of the country. As described in *Labour in Settler South Africa* on page 23, different types of forced labour developed. There was the out-right slavery of the early Cape Colony. The system of *inboekselings* was little more than child slavery, as shown by the story of *How Mozane Became Valentyn* on page 25. The words 'labour tenancy' describe a system in which dispossessed Africans from the con-quered chiefdoms were forced to work land which had once been their own for the settler farmers who had taken it over.

Colonial labour was transformed by the new form of production that came with the discovery of diamonds and gold and the new political system that

industrial capitalism brought with it. When this happened, many of the colonial forms of unfree labour (including the early pass system) were taken over and changed to suit the labour needs of the new economy.

Wages for taxes

A number of chiefdoms had managed to remain aloof from colonial labour for a long time. In the case of the Zulu people, there was almost no wage labour before the 1878 war. The Zulu economy was firm. Nor did they need to earn wages for guns, because the Zulu continued to fight successfully in the traditional way.

Labour in Settler South Africa describes the settlers' growing need for labour, even before industrial times. In Natal, the British colonists began to clash with the powerful and growing Zulu state, as described in

Msilana Refuses. Eventually the two states went to war. After gaining a memorable victory at Isandlhwana, the Zulu were finally defeated. The British government tried to claim the king's power over the labour of the young men. It imposed a hut tax and then a poll tax. So, although the Zulu did not lose all their land after conquest, taxation forced them onto the labour market.

Taxes were imposed on all chiefdoms in South Africa, as one by one they lost their independence to Boer or British rule. Taxes not only drove more and more people into wage labour. They also separated a young man's wages from his father's control. For example, the poll tax was collected mostly in the labour centres in the towns. And when the young wage-earners came home, many insisted that they control their own wages, showing less respect to their elders. By the early 1930s, an old man was lamenting lost traditions:

> 'Formerly an *umzi* (homestead) was under the thumb of the father, now it is under the thumb of the son. Things are bad now.'[8]

The result was that ties with the homestead were loosened, while the growing capitalist system benefited by a more readily available labour force.

Seasonal labour on the sugar plantations in the early years of this century.

Sharecroppers on borrowed land

There were many people, all over South Africa, who managed to avoid wage labour for an even longer time.

There were peasant farmers in Natal and the eastern Cape who were making a living from the sale of their own products, and did not need to look for outside jobs. Some Thembu, for example – those living in the Queenstown area – were producing wool, hides, horns, tobacco and cattle worth one and a half million rands a year in the 1860s.[9]

A good number who had lost all their land were able to make use of the settler economy itself. For example, Nkgono Mma-Pooe, whose story is told on page 28, was able to stay and work on land claimed by white settlers who were not actually using all of the land themselves. The system of sharecropping meant that though they no longer had their own land, share-croppers still had the *use* of the land.

Sharecropping was described by a white farmer in 1908 in the following way:

> 'Very few of us Boers can afford to keep more than one span of oxen to plough with ... it means too much capital locked up in animals which do

A sharecropper's family, 1916.

not increase. This means that in our extremely short ploughing seasons we cannot bring enough land under cultivation.... The farmer therefore gives one or more of these natives, who own perhaps three span of oxen between them, a certain amount of land to plough. The boy finds the labour and often the seed, and gives the owner of the farm half the crop grown.'[10]

The Pooe family lived in this way. The system was practised by landless whites, too, as the stories of *Two Bywoner Families* show on pages 31 and 32.

Sharecroppers were able to avoid direct wage labour, although life was often hard and never settled. The story of the second bywoner family illustrates how uncertain was the life of sharecropping. The death of the father broke up the family and scattered the children.

All the sharecroppers in our examples moved many times in search of independent working conditions. Nevertheless, a sharecropper was his own master. As one government official expressed it in 1913:

 'When the boy [meaning black man] had his whole piece of ground to sow and be given half of the crops, he was not a servant but a partner – a master.... As soon as you draw the line on your farm and say, "You can sow this land for yourself", he is your servant.'[11]

The land is taken

But there was a growing class of commercial farmers who were doing well enough not to need the services of sharecroppers. These landowners had acquired enough capital to get their own equipment and oxen – they were short only of labour.

'There is a great scarcity of labour in the Free State, and of course the competition with the gold mines is felt', reported a government commission on the Land Act.[12]

Where could they get this labour? As one magistrate suggested as early as 1891:

'The labour question is bound up with the land question. The man who has no land and no trade must work for someone else who has.'[13]

In other words, the only way to get sharecroppers to work for others was to remove the use of the land. In that way they would be forced to turn to wage labour. In 1913, the government passed the Natives' Land Act. The Act prohibited Africans from owning land outside certain reserved areas – those areas like Zululand, the Transkei and Ciskei, and other pockets of land where resistance had once been strongest. Blacks were allowed to remain on white-owned land only if they stayed on as labourers and servants.

Some families who did not accept the change were lucky enough to find other landowners willing to take them. The Pooe family, for example, crossed into the Transvaal and continued to farm for themselves for many more years.

But for both blacks and whites, sharecropping gradually came to an end as commercial farming developed and grew strong enough to swallow up the small producers on the land, turning them into wage labourers, too.

The Land Act Song (R T Caluza)

We are children of Africa
We cry for our land
Zulu, Xhosa, Sotho
Zulu, Xhosa, Sotho unite
We are mad over the Land Act
A terrible law that allows sojourners
To deny us our land
Crying that we the people
Should pay to get our land back
We cry for the children of our fathers
Who roam around the world without a home
Even in the land of their forefathers.

R T Caluza was a music teacher at Ohlange School in Natal from 1909 – see Chapter 3 from D Coplan, *In Township Tonight! South Africa's Black City Music and Theatre* (Ravan Press, 1985), p.73.

Migrant workers outside a Kimberley compound.

The later migrant system

Most Africans, however, still had a little land left,
for the Natives' Land Act worked in two ways. While
it removed the use of land in most places, it also
reserved land for black ownership. (In fact, some
Africans supported the Act, arguing that blacks should
hold on to the little land that was left to them before
whites took that over, too.)[14]

For the South African capitalist system, the land
reserved for blacks was essential to keep migrant
labour going. The homestead remained the base of the
family, while wage-earning took the form of migrating
between the workplace in the industrial areas and the
homestead in the reserves.

We see the first stage in the development of the
migrant labour system in Jonas Podumo's story. At
that time, most migrant workers and their chiefs were
in a position of strength, for the colonies needed their
labour and many chiefdoms were not yet defeated.
Mduduma: A Migrant Worker's Story gives us a
glimpse of how things stood 60 to 80 years later,
between 1920 and 1942. By this time migrant labour
has been established as a system, and during
Mduduma's lifetime we can see further changes in the
system taking place.

In the nineteenth century, migrant workers were
mostly independent enough to *choose* to enter wage
labour on their own terms for a short time when conditions made it necessary. They were able to use their
independence as a weapon to fight low wages. For
example, when the Chamber of Mines dropped the
wages of black miners in 1890-91, thousands of
Mozambicans were able to withdraw their labour by
going home. The mine owners were forced to offer
higher wages in order to get them to return.

We see from *A Message from the Queen of Mabudu*
on page 32, that for others wage labour became an
escape from the divisions in their own society. As the
homestead economy gradually broke down, it lost its
value and meaning, especially for young people.

It was not in the interest of the capitalist system to
smash the homestead economy completely, however. It
was needed to supply the growing mines and industries
with a ready-made, cheap labour force, as later
chapters in this book will show.

Heartless

Mtandizi (local recruiting agency) is not sorry
for taking taking my husband away to work.

(Nyanja folk song. Hugh Tracey record collection AMA
TR-96.)

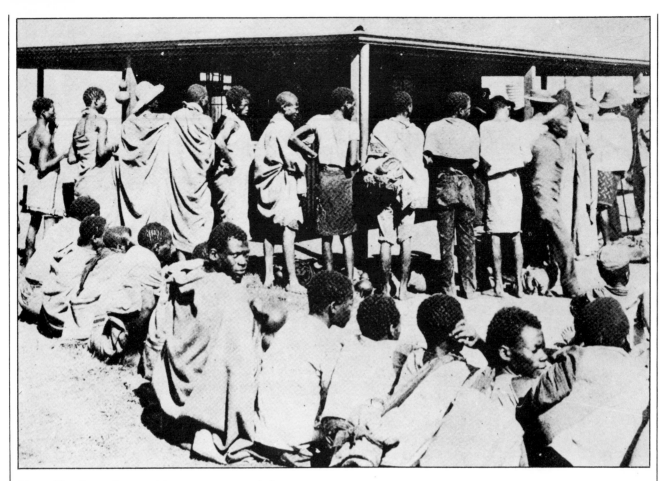

Above: The change to wage labour — young men being recruited for their first job, 1906.

Below: Tswana wives, mothers and daughters wait for their men to return from migrant labour — 1912.

A trading store in the Ciskei in the 1930s.

Traders and missionaries

The presence of traders and missionaries often accelerated the break-down of rural societies and the change to wage labour. Nineteenth-century traders soon realised the profits to be made from Africans, both as suppliers of goods such as ivory, cattle and skins, and as customers for manufactured goods. Gradually many chiefdoms became dependent on trade and began to build their economies on trade — with mixed results.

In 1866, a settler observed that people were 'surrounded' by traders who seemed happy to give easy credit. The result was that often wagons, oxen and cattled had to be sold to repay the traders.[15]

Most missionaries, too, insisted on European dress, at least for church-going. They also encouraged the building of square, stone houses, and introduced the use of tea and sugar.[16]

One British colonial reported in 1896:

'As the Natives came under the influence and teaching of the missionaries, they at once abandoned red clay, and sought to cover themselves with European clothing; and thus, in proportion to the spread of missionary influence, the desire for articles of European manufacture grew and spread, and I think will well satisfy this meeting that to the missionaries we owe the great revenue we now derive from the native trade.'[17]

Bemba Song

The white people have come, father,
They are flying in the sky,
They have made the smelter,
They have made the shaft,
They have brought money,
They have brought clothing,
They have come here for food,
They will never turn back from our country.
They have settled in our country
These settlers of the Copper Belt.

Hugh Tracey record, AMA TR 182.

A Christian wedding in the 1930s.

Let's go home

A he makawasa-kwasa makwasa
Shake hands dear friend
Here is a handkerchief, wipe your sweat away.
Let's go to the station,
I am waiting for him.
He alights from the train of the European.
He comes from town.
Don't you see how he has polished his shoes?
Come to me, come near me, mine
Greetings, mine
Let us go my darling
Let's go home.

Get to the shop
And buy sweets
and buy a handkerchief
Let's go dear friend
Mine, give me sweets
Let us reach home,
Shall we dear friend.

My friend you have caused me to spend
I will show you my money.
We shall marry, shall we not?
Come on home.
Come and pay my lobola.
I shall tell my mother.
Let's go home, my spouse.
Xayisa makwasa.

From *The Music of the Shangana-Tsonga*, Thomas F. Johnstone, Ph.D. thesis, University of the Witwatersrand, 1971, p.153.

A poem about migrant labour

While migrancy to the towns meant escape and new opportunities for some, migrant labour soon lost its glamour for others. The following Mozambican poem compares migrants to stupid cattle, allowing themselves to be used and abused for the benefit of others.

Mamparra m'gaiza*

The cattle are selected
counted, marked
and get on the train, stupid cattle.

In the pen the females stay behind
to breed new cattle.

The train is back from 'migoudini'**
and they come rotten with diseases,
the old cattle of Africa
oh, and they've lost their heads,
these cattle 'm'gaiza'.

Come and see
the sold cattle have lost their heads
my god of my land
the cattle have lost their heads.

Again
the cattle are selected, marked
and the train is ready to take away meek cattle.

Stupid cattle
mine cattle
cattle of
Africa, marked and sold.

Jose Craveirinha

* *mamparra* – stupid; *mgaiza* is a Mozambican expression for a man just returned from the mines, his pockets full of money but his health broken.
** *migoudini* – dialect for the mines.

From *Poems of Black Africa* edited by Wole Soyinka (Secker and Warburg, London, 1975), p.114. Jose Craveirinha was born in 1922 in Maputo (then Lourenco Marques). A journalist and poet, he was an outspoken critic of the colonial regime, and in 1966 was tried and imprisoned as a supporter of FRELIMO.

Conclusion

We have seen how migrant labour became a central feature in the political economy of South Africa. Its beginnings lay in the period before most chiefdoms lost their independence, when migrant labour was shaped by the economic and political conditions in the chiefdoms themselves.

However, as the nineteenth century progressed, there were a number of changes which served to lock these communities into a migrant labour system. The most decisive change was the impact of colonial conquest and the taxation which followed. The discovery of diamonds speeded up colonial conquest. Control over labour sources and mineral-bearing land became a priority for the colonial government. By 1880 few African chiefdoms remained independent.

There were other factors. For example, the destruction of game changed the hunting and trading patterns of many communities, pushing more and more people into migrant labour. Natural disasters such as drought and disease hit hard – especially the cattle diseases of Rinderpest and East Coast Fever, which spread across the countryside between 1896 and 1905.

These factors, alongside mounting pressure on agricultural resources, broke down the economic independence of African societies. By the 1930s, the state itself was concerned about the growing poverty of the reserve areas from which migrants came.[18]

The making of wage-earning workers was not altogether one-sided. Communities were also able to determine how and when they could become workers. As the examples in this chapter show:

- some people fought for their independence to the bitter end;
- some used wage labour to restock their cattle supplies and strengthen the homestead economies;
- some, like the sharecroppers, adapted to the market needs and remained independent for a longer or shorter time;
- others left home and settled in the towns – over the years more and more people left the land, never to return, although many elders and chiefs, and commercial farmers too, opposed black settlement in the towns.

Thus different historical processes, working in different communities, shaped the development of migrancy. The overall result was the creation of a large force of migrant and town-based workers who laboured in the new capitalist economy.

Chapters 2 – 7 will deal with the nature of their work in the Rand towns, and the organisations they developed to challenge their conditions and their place in the system.

Topics

Labour in Settler South Africa

By the 1860s, South Africa had a large settler population – people not of African stock who from 1652 onwards had come from Europe and colonised the Cape.[19]

Slave and Khoikhoi labour

The settlers soon took over land for their own cultivation, so that they could sell supplies to passing ships. But to do this on a large scale they needed labour. As the new commercial farmers were forbidden by the Netherlands East India Company (VOC) to use Khoikhoi labour, they began to import slaves from West Africa and Asia to work for them. For the farmers, slaves were cheap – R12 each – and easier to control than wage workers. They could be maintained from the land they worked, and the owners could also keep the children.

The slaves that were brought to the Cape were mostly political prisoners or convicts, captured from the Company's possessions in the east. Other slaves had been captured in West Africa, Madagascar and Angola. Many of the Malay slaves were skilled artisans – bricklayers, masons, painters, saddlers, carpenters, cabinet-makers, wagon-makers and shoe-makers. Their work was often hired out by the slave masters. Other slaves were put to work in the wheat fields and on the wine farms.

In time, the commercial farmers acquired many Khoikhoi workers, too. Only a few years after the settlers arrived, there were clashes between the Khoikhoi and the settlers, mainly over the use of the land. After a war lasting five years, the Dutch defeated the Khoikhoi in 1677, seized their sheep and cattle, and took the land on the other side of Table Mountain. The Khoikhoi lost more and more land. In the following hundred years, their numbers were cut down from 200 000 to 20 000 by the deadly waves of small pox epidemics brought by passing ships, and also by war and starvation. Those who did not flee to the deserts in the west were forced to offer themselves to the settlers as domestic servants and herders.

East African men and women captured in the 17th and 18th centuries were sold as valuable slave labour, mostly to plantation owners in the north and south Americas.
(A 19th-century depiction, complete with racial stereotypes.)

The spread of colonies

In the years that followed, the settlers spread out, especially along the east coast and into the interior.

By the 1860s, the British had established the two colonies of Natal and the Cape, and Dutch-speaking settlers were struggling to establish a number of small Boer states in the interior. (Strictly speaking, the Boer republics were not colonies, for they were not ruled by a foreign power, but by white 'Africans', or Afrikaners, as some had already begun to call themselves.)

The trekkers had many clashes with the people of African chiefdoms during their trek in search of new land and freedom from British rule. Many of the Africans were still suffering the after-effects of the *difaqane*. This had been a series of wars started by chiefdoms that were growing in power and attempting to centralise large numbers under their control.

The British colonies, too, had been engaged in a number of wars over land and cattle ever since the late eighteenth century. By the 1860s, most of the chiefdoms and settler states were still engaged in struggles over land and power.

Forms of unfree labour

As settlers took over more and more land, they found they needed more labour. The 'apprenticeship' system allowed Boers to keep homeless black children as unpaid 'apprentices' until the age of 25. But often this turned out to be nothing less than slavery, as a number of missionaries, including Livingstone, reported. In 1868 the Transvaal newspaper, *De Republikein*, deplored the fact that 'whole wagon loads' of children were 'continually being hawked around the country'.[20] There were men, both black and white, who had become traders in children, kidnapping them in raids and then selling them to Boers for domestic labour. (See the story of *How Mozane Became Valentyn* on page 25.)

Black families who had lost land to white settlers had nowhere to go, and stayed on the land as labourers for the new owners. There were different labour arrangements. Much of this kind of labour took the form of 'labour tax' — families laboured for their masters and gave them a share of their crops, or they worked part of the year for the land-owners, in return for being allowed to live on the land. *Mma-Pooe's Family: Sharecroppers* is one example of how people managed to survive on land that was not their own.

In Natal, the commercial farmers developed large sugar plantations which supplied the British sweet industry. However, they could not find enough labour to suit their needs. The neighbouring Zulu were not interested in working for wages (*Msilana Refuses* on page 26 shows that the Zulu had not yet lost their

independence). Eventually, the sugar plantation owners imported thousands of workers from India on contract as indentured labourers at ultra-low wages.

A number of different forms of labour had developed, therefore, in the different settler states before the discovery of minerals. Labour was scarce because most people still had access to productive land. But the shortage of labour for the commercial farmers had two results.

On one hand, where their governments were in a strong position over conquered peoples, these farmers were able to develop systems of forced labour. With the help of passes and policemen or soldiers, they were able to break down the economic independence of those who became their labourers.

Migrant labour before industrial times

On the other hand, they also had to make arrangements with the more powerful chiefs who were able to supply them with whole regiments of seasonal labour during the summer months, on favourable terms to the chiefs. So when the diamond and gold mines opened between the 1860s and the 1890s, and were desperate for labour, black farm workers were able to demand similar wages. These compared well with the wages of farm workers in Britain, and were double the wages of Irish workers in England at that time.[21]

Some chiefs were powerful enough to protect the interests of their regiments, and could recall them if they felt that the workers were not getting satisfactory treatment. So in the years before mining capitalism reached the peak of its power, migrant labour was an expensive form of labour for employers, and a bargaining issue for chiefs and migrant workers alike.

Indian indentured labourers came to Natal from 1859 onwards, mainly to work in the sugar industry. It was very difficult to avoid re-indenture once the first contract had been completed, especially after the R6 annual tax was imposed (a major cause of the Natal Indian Strike in 1913). Some indentured workers, like this field hand on a banana plantation, ended up in other sectors of agriculture.

The arrival and spread of settlers and the upheaval of the *difaqane* resulted in war and conquest of land and people, destroying chiefdoms and creating stronger new ones. Out of the turmoil, several forms of forced labour — including slavery, indentured labour and labour tax — developed. In addition, the system of sharecropping developed, as well as migrant or seasonal labour, which was often an arrangement made between chiefs and the settler land-owners.

This, then, is the background to the labour history of South Africa before industrial times. The discovery of minerals — of diamonds, gold and coal — transformed the economy into a capitalist system needing to exploit a massive labour force to extract the wealth of these valuable minerals.

How Mozane Became Valentyn

In the turmoil of the *difaqane* and the Boer trek, there were many tragedies and strange, heart-breaking experiences. The following is a story of the *inboekseling* Mozane, which he related years later to a German missionary named Nachtigal.[22]

Mozane was eight years old when the Boers defeated Dingane in 1839. In the confusion after the war, a number of Zulu women and children fled to the hills. Mozane's mother, Mpindo, was one of these women. They hid for three days in a cave without food.

'Then the followers of Mpande arrived. They sat below the fugitives among the bushes, slaughtered an ox and started to roast the flesh, giving the impression that they had come to assist the refugees. Two of Mpindo's children, Mozane and Nzunzu, were so attracted by the sight and smell of food that they left their hiding place to join them. The warriors were very kind to them and more and more went to join them. Finally, when no more children emerged, the warriors enticed the children further and further away from the hiding place.

Then, suddenly, a group of Boers on horseback appeared nearby, and although the children wanted to flee it was now too late. They were captured and taken to the Boer *laager* where, quaking with fear, they awaited execution. To their great relief they were not killed but were given food.

The children soon realised that each had a Boer as a master and these gave them new names. Mozane . . . was thenceforth called Valentyn. His brother Nzunzu was called Kibit and his sister Lutika was called Kaatjie. Valentyn and Kaatjie belonged to a Boer called Gerrit Schoeman. Eventually they became used to their new masters and their new life and were no longer as upset as they had been when they were seized.'

By a strange twist of fate,

'Valentyn was given over to play with and attend to the young Hermanus Steyn whose father had been murdered by Dingane. The young white Hermanus and the young black Valentyn soon got to know each other and were always together. They caught mice and roasted and ate the birds and locusts which they captured. They raided hives and removed the honey. The one learned from the other, bad as well as good.'

And so Valentyn grew up. When he was about eighteen, he became part of the Boer trek to the Lydenburg district, and worked on the farm of his master close to the town of Ohrigstad. This is not to say that inboekselings never enjoyed a break.

A Boer homestead, a visitor — and a servant.

'When their masters slept, a large number of inboekselings came together to dance and sing. When all was quiet at his master's place Valentyn would take a riding ox from the cattle kraal and would soon be in the middle of the dancing.'

At one of these dances, Valentyn met Lys, an inboekseling herself and the daughter of a freed slave brought from the Cape during the trek. Luckily for the couple, their masters gave them permission to marry, and Lys's master himself performed the marriage ceremony.

But within a few years, Valentyn became restless. It seemed that there would be no end to his life of bondage — although young men were supposed to be freed at the age of twenty-five, many masters openly ignored the law. As Nachtigal observed about inboekselings, 'some appear to remain young forever'. So, in the early 1850s, like hundreds of other inboekselings, Valentyn and his sister escaped. It is possible that the brother and sister wanted to find their father again, since they headed south for Natal. At the Vaal river, they met up with a group of 'Maferi' people, who held them captive and would not let them go further. But eventually they managed to escape. After many troubles and hardships, they met a Boer who knew Valentyn and took him back to his master in Lydenburg. It seems that Valentyn was pleased to return. He had been missing his wife, and his master did not punish him cruelly, as happened to other runaways who were caught and returned.

Also, his unhappy experiences with the 'Maferi' made him throw his lot in with the Boers, and he began to see his own people through the eyes of his masters. Years later, he told Nachtigal that he no longer wished to seek out his father as he had become used 'to the good life of his master and did not wish to return to the uncivilised Kaffirs'. Valentyn's poor opinion of African society deteriorated further when his brother Kibit ran away a few years later, only to be killed amongst the Ndzundza Ndebele.

Not all runaway inboekselings met with tragedy. Some were able to return to their former chiefdoms. Others escaped to the towns or diamond fields, or were adopted by other chiefdoms (for example the Pedi) where they made themselves useful as writers and translators or as experts in the use of Boer weapons.

As for Valentyn, he settled with his family in service to the Boers. By 1865, he was a 'free' man and the owner of a wagon and a team of oxen. By the early 1870s he was put in charge of a farm by the Boer owner and was using part of it to cultivate and sell his own crops.

Msilana Refuses

'In December 1888, ten years after the British invasion of the Zulu kingdom, a Zulu, Msilana, was brought before the Resident Magistrate of the Lower Mfolozi district in the British colony of Zululand. Msilana was the son of a chief. His father was then in hiding, charged with rebellion against Her Majesty's Government. Msilana was accused of refusing to assist a party of Zulu who, in the charge of a court policeman, were on their way to work for the Natal Government Railways.

It was alleged that Msilana had abused and threatened the labourers. [He told them that] by going to work on the railway they had deserted the cause of the Zulu royal house and allied themselves with the [British Colonial] government.'[23]

Many of these young men were having their first taste of wage labour. They were building the railway line from Natal to the Rand, where gold had just been discovered.

'They were recruited by the Zululand officials, gathered into labour gangs and marched to the railway works in the charge of a government *induna*, driving the cattle they needed for their subsistence with them.'[24]

The background

Only ten years before this incident, the people of Zululand belonged to an independent kingdom. In spite of many wars and a growing outside trade, the Zulu economy was not shaken.

Before 1878, the homestead, where the family lived and worked, was still the most important source of production. It was able to produce nearly all the needs of the head of the homestead, his wives and children.

Production for the king

But while the homestead was the basis of production, the king, too, was a necessary part of the system. He reigned over all the chiefs in Zululand and therefore united the chiefdoms into an orderly and powerful kingdom.

The basis of the king's power rested on his army. All the young men from the different chiefdoms in the kingdom gave service to the king as soldiers and workers. As well as going out to war, they tended the king's cattle, tilled his fields and helped keep order in the kingdom.

When they had finished their service (which could take up to twenty years) the king gave them permission to marry. He allocated them land to start their own productive homesteads. The king therefore took the labour of the young men from the homesteads and the different chiefdoms. This labour was used to maintain the system of the Zulu kingdom and keep it powerful.

How the Zulu economy was destroyed

The Zulu kingdom was too powerful for the comfort of its British neighbour, the colony of Natal. It also stood in the way of British plans for a federation of Southern African states under their control.

In 1879 war broke out. The British suffered serious losses, particularly at the battle of Isandhlwana, but eventually defeated the Zulu. Zulu resistance had been strong and the British dared not take away land directly. Nevertheless, the king was removed and the kingdom was divided into thirteen chiefdoms.

A scene from one of the wars of the *difaqane*. The Zulus played an important part in the restructuring of power in the 18th and 19th centuries in Southern Africa.

This act had two serious results:

1. Division

The kingdom lost its unity when the king was removed. The chiefs now owed their position to the British colonial government. Within a few years there was civil war amongst the chiefdoms, growing weakness and attacks from the Transvaal.

By 1887, the British had the excuse to step in and 'sort out the mess'. They handed a district in the north-west to the Transvaal and took over the rest of the country themselves. This became known as British Zululand. In 1897, it became part of Natal.

2. Taxation

Secondly, the British took over the function of the king. While they allowed the homestead system of production to continue, they disbanded the army and used the labour of the young men to pay for the new system.

The way they did this was to demand **hut taxes**. That is, each homestead had to pay tax for every hut in the homestead. The tax had to be collected by the chief and handed over. In 1889, the government no longer accepted cattle as payment – it had to be cash.

The result was what the government wanted – large numbers of young men had to leave to become wage labourers to earn cash for the homestead.

This method worked very well for the British. The taxes brought in up to R100 000 every year. In addition, it made a new labour force available to the growing commercial farms and towns.

At the same time, the homesteads continued to produce. They supported the young men — as well as the rest of the family — until they were ready to join the labour market, with their own labour, and at their own expense.

Breakdown

But gradually the importance of the homesteads began to break down. Men left home for places all over South Africa — as miners, labourers, domestic workers or workers in other service industries in the towns. (Chapter 2 describes the early town lives of Zulu and other workers on the Rand.) They began to serve the needs of the capitalist system more, and their own homesteads less and less.

The head of the homestead, no longer able to control production and labour as before, began to lose his authority over the family. Also, the homesteads were drained by the never-ending need to produce cash for the hut tax, and they came more and more to depend on the cash wages brought home by the new class of people created by the growing capitalist system — wage-earning workers.

Many people failed to return to the homesteads — they remained in the towns as permanent workers. The government income from hut tax declined, especially with rising costs after the Anglo-Boer War.

In 1905, the government decided to impose a new tax, the *poll tax*, on all men not already paying the hut tax — that is, on the young unmarried wage earners. For many, this was the final insult to the system of home production. As one old man said bitterly:

> 'although a man had a son who by rights ought to work for him, the son was obliged, on account of this tax, to go and work for himself'.[25]

In 1906, Chief Bambatha called for an uprising to resist the tax system. Hundreds of Zulu-speaking workers left the towns to join the rebellion. The rebellion was crushed later the same year.

The destruction of the Zulu Economy

The destruction of the king destroyed the Zulu army and its system of order. More important, the British broke the Zulu economy by removing the productive labour of the young men — those very people it claimed to be freeing from the 'tyranny' of the king.

Very rapidly, the Zulu people became more and more dependent on cash wages and the migrant labour system. By 1897, when rinderpest, following drought, epidemics and plague, killed off most of the cattle, the homesteads were too weak to recover without outside help. They were no longer able to help one another in times of hardship, because the colonial government demanded its taxes year in and year out, without regard for the economic well-being of the homesteads.

In the year of the great cattle disaster, magistrates were pitilessly ordered to:

> 'remind all the Chiefs . . . of the necessity for preparing their people to pay the Hut Tax next year by encouraging the young men to go out to work.'[26]

Thus, although the Zulu did not lose their land, they lost their independence, and their economy was destroyed. It is this tragic outcome which Msilana saw so clearly, and which he so bitterly opposed.

British officials collect poll and dog taxes from Zulu chieftains, 1906.

Mma-Pooe's Family: Sharecroppers

The following is the family history of a sharecropper as she told it to an interviewer in 1979, when she was nearly 100 years old. As a mark of respect for her age, she was commonly addressed as 'Nkgono' which means 'grandmother' in Sotho.

The ancestors of Nkgono Mma-Pooe settled in the area north of the Orange River (now the Orange Free State) nearly 200 years ago, before the *difaqane* and the coming of Mzilikazi. Mrs Pooe was born Emelia Mahlodi wa Molefe-wa-Motsisi, of Phuting-Kwena origin. Her husband, from the Pooe clan, was descended from the Ngwato-Kwena.

During the *difaqane*, both the Pooe and the Molefe clans fled from what is now the western Transvaal and the Orange Free State highveld. They put themselves under the protection of Moshoeshoe, and settled around the slopes of the Lesotho mountains. They became part of the new Sotho nation, dropping their Ngwato-Kwena origin.

Mma-Pooe remembers old people telling of the hard times of the **difaqane** – how they depended on hunting to survive; and how children who were born after their people found safety were called 'maja-kgomo-a-basimane-le-a-banana' – people who had returned to meat-eating after the starvation of the **difaqane**.

After a few years, when things had settled a little, Nkgono Mma-Pooe's grandparents moved down into the Caledon River valley, growing crops and trying to build up their numbers of cattle. Nkgono Mma-Pooe's parents were born in the 1850s and 1860s, during the wars between the Sotho and the trekkers. The Molefe family moved in and out of Lesotho a number of times because of these wars.

By 1882, when Mma-Pooe was born, the Sotho had lost the land on one side of the Caledon River. Her parents were living on a farm south of Heilbron that was then claimed by a Boer. The family moved many times in search of a secure place to live. In 1897, at the time of the rinderpest plague, the family again moved to another farm near Heilbron. It was here that Mrs Pooe's father started sharecropping. Nkgono Mma-Pooe described what happened:

> 'My father had cattle . . . I still remember precisely the period when the disease was rampaging through the area. We would wake up in the morning to find some of our oxen had fallen headlong and stone dead in the kraal manure.
>
> . . . We trekked in February and went up to Zaaiplaas [a farm] to join my uncle who was already staying there.
>
> . . . It's here where my father started sharecropping. His eldest brother, Rankwe, remained, though. He argued that he wouldn't go to settle on a farm where he could work so hard to cultivate the lands to produce a lot of crops that he would have to share . . . "to share your full harvest with a boer!" That he wouldn't do.'[27]

Mrs Pooe's father proved to be a successful farmer. Mrs Pooe remembered clearly the first sharecropping ceremony – half of her father's product went to the farmer, and he was left with 45 bags of maize.

But skilful farming was not always enough. The first season was followed by a great drought and then locusts which ate up the remaining corn. Mma-Pooe and her mother went to stay with Mrs Molefe's younger sister near Heidelberg where they helped to harvest the corn. At the end of the season, they were able to take ten bags of sorghum.

Then the Anglo-Boer War broke out. One day, black soldiers working for the British (**spijoene**) arrived and drove off all their cattle, fowls and pigs. They set the huts and corn on fire and sent the family (except the father, who joined the army) to an army camp near

A sharecropper, 1916. After the 1913 Land Act, the growth of commercial farming created a demand for more land and labour. Sharecroppers found it harder to remain independent. Many succumbed to labour tenancy, or left for the towns.

Vredefort. There they met people from all over the Orange Free State. The camp, said Mrs Pooe, was her first taste of 'location life'.

After the war, the owner of Zaaiplaas came to find Mrs Pooe's father. He asked him to return as a sharecropper. But now the terms were different – because Mr Molefe had lost his oxen and all his ploughing equipment during the war, the land-owner would provide these. In return, he demanded two-thirds of the harvest. Her father had no choice but to accept the new conditions. At the sharecropping ceremony, 'We watched tens and tens of bags of maize and sorghum going to the side of the Boer.'[28]

In 1906 Mrs Pooe (then Miss Molefe) married Naphtali Pooe, who lived on a farm near Parys. The young couple began married life as sharecroppers in Driefontein. But it was too crowded there, so they moved after a while to another farm, where Naphtali's brother was a sharecropper. There, with the two brothers' savings and through sharecropping, they acquired a full span of oxen, some horses and a horse cart, a plough and some other farming tools.

Sharecropping was hard work. One had to plough properly, which was a hard task, and select good seed. The field had to be perfectly hoed, and the crop harvested and threshed before the winter rains. Hoeing, harvesting and threshing could not be done alone. They needed strong work parties. For each work party, a sheep would be slaughtered and food and drink served. A sharecropper had to be able to afford the expense of work parties.

A sharecropper therefore needed the following: farming skill; oxen, a plough and other equipment; and capital with which to reward his labourers.

Naphtali continued to do well at that farm until 1913, when they were forced to move. The landlord wanted Naphtali to sell some of his cattle, Naphtali refused, and the family left.

However the Natives' Land Act had been passed. It was difficult to find a place to stay. Naphtali joined the many wanderers who were looking for a new home as a result of the Act.

'Oh! As if all the Boers had all formed a conspiracy whereby they vowed never to take any black man on sharecropping terms. They went for many long days using bicycles for travelling on some occasions and horses on others . . . .

Ultimately my husband found a place called Orbietjiesfontein on the northern bank of the Vaal River (in the Transvaal).'[29]

They remained in the area for many years. There were three other sharecroppers, one of them a *bywoner* – a landless white sharecropper. (See page 31 for more information on landless whites.) There was strong competition amongst the sharecroppers as to who could produce the most:

'We beat the *bywoner* by far.'
'How did you do that?'
'With us blacks, I could go out into the fields with my husband and perhaps with my children if they were already old enough. With the Boers as *bywoners* it was different. Normally their wives wouldn't go out into the fields to hoe. The husband would have to do the hoeing alone. Or sometimes he would take out money to pay for whomever he could hire. With us we would hoe together with Naphtali or organise a work-party. In fact, our competition with the *bywoner* was appreciated by Theuns [the land-owner] himself. Theuns would remark that he had at last got the real '*Vrystaat mense*' [Free State people] – people who are used to work and did do proper farming wherever they came from.'

The homestead of a black farmer.

The family continued to farm successfully in this way for many years. In 1935, when the landowner died, his widow appointed Naphtali as general overseer, and allowed him to continue his sharecropping. But in 1939, after white farmers objected to Naphtali's doing two jobs, he sharecropped for the last time. He kept his job as a foreman on the farm and was given only three acres of ploughing for his own family to use.

By that time the four eldest Pooe sons had already left home to work as labourers in Johannesburg. There was no longer any future in sharecropping. Commercial farmers had developed enough capital to purchase modern mechanical equipment. They no longer needed to share profits with those who worked 'on the halves'.

Reaping mealies in a 'half-share' field.

Two Bywoner Families

The following are two stories of 'bywoners' – white, sharecropper families – who turned to wage labour. They told their stories to an investigation into the problems of poor white people in the 1920s.[30]

Story 1

Mr A was born in the 1860s. His grandfather had a farm, but his father had no land. As a child he helped his father to rear sheep on a hired farm near his grandfather's.

By the time Mr A married, he had earned many sheep. His wife also brought sheep with her into the marriage. Between them, they had 100 sheep. Then the Anglo-Boer War came, and the family lost all their stock – we do not know exactly how.

After the war, Mr A became a bywoner. He worked for Mr O for three years. He was given a free house and allowed to graze twelve cattle. He had to provide a team of oxen and a plough as well as half of the seed. He then received half the harvest he produced.

In the first year of sharecropping, Mr A received very little. The second year was better – 100 bags, each worth R2. In the third year the crops were just enough to provide bread for the family.

He then moved to Mr C's farm. There he was given some ploughland for his family. In return he had to tend the landowner's sheep and cattle. The family lived on that farm for seven years.

'It was just about your bread and a little more', said Mr A.

By then Mr and Mrs A had eight daughters and no sons. The children helped with the ploughing and other farm work. But the school was too far away and the family moved to another farm, owned by an Englishman. There he received R6 a month and two sheep or goats for slaughtering, some ploughland for his family, and enough grazing for eight cattle. He stayed there for two years, then moved to a farm in another district, nearer to a school for the children. There he worked for six years on the same terms. They were very happy on this farm, but when the landowner died the family had to leave.

Mr A decided to give up farm work and found a job in a small town. His daughters grew up and married steady husbands, who also worked in the towns.

Story 2

Mr V was born in 1885. His father did not have his own land but owned cattle and sheep. With his animals, he would trek in search of grazing, whenever he could hire land.

Mr V had a hard life. His mother died when he was eleven years old, and he had to mind sheep in the veld all day, while his sisters went to the farm school. In the evenings, they taught him to read and write a little.

By the time Mr V was old enough to marry, he had earned 26 sheep. He married a woman who had also looked after sheep all her life. She brought 30 sheep into the marriage.

The young couple worked on Mr V's uncle's farm. They had a small, three-roomed house and were allowed to water their sheep. If the dam dried up, they moved to some grazing ground and lived in a tent. As soon as the rains came, they would pack up and return home.

When it was time for Mrs V's first child to be born, they moved to a farm near a village. Mr V found work on Mr S's farm, putting up fencing. This job ended when the First World War broke out.

A *bywoner* family.

Next, they found work on Mrs V's brother's farm. He was a shepherd, and was allowed to water his own sheep there. They lived in a room in her brother's house, but she did her cooking outside. They stayed on that farm until Mr V had 500 sheep. But then, in 1916, there was a long drought and only 20 sheep survived. They were forced to trek to the Knysna district. There he was offered work on a farm clearing forest ground. In return, he could keep all the produce from this land for two years. After that, they had to share the crops.

They were happy in Knysna and prospered. After three years Mr V went to Riversdale and bought eight oxen. Not long after he had a span of 16.

Then a dealer in wood offered him a job on good terms. Mr V sold his oxen for a good price and drew R70 from the bank to buy equipment and pay for labour. Mr and Mrs V also built a neat little house for themselves on part of the cleared ground. He cut the wood, and she trod the clay and plastered the walls. The roof was made of rushes (grass).

They had a good season, and they got all their money back. It was a good time. There was always enough for the family to eat — vegetables, milk and eggs.

Suddenly the husband fell ill. He was taken to hospital and died. Mrs V could not work on her own. She found a job taking care of a sick woman. Her children were either adopted by other families, or put into an orphanage in town.

A Message from the Queen of Mabudu

'The queen is very much indebted to the Natal Government for the licence granted to her subjects to enter, pass through or work in Natal without interference or being bound (on contract) for three years . . . however at the same time she would be pleased to know that the said government made it compulsory for her subjects to return home after two or three years' service in Natal as so many of them forsake their homes, wives and children and never return.'[31]

During the 1880s and 1890s more than a third of the migrants who had come to work in South Africa from Mozambique settled permanently in South Africa.[32] What was the reason for this high loss of productive men?

The background

The answer lies partly in the conditions of the chiefdoms in the Delagoa Bay area. Most of the area had become greatly weakened through natural disasters and war. In the early 1860s, war and drought wiped out the cattle in the area, and lobola came to be measured in goods brought in from the outside. At first it was iron hoes, imported from the Venda. But

The surface works of a Rand mine. By the early part of this century up to half of Mozambique's wage earners were working in South Africa, many on the gold mines.

more and more, the value of lobola took on a cash form.

During the 1870s, the Mpfumo brideprice was fixed at R16.[33] More and more young men entered the wage labour market to earn cash for lobola. At first they moved to nearby areas. For example, a group of young men might find work on the Nkomati railway, where they could earn R1,20 a week. Then they would most likely move to the Barberton gold diggings, where the wages were higher at R1,80 a week. Barberton was the stopping place before people moved on to the Rand. Others made their way to the labour markets of Kimberley or the Cape railways and docks.

By the late 1880s, more than half the working men of Mozambique were in South Africa.[34]

'And never return'

But why did these workers not return to their homes? As we have seen, most of the area had become poorer and was relying heavily on wage labour, even for lobola itself. Furthermore, the tsetse fly was a constant plague, making it difficult to return to a cattle system of lobola, which might have strengthened the homestead economy again.

But there was also inequality within the society itself. For younger brothers, especially, the chances of becoming a household head — an *umnumzane* — soon after marriage were not high, because they could not inherit their fathers' wealth. They had to submit themselves and their families to the control of their elder brothers after their fathers died, until they had enough wealth of their own to break away.

The *abanumzane* who had been eldest sons had got their wealth at an earlier age. They also had important privileges. They controlled production through the wives, the tools and the land, and also acted as magistrates for the chief. They could levy fines and taxes on behalf of the chief, and could demand presents. They often received cash payments from labour recruiters. The abanumzane also fixed the bride price. By 1890, lobola had risen to R30 to R40 in the Delagoa Bay area.

When migrant workers returned home, they generally had to pay a tax of R2 to the chief and at least 20 cents to the umnumzane.

Migrant workers were exploited twice over — once as low-paid workers in the mines and towns, and again as taxpayers and men trying to earn wealth for lobola.

Song of the Herd Boy

We just take care of the cattle,
But they belong to other people.
The one who cooks does not eat the food.

(Hugh Tracey Collection, AMA TR-77.)

The appeal of the towns

Young men came to regard the towns with desire, as dangerous and exciting places. There, young people could earn money and be free of the restrictions of the elders.

By the 1890s, people were noticing an increasing lack of respect for the abanumzane. Young men returning from the towns were refusing to perform certain tasks for the chiefs and the elders. Manhood and initiation came to be measured according to experience gained in the towns, especially after the chiefdoms lost their military power.

> 'After a period of service on the mines, young men were treated with new respect as *m'gaiza*, those who have returned from the mines and are a source of wealth. Red coats, smoking-jackets, hats and trousers bought on the mines were symbols of their new status. Men who remained at home and refused to work on the mines were looked down on as *mamparras*, narrow-minded and ignorant provincials.'[35]

In these early years, therefore, many of these migrant workers felt that the only way to escape stagnation at home was to leave for ever and join the working class in the towns.

A lone migrant from Mozambique, 1909.

Mduduma: A Migrant Worker's Story

'I ran away from school during the East Coast Fever [a cattle disease] and am illiterate. I was married before I went to the mines [about 1920]. Joyi [his father's eldest brother] paid the bridewealth, seven heads in one day. That was not the end: I paid twelve head for the first and nine for the second, whose bridewealth I paid myself.

Things were hard so I went to the compounds. We did not have [drilling] machines at first but after getting them the money was better. That is how I got enough money to build a kraal, and that got me my second wife.

I went twelve times and finished before I was old [about 1942]. I had a second wife when I finished. I bought cattle, cattle. They were cheap. Clothes were cheap. When I was putting up my kraal I got some cattle belonging to my late father. I bought a plough, I had six oxen for it and there were more, too. I also had enough milk.'[36]

Like other Mpondo men, Mduduma used the migrant labour system to benefit the homestead. The Mpondo had a tradition of wage labouring in exchange for cattle. Cattle helped to support the homestead economy, and the Mpondo still had enough fertile land. They were skilful farmers and their crops grew well.

Yet, there had been changes. By the time of Mduduma the position of the Mpondo was not as strong as it had been. Mduduma leaves home as a young man but he is **already married**. Earlier, migrant workers had been the young, unmarried men. Mduduma comes and goes many times. He does so because 'things were hard' and also to earn money for lobola.

The story of Mduduma shows that, by the 1920s, the head of the homestead could be a migrant worker. In the 50 or 60 years since the discovery of diamonds (when migrant labour began on a large scale) the homestead economy itself had become part of the migrant labour system. The homestead could no longer survive without it.

The homecoming. A migrant returns with gifts for his family.

Notes

1) I am grateful to Dr Peter Delius for the details of Jonas Podumo's story, which is related in the Berlin Mission records of 1867.

2) Cited by P Delius, *The Land Belongs To Us* (Ravan Press, Johannesburg, 1983), p.64.

3) P Delius, 'Migrant labour and the Pedi', in eds. Marks and Atmore, *Economy and Society in Pre-industrial South Africa* (Longman, London, 1980), p.301.

4) Cited by P Delius, *The Land Belongs to Us*, p.111.

5) Cited by P Delius, as above, p.110.

6) In later years, Podumo played a central role in the conversion of a man condemned to death in Swaziland — see P Delius, *The Conversion* (Ravan Press, Johannesburg, 1983).

7) Cited in P Delius, *The Land Belongs To Us*, p.65.

8) Monica Hunter, *Reaction to Conquest* (OUP, London, 1980), p.60.

9) S Van der Horst, *Native Labour in South Africa* ((Juta and Co., Cape Town, 1942), p.27.

10) Cited by T Keegan, 'The sharecropping economy' in eds. Marks and Rathbone, *Industrialisation and Social Change in South Africa*, p.199.

11) Cited by T Keegan, as above, p.206.

12) Report of the Natives Land Commission UG-'16, p.31.

13) Cited by Marian Lacey, *Working for Boroko* (Ravan Press, Johannesburg, 1981), p.121.

14) See, for example, William Beinart, *The Political Economy of Pondoland* (Ravan Press, Johannesburg, 1982), p.123.

15) Van der Horst, as above, p.19.

16) Van der Horst, as above, p.20.

17) Van der Horst, as above, p.20.

18) For example, the Report of the Native Economic Commission 1930-32, UG 22-32, and the Report of the Farms Labour Committee, 1937-39.

19) A colony is a land or country that is controlled economically and politically by a foreign power.

20) Van der Horst, as above, p.29.

21) Patrick Harries, 'Kinship, ideology and the nature of pre-colonial labour migration from the Delagoa Bay hinterland to South Africa up to 1895' in eds. Marks and Rathbone, as above, p.154.

22) The story is told in Chapter 6 of P Delius's book, *The Land Belongs to Us* and is translated from Nachtigal's diary by Dr Delius.

23) Jeff Guy, 'The destruction and reconstruction of Zulu society' in eds. Marks and Rathbone, *Industrialisation and Social Change in South Africa*, p.167.

24) J Guy, as above, p.177.

25) J Guy, as above, p.190.

26) J Guy, as above, p.184.

27) Ted Matsetela, 'The life story of Nkgono Mma Pooe' in eds. Marks and Rathbone, as above, p.217.

28) T Matsetela, as above, p.218.

29) T Matsetela, as above, p.221.

30) These case studies are taken from the 'Report of the Carnegie Commission of Investigation on the poor white question in South Africa', Part V: 'Sociological Report' by J R Albertyn and M E Rothman (Pro Ecclesia Drukkery, Stellenbosch, 1932).

31) Cited by Patrick Harries, as above, p.154.

32) P. Harries, as above, p.154.

33) P Harries, as above, p.152.

34) P Harries, as above, p.154.

35) P Harries, as above, pp.157-58.

36) William Beinart, as above, p.98.

Chapter 2
The Early Years

Chapter 1 has described some of the different ways in which people lost the use of the land and entered wage labour. This happened over a number of years. Natural disasters such as drought, cattle disease and locusts played a part in the process. But the decisive push came from wars of conquest and the taxes and laws imposed by the government when the independent chiefdoms had been defeated.

The discovery of gold on the Rand in 1886 speeded up the breakdown of the old, land-based economy. The new industry expanded rapidly – it moved from outcrop to deep-level mining within ten years – and demanded a massive labour force.

This chapter describes the economy of the early Rand, and examines the working lives of some of the people who came there hoping to earn a living, either independently or as wage labourers.

The birth of the Rand towns

Within a few years of the first outcrop gold mine on the Rand, a most remarkable change took place. Out of the veld emerged mine shafts, tents, shacks and rough tracks. Then came the market square, noisy with traders, farmers, peddlers and transport riders. Their customers needed mining supplies of all kinds, and goods to sustain the life of this growing camp on the veld. Around the square, dusty streets were measured out, and plots were sold for shops, banks, offices, bars and eating houses.

Within twenty years, a string of solid mining towns marked out the gold-bearing Reef, running some 60 kilometres from Springs in the east to Krugersdorp in the west. During that time, thousands of people were attracted to the Rand. Some of them came eagerly, most out of necessity. In Johannesburg alone, there were over 100 000 people by 1899 and nearly a quarter of a million black miners in compounds away from the towns, next to the mines. (The conditions of their existence there are described in detail in *Gold and Workers*.)

As the city grew, it created new needs and jobs for people who could supply these needs. Houses had to be built, food had to be grown and transported, water had to be supplied. Shops were needed to sell food, clothes and everyday requirements.

The growth of the Rand economy

The Rand came into being because the mines were there. Their needs came first. They needed labour; machines and supplies; transport; banks and postal services – and all these things supplied the *infrastructure* needed for an industrial city. *The Economy of the Rand* on page 48 gives the background to the power and influence of the mining companies.

Then, out of the needs of the mines, another form of capital developed. 'South Africa's "merchant princes"' on page 50 describes how big trading businesses flourished under the wing of mining capital.

These were the two main forms of capital in the early years of the Rand – mining capital and merchant capital. The manufacturing industry hardly existed – as 'Manufacturing for the mines' shows on page 50, most factories were really craft industries serving the needs of the mines as repair shops; otherwise they produced simple consumer goods, and were unable to develop because the interests of merchant capital blocked them.

However, the Rand was growing so rapidly that there were many ways of earning a living, even for those who arrived with empty pockets.

Indian hawkers in Johannesburg's first market.

Newmarket square, where farmers auctioned animals
and produce.

Commissioner Street in the late 1890s. With the rapid
development of Johannesburg came the urgent need for
transport — horse-drawn trams to carry passengers from the
residential areas to work, and carts to deliver produce and
goods to the business centre.

Newcomers

Many of the newcomers to the Rand had never lived in towns before. For instance, most blacks and Afrikaners came to the Rand because they had lost land which had been their only means of production.

Some brought with them the traditional skills of peasant farmers, as described in *The Rand's Early Afrikaner Workers* on page 51. Many new arrivals from the land, both black and white, were able to make an independent living in transport as ricksha runners, transport riders or cab drivers. Others worked the clay to produce and sell bricks for the constant building taking place in the fast-growing towns; or they washed clothes in the rivers for a fee, as described in *The 'Amawasha' Laundry Service* on page 53.

Other newcomers had some experience of town life – among them Jews, Germans, Greeks, the British and other Europeans, as well as Indians from India or Natal. These people provided supplies through trade, either as travelling hawkers or as small shopkeepers. By 1899 Johannesburg had a population of over 100 000. About half were blacks – Africans from all over southern Africa (with nearly 29 000 mine workers in the compounds), 'coloureds' and 'Asians'. Of the fifty thousand whites, only only about 6 000 had lived in the Transvaal before the discovery of gold on the Rand. The rest were newcomers (*uitlanders*) from near and far – some from the Cape and Natal; as many from Britain; about 3 000 Jews from Russia and Poland; 2 000 Germans; a few hundred each of Australians, Hollanders, Americans and French, and a sprinkling from other European countries. Typically, these immigrant communities established organisations for mutual support. The Greeks (page 42) will serve as an example.

Early Johannesburg's flower sellers, many originally from Cape Town and Natal.

Packing butter in a dairy. Many young working girls were Jewish immigrants from Eastern Europe, or *platteland* Afrikaners whose families were losing the struggle to survive on the land.

Young migrants on the long walk to the Rand, led by the employee of a recruiting agency, 1905.

A cane seller — one of the thousands of travelling salesmen and hawkers who hoped to make an independent living on the Rand.

A policeman, 1903.

Two tailors pose in their doorway with the local children. If newcomers could make commodities which people would buy, they had a better chance of succeeding in the towns.

A British immigrant dreams of home, plum pudding and a 'White Christmas' in the snow.

A seamstress, 1909.

Women and children, 1903. Johannesburg's census of that year found that 1 131 women and 1 280 children out of a total of 5 125 were living in the African 'location'. Johannesburg thus had an early permanent black population.

Johannesburg's Greek community on their way to a picnic to celebrate the New Year festival, 5 January, 1905.

A typical immigrant community

In 1950 there were some 330 'economically active' Greeks in the Transvaal. While a few were artisans – tailors, cabinet makers, blacksmiths and shoe makers – most were trading as general dealers, fruiterers, bakers and confectioners, tobacconists, bottle-store owners and, more familiarly, tea room or restaurant owners. There were fifty-one shop assistants. (There were only 20 to 30 women.)

Another 120 Greeks on the Rand were miners who were recruited from the ranks of the unemployed, or who came as experienced miners from the Belgian Congo. They worked as blasters, drillers, pumpmen and stoppers. Most were living in overcrowded, squalid rooms in Ferreirastown, Fordsburg and Vrededorp. In 1902 they formed their own Greek Miners' Association, because the Transvaal Miners' Association was hostile to unqualified immigrants who might undercut their own wages. Greek miners earned high wages – up to R60 a month with overtime – and were considered to be 'highly efficient'. Many were involved in the labour activities of the times – for example, Greeks were prominent in the May Day parade of 1904. But by 1924, Greek miners had disappeared – all but one had died of miners' phthisis.[1]

Service industries

Many newcomers were able to make an independent living by offering much-needed services in new towns which had not yet developed service industries on a large scale.

Domestic services were among the most important in those early Rand days. This was mainly because the mining towns had so few women living in them at first, and women have traditionally provided the services needed by men.

Working people needed to be maintained. Their food had to be prepared, clothes washed and mended, their dwelling places kept clean, so that they were ready and able to present themselves in a fit state at the start of a working shift.

In the early 'bachelor' days of the Rand, these services were missing, so they soon became *commodities* that people had to buy. For example, men had to pay others to do their cooking, cleaning and washing. Many were even prepared to pay prostitutes for sexual services.

So while most people on the Rand worked in the mines, there was a growing number of people who earned a living by selling services.

A horse-drawn tram makes its way to the fashionable suburb of Doornfontein. To the right is a cab, a means of livelihood for those who could afford to invest in a horse and cart.

An African in his 'houseboy' uniform. In a letter to *The Star* in 1911 a reader wrote: 'No native should be allowed to wear ordinary European dress during working hours, and employers should combine to this end. European dress gives him an inflated sense of importance and equality.'

A milkman on his delivery round.

Wage labour

As the towns developed further, however, many of the small independent concerns were crushed. Capitalism had attracted most of these people to the towns, but growing technology and expanding investments in service businesses crushed the small-scale efforts of the self-employed to earn an independent living. The brickmakers, the transport riders, the washermen and women, and many of the small traders were swallowed up by larger firms which had the capital to invest in technology (such as washing machines, which speeded up production; or vans and buses, which transported goods and people more efficiently and quickly).

So capitalist expansion, plus a number of other factors, such as drought and racial segregation in the towns, worked against the self-employed. People lost their new-found independence. No longer able to continue as producers, they were forced into wage labour.

Wage labourers

The great majority of people went straight into wage labour. Most blacks had made the long and dangerous trek to the Rand to be hired as low-paid labourers. They went into the building trade as diggers, shovellers and carriers of heavy goods. They delivered goods and undertook other kinds of manual work in the commercial firms. Or they went into domestic service, as described in *Early Domestic Workers* on page 56. Often, their aim was to make a certain amount of money for a specific reason, and then to go home again.

The unskilled whites who came to town found it more difficult to get jobs as labourers. Labouring jobs in the mines were closed to them, because the mine owners had worked out a system of cheap black labour based on the contract, the compound and the pass system, as described in *Gold and Workers*. Nor were they able to find work as semi-skilled workers, because the craft unions of the (mainly) British workers kept them out. And on the farms, as we saw in the last chapter, the small *bywoners* were edged off the land by commercial farming, which preferred the much cheaper labour of blacks.

As opportunities for self-employment declined, unskilled whites were trapped by the racism that had been developing in South Africa since early colonial times – fresh from the land, they lacked industrial skills, but because they were white, they could not be employed as ordinary labourers. The result was large-scale unemployment of whites, and poverty.

Help for whites

However, the suffering of the white unemployed did get some attention. It was pointed out that many of them had lost all ties with the land. They had come to the towns with their families, and were therefore totally dependent on wage labour. Furthermore, they could not be completely ignored by the political parties, because they were whites and they had the vote.

The government and some municipalities tried to help by setting aside labouring jobs on the railways and the roads for whites only, but during the depression which came after the Anglo-Boer War, thousands still remained unemployed.

As it happened, these unemployed whites had another use – they served as 'reserves of white labour', and were used in a time of emergency a few years later during the white miners' strike in 1907. After expressing an unwillingness to 'scab', hundreds of unemployed whites were persuaded to fill the jobs of the strikers. They safeguarded themselves by insisting on two-year contracts. After the strike was over, these new miners were kept on and were gradually trained to perform semi-skilled as well as supervisory jobs. With further strikes in later years, the mines employed more Afrikaners, but thousands continued to remain unskilled, unemployed and desperately poor.

In later years, the different governments of South Africa passed a series of laws protecting jobs for whites only. (See Chapters 5 and 6 for a further discussion of government policy on white labour).

Craft workers

Another important group of wage-earning workers who arrived on the Rand were the craft workers. They were trained in a particular craft (or skill) and had years of experience in industry.

Few South Africans had industrial skills at that early stage, so craft workers were imported from industrialised countries like Britain and other parts of Europe, the United States of America and Australia. In those countries they had served five to seven years of apprenticeship, learning their crafts as electricians, fitters and turners, moulders, pattern-makers and plumbers.

Craft workers held a strong position in South Africa.

Firstly, their skills were scarce and valuable, particularly to the gold mines, for deep-level mining required the cooperation of many skills. In later years, craft workers were also important in developing the manufacturing industry, as we shall see in Chapter 5.

The staff of a merchant firm. Most unskilled newcomers found work for wages as labourers or delivery men.

Black staff at lunch, 1912. Soap, along with the laundry service, was in great demand on the Rand. In 1912 the Transvaal Soap Company in Richmond, Johannesburg, was bought by the international giant, Lever Brothers.

The craft workers also brought with them from the industrialised countries a history of craft unions. As described in *Why Trade Unions Emerged* on page 58, craft workers had control over the tools of the trade. On the Rand, their strong position as workers with scarce and valuable skills helped them to form powerful unions. These unions were to have a strong influence on other workers in years to come, as we shall see later in this book.

A Johannesburg shop in the era of bicycle transport.

Early unskilled labourers on the railways, with the supervisor (seated).

Conclusion

The early period on the Rand was a time of constant movement – people came and people left. They came from far and near, bringing their work experiences and skills with them, and trying to fit these into the needs of the Rand.

This was also an open-ended time. In this new economy, many industries had not yet developed, and people felt they might become rich if they could supply a need that was missing on the Rand, such as the need for laundry services, transport or building supplies.

Most food and general stores remained fairly small for many years to come. Only much later in the century were they taken over by the large chain store and supermarket concerns that we know today. In the early years there were many bankruptcies, but those shopkeepers who survived (as opposed to the poorer hawkers) generally prospered, and in time became comfortable middle-class businessmen who employed the labour of others.

This period, then, was a time of *class formation*. A small middle class managed to survive and develop.

But it was also a time of *class suppression*. While it seemed for a time as if even black enterprises like the *Amawasha* might survive, race discrimination and large capitalist concerns overtook them and they were forced to retreat to wage labour. Many other small, self-employed people, like those in the brickmaking and transport businesses also disappeared.

In the years that followed, people continued to start their own enterprises – mostly they failed, though some succeeded in making an independent living. But within forty years from the time of the discovery of gold on the Rand, the process of *proletarianisation* was rapidly taking place. The great majority of people living there were wage-earning workers – for the rapid growth of capitalism demanded a large, hard-working and disciplined army of labourers, forced by need to go regularly to work, and to work productively once they were there.

Topics

The Economy of the Rand

Capital from mining

At the end of the 1860s, mining took hold of the economy of South Africa and changed its very nature. The prevailing system of production itself was changed. In the new system, goods were produced firstly for *profit*, and not for *use*. The measure of wealth became money, instead of the control of land and cattle as in the old society. When this money was used to make more money, through profit, the resulting *capital* became the key force in the new economy.

Capital began to grow rapidly in South Africa after the discovery of diamonds in Griqualand West, and then gold in the Transvaal.

Capital came from two sources:

1. Firstly, capital was brought in from other countries by capitalists hoping to profit from the new mining industries.
2. Secondly, it grew out of actual profits created in the mines through the super-exploitation of cheap black labour, as well as the use of special machinery to speed up the production of diamonds and gold.

The mining industry therefore established a *capitalist system* in South Africa by attracting and creating capital.

Mining capital in South Africa

But capital does not grow without labour, for workers are needed to produce the goods, which are then sold for a profit. In South Africa, the mining companies needed workers to mine diamonds and gold. To get enough workers, the mine owners had to speed up the

The gold mining industry was of central importance to the Rand. Its profits, its vast capital investments, and its massive labour needs laid the economic and social foundations of the region, and transformed the development of South Africa.

creation of the migrant labour system. (Volume 1 of this history, *Gold and Workers*, describes in detail how the mines got their labour.)

So the mining industry brought into being a class of capitalists who controlled the mines and capital, and a class of workers, separated from their families and from the land while they were working for wages.

Government help

The mines needed thousands of workers. To get this massive labour force they needed the help of the government. They could get this help because their enormous profits benefited the government through taxation. For example, through the mining industry, the Transvaal was converted in less that 20 years from a poor, struggling Boer republic, into a rapidly growing modern state.

But soon a clash developed between the new capitalists and the land-owning rulers of the Transvaal.

'Between the Chains', the cordoned-off part of Simmonds Street (between Market and Commissioner) which held the overflow from Johannesburg's early Stock Exchange. As international trade developed, finance capital had to be regulated and directed.

The question was: who would control the new, profitable system — the mine owners or the Boer rulers? In the end, this was settled by a war, the Anglo-Boer War, which lasted for three years (1899-1902).

The British connection

The British won the war and the Transvaal became a British colony, part of the British Empire. The new rulers looked well set to establish a modern, capitalist state in the whole of South Africa. The victory of the British in the war also meant that the mine owners had influence in the British government — British capital was invested in the mines and British manufacturers and merchants had a flourishing trade with the Rand mines and businesses, as 'South Africa's "merchant princes"' shows on page 50.

The mines were therefore valuable to the British economy, and the mine owners could call on the British state for help. For example, soon after the war, when the mines found they were short of cheap labour, mine owners were able, through the British government, to recruit 80 000 workers from China to work on long contracts.

The result was a massive increase in productivity and profits — the gold mines increased production from

R150 million in 1899 to an amazing R250 million in 1914.[2] With this kind of money, it was no wonder that the Rand gold mines had a powerful say in the capitalist world of Britain and her colonies.

South Africa's 'merchant princes'

Besides the mine owners there was another group of businessmen who did very well out of the mining industry – the large traders, or 'merchant princes' as they have been called.[3] Their wealth and capital grew out of the growing trade between Britain and South Africa.

After the Anglo-Boer War, trade with Britain flourished. By 1903, South Africa was Britain's second-largest customer – the biggest was India – and was importing goods worth R52 million from British factories.[4]

Much of this trade was between British industries and the gold mines, for mining equipment and stores. The building industry also imported much of its material, such as building tools and equipment, ceilings, baths and other household and shop fittings. All the equipment for railway and road construction, too, was imported. The growing number of townspeople also bought many imported goods, such as clothes, furniture and household appliances, from the shops.

Early importers and suppliers to the mining and building industries.

The traders established large importing firms at the coastal towns to receive the goods shipped from Britain. As their wealth grew, so did their influence. In the social clubs to which they belonged, which excluded retail shopkeepers and artisans, they sewed up business deals and consolidated their alliances. Many were also active in politics. They had strong pro-British feelings. One South African factory owner complained:

> 'The majority [of these wealthy traders] have been educated and trained in Great Britain, and in whatever community they may be, we find them taking the lead in public affairs. In some cases these merchants are looked up to as oracles on every question under the sun and their influence is almost absolute.'[5]

As their wealth depended on importing manufactured goods from Britain, it is not surprising that these 'merchant princes' were strong supporters of the 'free trade system', and tried to discourage the government from taxing imported goods.[6] They believed that the South African manufacturing industry had little future in the economic development of South Africa.

Manufacturing for the mines

It usually happens that a large successful industry, such as South Africa's mining industry, encourages the growth of other industries. In South Africa, however, this growth occurred slowly, because most of the needs of the mines were satisfied by trade with

A cement factory. The mining industry directly stimulated the manufacture of building materials and explosives to supply its own needs.

Britain, and a large share of the profits went back to Britain.

At the beginning of this century, Britain was 'the workshop of the world' — it seemed no other country could produce manufactured goods as quickly or as cheaply as Britain. Most people supposed that South Africa, as part of the British Empire, would always remain a supplier of raw materials to Britain and a buyer of her finished products.

There were some supplies, though, that were easier to obtain locally. For example, it was easier and quicker to manufacture dynamite, bricks and cement in South Africa, and the mining companies themselves started their own factories for these products. (*The Rand's Early Afrikaner Workers* on pages 51-53 shows how Afrikaner brick makers were squeezed out by the new brick factories.)

Small repair shops also emerged, especially to service the machinery of the mines, or to replace small parts. Other small factories slowly developed, too. These produced *light consumer goods* — like boots, saddles, blankets, candles and soap — which mine workers (especially) needed to buy.

By 1907, a small manufacturers' association had been formed with 53 members. Their aim was to support a policy of industrial development in South Africa.

Craft industries

Who were the owners of these small factories? Unlike the merchants (see 'South Africa's "Merchant Princes"' on page 50) most were newcomers to business. Many of them had, in fact, started off their working lives as craftsmen or artisans — and then used their skills and their savings to open up small factories. They themselves worked. They usually employed a few labourers and perhaps one or two artisans to produce the clothes, or window frames, or whatever goods they were producing.

Most were proud to call themselves 'self-made men' — people who had started with little capital, but had built up a profitable industry. To the wealthy merchants and mine owners, these early manufacturers belonged to a lower class. Not one of them was a member of the exclusive clubs of the Rand and the Cape, and not one was on the 'Who's Who' list of successful people.[6]

'Manufacturers were hardly recognised as respectable people', recalls the man who founded the Cape Manufacturers Association in 1913. 'Bank managers were sceptical . . . and traders turned away from their wares.'[7]

The early manufacturers, therefore, had not yet joined the ranks of the big capitalists in South Africa, and most of these small factories could still be called *craft industries*.

A small workshop manufacturer using spare parts for the repair of machinery.

The Rand's Early Afrikaner Workers

Afrikaner farmers were among the first arrivals on the Rand after the discovery of gold in 1886. Some of them soon set themselves up, as they had on the Kimberley diamond fields, as claim-holders of mining land, and independent 'diggers'. However, like other diggers, few of these Afrikaners could compete with the capital and know-how possessed by foreign capitalists, and they were soon overtaken by the large mining companies that were formed in the early 1890s.

Afrikaners were also unable to compete with the more commercially experienced European, Indian and Chinese traders, who set themselves up as shopkeepers or hawkers, and brought out young relatives to serve as apprentices. Small trade was soon cornered by groups of different nationalities: the Jewish 'concession' mining stores; the Greek cafes in later years; and the fruit and vegetables stores developed by the Indians and the Portuguese.

The police force

Afrikaners did have one advantage over foreigners in the early years. President Kruger, President of the Transvaal before the Anglo-Boer War, insisted that only citizens be allowed to serve in the police force. By 1899, nearly 900 young Afrikaners had found jobs as 'ZARPS' – members of the 'Zuid Afrikaansche Republiekeinsche Polisie'. In those days, however, their general lack of clerical skills prevented most rural Afrikaners from finding jobs as clerks in government posts, such as post office jobs in the new towns.

The South African Railways police force, Johannesburg, 1911.

Rural skills in town

Rural people, however, were not without skills. They knew how to be timbermen, riders, wagon drivers, tanners of leather, builders, bakers and brewers. Many of their skills were not needed in the towns, but some they adapted and used in the new conditions of town life, and so managed to avoid wage labour.

For example, many made an independent living in transport as mule and ox-wagon drivers. The services of transport riders were sought after by traders and travellers. Before the arrival of the railway line the mines relied on transport riders for a constant supply of machinery, coal and food for the workers.

In the towns themselves, Afrikaners used the smaller 'scotch cart' to transport supplies of building materials to and from railway yards, building sites and brickworks. They also operated horse-drawn cabs in the towns, transporting people from their work to their homes.[9]

The brickmakers

In addition, a number of Afrikaner newcomers succeeded in small-scale brickmaking. People who had once been **bywoners** brought with them a knowledge of clay and drying processes, and they were able to benefit from the building activities of the mines all along the Reef. From 1890 onwards, Johannesburg's builders began to erect hundreds of new brick buildings every year. There was a desperate need for building materials – the mining companies began to manufacture cement themselves, because it was in such short supply.

The President himself granted the brickmakers a site with good clay soil near Johannesburg's centre. The area became known as 'Brickfields'. (See page 74, Chapter 3, for a description of Brickfields). Other brick fields were established in the Johannesburg areas of Ophirton, City and Suburban and Turffontein. Afrikaner newcomers made their way to these brick fields. If they had a horse and cart and some capital to buy a mixing machine and pay for labour, they were able to start up their own businesses. Otherwise, they could be employed by other Afrikaners as brickmakers at a piece-work rate of 80 cents to R1 for every thousand bricks they manufactured.[10]

Hardship

However, the small businesses of the transport men and the brickmakers were not able to withstand the forces of capitalist progress. In the 1890s, the railway lines from Cape Town and Durban reached Johannesburg. Then in 1896, drought and rinderpest cut down the number of transport animals, and the price of their fodder was pushed up. In twelve months, 500 out of 1 200 men were forced out of business. They were obliged to work as wage earners for the more successful transport riders and cab drivers.[11]

The brickmakers also suffered misfortune, especially during the disruption of the Anglo-Boer War. Building

Morning market in Johannesburg, when farmers came to town to sell their produce. The rapid development of the Rand resulted in the stimulation of commercial agriculture.

almost came to a standstill between 1898 and 1902. After the war, large mining companies moved into the brickmaking industry. They introduced expensive, labour-saving machines which could produce many thousands of bricks a day 'with a minimum of hand manipulation'.[12] In the competition for customers after the war, the price of bricks dropped by half, yet one large firm (financed by a mining company) made a R20 000 profit in 1904.

The small brickmakers could not hope to match this

The aged, the poor and the unemployed line up for charity hand-outs. Particularly hard hit were the brickmakers, the cabbies, the transport drivers and the washermen and women who were thrown out of work by the arrival of large capitalist concerns.

competition, and soon they were looking for jobs, either in the companies that had put them out of business, or as unskilled road or railway workers.

The 'Amawasha' Laundry Service

There were several reasons why Johannesburg urgently needed a laundry service.

- Water was not easily obtainable — the nearest natural supply was the Braamfontein spruit, or stream, but even that had an uneven flow.
- To make things worse, until 1906 there were not enough drains in the town. For health reasons, slops (dirty water) were not allowed to be thrown into the streets. The washing of clothes thus had to be done at some distance from the houses.
- In the early years, most of the people in Johannesburg were single or unmarried men. The white miners worked long hours and most lived in boarding houses. They did not have the time or the inclination to do their own washing, and there were few women to provide the traditional maintenance services such as cooking and washing.

The rise of the 'Amawasha'

The 'Amawasha' stepped in to fill the need. The Amawasha were mostly Zulu-speaking men who came to provide a laundry service in the Rand towns. They

White launderers at a Westdene stream. In the background, the long washing lines and the homes of the washermen and women.

The *amawasha* come to town to renew their licences, 1895. Their uniform of turbans and long sticks and their allegiance to an *induna* showed their degree of organisation. As self-employed men, *amawasha* did not need to carry passes, and were permitted to bear weapons and brew beer.

Washermen at the municipal washing site, Klipspruit. It was a long way from town, and transport pushed up working costs. Ultimately, this forced move drove the *amawasha* out of business, for they could not compete with the steam laundries established in town.

had learned their trade from the Indian 'dhobis', or washermen who were making an independent living washing clothes in the Umgeni River in Durban.

The Amawasha came to the Rand because by the 1890s they had been pushed off the land by a number of bad droughts as well as the cattle-killing rinderpest disease (as described in Chapter 1). The nearest jobs were on the Natal railways, but they were not attractive to many because the wages of labourers were fixed at 25 cents a day.

When, therefore, the news came of Egoli, the 'City of Gold' in the Transvaal, many took the walk to the Rand to make a living as washermen. These early newcomers were so successful that they sent for their brothers and friends, too. Most of the Amawasha belonged to the clans of Kanyile, Buthelezi, Mchunu, Vilakazi and Sithole. By 1896, there were over 1 000 Amawasha in Johannesburg alone.

The organisation

The Amawasha were well organised. They made common cause to protect their interests. They were led by respected elders, or *indunas*, who would speak on their behalf, organise the smooth running of the washing process and enlist new recruits. They were organised into regiments, and would march into town every month to pay their licence fees, proudly singing their regimental songs. Customers could recognise the Amawasha by their uniforms, with their turbans modelled on the headwear of the dhobi washermen.

As businessmen who paid the monthly 10-cent licence fee, the Amawasha had certain privileges. They were not subject to the Masters and Servants Act, so they were free from passes. They could also carry a weapon for protection and were allowed to brew beer for themselves.

By 1896 the Amawasha had 8 different waterside sites. Most had rented places along the Braamfontein spruit, but there were also washing sites at Elandsfontein, Concordia and Booysens. The rental was very high for those days — 50 cents a week for a hut. In addition, they had the expense of the washing soap and the licence fee.

The working week

The Amawasha worked hard to earn a living. On Mondays, they would walk 5 to 12 kilometres to town and back, delivering and collecting bundles of washing. From Tuesday to Saturday they would do the washing, except for special deliveries on Wednesday. Most Amawasha managed to wash 18 large bundles of washing a week, and charged 80 cents to R1 a bundle.

In addition, they grew their own vegetables and kept their own pigs and cattle. The 1896 figures show that the Braamfontein site near Auckland Park was like a small village, consisting of 546 Zulu-speaking washermen, 14 Hindu dhobis, 64 African women and 4 Indian women. There were also 4 horses and carts.[13]

Capital moves in

But the independence of the Amawasha was not to last. Their success attracted the attention of investors looking for bigger profits. In October 1895, the first modern steam laundry company started, and the following year the Auckland Park Steam Laundry was started with a capital of R25 000.

In that same year, the Amawasha were instructed to move to a site on the Klip River, 25 kilometres away. There had been a drought, which dried up much of the water supply, causing the washing sites to become filthy. The health inspectors demanded that the sites close down until the water pits could be cleaned again.

The Amawasha organised a mass meeting of protest, but their demands were curtly refused. After this, nearly half the Amawasha left for their homes in Natal. Most of those who stayed moved 25 kilometres to the new washing site at Klip River, but had to double their prices to pay for the extra transport costs. Customers turned more and more to local laundries. By 1898, there was enough laundry to keep 8 laundry companies in business, as well as a number of Indian and Chinese hand laundries.

The Amawasha managed to keep going for a number of years, resisting through petitions, court cases, refusal to move and mass meetings. But too many interest groups were against them.

Firstly there was the competition from the laundry companies. Then, too, after the Anglo-Boer War thousands of white workers married and established households. Cheap domestic labour was employed to service the homes and do the washing. (See *Early Domestic Workers* on page 56.)

The new British administration was also determined to remove the Amawasha and put them in 'locations' along with other Africans. In 1906, the Amawasha were again forced to move, this time to a specially built washing site — next to Johannesburg's sewerage system! — at Klipspruit. At the same time, the monthly licence fee jumped up to 75 cents, while the Amawasha had to pay return train fares to town for themselves, plus a 5-cent charge for every 100-pound bundle of washing.

These conditions were so harsh that even the Chief Pass Officer was moved to comment that Johannesburg's 'white labour policy . . . was causing the Council deliberately to make conditions impossible for the Zulu washermen'.[14]

By 1914, only about 93 Amawasha had survived.

Many had gone home. They had benefited from their time as Amawasha, using their earnings to buy more land and cattle and settle down at a time when others were being forced off the land. For example, Bhamu Buthelezi, who had been a washerman on the Rand between 1893 and 1908, returned home and bought land in the Bergville district. His son, N. H. Buthelezi, joined the South African police force, while the daughter of N. H. received an education and went on to study at an American University.[15]

Others were not so successful. They had to stay on and find some other way of earning a living. Many became domestic workers or nightwatchmen, while others joined the ranks of wage earners in the newer and flourishing laundry companies.

Early Domestic Workers

Domestic workers are employed to provide services to people at home. They clean houses, wash clothes, cook, look after children and are at the beck and call of the adults.

In South Africa domestic service has been one of the largest employers of labour, along with the mines and the farms. As early as 1896, Johannesburg alone employed 8 375 servants, both black and white.[16]

The gold mines very soon made some people very rich. They lived in grand, many-roomed houses which needed the services of many people. Some of the servants in these houses were trained specialists, imported from Britain. Their presence brought their employers greater social standing.

Race and class relations in the kitchen

Before 1914, black and white servants worked side by side. Most unskilled male servants were black and many female servants were white. There are a number of instances on record of close friendships developing across the colour line between some black and white workers, and some sexual relationships amongst these workers. Servants, despite the colour of their skins, tended to identify along class lines.[17]

But in South Africa, where laws and society discriminated along both race and class lines, white women servants soon learnt to avoid contact with their fellow black workers. For instance, an article in a journal, *Imperial Colonist*, urged mistresses to teach their white housemaids how to behave towards the black servants:

'They should be civil and kind . . . but they should never allow any familiarity. They should not touch their hands, or sit in a room where there are boys, or do anything whereby an insolent native may take liberties.'[18]

Clearly the imperial message was that white house-maids ought to be divided from their fellow workers because they belonged to the conquering race, and therefore should behave as superiors. As attitudes of this kind became more widespread, tensions developed amongst domestic workers. Many white semi-skilled housemaids gradually left more and more of the work to the unskilled 'house boy' and were happy to give orders instead. Not surprisingly, the black workers became resentful, and many arguments followed.

As time went by, white housemaids gradually disappeared from most households — there was a shortage of white women on the Rand, and most of them found themselves husbands and settled into homes with servants of their own. White servants became more and more scarce, except for specialists like the trained English nannies who brought up the children of the rich.

By 1914, domestic workers in the kitchen were largely black, their employers white.

Control

Employers of domestic servants had tight control over their workers, more so than other employers, except perhaps for the managers of the mine compounds. The domestic workers lived and worked in the same place, under the watchful eye of the employer. Off-duty hours were almost as closely supervised as working hours:

'Employers of all classes did not hesitate to invade and inspect their servants' rooms and goods if they suspected them of theft or any other misdemeanour. Servants were always visible to their employers.'[19]

Opposite: Domestic staff Employed in Some Typical Households. *1. (Top left) A Wealthy Household. a.* A nanny holds the youngest child in this family group. A wealthy household would often employ a housekeeper (R10-14 per month) who would supervise the nanny and the other servants. *b.* A valet, a steward, a cook and a lady's maid. Like the nanny, these servants earned R8-10 per month under one-year contracts. *c.* The laundresses, waiters, and general servants who made up the rest of the staff earned far lower wages. *2. (Top right) The Home of a Trader or Professional.* The woman of the house usually did her own housekeeping, supervising *a.* the cook or housemaid and *b.* one or two general servants/'house boys'. *3. (Bottom left) A Typical Boarding House in the Early Years. a.* Housekeeper surrounded by waiter, housemaids and cook (R8-10 per month). *b.* Black 'house boys' could earn as much as R7 per month in the early years, but their wages fell below R4 from 1914 as this kind of labour became more plentiful. *4. The Home of a White Working-Class Family.* In a colonial society even working-class whites expected servants. Often a group of men shared a house and employed a housekeeper and a 'house boy'. *a.* A working-class family typically included a lodger. *b.* The wife did the domestic work, assisted by a 'house boy'.

1.

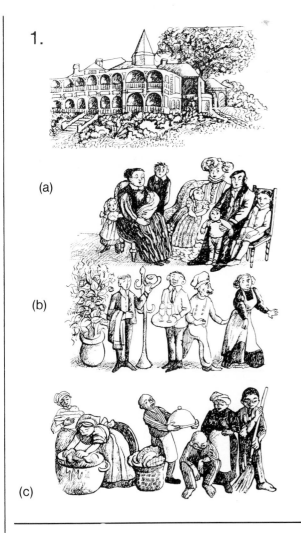

(a)

(b)

(c)

2.

(a)

(b)

3.

(a)

(b)

4.

(a)

(b)

Workers thus had very little private life. Visitors, especially of the opposite sex, were usually not allowed – more especially so if the workers were female.

In general, black servants were more easily controlled than white servants. They were subject to the pass laws – an employer's bad reference on the pass of a black worker could make it difficult to get work outside the mines. The pass system also controlled the movements of domestics in town during off-duty hours.

The rise and fall
of black domestic wages

'Since the reduction of mineboys' wages there has been a much larger supply of kitchen boys.'*The Star*, 3 May 1897.

When domestic labour was in short supply, the wages of black 'house boys' were as high as those of white housemaids – at R7 to R8 a month.

After the Anglo-Boer War the mines dropped the wages, and many young black men chose to go into domestic service rather than mining. But then, because there was no shortage of servants and a depressed economy, domestics' wages dropped, too.

New households

From about 1903, the wages of 'house boys' picked up again with the arrival of many more white women in the towns. The well-paid white artisans were more settled after the war. They could afford to get married and set up their own homes. There they required the services of at least one 'house boy'. Because of the increased demand, the wages of domestic workers rose again, as 'high' as R8 a month.

At this point, mine owners began to complain that the labour shortage was getting worse because of the number of black men working as 'house boys'. They suggested that black women be recruited so that the wages would fall and the men would be forced back into the mines. But white women employers resisted this idea. Many claimed that black women servants might be 'immoral'. An article in *The Star* warned of the danger of a new 'bastard population' if black women were brought into white homes.

But they need not have worried. Few black women were seeking employment at that time. Black families still living on the land resisted sending their daughters to the 'immoral' towns. The women were necessary to the homestead economy, as Chapter 1 describes. Parents much preferred to send their sons to earn money to help the family.

Child labour

Labour recruiting agents, helped by the government, then stepped in to profit from the demand for domestic labour. They turned to a still cheaper form of labour – child labour.

Labour bureaux began to recruit youngsters of 10 to 15 years of age for domestic service – most whites called them 'piccanins'. The recruiters undertook to supply householders with 'piccanins' for a fee of R4 plus the cost of a train fare. These young boys usually came from the Pietersburg area, where the Bapedi in particular had been hard hit by cattle disease, drought, and locusts at that time.

For this investment, employers got a 'piccanin' to work for them under contract for a cash wage of R1 to R2, 'according to size'.[20]

The drop in wages

These new recruits, together with the gradual entry of black women into the towns in the years thereafter, caused the wages of domestic workers to drop. By 1914, the average 'house boy's' monthly wage had fallen to below R4, where it stayed for many years.

At this rate of cheap labour, even less-skilled white workers could afford domestic service, and came to expect it as the right of all their race.

Why Trade Unions Emerged

The rise of mining capitalism created a class of people who owned the mines – the capitalists – and a growing class of workers who had only their labour to sell.

In Britain, the factories and mines had brought workers together in large numbers. The workers soon realised that they could bargain for better conditions and wages if they closed ranks to form trade unions. These unions set out to strengthen the position of the workers through united action. The main ways of doing this were:

- by limiting competition amongst workers so as to maintain and raise wages;
- by preventing the undercutting of wages;
- by organising to bargain with the employers;
- by withdrawing their labour, if all else failed in collective bargaining – in other words, by going on strike.

However, the workers had no real power until they were able to stop 'scabbing'. Scabs are workers who

A May Day demonstration in Market Square, 1904. Skilled workers from Britain and other industrialised countries brought with them the experience of craft and trade unions, and strong labour traditions which challenged the power of the employer.

take the jobs of other workers while they are on strike. So trade unions, as worker organisations, had to be able to control the labour supply to be really effective. The early craft unions had this control in the early years on the Rand.

Craft unions

The earliest worker organisations on the Rand were the craft unions. Craft workers, or artisans, were trained in a certain craft or skill, such as furniture making, iron moulding, printing, plastering, machine drilling and so on. Workers were trained in these skills on the job, and when they qualified they became 'journeymen' and were admitted as members into the craft union.

In South Africa, craft unions were at their most powerful in the twenty or thirty years after deep-level mining was started; that is, from the 1890s onwards, when there was a great need for industrial skills and the

Rand was growing very rapidly. The great majority of craftworkers came from industrialised centres in Britain and Australia, where there were strong union traditions.

A number of craft unions were established soon after craft workers arrived on the Rand: the Witwatersrand Mining Employees' and Mechanics' Union (1892), the South African Engine Drivers' Association (1896) and the Amalgamated Engineering Union (1898) are some examples.[21]

Craft control

The craft workers were able to control both the content and the pace of work through their unions. How did they get and keep this craft control?

In the early phase of industrialisation, people continued to produce in much the same way as they had done before. Craft workers made such things as shoes, furniture or metal objects, using the skills they had been taught during their five- to seven-year apprenticeships. They controlled production because only they had these skills.

Craft workers maintained control over the job in four

The Plasterers' Union, 1914. Craft unions increased their bargaining power by controlling the training of workers and negotiating the rates of pay. They were able to enforce a closed shop, so that no worker could be employed unless he was a member of the union of his craft.

important ways, which are discussed below.

1. The closed shop

Firstly, the unions had the power to enforce a closed shop — no worker could be employed as a craft worker unless he was a member of a craft union. In this way, the unions were able to stop scabbing. For example, a newspaper was not allowed to hire a printer who was not a member of the printers' Typographical Union. If it did, the union had the power to call a strike, and the newspaper would lose the labour of all its printers.

The closed shop system meant that the craft union had a monopoly over labour — in other words, it had exclusive control over the labour supply for that craft. The Iron Moulders' Society, for example, imposed a fine or 'late entry fee' of up to R40 (or a month's wages) on any member who had worked as a moulder before joining the union.[22]

Monopoly over labour was vital to the strength of a craft union and its members jealously guarded it. The closed shop system gave the unions the power to control the rates of pay, the standards of work and the apprenticeship system.

2. Control over rates of pay

The craft unions insisted that *they* fix the rates of pay for each category of craft worker. They decided on the hourly or daily rates of their members.

The rate of pay was guided by the idea of 'a fair day's pay for a fair day's work'; but, in practice, the wage depended on the strength of the union. For example,

every qualified moulder in the Transvaal belonged to the Iron Moulders' Society in 1913. As a result, the union was able to fix the rate of pay at R2 a day. In other trades, craft workers earned R8 a week.[23]

3. Control over tasks

The craft unions claimed the right to control the kinds of task done by the workers. The unions monitored closely the work of their members. For example, in 1918, the records of the Iron Moulders' Society show that the Executive Committee summoned a member to explain why he had carried castings, which was defined as a labourer's job.[24] In 1909, a moulder was fined by the union itself for doing poor work.[25] And, in 1915, we find the union's secretary writing to a shop steward at ERP Mines:

> 'It has been brought to the knowledge of our Society that in the making of white metal bearings...the usual moulder's tools are used by a plumber — we do not know how this has been initiated and allowed to continue by our moulders in the ERPM as my Society has always considered anything of this nature an infringement of our trade'.[26]

Craft workers were not supposed to allow anyone else to perform certain tasks, or to do work that had not been defined by the union. In this way, they kept tight control over who should do the productive work and over the tools themselves, the instruments of production.

4. The apprenticeship system

The craft unions also controlled the training of craft workers through apprentices. It was the responsibility of the journeymen (the qualified craftworkers) to train apprentices on the job. An over-supply might weaken the bargaining position of the craft workers and lower

their wages. So, for example, the craft unions in the engineering industry would not allow more than one apprentice to every four journeymen.

The power of the craft unions rested on their monopoly over the labour supply, their control over the tools of the trade, and their strong organisation.

Wagon making. The craft workers kept strict control over the tools — the assistant was permitted to carry or hold the tools only.

Management, clerks, packers and delivery men.

Notes

1) See E.A. Mantzaris, 'Class and ethnicity: the politics and ideologies of the Greek community in South Africa, 1890-1924', Ph.D Thesis, University of Cape Town, 1982.

2) Cited by C van Onselen, *Studies in the Social and Economic History of the Witwatersrand 1886-1914*, Vol. 1, *New Babylon* (Ravan Press, Johannesburg, 1982), p.1.

3) See B Bozzoli, *The Political Nature of a Ruling Class: Capital and Ideology in South Africa 1890-1933* (London, 1981), Chapter 3.

4) B Bozzoli, as above, p.108.

5) B Bozzoli, as above, p.118.

6) The conflict between 'free trade' and import control is discussed in Chapter 4.

7) B Bozzoli, as above, footnote 45, p.317.

8) B Bozzoli, as above, p.317.

9) C van Onselen, 'The Main Reef Road into the Working Class', in *Studies in the Social and Economic History of the Witwatersrand 1886-1914*, Vol.2, *New Nineveh*, pp.114-15.

10) C van Onselen, as above, Vol.2, pp.116-18.

11) C van Onselen, as above, Vol.2, p.112.

12) C van Onselen, as above, Vol.2, p.124.

13) C van Onselen, as above, Vol.2, p.79.

14) C van Onselen, as above, Vol.2, p.99.

15) Interview by C van Onselen, as above, Vol.2, p.101, and footnote 131, p.110.

16) C van Onselen, as above, Vol.2, p.3.

17) C van Onselen, as above, Vol.2, p.46.

18) *Imperial Colonist*, May 1903, quoted by C van Onselen, as above, Vol.2, p.41.

19) C van Onselen, as above, Vol.2, p.38.

20) *The Star*, 23.1.1908, quoted by C van Onselen, as above, Vol. 2, p.18.

21) Eddie Webster, *Cast in a Racial Mould* (Ravan Press, Johannesburg, 1985), p.41.

22) Jon Lewis, *Industrialisation and Trade Union Organisation 1925-1955: The Rise and Fall of the South African Trades and Labour Council* (Cambridge, 1984), p.23.

23) E Webster, as above, p.27.

24) E Webster, as above, p.26.

25) E Webster, as above, p.42.

26) E Webster, as above, p.26.

Chapter 3
Where Working People Lived

This chapter describes the nature of housing and shows how it was related to the labour needs of the employers on the Rand.

Housing before industrial times

In traditional society, families built their own houses, using materials freely available from the land around them – clay, water, wood, reeds and grass. Their houses were warm in winter, cool and airy in summer, and spacious. Overcrowding was fairly easily overcome – it was not difficult to build another hut if the family got bigger.

With more space available, it was easier to keep the living area clean, and to dispose of rubbish and sewage at a healthy distance. In the old society life was often hard, but it was much easier to organise living arrangements, and families were able to supply most of their own needs.

New needs in the towns

In the towns, people's lives were separated from their work-places. Large numbers of people lived close together, and this new way of life created new needs – while the nature of these needs created new markets for businessmen.

In the emerging capitalist system, nearly every need became a *commodity*, something to buy and sell – even space itself. People had to pay with money for land, for materials for a house, and usually for the people to build it, too. In the early years, water had to be bought by the bucket (as the photograph on the next page shows). The Rand towns were not built near large rivers, so water had to be transported from afar and pumped, cleaned and piped to all parts of the growing town. Heating and lighting – whether in the form of gas and electricity, or more simply as candles, paraffin and coal – also had to be paid for.

In the towns, most of these services were difficult for individual families to obtain – they had to be organised on a large scale. In other words, they were run by the government of the town – the town council or municipality – and shared by the people, provided they could pay.

From the beginning, the town council in Johannesburg was responsible for sewage and rubbish disposal. At first, water, gas and electricity were supplied by private companies holding special licences from the government. Then the companies found that these services were not profitable enough, and the municipality took over the supply of gas and electricity in 1895, and the supply of water in 1903.

Other services like roads, transport, education and hospitals were also developed to some extent by municipalities, the provincial administration of the Transvaal, or by the central government itself.

Part of a traditional homestead. Houses were built by members of the families that lived in them, using the materials freely available around them. The Rand municipalities forbade the construction of 'reed huts', and the traditional skills of house-building therefore lost their usefulness in the towns. Most self-built houses were tin shacks.

Corner Pritchard and Joubert Streets on a rainy day, 1907. In the background, labourers are laying water pipes. 'When it rained – and didn't it! – the blessed village was submerged by fearful floods, and when dry it was hidden by the most terrible dust storms, born in the sanitary settlements, that were ever invoked by the devil.' Louis Cohen, in *Reminiscences of Johannesburg & London*. See also quote on opposite page.

Water for sale by the bucket during the drought of 1895-1896, before reservoirs and pipelines became the responsibility of the town council. 'Although at times there was enough water in the town to float a ship, at other periods there was not sufficient to drown a flea — except at prohibitive prices — and a good wholesome bath was generally out of the question.'

Main Road, Fordsburg, in the early years of this century. Fordsburg was one of Johannesburg's first working-class suburbs, and most of the men rode bicycles to work.

Mainroad   FORDSBURG

Housing in the towns

We must therefore see services as part of the basic issue of housing in the towns. And to understand the development of housing in the towns it will be useful to remember two points:

- Every material need – space, housing, services, food and clothes – had to be paid for. Most of these needs became commodities, to be bought and sold for profit.
- It was so difficult for individuals to obtain certain services by themselves that they had to share the cost of these services with others. A municipality or some other central body then organised the service and decided who could use it and how much they would pay.

These two points help to explain why and how housing and services were unequally shared in the towns, as we shall see later in this chapter. Some people got better houses and services than others. The quality of housing and everyday living depended on having enough money. For workers, this depended on having a well-paid job.

Homes for skilled workers

We have seen how there were two kinds of workers on the early Rand – skilled and unskilled. The skilled workers were experienced. They had worked in industry before, mostly in England or one of the other English-speaking countries. They could command higher wages because they were few and there was a great demand for their skills. They thus earned enough to find reasonable homes.

In the early years, these artisans tended to come alone and would either club together to share a house, or live in boarding houses, as described in *Early Domestic Workers* in Chapter 2. In 1902, a British labour politician visiting the Rand gave his impressions of the life white workers lived on the Rand:

'You have simply to walk through the wage-earning districts of the town to see the numerous dining rooms; you have simply to try and find a workman at home in Johannesburg to discover that his home is only a bedroom, which he generally shares with a fellow workman, and that family life – upon which the state is built – may be said to hardly exist amongst great sections of the population. Men rent beds, not houses, in the Golden City.'[1]

After the Anglo-Boer War established that Britain was to control the economy and build up a modern, capitalist state, many artisans returned to the Rand, some of them with wives. Artisans grew more confident about holding down steady jobs. Hundreds more sent for their wives and families as the economy picked up again, especially from 1909. Between 1902 and 1912 the number of married white miners nearly doubled.

But the great influx of people after the war led to a serious shortage of accommodation. Some of the skilled white workers were able to find housing in married quarters on the mines. Others had to squeeze into the small houses in the poorer areas near the centre of town (as the map of Johannesburg shows on page 69).

But the British members of the Transvaal government were anxious to secure a stable, settled working-class. They wanted to encourage the building of family housing. They were also anxious to avoid the division of Johannesburg into rich and poor areas, and to prevent slums of the kind that had developed in English cities during the rapid industrialisation of the 19th century (see page 80). As the town clerk pointed out to the governor, Lord Milner (thinking only of white workers):

'What we have to fear and avoid is a similar state of things in Johannesburg – where the area north of the reef would be covered by residences of the well-to-do, and by streets of shops supplying their wants – while the area south of the reef would be inhabited solely by the poorer employees of the mines and by an inferior class of local shopkeepers'.[2]

In 1903 Johannesburg's boundaries were extended to include an area of 82 square miles. Neat, white working-class suburbs like Jeppe, Malvern, Troyeville, Bez Valley and Belgravia were established, as shown on page 69. Roads and trams made the journey to work quick and cheap.

Most of these suburbs had no freehold rights, but were owned by the municipality or by the mining companies. But in 1912, the houses in these working-class suburbs were put up for sale to encourage a stable, orderly, property-owning white artisan class.

Where the unskilled lived

Chapter 2 has described the struggle for existence of many unskilled Afrikaners in the towns. However in Johannesburg's early years, as 'burghers' (the only people allowed to vote in the old Transvaal Republic) they were able to appeal to the government for special assistance in setting up their homes cheaply, as the stories of Brickfields and Vrededorp on pages 74 and 76 show.

But these special conditions were not to last – the steady influx of unskilled workers placed them in competition with low-paid black workers.

Artisans without their families, residents of a boarding house.

A Johannesburg advertisement in 1913. By then, freehold land was being offered to encourage the growth of a stable, productive, property-owning artisan class — the wild bachelor days of wine and women were meant to be over.

THE Building Scheme the Working Man Has Been Looking For!

THE GROUND IS FREEHOLD.   ONE-QUARTER ACRE IN EXTENT.
NEAR TRAM LINE.   FULL PRICE, £500.

CARDIGAN ROAD, PARKWOOD.

NO DEPOSIT.—£8 17s. 6d. monthly.   Only £8 17s. 6d. per month and NO DEPOSIT secures

A NEW MODERN VILLA BUILT TO ORDER.

Box 3454.   Apply—F. T. RICHARDS, Rand Club Buildings.   'Phone 2695.

Housing for migrant workers

For black workers, the housing available in the towns depended on the labour needs of employers. The migrant labour system of the mines, for example, led to the development of the compounds. Later, compounds were also used by other employers of migrant workers in the towns – by the growing municipalities on the Rand, for instance, and by other employers of large numbers of unskilled workers, like those in the building industry. Conditions in the compounds are described on page 77.

There were also many black workers who lived at their places of work. Domestic workers lived in the back yards of the houses they cleaned; cooks, waiters and cleaners lived behind or at the top of the hotels and boarding houses they serviced. Most of these workers were migrant workers. Their homes were in the Reserves or on the farms where their families lived, to which they returned whenever they could.

Housing for town-based workers

But with greater hardships on the land, especially after the 1913 Land Act and the droughts in the following few years, more people made the trek to the Rand to look for work. Many eventually settled in the towns.

After World War I the economy of the Rand began to develop more rapidly. (This is discussed in more detail in Chapter 5.) As industries developed, they began to require more settled, semi-skilled workers who would not leave after a few months. They wanted to retain the services of the delivery man who was trusted to use the firm's bicycle, or the worker who had learnt to use a new machine. So it was more profitable to encourage trained workers, both black and white, to stay in town for as long as possible.

These workers needed homes for themselves and their families. The small 'locations' set aside for blacks were soon outgrown and usually, like white workers, they settled as near as they could to their places of work.

Overcrowding

The new working-class suburbs helped to create a greater distance between the skilled artisans and the new, unskilled workers. The residential divisions (which the town clerk had been so anxious to avoid) remained, and working-class areas in the inner city did indeed grow into slums as more people settled in Johannesburg.

An early domestic worker. A Town Regulation of 1899 ruled that 'coloured persons [blacks] may not reside in any place abutting on the public street in any town or village, but every householder or owner of an erf may keep in his backyard whatever servants he requires for domestic service'.

The map of early Johannesburg shows that the places nearest to the centre of town were working class and poorer areas – the Brickfields and Vrededorp areas to the west and (later) the Doornfontein and Jeppe areas to the east. They all developed into cheap, inner city housing areas for poor people of all colours.

The houses in these areas were mostly very small. The stands in the areas originally set aside for blacks were even smaller. Yet, to be able to live on their miserably low wages, black workers had to share more and more of their space in order to pay less rent.

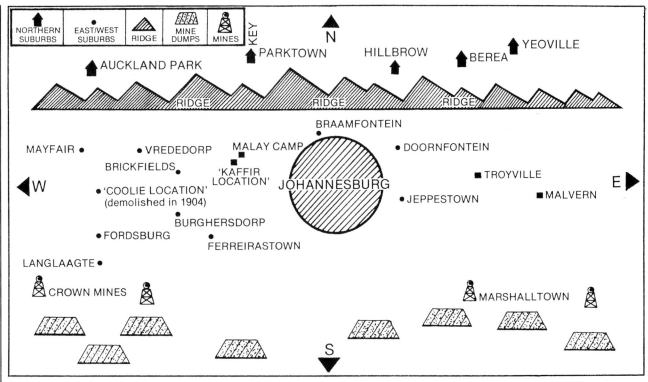

Johannesburg, about 1910.

By 1910, the main suburbs in Johannesburg had been laid out. The town ran from east to west, in the same direction as the gold reef. Suburbs north of the ridge became upper-class and middle-class areas. The area south of the town developed slowly, because most of that land was the property of the mines.

Space for workers, therefore, was expensive because it was limited. Blocked from settling north of the ridge (see map) and south of the town, which was mining property, they had to squeeze into areas immediately east and west of the shopping centre. It was hard for black workers, particularly, to find a place to live.

A rural family treks to town. Many white peasants lost their land during the Anglo-Boer War. Others could not survive the depression that followed. The disastrous droughts and cattle diseases in the years 1913-1916 wiped out many more of the small farmers and bywoners, forcing them to move to the towns or the diamond diggings in search of a living.

Soon there was overcrowding, and from the earliest years blacks began to spill into 'white' areas, often only a street away.

Lack of services

In these areas – the 'slums', the 'camps', the 'yards' and the 'locations' – there were few services provided, even though these services were basic needs for health and even life itself.

As described in *The Diseases of Poverty* on page 78, time and again the Medical Officers of Health in the Rand towns complained about the conditions people had to live under. What was the attitude of the government and the town councils towards the housing of the poor? What steps did they take to improve conditions?

Official housing policy

From the earliest years of colonial government, it was customary to keep the housing of different race groups separate – in other words, the policy was one of *segregation*. The Transvaal government too would always place black townships or 'locations' just outside the boundaries of each town – the first map of Johannesburg shows clearly the separate living areas marked out for Indians, 'coloureds', Africans and whites.

Indeed, in the early years some camps were established on the basis of ethnic groups. The name 'Malay Camp' goes back to this time. It was easier at first for people to set up homes near to friends and relatives, or people who had the same background.

Yet, as we see in the histories of Vrededorp, Doornfontein and Brickfields, and in other Rand towns, too, racial mixing soon developed amongst the poor and amongst the lower-paid workers, desperate for cheaper living space.

While *in theory* Vrededorp was a separate 'Afrikaner location', it was also situated next to the other workers' 'locations'.

The housing of Johannesburg was thus *in practice* divided along class lines – the working class poor of all racial groups had a clearly defined area of their own, set apart from the upper and middle classes. For instance, in Doornfontein the working class and middle class areas were separated by the railway line.

1905: a typical middle-class home. Its owner would have been represented on the Johannesburg Town Council.

Mixed housing

Why was 'mixed' housing allowed in a racial system like South Africa, where people are defined according to their colour?

Firstly, the Rand – Johannesburg in particular – was the centre of the industrial revolution in South Africa. This powerful force of change was beginning to weaken the old, colonial economy based on land and conquest. Instead, driven by profits, the fast-growing capitalist system was attracting work seekers, both black and white, from all over the country. Many came without capital or skills. They had only their labour to sell. Regardless of race, that was what they had in common as unskilled workers.

In this first period of Johannesburg's history, therefore, the town's housing pattern was that of most other industrial towns in the world, with more or less separate areas for the rich and the poor – the upper and middle classes, and the workers.

The town councils

For many years, official housing policy on the Rand was not clear cut. Rather, it reflected the struggles amongst people with different interests in the town councils.

The councils were run in the following way. Each municipality was responsible for the housing and servicing of its town. The money for the services came from the rates – mostly taxes on homeowners and other property owners. These people were of course either upper or middle-class, or they were better-paid workers who could afford their own homes. Their representatives sat on the town councils.

The money from these rates was used to run the towns, to build roads, and to supply the services described at the beginning of the chapter – as well as to beautify the town with parks and pools where people could relax.

The town councils, therefore, tended to be controlled by the rich and comfortable. The poor people, on the other hand, had little say in the running of the town, or how money should be spent, because they did not pay rates.

In the racially divided society of South Africa, the property owners were nearly all white. Those whites who were poor were at least allowed to share some of the recreational space and transport provided by the municipality.

Most blacks were too poor to be taxed – they certainly got few of the services or benefits. (In the early years, even the pavements were forbidden territory – blacks had to walk on the side of the road so as not to brush against white passers-by.) Their needs were neglected, and they had to manage as best they could with a minimum of help from the society and the towns they served.

Strolling in the park, reserved for (respectable) whites only.

Interest groups

In the early years after the Anglo-Boer War, most Rand town councils were controlled by mining capitalists. Mine owners had no specific interest in the housing of black workers, because black miners lived in the compounds while they were working their contracts.

But the living arrangements arrived at in Johannesburg suited a number of other interest groups that had emerged in the new capitalist system.

Employers wanted to keep their workers as near to their places of work as possible. They did not want extra transport costs and higher rents to push up the workers' cost of living, for that would oblige the employers to raise the wages of the workers. For example, when the Johannesburg municipality chose Klipspruit as a future 'location' for black workers, the government and employers expressed concern that the distance from town 'would have a depressing effect on the labour market'.[3]

Many *ratepayers*, who paid rates to the town council, objected to changes in the housing of the poor if the town council had to pay for these changes out of the rates.

Spending on black housing was kept to a minimum. Only when disease struck down too many workers and threatened to spread, as happened in Brickfields, was any attempt made to improve the conditions of the poor. Even then the council offered black residents a 'location', known as Nancefield, outside the town right next to a sewage dump.

Slum landlords, too, were benefiting from black workers living in town, and did not want them to move to improved housing. (See, for example, how slum removals were delayed in the histories of Brickfields and Doornfontein.) Nor were they prepared to spend extra money on improving existing property.

A 'yard' in Ferreirastown, originally a fashionable suburb. Rents soared so high that tenants began to move out and the empty buildings became run-down. When these properties were sold, the buyers extracted as much rent as possible from them. It did not matter who the new tenants were, or how many there were, as long as the weekly rent was paid. With many workers desperate for a roof over their heads, whole families would rent a single room — they could not afford to pay more — and the properties soon became packed with poor people, mostly black. In time, the whole area became a 'slum'. By 1916, black tenants as a whole were paying R100 000 in rent in Ferreirastown alone. (*The Star*, 13.1.1916.)

A cartoon illustrates the acute shortage of housing in the 1890s, and the building boom that went with it. Top: The speculator buys land from the Boer farmer. Middle: An old South African custom – black labour under white supervision. Bottom: Families move into the hastily erected houses before the last roof-sheet is nailed down.

Conclusion

In this chapter we have seen that the crowded environment of industrial towns creates a new kind of living. In a town, people work for a wage and the individual or the family unit cannot provide for all its basic needs. Services have to be organised by the town or the state if the people are to stay healthy and ready to report for work every day.

In the first stage of industrialisation in South Africa, and in other countries too as these pages show, services were not adequately provided for the poor and the lower-paid workers. The result was 'slum' living conditions, diseases and a high number of deaths, especially amongst children.

The industrialised towns quickly developed an inequality so great that it outstripped the older racial inequalities of the colonial farm labour system of the nineteenth century. While the lowest-paid workers – black and white – lived in dangerously over-crowded, under-serviced 'slums', the middle and upper classes lived comfortably in spacious, separate areas. And while the town councils developed to organise services for those they represented, they ignored the needs of the poor, especially the black poor.

The town councils allowed the housing and the servicing of the poor to remain more or less unregulated for many years, guided mainly by the needs of business and the job market.

But as the capitalist economy began to expand, industrialists, businessmen and the state itself were forced to pay more attention to the needs of the growing number of workers at their homes. These changes in housing are discussed in chapter 7.

Topics

Life in Early Johannesburg

This is how two English speakers remembered childhood in early Johannesburg:

'In place of a large, comfortable farm house on the open veld — a five-roomed cottage abutting on a dusty street. Where buckets of frothy milk came daily to our dairy, now ordinary dark bottles, none too clean, were taken from under wet sacks and sold for ninepence or a shilling each. Instead of the pleasant chug-chug of the churn and the large dish of fresh butter, we bought from the Chinaman's shop oily stuff imported from Australia. Instead of wagon-loads of sweet-smelling firewood — our bag of stony coal which was very slow in burning. No longer the great pot of boiling water on the river bank where women chatted as they washed the family clothing and hung it on thorn-bushes to dry. We gave our bundles of washing to native "boys" with number discs on their arms, who carried them away to God knows where . . . .

There were some taps from which we were sometimes able to get water, but this was often in short supply. We were mostly dependent on wells from which we drew water in a bucket by windlass, so different from the sun-kissed Fish River. If the yards were small, the water was often polluted by the close proximity of a pit-lavatory. Dysentery, fever and even small-pox were prevalent and as time passed, so the yellow small-pox warning flags increased. We children on our way to school were told to avoid streets where yellow flags hung out on bamboo poles from verandahs, but in time they became so numerous that we just held our breath and ran.'[4]

'There came a time of great hardship in Johannesburg. The population was increasing very rapidly and becoming more cosmopolitan. Food was very scarce and expensive and water difficult to obtain. In an attempt to keep out the hordes of "uitlanders" who, by their advent, were endangering the hard-won independence of the Boer Republic, President Kruger closed the drifts over the Vaal and so precipitated a crisis in Johannesburg.

Weeks of desperate famine resulted and food prices soared until a bag of mealie-meal cost R25 and a bucket of water was sold for half a crown [25 cents]! My family lived chiefly on a bag of rice and some tins of golden syrup which my father had been able to buy before the supplies ran out, while around the corner from our house the Chinese shopkeeper had rats strung up for sale outside his store — a source of delightful horror to my elder brothers and sisters.'[5]

The Brickfields Area

The Brickfields area was originally set aside for poorer white people. Brickfields was a marshy piece of ground granted to displaced Afrikaners who had taken up brick making for a living. Next to it was Burghersdorp, planned in 1891 to house the brick makers.

Burghersdorp-Brickfields was close to town and cheap. As the Johannesburg housing shortage grew, the government offered stands at lower prices to licensed brick makers and their employees. In the 1890s, as poverty increased in the countryside, more and more Afrikaners were forced to seek work in the towns. Many made their way to Johannesburg for jobs and shelter, and ended up in the cheapest living areas, like Brickfields.

Early Johannesburg families, before the advent of brick housing.

Brickfields in the 1890s. Puddles of water stood for months in the clay soil. To the left, raw bricks are lying in the sun. The houses varied in construction and quality, but every house had an oven for baking bricks.

Simple dwellings

Early reports describe houses of tin and iron, or very simple brick sheds, most of them built close together. By 1894 the area was so overcrowded that health inspectors had to use force to stop people from building any more houses. Rooms were very small, with very little air, and earth floors. The marshy ground was often pitted with puddles of stagnant water.

After the Anglo-Boer War, overcrowding became an even more serious problem. Buildings had been neglected during the war, and many collapsed. A census taken in 1903 shows that there were 5 651 people crammed into this small area — 1 811 were whites, mostly Afrikaners, the rest being Africans, 'coloureds' and Asians. The area had thus become a slum for the poor of all colours.

The brick industry was forced to close down (as we saw in Chapter 2), but it left behind a large, shallow dip of land which did not drain well. The area was often flooded during the rainy summer months. Water supplies came from shallow wells in private yards. Lavatories were holes in the ground and much of the water had been made unusable because some wells had been used as lavatories, or polluted by manure and dead animals.

So bad was the situation that the municipal council was forced, in 1902, to appoint an 'Insanitary Area Improvement Commission' to inquire into the Brickfields-Burghersdorp area. The 'insanitary area' included the 'Coolie Location' where 3 000 people lived. Only about 630 were Indians. The rest were a mixture of other black and white groups, the majority being African.[6] The medical officer reported:

'It consists of narrow courtyards, containing dilapidated and dirty tin huts, without adequate means of lighting and ventilation, and constructed without any regard to sanitary considerations of any kind. In the middle of each slop-sodden and filth-bestrewn yard there is a well from which the people get their water supply, and they choose this place for washing purposes, urinals and closets [lavatories] sometimes being in the immediate vicinity. In one case the closet is about one pace from the well.'[7]

Yet the Brickfields area was close to town and therefore valuable. The new governor of the Transvaal, Lord Milner, had plans to expand Johannesburg and encourage the development of industry. In 1902 the town council suggested that the whole area be demolished and redeveloped. But these plans were delayed by the objections of the landlords in Brickfields. At last, the owners of the area agreed to accept more than one million pounds for land that the town council valued at a third of that amount.

Even then, the people of Brickfields were not immediately moved to improved houses, because the white voters opposed every new area of settlement proposed by the town council.

The plague

But in March 1904, the bubonic plague broke out. This is the disease which swept over Europe a few hundred years ago and took the lives of millions of people. The bubonic plague flourishes in dirty and unhealthy living conditions amongst underfed, poor people. The news of the plague horrified the wealthier Johannesburgers, for the disease spreads quickly. Their action was swift.

The people of the 'Coolie Location' and Brickfields were removed overnight. The shacks and houses were burnt to the ground. The black inhabitants were moved to a 'temporary camp' (it did not turn out to be temporary) next to a sewage farm called Klipspruit, on a site about 20 kilometres from Johannesburg. Known as Nancefield, this site eventually developed into a 'location' called Orlando in the 1930s, and was to become the first suburb of Soweto many years later.

In the place of Brickfields, Newtown was built, with a new Johannesburg market at its centre.

The Vrededorp-Malay Camp Area

In 1895 the government of the South African Republic (the Transvaal) decided to set aside some vacant land west of the Braamfontein cemetery for the housing of various black groups. However, poor Afrikaners (or 'burghers') sent a petition to the government to ask for land in that area at a special price. The black housing areas were then shifted to make space for an Afrikaner housing settlement called 'Vrededorp', the 'village of peace'.

Only poor burghers or their widows were allowed to occupy the land. They had to pay 2s6d (25 cents) a month for a licence and were evicted if they fell behind more than three months with their payments. During the hard times of the Anglo-Boer War, many of these desperately poor burghers sold their licences. After the war, the new government allowed the Vrededorp stands to be sold without restriction. Most of the new people who moved into Vrededorp came from Fordsburg and Brickfields after the plague (1904). Most were Afrikaners — there were very few English names on the register.

But Vrededorp was not an all-white suburb. A survey taken in 1910 showed that nearly 100 black tenants were living there amongst the whites. A few were shopkeepers, and the rent paid for their shops was an important source of income to the white licence-holders. In 1912 all blacks (except servants) were forced to move out of Vrededorp, but within a few years yards were being divided and let to black tenants again. In 1913, the government actually built schools for coloured children in Vrededorp and more coloureds moved into the area.

A Vrededorp street in the 1920s. By then it had developed into a largely multi-racial suburb for the poor.

The 'Malay Camp'

The 'Malay Camp' was established in 1894. The 'location' was divided into 279 small stands, each fifty feet square. It is reported that when President Kruger saw the plans, he drew a line through the stands, dividing them in half, and said, 'Ek sal nie hulle plase gee nie, maar net sitplekke.'[8]

The stands cost seven shillings and sixpence (seventy-five cents) plus another 7s6d for rates, and only 'Malays' or coloureds were allowed to buy them. However, in time Indians bought over stands, and by 1905 nearly half the population was 'Asian'.

The 'Malay Camp' (Pageview), which adjoined Vrededorp.

As the housing shortage got worse for blacks, more and more people were crowded into the Malay Location. Conditions were very bad. There was a primitive sewerage and drainage system, and people were forced to throw their slop water out into the streets. In 1908 the **Rand Daily Mail** described the Malay Location as 'the worst slum in Johannesburg'. When small-pox broke out in the area the municipality sent a rat catcher and installed a modern sewerage system — but only about half a dozen families could afford to install new lavatories.

Things never really improved in the Malay Location. In the first place, the South African Railways announced in 1906 that it would be needing the area for new railway sidings within the next ten years. It seemed as if people of the location would have to go, and landlords

Recruiting labour for the mines, 1905. These workers were destined to be housed in compounds. Other large employers, like municipalities and construction firms, followed the example of the mines and provided accommodation. Usually this was of the most basic kind – concrete bunks, no heating, no lighting, no running water. Food had to be cooked outside.

and the municipal council were not prepared to spend money on improvements.

Secondly, after the bubonic plague (see *The Brickfields Area*) many of those evicted from Brickfields trickled into the Malay Location, which was nearer than Klipspruit to their workplaces, and therefore cheaper for them. And so, by removing one slum (in the Brickfields area) yet not providing convenient alternative housing, the municipal council was responsible for the making of another slum, just across the railway line.

In 1912 the Medical Officer of Health wrote a report on conditions in the Malay Location. He found an overcrowded district, with more than ten people living on each small stand – in the main house, in the stables and other outbuildings, and even in the shops. For heating and cooking, most people used old paraffin tins, without chimneys.

In 1920 the municipal council finally decided to set aside R200 000 for the improvement of the Malay Location. They aimed to establish sports grounds and lay out a park. But these plans came to nothing – a petition by 4 000 whites from neighbouring suburbs called for the removal of the Malay Location because it was 'a danger to health, life and morals'. Instead of improving conditions to help remove these dangers, the council postponed their plans.

Compounds For Migrant Workers

For many years, most black workers on the Rand were migrant workers. The migrant labour system was a cheap form of labour for the employer because the migrant worker was not paid a family wage, but barely enough for a single person to stay alive on.

In the mines, compounds were provided for the workers. This reduced costs even further, and enabled the mining companies to keep down wages for over 50 years. The system worked so well from the employer's point of view that a number of municipalities on the Rand tried the same thing. They built compounds – or hostels – to house their municipal workers while they were employed by the municipality.

The earliest compounds in Johannesburg were camps of tents or low iron huts in rows. As industry developed, employers of 50 or more black workers were obliged by municipal regulations to provide accommodation for them. Company hostels were convenient for the employers as they provided cheap accommodation as well as saving on transport costs, thus keeping the cost of wages low. Also, workers could be better regulated in compounds, as they depended on the employer for both their wages and the roof over their heads.

Municipal compounds

The compounds differed in quality. In the early years of the newly built municipal hostels, conditions were reasonable, although not comfortable. One report gave glowing descriptions of the Smit Street compound in Johannesburg, built in 1915 to house 1 100 workers employed by the Department of the Town Engineer.

> 'It can truly be stated as a model . . . . Each dormitory (sleeping room) accommodates 40 boys. The rooms are arranged round a quadrangle (square) with a wide verandah; each room is well ventilated and heated by a complete system of hot water installation by means of radiators. There is also an up-to-date cooking plant and the sanitary arrangements leave nothing to be desired. The only defect is the lack of a large area for sport and recreation to which the manager of the compound told us the natives quickly respond. This compound reflects great credit to all concerned.'[9]

On the other hand, the Sanitary Department compound was described as 'a slum. The existence of such a compound is a disgrace . . . .'[10]

Both the old and the new compounds signified that the black workers staying there were not meant to settle in the towns.

A municipal officer supervises the fumigation of houses in the so-called 'Coolie Location' during the plague of 1904.

The Diseases of Poverty

From time to time, epidemics would strike the poorer areas of the town. Early Johannesburg saw the outbreak of cholera, the bubonic plague, a number of smallpox epidemics and other infectious diseases. Some of these are discussed in other sections of this chapter. There were also other diseases of poverty which never went away.

In 1904, for example, the Johannesburg Medical Officer of Health reported that 17 out of 1 000 whites had died in that year, compared with 33 out of 1 000 blacks. There were thus nearly twice as many deaths amongst the black population, who were poorer.

Pneumonia

One of the main killers was the lung disease of pneumonia — on the mines, but also in the crowded towns.

'Pneumonia is an infectious disease', commented the medical officer, and went on to describe how an 'insanitary environment, overcrowding, air pollution, as well as inferior and insufficient food, and neglect of precautions against the sudden changes of temperature' increased the chances of contracting this disease.

The conditions he was describing had a simple cause: poverty. People were breathing in disease-carrying germs all the time, but the poorest were least able to resist these diseases.

Typhoid

In 1904, typhoid killed off nearly 2 000 people in Johannesburg. The Medical Officer of Health reported that this disease, too, bred more easily where there was 'pollution of soil and air by the present bucket system, extensive soil pollution by slops and by natives promiscuously defecating in outlying districts.'[11]

Lack of services

All these conditions pointed to the lack of sewerage and water services for the poor. The medical officer also noted that the killer disease of the stomach (enteritis) struck down most of its victims in households that did not have plumbing but drew their drinking water from unprotected wells which could be contaminated by animals and people.

Earlier, in 1902, the medical officer had warned the Insanitary Area Committee against conditions in the 'Coolie Location' near Brickfields. His warning was ignored until the outbreak of bubonic plague. It was feared that the disease would spread, and the result was that Brickfields was burnt down, as described on page 76.

The T.B. Commission

Another regular disease amongst the poor was tuberculosis of the lungs (T.B.). This was so widespread that eventually the government was forced to appoint a commission to examine its causes. In 1914 the commission made its report. It found that the disease was caused by lack of food and clean water, by dirt and by overcrowding — in short, the living conditions caused by poverty.

The commission made a special point of examining black 'locations' throughout the country. They found a remarkable sameness in most of them. In the urban areas, the commission found that 'the majority . . . are a menace to the health of their inhabitants, and indirectly to the health of those in the towns'.[12] It went on to report that the sites were badly chosen, often in some donga, on stony ground, or near sewerage works or garbage tips outside of town. Also, a proper water supply and street lights were usually lacking.

A Johannesburg yard. The drums are for storing water or for cooking food. Overcrowding, poverty, and the lack of services — clean water, sewerage and rubbish collection — were major causes of disease.

There were few public lavatories. Most people had to share a hole in the ground. Garbage was not collected — people were expected to dump their rubbish in a donga or a sluit.

But the commission found the worst fault with the houses themselves:

'With few exceptions they are a disgrace, and the majority are quite unfit for human habitation . . . the dwellings are mere shanties, often nothing more than hovels, constructed out of bits of packing lining, flattened kerosene tins, sacking and other scraps of odds and ends. The dwellings are low, dark and dirty, generally encumbered with unclean and useless rubbish, mud floors the rule, often below ground level and consequently sometimes apt to be flooded in wet weather. Overcrowding is frequent; and altogether one could hardly imagine more suitable conditions for the spread of tuberculosis'.[13]

The 1918 'flu epidemic

The overcrowded, under-serviced and poverty-stricken living conditions in the towns left the poor weak. Their bodies were not able to resist the infectious diseases introduced by the many newcomers to the towns.

In 1918, a great 'flu epidemic spread from Europe to other parts of the world. When it hit South Africa, thousands of people, especially blacks, died within a few weeks. It was the shock of these sudden deaths, plus the fears of the neighbouring middle-class areas, that forced the government to examine the conditions of the slums. Their 'solution' to the problem was to plan for racially segregated, cheap housing for the poor, both blacks and whites.

However, housing of this kind was a long time in coming to the Rand, and when it was built at last, the black population had grown so rapidly that the municipalities could not hope to keep up an adequate supply of houses. As more and more women and children joined the urban population, so overcrowding in the inner city increased. New diseases and higher death rates, especially the deaths of babies, added to the tragedy of poverty in the towns.[14]

Influenza

Song Composed by R T Caluza

In the year of 1918
We were wiped out
By a disease which they call influenza
It took friends which we loved
Mothers, fathers, sisters, and brothers

In other homes, nobody survived
It took maidens, and young men
Taking the beautiful
It took the most coveted
The cream of our youth
It took even the handsome virile men
It took even virgins
Who were pleasing to the eye
It took those with home and promise
It took young brides and grooms

It was as if there were a black cloud
Hanging over this earth
Which had come to take our youth
It burnt the elderly out
Mothers and fathers left orphans
Sad and suffering
With no one to help them out

It was like this in the wilderness
For those who were travelling to Canaan
When they started to suffer on the journey
They pitied themselves
Because when they ruled
They were happy
They forgot their maker
Only those who worshipped him constantly
Pulled through
The rest were destroyed,
Out there in the wilderness

Now we want to warn our sons and daughters
Do not let your hearts rule your heads
Because it can never be satisfied.[15]

The Effects of the Industrial Revolution in Britain

It was not only in South Africa that working-class slums developed. Wherever industrialisation and capitalism went hand in hand, thousands of people were forced to leave the land and seek work in the towns. The new conditions of town life, overcrowding, and low wages led to miserable living standards.

A typical report on conditions of working-class life in Edinburgh, the capital of Scotland, 1836:

'He had never before seen such misery, where people were without everything, two married couples often sharing one room. In a single day he had visited seven houses in which there was not a bed, in some of them not even a heap of straw. Old people sleep on the board floor, nearly all slept in their day clothes. In one cellar room he found two families from a Scotch country district; soon after their removal to the city two of the children had died, and a third was dying at the time of his visit.'

Notes

1) J Ramsay Macdonald, *What I Saw in South Africa* (London, 1902), cited by C van Onselen, *Studies in the Social and Economic History of the Witwatersrand*, Vol.1, *New Babylon*, p.27.
2) Cited by C van Onselen, as above, p.30.
3) N Kagan, 'African Settlements in the Johannesburg Area, 1903-1923', MA Thesis, University of the Witwatersrand, 1978, p.157.
4) Ralls and Gordon, *Daughter of Yesterday* (Howard Timmins, Cape Town, 1975), p.34.
5) Fred Hoskings, 'Come Wind, Come Weather', unpublished diary.
6) N Kagan, as above, p.21.
7) Report of the Medical Officer of Health to the Insanitary Area Commission, 18.11.1902, para.838.
8) F Frescura, 'Witwatersrand Townships, Labour and Protest', paper presented to History Workshop, University of the Witwatersrand, 1978, p.3.
9) N Kagan, as above, p.111.
10) N Kagan, as above, p.112.
11) Report of the Johannesburg Medical Officer of Health, 1903-1904, p.31.
12) Report of the Tuberculosis Commission, 1914.
13) Cited by J S Allison, 'Urban Native Legislation', UX (South African Institute of Race Relations), Vol.vii, No.4, 1940.
14) Chapters 7 and 8 include a discussion of infant mortality in later years.
15) R T Caluza was a music teacher at Ohlange School in Natal from 1909. See too Chapter 1, p.18, from D Coplan, *In Township Tonight! South Africa's Black City Music and Theatre*, (Ravan Press, Johannesburg, 1985). Song translated by Fatima Dike.

Chapter 4
Protest and Resistance

Chapters 1 to 3 have described how people worked and lived on the early Rand, and where all these people had come from. Between 1886 and 1914 they continued to arrive in a steady stream. From about 1914, the population of newcomers to the Rand increased even more rapidly. With their different backgrounds and experiences, many of the settlers on the Rand had one thing in common – this was their first experience of urban life. As described in Chapter 3, the poor, the unemployed and the lowest-paid workers suffered the greatest hardships, yet they got very little help or understanding either from those who controlled the town councils, or from the government itself.

This chapter looks at how the workers and the urban poor fought back, and how those in power responded to them. While some challenged their condition of life through organised labour resistance, others expressed their grievances in less obvious ways.

A clash between strikers and police, 1913.

Newcomers from the land

Anti-pass meeting, March 1919.

The rapid development of the Rand brought regular waves of newcomers. One such 'wave' came from the rural areas after a series of droughts, diseases and locusts attacked the land. The years 1912, 1913, 1914 and 1916 ruined many small farmers and eventually pushed more rural people, including whites, into the towns.

Growing agricultural capitalism (bigger farms, more investments in machines, etc.) was also steadily removing the independent small farmers. The 1913 Land Act described in Chapter 1 accelerated the change from sharecropping to labour tenancy. White-owned land used for commercial farming almost doubled in the 1920s. By 1930, the Institute of Race Relations was pointing out that

> 'The white farmer is making more use than he did originally of his farm and the farm is becoming too small for himself, his children and the natives.'[1]

As land became more profitable and scarce, more and more sharecroppers were evicted, or else turned into labour tenants. Unlike sharecroppers, labour tenants could not work the land for themselves and share their crops with the landlord. They had to work directly for the landowner in return for being allowed to live on the land, usually without wages. Labour tenancy was often half-yearly labour, during the summer months. The rest of the year, many labour tenants went to find work in the towns, and formed a 'floating population' in the industrial areas. Some capitalist farmers, like the fruit, tobacco and cotton farmers around White River, Nelspruit and Barberton, went so far as to expel their labour tenants because it was more profitable to hire migrant labour. The result was that from about 1918 onwards, many people left the farms permanently and moved into the towns.

Settled townspeople

For whatever reasons they left the land, people continued to come to the Rand because of the job opportunities there. Many people avoided the mines and clustered in the towns. Between 1911 and 1921, the town population nearly doubled. During that same period, the population of African townswomen grew by 30 000. Between 1918 and 1920, the number of Africans *not* working in the mines grew from 67 111 to 92 597.[2] The numbers of African women grew even more rapidly, from 98 000 to 147 000.[3]

The beginning of the migration of black women to the towns is significant because their arrival began to change the pattern of black urban living. With women came children and families, and a steadier way of life. Once men had their families with them in the towns, they were even more concerned to keep permanent jobs. At the same time, more and more jobs outside of mining were becoming available – the towns and the

Women employees at a Rand mine. The arrival of women and children began to change the pattern of life in the towns, and blacks began to see themselves as townspeople.

municipalities were growing, and more industries were being set up, as we shall see in the next chapter. The table on this page showing the number of labourers registered every day in Johannesburg gives an idea of the kind of jobs available to black workers – as well as the opportunities open to self-employed blacks – in 1923.

Economic effects of the World War

In the period we are examining, a world event was having an important effect on the economy of the Rand. In 1914, Britain went to war against Germany, a rival power in trade and colonies. Britain's large empire, including South Africa, was drawn into the war, too.

British manufacturing was now geared to supplying war needs – tanks, guns, bombs and other weapons, as well as uniforms, boots, helmets and food supplies for the soldiers. The seas became battlefields too, and few trading ships were allowed to cross the oceans. One effect on South Africa was that the war cut off imported goods from Britain. Only urgent goods were supplied – the rest would have to be produced inside the country.

The result was a rapid development of the small factories that had been started on the Rand since the South African War, as described in Chapter 2, pages 50 and 51. In the long term, this was a very important development because factories were to provide many new jobs for unskilled and semi-skilled workers in the years to come. (Chapter 6 describes these jobs, the workers and their organisations.)

There was also a great jump in the cost of living. The value of money dropped. For the lowest paid town workers, this was particularly hard. According to government statistics, the average value of the wages of Africans working in factories dropped by just over 13

Wages of Black Workers on the Rand, July 1918*

Job	%Non-mining population	Average wage	Conditions
House boys	50%	R4-6 per month	with food and accommodation
Store boys	23%	R7-8 per month	without accommodation
Stable boys	9%	R5-6	with food and accommodation
Industrial workers	15%	R1,50-R2,20 per week	no food or accommodation

* Source: Director of Native Labour, July 1918

percent between 1916 and 1917. In other words, a wage of R8 per month in 1916 could have been worth only R7 in 1917.[4]

Hardship and control

Most newcomers found themselves squeezed into freehold areas such as Sophiatown, Martindale or Newclare, or forced to live in the squalid housing conditions of the slums described in Chapter 3. Their arrival aggravated the growing shortage of housing on the Rand, and pushed up the rents.

Added to these hardships, the pass system made the life of every African town worker a misery. The harsh manner in which passes were checked by the police became a bitterly sore point. Even the Native Affairs Inspector for Krugersdorp commented:

'The Pass Laws as applied in the Labour Districts appear to be based on the assumption that every native is a criminal from whom the rest of the community has to be protected.'[5]

The pass system was being used to control the rapid movement of black labour to the towns, and to help employers to hold African workers to their contracts. As every pass-bearer also had his wages written on his pass, every new job tended to be pegged to the wage of the first job. The pass system therefore delivered a low-paid work-force into the hands of the employers. In 1919, two Transvaal Congress leaders, H.L. Bud-Mbelle and C. Mabaso, announced:

A scene showing hundreds of anti-pass demonstrators under arrest, 1919. The Transvaal Congress and the IWA (Industrial Workers of Africa), the organisations which led the campaign, blamed the pass system for low wages.

'At our meeting at Vrededorp on 30 March 1919 we came to the conclusion that passes prevented money.'[6]

Passes did in fact 'prevent money'. They were related to the Masters and Servants Act, which tied a worker to a contract at a fixed wage, regardless of growing inflation. A clerk, Benjamin Phooko, representing 5 000 municipal labourers, put it this way:

'Allowing prices to rise alarms us because we have entered into contracts that cannot be broken, so as to demand a higher price for our labour.'[7]

The miserable wages and living conditions of black workers reached a crisis point in 1918 to 1919. Not fit enough to resist sickness, 127 745 black people died during the influenza epidemic. In the towns, 11 out of every 1 000 Africans died that year, while over 400 out of every 1 000 black babies in the towns lost their lives.[8]

Protest

Clearly, the wages and living conditions of black workers were insufficient to maintain them in good health. A groundswell of anger began to grow, and the years after the war saw a series of militant campaigns. In Nancefield (Klipspruit) numerous petitions were ignored until eventually there was a violent outburst and a stayaway, described on page 92.

On the East Rand, boycotts against high prices in the mine stores were a protest against the rising cost of living. There was also the 1918 'shilling-a-day' campaign for higher wages, as described in *Collective Resistance* on page 89, and for a time there was united black action, drawn from all classes, against the hated

The staff of *Bantu World*, about 1920, in Westdene, Johannesburg.

pass system. Added to these protests, there was the succession of strikes described on page 86.

This period of unrest shows that there was a growing awareness of the strength of *organised* resistance. It also shows that thousands of blacks were beginning to fight issues in the towns, and see themselves as part of the towns. Even one of the more cautious Congress leaders, Saul Msane, pointed out:

> 'The masses in the native population are beginning to realise that they are an indispensable factor in the natural and social fabric of South Africa. They are beginning to see that the whole industrial system in this land is based and must be based on their willing cooperation.'[9]

This town-based consciousness was growing more rapidly on the Rand, where a huge black population was massed together in one industrial centre. It is significant that the leadership of the ANC shifted in June 1917 to the Rand, when John Dube and R. Selope Thema were replaced by Johannesburgers S.M. Makgato as president and Saul Msane as secretary-general. Johannesburg also published the Congress newspaper, *Abantu-Batho*, which was controlled by the Transvaal branch of Congress and read by the growing numbers of literate townspeople on the Rand.[10]

For thousands of blacks, the Rand was their only home. They were dispossessed of land, yet not accepted in the white-controlled towns. In one sense they were worse off than migrant workers because their wages had to support their families in full, yet these wages were based on the ultra-low wages fixed by

the mines, with the excuse that all black workers were supported by a rural economy.

Yet, as the wave of strikes by municipal workers showed during 1918 and 1919, even migrant workers living in the compounds were unable to come out on their low wages. The table of average black wages on the Rand on page 83 gives an idea of the level of their exploitation.

In the ten years after the 1920 strike, organised resistance developed in the form of the *Industrial and Commercial Workers Union* (the ICU), whose history is given from page 107. There we see that the activities of the ICU were far-ranging and country-wide, starting in Cape Town, then moving rapidly towards the industrial centre of the Rand, but serving also the needs of rural workers and poor peasants, who as we have seen were struggling against the encroachment of capitalist farming. At that stage many still hoped to get their land back.

The ICU reflected the in-between position of millions of blacks in those years as people of two worlds — as workers in the industrial centres or on white-owned farms, and as cultivators of the land for the survival of their families. It was able to express different grievances, hopes and dreams for different people, whether they were workers settled in the towns, migrants, farm workers or poor peasants struggling to make ends meet in the reserves.

Capitalism in crisis

The period after World War I was also a time of crisis for capitalism. Throughout the world there was a depression. At the same time, South Africa was feeling the pinch of inflation.

On the mines, inflation pushed up production costs, yet the price of gold remained fixed. The mine owners were looking for ways to save money so that they could prevent their profits from dropping so low that some of the less profitable mines would have to close down. So they would not allow black miners' wages to go up. Their tight profit squeeze helps to explain the brutal way in which the black miners' strike was crushed in 1920. (See *Gold and Workers* for further discussion of this strike.)

The crisis of profits also affected other sectors of capital – trade and industry – so that workers throughout South Africa were not getting the rises they were asking for.

Militant action

The result of this refusal to raise wages was that workers turned to militant collective action. White as well as black workers were going on strike throughout South Africa during this period. On the Rand, there had been a struggle over union recognition ever since the Transvaal Mine Workers Union was formed in 1902. There was a series of bitter campaigns against the mining companies. The 1907 strike was followed by the Transvaal Industrial Disputes Prevention Act of 1909, which tried to outlaw strikes. The 1913 strike over union recognition spread to the railway and power station workers, and led in 1914 to a general strike. The government responded with the Act of Indemnity and the Riotous Assemblies Act, designed to make strikes in public services illegal and to outlaw peaceful picketing.

But the industrial development of World War I brought more power to the unions. From 1915 to 1918 union membership increased from 10 538 to 77 819. Militant action included the strike of the ironmoulders for paid annual leave in 1918, followed by the Johannesburg engineers' strike and the builders' strike of 1919. And at least twice before 1922, white unions took a vote on whether to go on general strike or not.

The years after the war were also a time of excitement and hope for many workers. They were inspired by the Russian socialist revolution of October 1917. (See page 106.) In South Africa, the International Workers of the World and the short-lived Industrial Workers of Africa were organisations that hoped to create a society where the mines and factories would be owned by those who produced the wealth – the workers.[11] Even those workers who did not support socialism became more critical of the capitalist system.

The 1922 Strike

The combination of the dwindling profits of the mining companies and the growing militancy of the unions came to a head in the general strike of white workers in 1922. As described in *Gold and Workers*, Chapter 15, the mining companies sought to cut costs by reorganising the work in the mines – they intro-

---

Miners outside a mine store. Situated next to the compounds, these stores had a monopoly over the custom of mineworkers. Rising prices after the war led to a widespread boycott.

The arrest of leaders during the 1920 mineworkers' strike.
They were later sentenced to three months' hard labour.

duced new, labour-saving machinery which would be operated by black miners at the same ultra-low wages. In addition, hundreds of white workers would be made redundant. The struggle for union recognition became increasingly tied to the job insecurity of white miners. Once again, the ultra-exploitation of black workers led to the insecurity of white workers, and a further racial division amongst workers.

As workers, most of the white miners wanted a fairer share of the profits they helped to create at considerable risk to their health and even their lives (see *Accident!* on page 102): as whites in a racially divided society, they wanted to deny this share to blacks because they feared that the blacks' low wages would undercut them. The white workers thus found themselves in a *contradiction* – a situation creating opposite effects. This contradiction was expressed in the socialist, yet racist, slogan of the strike:

'Workers of the World Unite for a White South Africa!'

In January 1922, 25 000 white workers went on strike. Black workers were prevented from working and so the mines stopped production. The strikers took up arms, the Smuts government called in the army, and hundreds of people were killed. The strike raged on for two months.

In the end the workers lost the strike. Over five thousand strikers were arrested and found guilty of sedition. Four men were hanged. The white miners had

Railway workers protest over union recognition, 1913.
This issue led to a general strike the following year.

to accept lower pay. Hundreds were laid off, while black workers took over more of the productive work – at the same wages as before.

A new government

The white workers lost the strike. However, they had another weapon – the political power of the vote. In the elections of 1924, the white workers turned against Smuts, and his government was swept from power.

The Labour Party, which represented most of the English-speaking craft workers, and the National Party, which had the support of Afrikaner workers, formed an alliance and together they won the elections.

Soldiers versus strikers in Braamfontein, Johannesburg, 1922.

Bomber aircraft flying over the working-class suburb of Fordsburg, 1922. The strike brought South Africa close to a civil war: thousands of white workers were on one side, the mineowners and the state on the other.

They called the new government the Pact Government, and the new Prime Minister was J.M.B. Hertzog, leader of the National Party.

In the years that followed, the new government developed a definite labour and economic policy. It aimed to *co-opt* the white working class — that is, to create a white working class willing to ally itself with capital. More importantly, it did all in its power to encourage the growth of South African capitalism and South African industry, as the next chapter will show.

Collective Resistance

For a long time, individual black workers had been asking for wage increases — especially since 1917, when inflation had begun to bite hard. Then came collective action. Workers were gaining experience and beginning to feel that they had some power through their labour.

Collective demands

What collective action could do was clearly illustrated in May 1917, when white municipal engineers went on strike. For five nights, Johannesburg was without lights. The Johannesburg municipality hastily granted a 23 percent increase to *all* white municipal workers. The ease of the white workers' gain made an impression on the black workers. It seemed as if the authorities were in a weak position, and black workers were quick to seize their chance.

On 13 May black railway workers demanded and got an increase of 2½ cents a day. This success triggered off a wave of collective demands right across the Rand. A week later, the workers at the Destructor Compound

Workers in the sanitation section of the Johannesburg municipality. In 1918 they went on strike for higher pay.

in Newtown demanded wage increases, followed by compound workers in nearly all the other municipal compounds. The Johannesburg Council was most alarmed at this 'concerted action'. The Inspector of Native Affairs said that

> 'It would appear to indicate that correspondence and organisation is being evolved among the natives employed in large concerns.'[12]

The Council was afraid that it might lose control of the black workers, and decided not to encourage collective demands by giving increases. On 1 June, it told the Vrededorp Sanitary Municipal workers that they could not get increases, but had to finish their contracts. If they were unhappy, they could leave. If they stayed on, a small increase would be considered.

These workers were the 'bucket boys'. Their job was to collect the sewage from the lavatories of all houses in Johannesburg. (This was before the days of flush toilets in the white suburbs.) For this necessary but unpleasant job, the workers received R5 a month for a seven-day working week on a contract of 180 days.[13]

Strikes

The result of this ultimatum was a wave of strikes that rippled through the Rand. The Natalspruit workers were the first to go on strike. Fifty were promptly arrested. Then the Vrededorp workers were asked to take over the jobs of the 'bucket boys' at double pay. But they refused to scab. The Wolhuter and Springfield compounds also stood firm. There were more arrests, followed by the trial of the 'bucket boys'. They were sentenced to three months' hard labour in their jobs (without pay) for breaking their contracts under the Masters and Servants Act.

Congress leaders arrested in 1919 for incitement during the strikes and anti-pass campaigns. From left to right: J Ngojo, A Cetyiwe, L T Mvabaza, H Kraai, L Masina and D S Letanka.

Black workers were outraged by this harsh sentence, and Congress leaders immediately arranged a protest meeting. The Industrial Workers of Africa, a black organisation inspired by the largely white International Socialist League, called for a general strike. The Transvaal Congress was divided. Some leaders called for moderation. They seemed to feel that black workers were not strong enough to challenge employers.

At the first protest meeting I. Bud-Mbelle (son of H.L. Bud-Mbelle) advised:

'My countrymen, do not forget we are in a critical time. Do not forget that we have not a single grey-headed man among us, therefore when the fat is in the fire we must remove it ourselves . . . the Congress at Bloemfontein decided that its sentiment was against any form of strike. If we do not stop the strike the whole of Johannesburg will be in flames . . . . I therefore entreat you to stop the strike. I entreat you to help those people financially, protect them in the appeal required against the magistrate's judgement. At the same time, let us make it quite clear that we are opposed to strikes.'[14]

When Bud-Mbelle voiced his fear that 'the whole of Johannesburg will be in flames', the audience's reply was, 'Let it burn!' Bud-Mbelle left the meeting in con-

fusion. After a few weeks' debate, L.T. Mvabasa (of Nancefield – see page 92) proposed that Congress stop their petitions and demand instead a wage increase of a shilling (10 cents) a day as of 1 July, and recommended class action if this was not granted:

'The capitalists and workers are at war everywhere in every country . . . . The white workers do not write to the Governor-General when they want more pay. They strike and get what they should.'[15]

In the meantime, black workers were taking matters into their own hands. On 13 June, 118 Premier Milling workers struck for higher pay, and nearly 500 workers from another eight firms demanded pay increases. And while Congress urged workers not to strike yet, but to wait for a reply to their 10-cent demand, workers from several Johannesburg firms as well as 6 000 mineworkers went on strike on 1 July.

The Johannesburg council became very uneasy and it seemed as if it might give in to the demands, but a letter from government officials warned them that

'For the council at the present time to consider even, much more to concede, any claim of bodies of native servants of the municipality for an increase in wages is a course which would, in our judgement, be fraught with the most serious danger, not only to industry but also to public safety on the Witwatersrand . . . the government is prepared to deal sternly and immediately with any criminal disorder by the Natives or the Europeans should any disorder follow from a refusal of the council.'[16]

Anti-pass demonstrators outside the Pass Office, 1919.

Mounted police assembling during the black mineworkers' strike, 1920.

Conciliation

Nevertheless, the council decided to adopt a policy of conciliation. It announced that the 'bucket boys' had been released and the prime minister agreed to hold discussions with a deputation of Congress leaders on 9 July. A list of grievances was presented. Another meeting followed with black residents from the Pretoria district on 24 July. During this time, Congress leaders urged the impatient workers to wait.

In September the government's commission on black disturbances announced its findings. The main recommendations were higher wages for black town residents (but not for compound workers) and the scrapping of two pass-law regulations: the 10-cent travelling pass, and night passes for women. But these concessions failed to satisfy most of the workers. Inflation continued to rise, and they began to see that black workers were hampered by a whole system of labour control, at the heart of which was the pass system. The black newspaper *Abantu-Batho* reported:

'It was agreed that passes be thrown away as passes are the foundation on which the refusal [of wages] is based.'[17]

The anti-pass campaign

Early in 1919, the Transvaal Congress announced an anti-pass campaign. This has been described in some detail in Chapter 16 of *Gold and Workers*. Thousands of passes were collected in Johannesburg alone in the next few days. Organisers were sent all over the Rand to hold meetings and collect passes from all workers. The anti-pass campaign spread as far as Springs in the East Rand, and to Maraisburg in the west. Violent clashes in a number of Rand towns resulted in hundreds of arrests, and in July some of the leaders announced a general strike on 1 October. In Middelburg, Potchefstroom and Rustenburg organisers began to campaign for the strike.

But again, the Congress leadership was divided. Some Congress leaders had a meeting with the Director of Native Labour. They were persuaded to drop the campaign because it was breaking the law, and arrests might lead to more suffering for black workers. They were also influenced by the news that most of the chiefs were not in favour of strikes — many chiefs were concerned to negotiate with the authorities from a rural base; they did not want people to get caught up in town life and town issues.

However, on the Rand, trouble was brewing amongst the black miners. It seemed to them that none of the campaigns had brought them any gains. The only thing for them to do was to strike.

In November 1919, the first strike began at Rose Deep Compound. It was to trigger off the largest strike in South African history, with a work stoppage of about 71 000 workers — the story is told in detail in *Gold and Workers*.

After the crushing of this strike twenty-six years passed before black mineworkers went on strike again. But in another part of the country, organised industrial resistance was taking place, and was to grow into a mass movement under the banner of the ICU. The history of this organisation is given on pages 107 to 116.

The Nancefield Stayaway

On 23 March 1919, a crowd of Nancefield residents in the Klipspruit area attacked and injured the superintendent of Nancefield Location and a number of police with choppers, picks, sticks, and stones. On the following morning of 24 March 1919, at 5.30 a.m., the special workers' train to Johannesburg left Klipspruit practically empty. On that day, the residents of Nancefield held a successful stayaway.[18] What was the cause of the trouble?

People of the town: they no longer had access to the land. Many such families lived in Nancefield, just outside Johannesburg.

Promises

The grievances of the Nancefield residents went back a long way, to the time of their arrival in 1904. People were first moved to Klipspruit after the outbreak of plague in the area around Vrededorp (as described in Chapter 3). Anxious to deal with the emergency speedily and smoothly, the town council persuaded people to move to Nancefield, assuring them that they would get:

> 'Security of tenure — healthy surroundings, a good water supply and lighting. Natives would be allowed to build their own houses, and municipal houses could be rented by single men unable to provide their own. [They were also] given to understand at the outset that their animals would graze on Klipspruit Farm free of charge and suitable land would be provided for any who desired to cultivate.'[19]

These were attractive features, for cattle and crops could help black townspeople to supplement their low incomes. But the newcomers were in for an unpleasant surprise. They found that Nancefield was 200 metres from a fly-infested sewage dump with an unbearable smell. There was not enough land for growing crops or grazing cattle — the location was soon surrounded by a fence — nor were there proper roads, lighting, lavatories or transport to town. Only three or four taps in the main street supplied water to about 5 000 people. The iron huts hurriedly erected in 1905 and 1906 were clearly not meant to be more than temporary shelters, yet they were never replaced with more solid houses.

Control

It was a bad start. To make things worse, the authorities did not respond to the residents' grievances. Unbelievably, the 'Location Superintendent' was responsible to the Johannesburg Parks Department — the town council did not get to hear directly of any complaints. The superintendent ignored the elected Residents' Committee of Nancefield and it soon stopped functioning. The superintendent replaced the committee with his own favourites.[20]

The superintendent's control over the 'location' was harsh and unfair. Many lost their houses as soon as their repayments were three months in arrears — often their homes were broken open while the owners were away and the furniture siezed, or the house sold to the municipality for a small sum. To give a few examples from many:

> 'Elizabeth Bekwa's house, sold 28 June 1916 for R6 [to the municipality] valued at R40, let at R2 a month, rent accrued [collected by municipality up to 30 September 1919] R72.
>
> William Mbeni's house, sold 2 November 1908 for R2, arrears R20,80, valued at R20, let at rentals varying from R2 to R6 a month, accrued rental R110,50.'[21]
>
> Evidence of Samson Ndaba: 'I lived in Stand 1922 for two years. I paid rent on 26th of each month. On Thursday 26 September I left for town. I was looking for a job in town. I had money to pay rent, about R6. My furniture was gone when I got back. I enquired and have not got my furniture yet. It is worth about R60. I don't know where the furniture is. I think Mr James took it for rent.'
>
> Henry Reid Mckaya: 'Stand 1922 — the furniture was taken out an hour after time was up, when the occupant was in town.'[22]

These were clear examples of gross exploitation of poor people by the municipality. Nor were people's cattle safe. There was nowhere except the small gardens or the streets for the cattle to graze. Yet if they were found on the roads, the superintendent had the cattle impounded, and they would only be returned on payment of a 60-cent fine. The superintendent also harassed people with surprise pass and liquor raids and fines.

Protest

The residents of Nancefield were quick to protest. Amongst them were settled townspeople and leaders active in community affairs, including the well-known L.T. Mvabaza, journalist and Congress leader; church ministers Henry Mckaya and Nqcayiya; Josiah Sibiya and Albert Myango, both shopkeepers; a headmaster named Thomas; a schoolteacher, Duzma; and Jan Folk, a driver.[23] After many applications and three petitions to the superintendent, starting in 1910, they employed a lawyer to challenge the 'location' by-laws and charge the superintendent with assaults on a young boy and others.

(Left) L T Mvabaza, editor of *Abantu-Batho*, Congress leader, and resident of Nancefield.

(Right) Rev. Henry Reed Ngcayiya, Methodist minister and a founder of the ANC, was also a resident of Nancefield and active in its affairs.

The events of the Sunday outburst and the stayaway that followed received much attention in the newspapers. The Transvaal Provincial Administration appointed its own investigation. At least two members of the three on the committee were radical labour leaders who were clearly sympathetic to the Nancefield residents, and criticised the town council for neglecting its duties towards the people of Nancefield:

> 'Frequent representations have been made by natives in regard to well-founded grievances, which they placed before the council through the town clerk. Later, the natives employed solicitors to assist them and, in October 1918, a municipal inquiry was held at Klipspruit . . . . The result of this inquiry appears to be known only to the municipal committee concerned, and the grievances complained of were not remedied . . . . It reflects very seriously on the attitude of the town council towards their responsibilities in respect of this location, and indicates a lack of even reasonable consideration of justifiable grievances.'[24]

The 1919 committee commented on the superintendent:

> 'There can be no doubt that he clearly embarked upon a systematic policy of "straffing" [victimizing] all those who attempted to oppose him. These were persons consisting principally of the educated and civilised class of native, and leaders of the principal native political organisation of the Transvaal, described by Mr James [the superintendent] as "political agitators and criminals".'

Recommendations

The committee made various recommendations: that provision be made for the grazing of cattle; that proper services such as roads, water, lighting and emergency water supplies should be 'carefully considered' by the town council; that the iron huts be removed and housing improved; that the unfair by-laws regarding rents be changed; that an elected committee should assist the superintendent; that the long sentences of those found guilty of rioting be carefully reconsidered; that residents get compensation for lost property and rents; and finally:

> 'There can be no alternative but to recommend the removal of this official [the superintendent] from the control and supervision of native locations, and that, if possible, he be found some appointment more suited to his qualifications.'

Conclusion

Many of these recommendations were never put into practice, but it is clear that the events of the two days in March shook the authorities. At last the Nancefield residents were taken seriously — at least for as long as there was a united stand against a system that allowed them no power to remedy oppression and exploitation. The residents had tried petitions and applications, and even tried the law courts to get a hearing — but in the end, it was the outburst of that Sunday, followed by the work stoppage, that spoke to town councillors and employers louder than words.

The Indian Resistance of 1913

In October and November of 1913, more than 20 000 Indian workers in Natal went on strike. The immediate reason for the strike was a R6 residence tax on all Indians no longer bound by contract to the sugar companies, but the workers had many other grievances.

The leader of the strike was an Indian, British-trained lawyer named Mohandas K Gandhi, who had been active in South Africa for a number of years. His famous *satyagraha* or *passive resistance* method of struggle was to defy unjust laws, without violence and in large numbers, and so to overflow the jails. The government would be unable to hold all the resisters, and then it would be forced to negotiate with them.

At first the movement with which Gandhi was associated concentrated mainly on middle-class grievances — the lack of trading licences, and discrimination against Indians in the civil service.

But *satyagraha* could only work when there was mass resistance. Eighty percent of Indians in South Africa were wage-earning workers. Gandhi began to realise that the movement would not succeed without the support of these workers; that the R6 tax was a greater hardship for them than for anyone else; and that on this issue a decisive stand could be made.

On 13 October 1913 a public meeting in Newcastle was addressed by a popular Indian leader, Thambi Naidoo, who had been sent there by Gandhi together with a number of women supporters. They appealed to the Indian mine workers to withdraw their labour. Naidoo and two others were arrested for trespassing on

Nancefield, 1902, before the erection of the 'temporary' tin shelters following the 1904 plague.

Indian protest meeting against the R6 labour tax.

railway property. The next day, the 78 Indian workers at the Farleigh coal mine went on strike. Resistance spread rapidly and inside two weeks 4 000 to 5 000 workers had struck work in northern Natal.

Gandhi and other organisers of the passive resistance movement rushed to northern Natal to encourage the strikers to stand firm. He also negotiated with the coal mine owners, putting forward the workers' demands. The mine owners responded by threatening to stop food supplies to the strikers (who were compound workers). But if the workers returned to work within 24 hours, they said:

> 'The time they had lost would be treated as a holiday, and no steps would be taken against them for breach of contract.'[25]

The strikers decided to leave the compounds and march to the Transvaal. By entering that province illegally, they would force the government to arrest them and thus keep their struggle alive. Four thousand strikers and their families were marching within four days. The march was hard and exhausting. There was not enough food, even though Indian traders supplied the enormous crowd with bread and sugar. General Smuts, however, very cleverly refused to arrest the marchers. He hoped that hunger would force them to abandon the march.

The strike of the sugar plantation workers

In the meantime, the strike spread to the south, to the 15 000 Indian workers on the sugar plantations. This had not been planned. It was a spontaneous development which caused great alarm among the plantation owners as well as whites in general.

There were rumours that the indentured workers would call on black workers for support – the Zulu uprising against taxes was still fresh in people's memories – and there were fears of 'cane fires and rioting'.[26] The sugar industry relied almost completely on Indian labour, and the crops had not been harvested when the strike began.

These fears resulted in panic and incidents of police brutality. In the most serious clash between strikers and the police, a number of workers were shot dead and many injured. One sugar farmer assaulted two innocent, unarmed workers and nearly killed them.

General strike

The strike spread and became a general strike of Indian workers in Natal. The Durban and Pietermaritzburg produce markets were paralysed. Some of the sugar mills closed down. Hotels, restaurants and private homes lost the labour of their workers. The railway and coal mining industries had to slow down. During the month of November, 150 acres of sugar cane were burned.

The government took action. Gandhi, other leaders, and some strikers were arrested. But most of the

At the prison gates: the release of Gandhi and other resisters. Gandhi is sixth from the left in the back row.

strikers were forced back into the mines. The mine shafts were turned into short-term prisons, and Indian miners were sentenced to hard labour in the mines. Those who resisted were met with violence – a riot in Ladysmith was met by police batons. In a coal mine nearby, workers were driven down the shaft by sjambok.

All these events received a lot of publicity. The British and Indian press caused a public outcry, and the British viceroy (governor) of India was obliged to criticise the South African government for its treatment of Indians. Eventually, Smuts appointed a commission to investigate the causes of the strike. In April 1914, the commission recommended the abolition of the R6 tax and brought about a settlement with Gandhi's passive resistance movement.

The results of the strike

The 1913 strike succeeded in removing the hated R6 tax on Indians, and to that extent it was successful. The strike also gave Gandhi valuable experience. It made him realise the importance of a mass base if passive resistance were to succeed. After the settlement in 1914, Gandhi felt free to leave for India, where he developed his *satyagraha* ideas and became the most important leader in India's movement for independence against British rule. In South Africa, *satyagraha* was to prove an important legacy. Tactics like these were used repeatedly by the mass movements of later years.

For the Indian workers in South Africa, the struggle to survive continued. While the tax removal eased their burden of poverty, low wages forced more and more Indian families onto the job market, where they joined the working class and eventually organised themselves into trade unions to fight for better wages and working conditions.

The Stormy Years

The years 1911-14 and 1918-22 were the stormiest in South Africa's early labour history. The angry confrontations between workers and the state (seen by workers as acting on behalf of capital) find echoes today in clashes between black labour, capital and the state.

The 1913 strike

The following is an eye-witness account of the events of the strike on that day:

'On July 4 – Black Friday – a great demonstration [was organised] on the Market Square [Johannesburg]. Masses of determined men rolled on to the square, and a German workers' band swung along playing the *Marsellaise* [the song of the French revolution]. At the eastern end were drawn up the ominous ranks of police and mounted dragoons [soldiers on horses]. Nobody anticipated trouble from the armed forces while the crowd kept in good order. After the meeting had started, however, the police announced its prohibition. Then started an orgy of violence. Police and dragoons charged the unarmed people, sweeping them off their feet, beating them down with batons, pick-handles and the flats of swords. Groups of workers formed up here and there and brought down a few police with stones and broken bottles.

'. . . Outside the Rand Club, which symbolised the luxury and callousness of the capitalists, small crowds gathered. A number of the more stupid club members stood on the balcony and jeered at the people, snapping their fingers at them. The situation became ugly. A few stones were thrown, and an attack was made on the club entrance. The street was cleared by dragoons. The crowd raided a bread-cart and pelted the troopers with loaves.

'Come on, shoot me!' was the original caption for this photo of a young miner, Labuschagne, seconds before he was shot down. Some people refused to accept that this was a genuine photograph of the tragedy, arguing that it was posed after the event, and that the man shown was not Labuschagne.

Demonstrators outside the Rand Club, where there were angry exchanges between the wealthy club members on the balcony and the strikers below. Later that day mounted police and soldiers fired on the crowd, killing about twenty people (including Labuschagne) and wounding many more.

Arrested strikers on the way to prison.

After patrolling the streets for some time, the dragoons were ordered to dismount. They formed a square on the corner of Loveday and Commissioner Streets, and began to pour volleys into the crowd. Scores fell, killed or wounded. From the windows and roof of the Rand Club, a number of unscrupulous members joined in the firing and accounted for a number of casualties.

'The fury and dismay of the crowd knew no bounds. Only a few carried hip-pocket pistols, as was common on the Rand at the time, and they tried to fire back, ineffectually. But the great majority were peacefully inclined and unarmed, and many had nothing to do with the industrial struggle. A dramatic and tragic interlude, which recoiled heavily afterwards on the heads of the government, was the death of the young Afrikaner miner, Labuschagne. Stepping from the pavement into the middle of the street, Labuschagne shouted: "Stop shooting women and children, you bastards. Shoot a man!" At the same time he tore open his shirt to bare his chest. From point-blank range a trooper deliberately shot him through the heart.

'A railway ambulance man who had come to the aid of the wounded described his experience afterwards: "The courtyard of the Victoria Chambers was a shambles. Blood was pouring out of the doorway, across the street and down the gutter. Wounded and dead were all around the court and on the wood staircase. I was putting a [bandage] on a man's leg, when a bullet grazed my back. A man standing near me saw me wounded, and leaped indignantly out into the street and shouted to the soldiers: 'See what you've done! Shot a man attending to the wounded!' He fell with a bullet through his body."

'As the volleys died down a rough dray was driven up. The dead lying stretched on the pavements were reverently laid on it. A red flag was draped over them, and a small procession moved off to the heart-rending strains of the people's song – *The Red Flag*.'[27]

The people's flag is deepest red,
It shrouded oft our martyred dead;
And 'ere their limbs grow stiff and cold
Their hearts' blood dyed to every fold.

Then raise the scarlet standard high,
Beneath its folds we'll live and die;
Though cowards flinch and traitors sneer
We'll keep the red flag flying here.

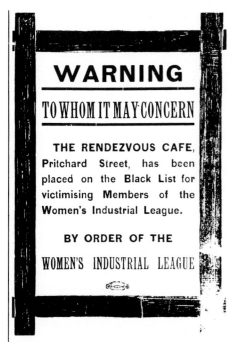

A boycott call to customers. The Women's Industrial League, formed in 1918, drew its support from laundry workers, women workers in Pretoria's mint, waitresses and shop assistants.

An election photograph of Mary Fitzgerald with her famous pickhandle. She can also be seen in the foreground of the photograph of page 81.

Pickhandle Mary[28]

'Pickhandle Mary', or Mary Fitzgerald, got her nickname at the time of the tramwaymen's strike over victimisation in 1911. Mounted police armed with swords and pickhandles broke up a meeting at Market Square. Mary and other strike supporters found that some of the pickhandles had been dropped. From then on, Mary addressed every protest meeting with a pickhandle, as a symbol of the brutality of the authorities.

Mary was a fierce labour fighter. A young Irish immigrant, she was converted to socialism during her first job in Johannesburg as a typist in the Mine Workers' Union (MWU). Mary was horrified at the slaughter of miners by phthisis during the five years she worked for the MWU.

In 1913, Mary was charged with incitement to public violence. The court heard that she had taken part in the mass demonstration on 4 July. She had been seen that day standing on a tub near the corner of Simmonds and Main Streets addressing the crowd and inciting them to throw stones at the police. She had stepped in front of a tram car, forced the driver to stop, grabbed the steering handle, and run off. The crowd followed her example, and other tramwaymen were forced to join the strike. Later that afternoon Mary addressed the crowd outside the Post Office. She is alleged to have said:

'If you want anything, take it; it belongs to you. Do not "pinch" it — take it: it is yours.' Pointing behind her, she added, 'Let them in Parktown starve.'

Mary was acquitted of the charge. She went on to become very active in labour and public organisations. She was a gifted public speaker, and her passionate defence of workers and the poor made her very popular. During Mary's life as an activist she was at various times the organiser of the Women's Industrial League, president of the South African branch of the IWW (the militant socialist International Workers of the World), the secretary of the United Socialist Party, the first woman member of the Johannesburg Town Council (during which time she served on the commission of enquiry into the grievances of the Nancefield residents), and head of Johannesburg's Public Health Committee. In the early 1920s she became Deputy Mayor of Johannesburg. She withdrew from public life after the death of her husband, Archie Crawford, a militant labour activist in earlier years.

Before the rush hour — waitresses and steward, 1916.

Scab cage or 'Home for Scabs' during the Johannesburg and Pretoria builders' strike in 1919. The dispute was over the length of the working week. During this strike, a large dog cage was mounted on a horse-drawn cart and driven to all the building sites. Strikers removed the scabs and locked them in the cage. The scabs were then taken for an uncomfortable ride around the town, to the sound of the jeers of the strikers.

Early Struggles over the Control of Production

The workplace was another area of growing conflict. As the demand for manufactured goods grew in South Africa, employers became more and more concerned to increase production, and in the early years they found two ways of getting the workers to produce more. One was to lengthen the hours of work each day; the other was to pay workers only for each product that they made. Craftworkers resisted both these tactics.

The length of the working day

A long dispute developed between craft workers and employers over the length of the working day. In 1908, the craft unions asked for an 8-hour instead of a 10-hour working day. The Transvaal government rejected this demand. But the start of World War I in 1914 put craft workers in a better bargaining position, because they were now in short supply — many skilled men had joined up as soldiers in the war and there was a greater demand for manufactured goods. In 1916, three big craft unions put forward a successful demand for a 48-hour week.

The following year, faced with growing pressure to produce more in the day, the Iron Moulders Society put forward five demands to the employers' Engineering Foundry Association. They demanded a minimum wage of R15 a week, a R1 war bonus, a ban on all overtime, and two weeks' paid holiday. The union then went on strike for 13½ weeks. They won the strike, paving the way for paid yearly holidays for all industrial workers.[29]

Resistance to piece work

Employers also tried to introduce the piece work system, in which work was rewarded according to the number of pieces produced — chairs, for example — rather than the amount of time worked. The craft workers resisted piece work, saying that in the end the system would force them to work harder for less money.

In 1902 there was a dispute over the piece work system introduced for moulders at Crown Mines.[30] In 1909 the railway workers went on strike over piece work. They argued that they had to work so hard that the result was that the working day was lengthened and their wages were cut. In the end, they lost the strike.

But many of the craft unions, including the Iron Moulders Society and the Furniture Workers Union, continued to resist piece work, believing that it

> 'delivered the worker into the hands of the employer, who now increased the surplus value [profits] through cutting piece work rates'.[31]

Piece work was a trap for the workers, because

Johannesburg's Park Station was sabotaged during the 1914 railwaymen's strike.

tomorrow the employer might change the rates and the worker would have to work harder for the same wage. The only way to avoid this trap was for workers to get together and reject it collectively.

The birth of a union

The following story is an example of how a furniture worker responded to the 'piece work trap'.

> 'I started working in 1915 at the age of fifteen at F. Hoppert. They made Bosch magnetos — it was before the days of motor car generators — and they repaired and maintained these instruments.
> 'I started with five bob a week [50 cents] as a

learner. One day an old school friend said to me, "What do you want to work these lousy wages?" He got me a job at £3 [R6] a week working for a Scotsman – De Wildes – making furniture.

'After a few years they introduced piece work. A wash stand was the easiest to make. We got 15s [R1,50] each for those, and 25s [R2,50] to make a gent's wardrobe. A hard worker could earn up to £5 or £6 a week [R10-12].

'You had to have your own tools, and a hand saw and a spindle – the factory owned the electric tools. You had to set out your own work, work out the holes, put it together.

'I worked with some nice chaps, a mixed crowd – Jews, Italians, Yugoslavs. Then the boss started price-cutting. He used to go secretly from one worker to another, saying we shouldn't talk about prices or compare what we got.

'I said to my Yugoslav friend we should do something about this. I wrote a letter to W.H. Andrews [Secretary of the Trades and Labour Council] that there were constant attacks on the piece work rates.

'We decided to start a union. [The old Allied Furniture Workers' Society had started in 1920 but it had lapsed after the 1922 Strike.] We had our inaugural meeting in Shakespeare House in Commissioner Street in 1924. Although I had no experience, I was appointed secretary.

'I continued to work, but went with my push bike during my lunch hour, recruiting members. We must have had several hundred members within the first year.'[32]

Effective

Eventually, after the Industrial Conciliation Act, the union successfully challenged piece work.[33] For thousands of workers, especially those with useful skills, the craft or trade union was the most effective form of resistance against exploitation, low wages and poor working conditions. The further development of worker organisations is discussed in Chapter 6.

Irate Passenger : " Just look at this bicycle, all broken to pieces ! How do you account for it?"

Stationmaster : " Can't account for it, unless it was built on the piecework system !"

A cartoon reflects workers' objections to the piecework system.

A wheel factory, showing craft workers and their assistant.

Accident!

In 1911, four out of every thousand miners were killed in accidents in the gold mines, both surface and underground. After 1913 – the year of a major miners' strike – the Chamber of Mines introduced an accident monitoring scheme, and the accident rate declined dramatically. By 1922, the number had dropped to less than 2½.[34] However, deep-level mining continued to take lives. By the early 1980s an average of six hundred workers were losing their lives every year on the gold mines.[35]

The following extracts are from the memoirs of Fred Hosking, a miner on the Rand from 1912 to 1925.[36] The harsh working conditions that he describes – the long hours, the constant danger, the horror of death at the rock face – were always with the miners, both black and white.

For white miners there was also the threat of being undercut by the ultra-exploited black workers. This job insecurity of the white miners caused them to view the black men they supervised more and more as units of labour, rather than as fellow workers in a struggle against common danger and exploitation, and they guarded jealously the privileges which they had won through union action in the years before the 1922 strike. Although Fred Hosking himself had mild opinions on labour relations – he was against the strike weapon – his experiences may give an idea of the conditions underground which turned thousands of white miners so bitterly against the Chamber of Mines and the capitalist system.

The shift

'When I started work at the Crown Mines, it was in the position of assistant banksman on what is known as a sinking shaft. The banksman and his assistant on a sinking shaft were responsible for the safe lowering of all men and material, for the disposal of all broken rock hauled to the surface, and for cutting fuses and affixing detonators in readiness for the blasting. They had a twelve-hour shift, and it can easily be understood that there were not many idle minutes in the twelve hours. To continue thus for seven days a week, and for weeks on end, was very exhausting; nevertheless I was happy to have regular employment.

'The shifts were arranged as follows. For five days of the week from Monday to Friday we worked from six in the morning to six at night. Then came a longer break from six on Friday evening till noon Saturday, during the whole of which time the night shift man was on duty. We would then take duty on Saturday at noon, and work right through to six on a Sunday morning, thus commencing a week of night duty. In my poor health I found this very fatiguing, but I was . . . determined not to risk unemployment.'

At the rock face. Standing in water, these miners are nearly two and a half kilometres underground.

Fred Hosking continued this job for two and a half years, without a single day off, seven days a week. When he asked for a two-week holiday, he had to leave, and was lucky to find a job again when he returned. He then worked as a skipman until he got his blasting certificate. During his time there he had at least two narrow escapes from fatal injury. After the start of World War I, Hosking joined up. When he returned from the war he got a job at Simmer and Jack mine.

Gassed

'Whilst on this mine I had an experience which might have proved fatal to me, as indeed it was to a native worker. When I arrived on duty one night there was a note from the mine captain, warning me that the air pipes had been blasted on one of the levels, and asking me to satisfy myself that a winze on that level had been cleared of gas and dust before anybody was allowed down. I called to the bar rigger, whose duty it was to work in the winze, and warned him not to go down until I had been down myself.

'I then left him while I saw some timbermen started on a job at lower levels, and whilst with them I heard air being turned on, on the level above. I hurriedly gave instructions to the timbermen and returned to the higher level to find, on approaching the winze, that the man in charge had gone down, contrary to my orders, with his boys.

'Here was an emergency with which I must deal immediately. Wetting my handkerchief to cover my nose and mouth, and having satisfied myself that the air had been turned on, I started to descend the winze. I had not got very far down before I came upon the prostrate forms of the European and one native. These I got to the level, and calling to a winch driver to run for help, I started artificial respiration. We managed to bring these two round, but only to discover that one other native had penetrated still further into the winze, and him we could not save.'

Ndau Song

'I go to die in Johannesburg.'
'Ndenda ndofira Joni.'

(Hugh Tracey collection A-TR-29)

Shortly after this incident 'it was found necessary to close down part of the mine, and as I was the junior shift boss I was the first to be retrenched.' He eventually found a job sinking a shaft in Brakpan.

Shaft sinking

Shaft sinking is one of the best paid jobs in mining due to the fact that a bonus is paid on all footage completed over the target set, and also because it is continuous throughout the year for seven days a week, the only holidays being Christmas Day and Good Friday. But while it is well paid it is also dangerous, on account of the nature of the work, and partly because, during the three shifts of eight hours each day, the sinkers are working at high pressure in order to complete their work in time for the change of shifts.

Drowned

'This shaft [at Brakpan Mine] was rather unfortunate for shortly after they had started to sink they drilled into an underground stream of water which I heard estimated as something like three million gallons a day. To sink this was of course impossible — in fact two natives were drowned during the few minutes it took to send the skip to the surface six hundred feet above the bottom of the shaft!'

Buried at the bottom of the shaft

'I went down with a gang clearing the sides of loose rock, and we cleared the bottom of the shaft in preparation for the drilling. It was my job to attend to all signals, on the knocker system — to signal the empty bucket from above our heads when ready for it and to attach the full bucket for hauling to the surface.

'In the small hours of the morning I was working with thirty natives on the shaft bottom. I had just signalled down an empty bucket and sent the full bucket up, and was standing at the side of the shaft next to the signal wire, when there was suddenly a tremendous crashing noise above me, and I imagined that the ascending bucket had become detached and was falling on us!

'I felt a knock and the lights went out. It took me some time to light my acetylene gas lamp, but in its light I found myself standing in the centre of the shaft — how I got there is still a mystery to me — and in the broken rock on which I was standing I could

Down the shaft.

see a head, an arm and a leg at intervals, protruding grimly . . . . I called together the survivors of the gang, and grabbing a spade I set to work to help them in the grim task of digging out the buried natives, seven in number, none of whom survived for more than a few hours.'

The death of a friend

After six weeks in hospital, Hosking was back at work.

'One night I was on the surface preparing for the blast when the accident signal of ten knocks was given from the bottom at about eight o'clock. I could not get down as both the buckets were at the bottom, so stood watching the bell wire for signals. The signal was given for the empty bucket to be lowered the last few feet to the bottom, and then there was a long silence, followed by the signal for the men to be raised to the surface.

'After a minute or two we at the surface heard a great deal of shouting as the bucket approached, and as it drew near we saw Sandy, [Hosking's close friend] supported by two natives, and he was shouting at the top of his voice. He was obviously badly injured. I got him out and had him carried to the First Aid Room, sending meanwhile an urgent call for a doctor. But when I examined his wound I knew he could not possibly live, for he had a compound fracture of his skull . . . with obvious brain damage. The doctor arrived and confirmed my prognosis, after which we removed poor Sandy to hospital where he died the next day.'

'The luckiest man alive'

'Shortly after Henderson's death I was again involved in an accident. I was on night shift. The blast was over. We loaded twelve natives into the bucket. The pumpman, my mate Jim, and I stood on the edge of the bucket holding on to the suspending chains, and in this way we were lowered . . . .

'We had gone about halfway — 2 000 feet — travelling at the rate of about 4 000 feet per minute, when there was a sudden stop, and our lights went out. I heard the pumpman give a shout as he lost his balance, I fell into the bucket on top of one of the boys, breaking his thigh with the force of my fall, and Jim fell off the bucket but managed to catch the edge as he fell — hanging there until we reached the bottom 2 000 feet below! On my arrival at the stage I groped about in the dark until I found the electric light connection and plugged it in, and the first thing I saw was the pumpman's body on the stage. He was quite dead, without any doubt . . . .

'At the enquiry held into the pumpman's death the magistrate complimented my mate and myself on our escape. He then turned to me.

'"I think you are the luckiest man alive", he said. "Not long ago I enquired into another fatal accident in which you were involved. I hope your luck will last!"'

'Tramming' — filling buckets with loose rock and ore, to be sent up the shaft and out of the mine.

'The fateful day'

His luck lasted until

'the fateful day of 1 June, 1925, a day which I was to remember all my life. When I reported for duty I was met by the mine captain and instructed to proceed to one of the old workings on the tenth level to close off an old stope. The procedure was to build a partition across the opening of what is known in mining parlance as "brattising" or planks.

'With my four native boys I worked my way down to the old stope, having collected the tools, brattising poles and other necessaries, and we commenced work . . . it took us until about half-past nine o'clock to complete this part of the work; and then we set about placing the upright poles into position and securing them.

'We had put in one and were busy on the second pole, my part being to steady the pole while one of the boys hammered a wedge between the hanging and the top of the pole. I became impatient with him, for he was just tapping the wedge instead of giving one or two good welts with the hammer, and when he seemed unable to grasp the idea, I grabbed the hammer from him and made a movement to hit

---

'The men I was working with were as good a crowd of fellows as could be found in any part of the world. I was the least robust of them all, yet strange to say I am the last survivor, for all this sinking gang have answered the last call — some succumbed through accidents, some through phthisis, and others with malaria while opening the copper mines in Northern Rhodesia [Zambia].'

the hammer myself. But the footwall was wet, and as I struck my boot slipped and I lost my footing, cannoning into the drive below. Right in the centre of the drive was a stick of timber supporting the hanging, which, left alone, might have gone on standing for years, but as I fell I pitched up against this stick, dislodging it and with it the rock hanging, and in a moment I was completely buried in rock.

'I was conscious of multiple injuries, my left foot was pinned painfully under the fallen rock, it was difficult to draw breath for the debris was crushing my chest, and my ribs were fractured, and what little air I had was full of dust, and in the darkness I was conscious of severe bleeding from my right upper arm, where the fractured bone had torn through the brachial artery.

'What had saved my life was the fact that the slab of rock had lodged above my head, and was partly supported by another slab to form a sort of cave, in which I had a little movement of my left arm — and with it I was able to catch my broken right arm and press the artery, thus controlling to some extent the haemorrhage.

'Oddly enough, in spite of loss of blood, I never lost consciousness. As I was struck I found myself breathing a prayer to God to care for my mother, for I thought my time had come at last!'

Fred Hosking's life was spared, but he was left with a lame right arm and a stump where his foot had once been. He continued his mining career, but was transferred to the chrome mines in Southern Rhodesia (Zimbabwe), where mining was mostly surface or shallow working.

The Influence of the Russian Revolution

The revolution in Russia was a massive experiment in socialist reconstruction, and excited the imagination of oppressed and exploited people in countries all over the world, including South Africa. In Johannesburg in 1917, people gathered on the steps of the city hall to celebrate the victory of the Bolsheviks, later known as communists. In 1921, the Communist Party of South Africa (later the SACP) was formed out of the International Socialist League, which had broken away from the South African Labour Party during World War I. The new party was affiliated to the international committee of marxists in the Soviet Union, called the Comintern. In the beginning, the SACP believed that the white working class would eventually carry out the revolution that Marx promised because it was the most organised section of the working class.

But in the 1922 strike (which was labelled 'The Red Revolt' by the press) the white workers were hostile to black workers, although they were militant in their struggle against the bosses. The white workers' slogan, 'Workers of the world unite for a white South Africa' showed this confusion. So at their third congress in 1924, the SACP decided to concentrate on black workers, and in particular to organise black workers into trade unions. (See *The Rise and Fall of the ICU* on page 107 and *Black Trade Unions After the ICU*, Chapter 6, page 161.)

The nature of Marxism

The idea of communism as a systematic and practical political programme first emerged in the middle of the last century. It was developed mainly by a German philosopher, Karl Marx, who was exiled in Britain when he wrote his most important works. Marx developed a scientific socialism around the idea of *class struggle*. He argued that history is a class struggle between those who control the wealth of society and those who produce it. Our period of industrial capitalism, Marx said, is characterised by two major classes – the bourgeois class, who own the means of production, and the workers, or *proletariat*, who produce the wealth in the factories, mines and farms. Marx believed that the working class would eventually win this struggle.

'Working People, Arise!' – a scene from the Bolshevik revolution in Russia in November 1917, by Soviet painter, V Serov.

The Revolution of 1917

Marx expected the industrial proletariat of western Europe and the United States of America to be the revolutionary class; but it was, surprisingly, in the more backward Tsarist Russian Empire that the first workers' revolution took place.

The first modern socialist experiment began under the leadership of Lenin, based on the ideas of Marx and his collaborator, Engels. The Union of Soviet Socialist Republics (the USSR) was established. The factories were taken over by the workers, and the capitalist class ceased to own the factories. Although thousands of socialists disagreed with the Soviet brand of socialism, for more than thirty years the USSR remained the dominant force in the socialist world.

The Rise and Fall of the ICU

'The ICU, to my mind, was not a trade union. It was really a political organisation with members recruited from every walk of life. The question here was whether we were prepared as a government to allow a native body like that to come and represent to us what wages should be paid to our employees in the service.' (General Barry Hertzog, Prime Minister, after a strike by members of the ICU at a state-funded service industry, Pretoria, 1926.)

In the above quotation the Prime Minister of South Africa was referring to the Industrial and Commercial Workers' Union (the ICU) the first nationally organised African general union in South Africa. At the height of its power, in 1927, it claimed a town and country membership of 100 000. Yet three short years later, it was a pale ghost of its former self. Splits and divisions had played havoc with its leadership and its member-ship was ebbing away. Yet the ICU remains a significant organisation because its experiences raised problems and questions that are still relevant today.

Was the Prime Minister right in his assessment? What sort of organisation was the ICU – was it 'just' a political organisation or was it a workers' union? Could a black worker organisation in a racially divided system of capitalism ever be 'just' a worker organisation? And why did it collapse so suddenly? These are questions that continue to interest black workers in South Africa today.

To find some answers, let us examine the record.

Strike on the docks

The ICU was born out of worker resistance. Formed in the stormy years after World War I in 1919, the ICU made its first powerful impact when the Cape Town dock workers went on strike. The strike was organised together with the white National Union of Railways and Harbours (the NUR&H) in order to stop food from being exported at a time when there was a shortage of food in the country. However, the ICU independently decided to use this opportunity to demand an increase in the minimum wage to 60 cents a day.

On the first day of the strike, 'coloured' workers downed tools, while Clements Kadalie, secretary of the ICU, borrowed a bicycle and went around the docks, calling on all workers to stop work and follow him to a meeting. A strike committee of black and white workers was formed at the offices of the Cape Federation of Labour.

The letterhead of the ICU, the first nation-wide general union for black working people.

INDUSTRIAL & COMMERCIAL WORKERS UNION OF AFRICA.

Established January, 1919.

Branches throughout the Union of South Africa and South-West Protectorate.

All Correspondence to be addressed to the General Secretary.

• HEAD OFFICE •
24 LOOP STREET, CAPE TOWN.

PHONE NO. 5320 CENTRAL.
TELEGRAPHIC ADDRESS: "ISEEYOU," CAPE TOWN.

Official Organ: "THE WORKERS HERALD."

A scene at the Cape docks, 1919, where the ICU's first strike took place.

Solidarity and success

This unusual solidarity of workers led to a successful work stoppage. The controversial food exports were stopped. A few months later, the ICU executive committee decided to press again for higher wages. They sent letters to all the dock companies, as well as to the South African Railways. The SAR refused to recognise the union. But the private companies, remembering the strike six months earlier, agreed to meet the ICU committee. The employers offered a minimum wage of 80 cents — more than the dockers had demanded during the strike.

The strike was successful in more ways than one. Not only did the dock workers get higher wages, but they proved that they could act in solidarity, regardless of tribal or colour differences. The success of the strike also gave hope to black workers at a time of stormy protest and resistance, including the anti-pass campaigns, boycotts, and strikes described in this chapter. Word of the ICU spread.

'One big union'

Kadalie linked up with other African worker organisations — Selby Msimang in Bloemfontein and Samuel Masabalala in the Eastern Cape. In 1920, fifty delegates from various black worker organisations held a conference in Bloemfontein. They decided to join together to form the Industrial and Commercial Workers' Union of Africa. They declared that their aim was to

> 'bring together all classes of labour, skilled and unskilled, in every sphere of life whatsoever . . . to obtain and maintain equitable rates of wages and reasonable conditions of labour, to regulate the relations between employer and employed and to endeavour to settle differences between them . . . and to promote cooperation, insurance, sick and out-of-work benefits and old-age pensions.'[37]

Tragedy in Port Elizabeth

In October 1920 in Port Elizabeth, workers held a meeting to demand higher wages. During a disturbance at the meeting the organiser, Masabalala, was arrested. A large protest meeting followed, during which police opened fire on the crowd. Twenty people were killed.

The shooting caused great bitterness amongst the workers and was remembered for a long time afterwards — four years later, in the next government elections, the ICU decided to support the Pact government (the Labour and Nationalist Parties) rather than Smuts's 'capitalist' party.

Political hopes

Their political support was significant because a number of members of the ICU had the vote in the Cape at that time. In fact General Hertzog, the leader of the Afrikaner nationalists, even sent the ICU a friendly letter and a donation for the families of the victims of the Port Elizabeth shootings. This was before the 1924 elections put his party into power.

At that stage, it seemed possible to many that some blacks in every province of the country might qualify for the vote and so exercise a little political power within the system. The Pact government, which included Labour Party leaders, came into power and some of the ICU leaders tended to pin their hopes on it. These hopes were to prove unfounded – but the ICU had several other ways of fighting exploitation.

Fighting exploitation

The ICU branch in Durban, led by organiser A W G Champion (a Zulu-speaking mine clerk), concentrated on fighting issues in the law courts rather than on the shop floor. He fought and won many workers' cases against the employers. Some employers were fined under the Masters and Servants Act for beating workers unfairly. The courts also forced many employers to improve the working conditions of their labourers. The most notable victory was the court decision that Africans entering Durban were no longer to be dipped with their belongings in disinfectant tanks, like animals.

In Bloemfontein, the ICU used the Wage Board (set up after the Wage Act – see Chapter 6, page 153). They managed to get a R2,10 minimum monthly wage for the city's black workers.

But it was on the Rand, where Kadalie opened a branch and appointed two organisers (a young communist named Thomas Mbeki and, later, a printer named Henry Tyamzashe) that the ICU began to adopt a more direct worker approach. The ICU newspaper, *The Workers' Herald*, was established and the ICU even set up a Workers' Hall, where workers could hold meetings and social events.

Soon after the ICU was established in Johannesburg, there was a strike which *The Star* called 'the native union's first strike on white lines'. The strike was at a metal factory in Mayfair, where 52 members of the ICU demanded an hour's break for breakfast. The workers got their demand.

It was in that year that the preamble to the constitution was drawn up. (See page 115.) It was heavily influenced by labour ideology. The South African economy was growing, and black workers in all types of employment pinned their hopes on the pressure of numbers and a large organisation.

Kadalie and Champion, the best known leaders of the ICU.

A W G Champion outside the ICU offices in Durban.

Membership of the ICU shot up to 30 000 in 1924, then 39 000 in 1926. The ICU got international attention, and Kadalie was invited to attend the international trade union conference in Geneva, Switzerland, as an observer. As the white trade union federations could not agree on which delegate to send, the ICU, with a higher membership than any of the other federations, was the only South African representative.

Organised farm workers

The success of the ICU was not confined to urban workers. News of the union spread to the countryside, to farm workers in Natal, the Free State and the Eastern Cape. Farm workers were the lowest paid workers in South Africa. Many were labour tenants who had to work for the farmers without any pay at all, in return for being allowed to stay on the land with their animals. So they were partly farm labourers, and partly peasants, struggling to make a living from the land left to them.

It was not long before Sunday meetings were attracting thousands of people who had walked many miles across the veld to hear the ICU leaders. Others, as described by Kadalie, streamed 'from all directions on horses as well as horse-drawn vehicles'.[38] In the countryside the ICU took on a new meaning.

To its members there, the ICU was a way of reclaiming their lost and conquered land — the last war over land had occurred only twenty years earlier. They had high hopes that the ICU would somehow help them to get rid of the farmers, and that the land would be returned to them. 'Man, we thought we were getting our country back from Kadalie!' exclaimed an old man years later.[39]

One chief, Diniso Nkosi of Barberton, even registered his entire people — nearly two thousand — as ICU members.

Wild hopes spread around the countryside. In the Eastern Transvaal, members were told that the ICU would restore freedom by Christmas, 1927. 'Redemption has come and that is the ICU', rejoiced a Nelspruit chief.[40]

Attacks on the ICU

The success of the ICU alarmed both the government and the employers in the towns and the countryside. A missionary was given much publicity when he spoke of that 'deadly threat to the peace of the country, the ICU'. While some of the better-off farmers nervously raised the wages of their workers, many simply forced ICU members off their land.

The government tried to control the development of the ICU. Kadalie was a powerful speaker, and often after a popular speech the government would act against him. In 1926 the Secretary of Native Affairs banned Kadalie under the pass laws from entering Natal. Kadalie ignored the ban, and when he was arrested in Natal, challenged it in court and won his case. However, the ICU was banned from operating in the Transkei, Lesotho (then known as Basutoland) and Namibia (South West Africa).

Kadalie and other organisers were also prosecuted under Section 1 of the Native Administration Act — the black vote was not powerful enough to prevent the state from passing legislation to control black political expression. Kadalie had given a speech against the government's pass laws in Marabastad, Pretoria.

'We shall teach them a damn good lesson and we'll burn our passes all over the country', he said.[41] He and the others were found not guilty of 'racial hostility'. But the government refused to recognise the ICU.

White workers were also afraid of the ICU. When Kadalie applied for the ICU to join the militant Trades and Labour Council, they turned him down. They were embarrassed by the huge membership of the ICU, compared with their membership of 3 000. Then, in 1929, the government used the Riotous Assembly Act to ban Kadalie from the Rand and Champion from Natal.

The ICU divided: Splits in the leadership

While the ICU was growing in many parts of the country, it was also showing signs of weakness. For instance, after the head office was moved from Cape Town to Johannesburg, the ICU gradually lost touch with Cape Town workers and the membership dropped there. And while the membership was growing so rapidly from one rural district to another, there was no time to consolidate — to go back to the members and discuss issues and problems with the rank-and-file.

An ICU speaker (Champion) addresses the crowd.

Audience at ICU meeting, July 1929.

There were also rumours that union money was not being managed properly. A Natal organiser, Sam Dunn, was actually jailed for taking union funds, and many others, including Champion, were also suspected of mismanagement.

The ICU had come to mean different things to different people. In 1926, an open split developed over tactics. The militants, many of them members of the Communist Party, wanted to challenge government laws like the pass laws, housing and education, through mass action. They criticised the 'hamba kahle' method of working through lawyers, who dealt with cases one by one. They claimed that in spite of fine speeches, Kadalie had often persuaded workers not to act together and strike, but to leave matters to the organisers — with few results. They also criticised the quality of some of the organisers, many of whom were school teachers with little interest in workers' problems. They were mainly in the ICU for the money, it was said.

On the other hand, some of the organisers felt that the communists were trying to push the ICU too far to the left. They felt that the Communist Party was a white-controlled party which did not understand fully the close ties of the black population to the land.

The dispute boiled down to a question which was to vex black organisations many times in the future: whether to organise as a class or as a race. Should the ICU concentrate on organising all blacks, regardless of their position — in short, become a national organisation ready to take on all issues which oppressed blacks generally; or should it concentrate on workers and use the power of their labour at the workplace to make demands?

Kadalie himself hoped that the Prime Minister as well as the white workers might recognise the ICU as a proper trade union, provided the ICU dropped the communists. From 1926 onwards, Kadalie turned more and more for guidance to white liberals who strongly disagreed with communism.

In 1926, at a meeting of the National Council, members of the Communist Party were expelled. Many of the ICU's most hard-working and experienced organisers were thus removed. As a result, the ICU branches in the bigger towns became weaker, because that was where the communists were strongest, and the strike weapon was dropped. The ICU began increasingly to shift to the countryside.

A trade union?

At this point, the ICU was finding its direction difficult to control. The movement was growing so fast that there were not enough experienced and reliable organisers to consolidate the new members, and the banning of the more experienced communists made things worse. Many branches were neglected, and as the ICU recruited new members in the countryside, old members in the towns were dropping off.

The more it grew, the more the ICU found itself trying to satisfy the aspirations of all groups and classes of blacks. There were the educated, professional and white-collar people who continued to hope that their

THE TRUTH

ABOUT

the I.C.U.

The
Industrial & Commercial
Workers' Union

Champion's reply to accusations of mismanagement of ICU funds.

protests would have some influence on the government and government-made laws. There were workers who wanted to rely on the power of the solidarity of their labour. And there were the many thousands in the countryside who wanted to avoid becoming workers at all, and simply wanted their land back.

In the meantime, Kadalie, worried about this loss of direction, and seeing that the ICU was a political threat to the ruling classes, tried to change the ICU from a mass, half-rural and half-urban popular organisation into a 'respectable' trade union along British lines. His overseas trip influenced him to try to learn methods of organising from British trade unions, especially as he was hearing reports of confusion in many ICU branches. In the following year, the British Trade Union Council sent Kadalie an assistant, William Ballinger, to advise the ICU on how to run a trade union.

Ballinger found the ICU accounts in a mess. He began to accuse Kadalie of poor leadership. Ballinger also wanted to make the ICU's image less threatening to the employers. In spite of the expulsion of the Communist Party members, businessmen still associated the ICU with them and with 'irresponsible elements'. Ballinger began to defend the ICU to white business groups to gain time to rebuild the organisation. 'Give the ICU a chance to prove itself in the new form with its new methods', he said, and urged them not to 'judge the movement by some of its old leaders who went about the country breathing fire and murder'.[42]

Leaders discredited

Kadalie was deeply hurt by the public criticism and quarrelled with Ballinger. Some of the organisers turned against Kadalie and he was eventually forced to resign.

In the meantime, Champion broke away. The ICU was thus split into three: The ICU of Africa (Ballinger's group); the Independent ICU (led by Kadalie with headquarters in East London); and the ICU yase Natal (led by Champion).

While the organisers were accusing one another of mismanagement, the members were neglected, and saw no results for their hard-won subscription money, not even the promised insurance and funeral benefits. Rumours of wastefulness and dishonesty seemed to prove that the ICU was lacking in democratic organisation. By 1928, thousands of members were leaving because they had lost faith in the ICU. People complained that the ICU 'promised the world's things and none of its promises has ever been fulfilled, so they are no more following'.[43]

Collapse

Dissension and loss of credibility among the leaders was the final blow to the ICU. The organisation had grown so rapidly, from region to region, and town to countryside, that it had no time to consolidate, or develop democratic structures to enable ordinary members to make decisions and keep in touch with the problems and progress of the organisation. So, when the leaders were removed or made ineffective, there was no one else to take over — too much depended on the few at the top.

Political and economic difficulties

There were also wider pressures on the ICU — the hostility of the government, the insecurity of white workers which led them to see the ICU as a threat, and the recession which started at the end of the 1920s. All these factors militated against the ICU as a black organisation. In racially divided South Africa especially, political and economic issues were closely linked – in his life history Kadalie wrote: 'As Karl Marx said, every economic question is, in the last analysis, a political question also.'[44] This seemed to be true of the issues faced by the ICU.

For example, blacks as workers were bound by the pass laws; yet a protest against passes was seen as a political threat, which the government would not allow. And while it is true that some black workers in the Cape had the vote, these votes were not enough to influence the government to change its labour policies – although we have seen how even the Afrikaner nationalists tried to woo black voters before the 1924 elections.

After the Pact government came into power, it passed some laws to protect white workers. These laws operated at the expense of black workers rather than employers, however. For example, the colour bar in the Mines and Works Amendment Act in 1926 excluded Africans from skilled and supervisors' jobs. And the 1924 Industrial Conciliation Act excluded all Africans from recognised trade unions because the Act did not define Africans as 'employees', and only 'employees' were allowed to join trade unions. (These laws are discussed more fully in Chapter 6.)

A new working class

Another set of reasons for the collapse of the ICU was related to the fact that the black working class was not yet fully formed.

Black workers had little organisational experience to draw on. Most were new to industrial society and had low-paid, short-term labouring jobs — few had a skill which they could use as a bargaining lever.

Blacks, of course, were not the only unskilled workers on the Rand – many Afrikaners, too, were new to the towns – but black workers had a different economic position from other unskilled workers. Thousands of ICU members were only partly workers – they also made a living from the land, and aimed to return permanently to the land as soon as their wage-earning days were over. Thus many of them thought of independence in terms of having more land, as we have seen, rather than in terms of building up a strong, organised working class through labour struggles.

On the farms, thousands of labour-tenants, sharecroppers and farm workers (who were not strictly speaking wage-earning workers) still hoped to find freedom and independence by getting back their lost land. The ICU therefore did not consistently organise its members as a class of workers.

The ICU members were a mixed group of oppressed and exploited people – there were industrial, municipal and government workers, domestic workers, farm labourers, and dock workers, as well as non-workers like poor peasants in the reserves, the better-off teachers, and even small traders – all in one

Delivering bread to the compound. In the 1920s, most workers were migrants, with ties to the land. At the peak of its membership, the ICU had more rural than urban supporters.

union. The ICU meant different things to all these different people, and was therefore forced to serve different needs in different ways.

The 1920s were early days for the black working class. It was only when their numbers increased in the towns, and when they began to get more stable jobs in the factories, that they were able to organise themselves more effectively to fight for a better deal.

There are those who argue that whatever the ICU might have done, the time was not yet ripe for strong black worker organisations because most of the black population was still at least partly dependent on the land.[45]

So, with the political and economic forces of the powerful ranged against it, together with the lack of experience and political and economic weakness of its members, the ICU was eventually crushed.

The contribution of the ICU

But the ICU did not fail completely. For one thing, the mistakes of the ICU were lessons which later trade unions tried to learn from. After this, black workers were organised into separate industrial trade unions which were more unified, and yet were linked to other unions through a federation. (See **Black Trade Unions After the ICU** on page 161.)

Rural workers on a commercial farm in the eastern Cape in the 1920s. Many rural workers hoped that the ICU would restore the land to them.

Separate trade unions could give a clearer direction to their members. Many of the later trade unions were started by organisers who had served their 'apprenticeship' in the ICU, so their experience was not wasted.

The ICU was the forerunner of black national organisations of the masses – at that time, the ANC was still a congress of professional and propertied people. Through demonstrations and mass meetings, the ICU expressed the grievances of thousands of exploited and oppressed people, and these protest methods left a tradition which later mass movements such as the ANC developed.

The ICU brought precious hope – perhaps its most enduring legacy. For a few exciting years, thousands of the oppressed and exploited, those without land or property or urban rights or decent wages, were able to believe that at last they had their own organisation – the ICU – which could resist the power of the ruling classes and win back their rights. One black writer recalled what the ICU meant to so many:

> 'Although the initials stood for a fancy title, to us Bantu it meant basically: when you ill-treat the African people, I See You; if you kick them off the pavements and say they must go together with the cars and the ox-carts, I See You; I See You when you do not protect the Bantu . . . I See You when you kick my brother, **I See You**.'[46]

Fifty years later, old workers were still pulling out their faded ICU cards and remembering the excitement of the ICU.[47] In the words of an old woman recalling her expectations of the ICU, for a short while at least, 'we too, tasted freedom'.[48]

Preamble to the ICU Constitution of 1925

'A struggle must always obtain about the division of the products of human labour, until the workers through their industrial organisations take from the capitalist class the means of production, to be owned and controlled by the workers for the benefit of all, instead of for the profit of a few. Under such a system he who does not work, does not eat. The basis of remuneration [payment] shall be the principle from every man according to his abilities, to every man according to his needs. This is the goal for which the ICU strives along with all other organised workers throughout the world.'

The ICU executive in 1925. Left to right (standing) are Thomas Mbeki, Jimmy la Guma, and John Gomas. Seated are Clements Kadalie and George Champion.

ICU Song

You young man of Kadalie,
You have come to unite
Flocks that spurn each other,
Shangaans, coloureds,
Son of a black man
In the land of our ancestors.

(From Pondoland)

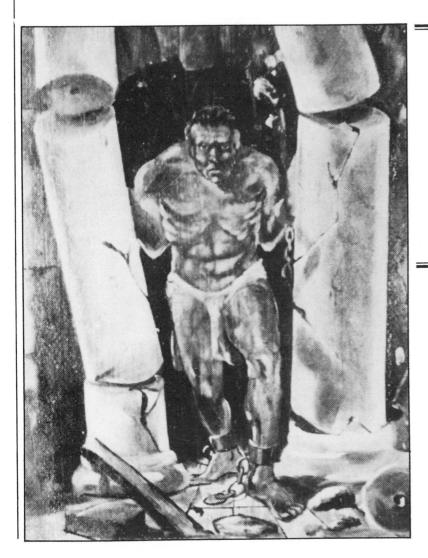

The mighty Samson breaks his chains, and the pillars of his prison crumble — the painting in the ICU hall, Johannesburg, in the 1930s.

Notes

1) Native Economic Commission 1930-1932, cited by H Bradford, 'A taste of freedom', in ed. B Bozzoli, *Town and Countryside in the Transvaal*, p.129.

2) P Bonner, 'The Transvaal Native Congress, 1917 – 1920', in eds. Marks and Rathbone, *Industrialisation and Social Change in South Africa*, p.272.

3) D Hindson, 'The pass system and the formation of an urban African proletariat in South Africa', Ph.D. thesis, University of Sussex, p.309.

4) D Hindson, as above, p.321.

5) Cited by P Bonner, as above, p.281.

6) Cited by P Bonner, as above, p.279.

7) Cited by P Bonner, as above, p.279.

8) Influenza Epidemic Commission, 1919, p.7, and Report of Medical Officer of Health for Johannesburg, 1916 – 1919, p.6. Cited by E Koch, M.A. thesis, Witwatersrand University, 1983, p.76.

9) Cited by P Bonner, as above, p.298.

10) See B Willan, *Sol Plaatje: A Biography* (Ravan Press, 1984), p.251.

11) A description of the Industrial Workers of Africa (the IWA) appears in *Gold and Workers*, p.93.

12) Cited by P Bonner, as above, p.290.

13) This strike and the period of general resistance has also been described in *Gold and Workers*, Chapter 16.

14) Cited by P Bonner, as above, p.291.

15) Cited in *Gold and Workers*, p.94, and also by P Bonner, as above, p.294.

16) Cited by P Bonner, as above, p.294.

17) Cited by P Bonner, as above, p.300.

18) *The Star*, 24.3.1919, cited by T Kagan, 'African settlements in the Johannesburg area, 1903 – 1923', M.A. thesis, University of the Witwatersrand, 1978, p.161.

19) 'Report of the Committee appointed by the Administrator of the Transvaal to inquire into any grievances of the Natives residing in the Nancefield Location', September 1919, p.2.

20) As above, p.8, and Municipal Inquiry at Klipspruit Location, 5.10.1918, Annexure 2 of report of committee, p.1.

21) As above, p.5.

22) Municipal Inquiry, October 1918, pages 5 and 2.

23) Municipal Inquiry, October 1918, as above, pp.1-4.

24) Report of the Committee, p.7.

25) M Swan, *Gandhi. The South African Experience* (Ravan Press, 1985), p.250.

26) M Swan, as above, p.253.

27) R J Cope, *Comrade Bill*, p.139.

28) I am indebted for this information to Lou Haysom's as yet unpublished study of Mary Fitzgerald.

29) E Webster, *Cast in a Racial Mould* (Ravan Press, 1985), p.31.

30) E Webster, as above, p.32.

31) E Webster, as above, p.34.

32) Interview, 16.6.1983.

33) See Chapter 6, pp.152-3 for a discussion of this Act.

34) Chamber of Mines Annual Report, Chamber of Mines, 1982, p.98.

35) L van der Bosch, *Mining Survey No.3/4*, 1983, pp.6-7.

36) 'Come Wind Come Weather'. I am grateful to Fred Hosking's nieces, Mrs Enid Webster and Dr Alison MacCutcheon, who transcribed these memoirs and generously made them available to me.

37) *SALB*, vol.1, no.6, p.8.

38) Kadalie, *My Life and Times in the ICU* (Frank Cass & Co Ltd , 1970), p.97.

39) H Bradford, as above, p.139.

40) H Bradford, as above, p.139.

41) Kadalie, as above, p.167.

42) *The Star*, 15.11.1928, cited by E Roux, as above, p.180.

43) Cited by H Bradford, as above, p.146.

44) Kadalie, as above, p.169.

45) See, for example, P Bonner's paper, 'The decline and fall of the ICU – a case of self-destruction?' in ed. Webster, *Essays in Southern African Labour History*.

46) J Jingoes, *A Chief is a Chief by the People*, cited by H Bradford, as above, p.135.

47) This has been evidenced from meetings in East London and Durban of new trade unions in the eighties. (Verbal communication, Robert Lambert.)

48) H Bradford, as above, p.147.

Chapter 5
New Factories, New Workers

Today the industrial working class is more numerous and better organised on the Rand than anywhere else in Africa. More and more workers are employed in factories, and their lives are shaped by this fact. Yet less than sixty years ago the manufacturing industry hardly existed except as small, craft-based industries, or repair shops for the mines. By 1943 South Africa's factories were producing more wealth than her gold mines.

How did this spectacular development occur so rapidly, especially in a colony whose capital resources were largely controlled by Britain? This chapter examines

- the growth of manufacturing which today employs such a large work force;
- how South African capital was developed with government help to finance the factories;
- how the changing labour needs of the manufacturing industry produced a new kind of worker.

Factories start manufacturing

In Chapter 4 we learned that World War I stimulated industry because Britain was unable to deliver goods to South Africa during the period of the war. Many new factories were set up in South Africa during this time. Many factory owners now became capitalists – they used their capital, which they had either accumulated or borrowed, to set up machines and employ a number of workers to do the productive work, while they themselves managed the factory and supervised the work.

Returning from the Rand Show.

(Newspaper reports state that the Kaiser is anxious for the cessation of hostilities).

FARMER (who is thriving on War prices): "Good gracious! Surely there's no danger of Peace!"

Commercial farming benefited greatly from economic development during World War I.

Imported goods

However, the progress of the manufacturing industry was uneven – it did not always develop at the same rate. In spite of the boost to South African manufacturing during the war, by 1920 more goods were imported than ever before. Why was this?

After the war, the British economy slowly recovered and went back into full production. American factories, too, were expanding and there was fierce competition for new customers. Many overseas factories were offering their products at 'bargain' prices. This was called 'dumping'. The new South African factories found it hard to match those prices and so could not sell their products easily. In 1923 the consultant engineer for Portland Cement pointed out:

> 'The demand for cement in South Africa is well maintained and were it not for the continuance of dumping by foreign manufacturers, the company's own business would show considerable expansion.'[1]

But the basic reason why so many goods continued to be imported was that South African factories had not developed sufficiently – in numbers or in output – to keep pace with steadily growing market demands. The most important drawback remained: South Africa did not have the capital to develop the factories that were needed. We have seen in Chapter 2 that much of the profit from the mining industry went back to investors in Britain.

The growing strength of manufacturers

But despite its uneven growth, the South African manufacturing industry had a long-term future. Manufacturers soon found that they were gaining important allies.

Some mining companies were beginning to invest capital into local industry for products that the mines needed all the time, like cement and dynamite.

Many traders also began to support the development of South African manufacturing. During the war, when imported goods were nearly all stopped, trade suffered badly. Traders were therefore grateful when South African factories began to produce and profits picked up again.

Among the large-scale commercial farmers, too, there were those who supported the development of local manufacturing. The farmers and manufacturers needed each other. A properly organised manufacturing industry would provide a regular market for the raw materials of the farmers.

White workers also supported the growth of local industry. They used their political weapon – the vote – to put pressure on government to create more factories and thus more jobs.

Government help

In 1924 the Smuts government was swept from power – we have seen how white workers voted against Smuts after the crushing of the 1922 strike. Others, too,

An early assembly line in a motor car plant, showing how mass production divided jobs into smaller tasks, thus speeding up production.

including some manufacturers, saw Smuts as a tool of the mine owners and British imperial capital. Over half the profits from the mines were going out to foreign countries. To make things worse, unemployment and inflation were rising.

The new Pact government, on the other hand, had a clear policy of supporting local industry. As we saw in Chapter 4, the Pact government was an alliance between two parties. The National Party wanted to develop South African, and not foreign, capital; the Labour Party wanted more industry in South Africa so that there would be more jobs for workers.

So the new government wanted to encourage local industry as much as possible. It wanted to develop a strong South African or *national* capitalist class which would keep its profits in South Africa. These profits would serve the needs of the country and especially the Afrikaner people. (See *The Birth of Afrikaner Capitalism* on page 125.)

In 1925 the Pact government passed the Tariff Act, which protected local industry by taxing many more imported goods. A tariff is a tax which makes foreign goods more expensive and thus encourages people to buy local goods because they are cheaper. Local businessmen are encouraged to build up more factories because they have a market for their goods.

The result of the Act was that the manufacturing industry began to grow again. The chart on this page shows the progress made by manufacturing in the four years after the Tariff Act. As the chart shows, the *established* factories grew in size and profits. Small

The Development of the Manufacturing Industry in the Four Years after the Pact Government came into Power

	1925	1929
Value of goods produced	R161 million	R230 million
Profits made	R98 million	R134 million
Number of factories	6 009	6 238
Number of workers	115 000	141 000

In only four years, the value of goods produced by South African factories jumped by R69 million, and profits by R36 million. These profits were then reinvested to develop the manufacturing industry further. Although this remarkable growth provided jobs for 26 000 more workers, the wages of the semi-skilled remained very low.

businesses grew into much bigger firms. In 1929 the President of the Federated Chamber of Industries remarked that fewer factories were being run by the owner – as the factories grew, experts in management and money control were directing the firms.

By 1931, the manufacturing industry was producing nearly one sixth of the country's wealth.[2] Furthermore, industries like food and canning, footwear and cigarettes were also helping the commercial farmers, because the manufacturers were turning more and more to local raw materials – local farming products received the greatest protection from the Tariff Act, so they were cheaper.

119

Horse Shoe
TOBACCO.

Horseshoe Tobacco
SOUTH AFRICA'S PRIDE.

Farming products were protected by the Pact government's Tariff Act. Local tobacco, leather and food crops supplied the cigarette, footwear and food and canning industries.

Labour policies

The Pact government's labour policy also helped the manufacturing industry, as this chapter will show later. However, since the government had strong white worker support, both from the largely English-speaking Labour Party and from Afrikaner workers who voted for the National Party, it had to balance the interests of the white workers against the labour needs of the manufacturers. This was not easy to do, because the interests of the employers were opposed to the interests of their workers. A wage was *income* for the worker, but a *cost* for the employer, and the employer was concerned to keep costs down as much as possible in order to increase profits.

The legacy of the mines

In South Africa, the manufacturer had inherited from the mines a system of cheap black labour.

As was shown in *Gold and Workers*, black labour was *cheap* because it was based on migrant labour, so that the land helped to support the low wages given by the mining companies.

It *remained* cheap through a system of control which included the pass system, contracts and compounds. This system made it very difficult for black workers to resist this ultra-exploitation by bargaining for better wages and conditions.

The system worked so well that it was adopted by other large employers of labour on the Rand – for example, the municipalities and the railways. (Chapters 3 and 4 have dealt with aspects of the wages and living conditions of some of these workers, and with the early history of worker organisation and resistance.)

The manufacturers inherited from the mines a more expensive white labour force. *Gold and Workers* traces the history of white labour on the mines – how at first they were able to charge more for their labour because their skills were badly needed and scarce; how they arrived from other industrialised countries with experience of worker organisation; and how (after the 1922 strike) they also used the power of the vote.

The manufacturing industry in South Africa therefore entered the capitalist system with a racially divided (cheap black and expensive white) system of labour.

Labour needs of the manufacturing industry

The labour needs of the factories were similar to those of the mines but also different in certain respects. The *labour process* of manufacturing – that is, the way work was organised to produce goods – was different. Before World War I, the labour process in manufacturing was based on jobbing.

In the early years, most factories made products to order (See Chapter 2, and *The Growth of a South African Factory* on page 137). But after the war the nature of production began to change in the new, larger factories (mostly clothing, footwear and furniture). As larger orders came in, factories began to produce fewer items in larger numbers. They began to *mass produce* with the aid of new machines.

Machines were expensive, but they had a number of advantages for the employer. They speeded up the work and they usually produced a more accurate product with a better finish. Even more important, machines enabled employers to cut down on the use of the organised, highly-paid, skilled workers.

With machines employers were able to reorganise production by breaking up jobs into smaller tasks done by large numbers of less skilled and lower-paid workers. As a result, large quantities of the same product were produced more cheaply in every shift.

The result of mass-production was that factories needed mainly *semi-skilled* labour (rather than the small group of craft workers, backed by a massive number of labourers, which the mines had required in their early years).[3]

The cheap black labour system of the mines left as its legacy the racial division of labour, and low wages.

As the factories developed from the mid-1920s onwards, they found, with the help of the government, a ready-made labour supply in the towns. Chapters 3 and 4 dealt with the growing number of townspeople settling on the Rand, and the hardships they suffered from unemployment.

These two factors – the use of semi-skilled labour, which was cheaper than skilled labour, and a reserve of labour in the towns – created a new kind of worker on the Rand. One result was that the position of the craft workers was weakened. They lost ground through the *deskilling* of their work.

The 'Civilised Labour' policy

Factory owners employed both black and white workers – all at low wages because they were new to industry and had little bargaining power. However, the Pact government stepped in to encourage manufacturers to employ whites in preference to blacks: the so-called 'civilised labour' policy (see page 127).

The Labour Party wing of the Pact government would not accept that Africans were workers. They argued that Africans were still tied to the land and were only part-time wage labourers. Nor would they accept that there was a large black population settled in the towns (as we saw in Chapter 4).

Depression

South African manufacturing received a hard knock when most of the industrialised, capitalist countries were hit by a severe depression. *South Africa in the Depression* on page 131 describes the causes and nature of this disaster. In South Africa, thousands of people were laid off – often, black workers were the first to be fired, as we shall see in Chapter 6.

Factories slowed down, or even stopped production. The Pact government's policy of putting 'South Africa first' did not guarantee steady profits. South Africa still relied heavily on British capital and world trade, and was influenced by the rise and fall of the business cycles of the capitalist world economy.

On the other hand, the South African economy recovered more rapidly than most other countries. South Africa's steady gold production saved her economy. *Money, The Gold Standard and Devaluation* on page 134 shows that gold remained profitable. As an international measure of wealth, it was always in demand.

New support

When the depression was over, the two leading political parties formed an alliance in order to work towards economic recovery for South Africa – the manufacturers and commercial farmers, and even the mining companies, were ready to get together to put the South African economy 'back on the road'.

Above: Cartoon expressing the concerns of white workers who feared that the Smuts Government would employ the cheaper labour of blacks. The ultra-low wages of black workers led to a job insecurity of whites which further intensified racial hostility.

A white worker during the Depression. Thousands of South Africans lost their jobs during this time. Black workers were usually fired first — between 1930 and 1932, nine thousand blacks in the manufacturing industry were laid off, whereas in the same period two thousand extra whites were employed.

Below: A gang of fitters on the railways. The 1926 Mines and Works Act reserved skilled jobs for whites only: Africans were not officially permitted to acquire or use industrial skills.

Hertzog, the Prime Minister, had lost a lot of popularity during the depression and he felt he could not govern the country without support. In 1933, the two main political parties, Hertzog's National Party and the South African Party led by Smuts, agreed to work together. A year later, they joined together to form a new party, the *United Party*.

The new government protected manufacturing and farming by raising even further the price of imported goods. It also gave bonuses to firms or farmers exporting goods (except gold, diamonds and sugar).

Furthermore, the government was worried that white militants might join forces with black workers to overthrow the capitalist system. Even if they did not succeed, their strikes and protests might set a bad example to black workers and plant the seed of violent resistance. This was a general anxiety amongst the ruling class. For example, after the 1922 strike described in Chapter 4, Smuts confessed to parliament:

> 'The fear that obsessed me above all things was that owing to the wanton provocation of the revolutionaries, there might be a wild, uncontrollable outbreak among the natives.'[4]

White workers and the white unemployed were therefore protected, segregated from blacks and brought into the fold of white ruling class society. The Industrial Conciliation Act of 1924 (passed by the Smuts government) recognised the organisations of white workers but not those of blacks, as we shall see in the next chapter.

The Pact government also backed up its 'civilised labour' policy with social welfare – help in education, health care, and later housing – for the general upliftment of poor white people.

The 'civilised labour' policy was supported by the 1926 'colour bar' act – the Mines and Works Act – which reserved skilled jobs for whites. The government further encouraged manufacturers to employ whites by rewarding them with lower taxes if they did so. In 1928, it also introduced the Wage Act, which was meant to push employers into paying 'civilised' wages. The idea was that if employers had to pay higher wages, they would prefer to employ whites. The Wage Act was only partly successful in this respect, as Chapter 6 will show.

The Wage Act did succeed, though, in encouraging manufacturers to modernise their factories and invest in machines for mass-production. In that way, they could afford to pay the higher, 'civilised' wages because production was speeded up. To that extent, the 'civilised labour' policy helped to develop the manufacturing industry.

The 'civilised labour' policy was most successful, however, in the large state industries, such as the railways. As we see on page 131, the white workers came to realise that their jobs depended on government protection, and thus their employers gained the advantage of a willing labour force.

A South African-made electrical product. The mines' need for massive supplies of energy encouraged the development of cheap electricity, which was also supplied to the white suburbs of the Rand. In turn, the electrical appliance industry was stimulated.

The government imposed a new tax on the mines, the Excess Profit Tax. This brought in more than twice as much revenue to the government – an extra R12 million – and provided most of the money to help local industries, including the state-run electricity supply (ESCOM), the railways, and ISCOR (the Iron and Steel Corporation of South Africa, see page 136).

How gold helped manufacturing

From 1933, there was a burst of industrial growth in South Africa. Production more than doubled between 1933 and 1939. As described on page 133, gold sales soared after devaluation. The profits of the gold mining companies rose from about R25 million a year between 1913 and 1932, to R65 million a year between 1933 and 1939.

The mining interests were not always happy with the heavy taxes on their extra profits and they complained to the government (and especially to Smuts) about this extra taxation. But as more gold mines were opened and developed (the most important being the Far West Rand goldfields) the extra taxation was absorbed by the mines.

The increased gold sales also helped state industries in another way – South Africa was able to pay in gold for the heavy machinery needed to develop ISCOR.

Mining and foreign investment

The capital from the gold mines was also used to help the growth of manufacturing more directly. The more far-seeing mining companies had already begun to invest in manufacturing materials such as dynamite and cement (as we saw earlier in this chapter).

In the 1930s, some mining companies invested capital in established factories, while others started industrial concerns − Anglo-American in fertilisers and the engineering industry, for example; Union Corporation in pulp and paper milling (SAPPI); and Anglo-Transvaal in engineering, glass, cement and fishing.[5]

South Africa's economic growth attracted outside capital, too. Most of this was invested by large British and American companies wanting to establish South African branches of their firms. They did this partly to avoid paying the heavy protective tariffs, but also because steel was inexpensive. For investors, these were important factors because they kept down the cost of production.

Branches of such big firms as Nestlé, Cadbury, Ford, General Motors, McKinnon Chain (US), Dunlop, Firestone, Siemens, Babcock and Wilcox, Dorman Long, Stewarts and Lloyds, Davy Ashmore, and General Electric were set up during this time.[6] These today are part of huge multi-national concerns with branches all over the world.

The Growth of the Manufacturing Industry Compared with Other Industries

The table below shows the national income in millions of Rand from the major industries, and the percentage of that income compared with the other industries.

Year	Farming, forestry, fishing	Mining	Manu-facturing	Trade
1912	R46m − 17%	R72m − 27%	R18m − 7%	R36 − 14%
1920	R102 − 21%	R104 − 21%	R52 − 11%	R82 − 17%
1925	R102 − 22%	R80 − 17%	R56 − 12%	R73 − 15%
1930	R70 − 14%	R88 − 17%	R78 − 15%	R73 − 15%
1935	R81 − 14%	R126 − 21%	R91 − 15%	R82 − 14%
1940	R101 − 12%	R196 − 23%	R151 − 18%	R123 − 14%
1945	R164 − 12%	R192 − 14%	R265 − 20%	R188 − 14%

(Union Statistics for Fifty Years, table S-3.)

The manufacturing industry made steady progress from World War I onwards − it more than doubled its income between 1912 and 1920. It continued to develop even during the Depression (see the figures for 1930-1935), and by 1945 had surpassed mining. (The value of gold mining, however, goes beyond the income it brings in, because gold is always in demand − see *Money, the Gold Standard and Devaluation*, page 134.)

Manufacturing in 1940

By the end of the 1930s, manufacturing had made very good progress. It had, in fact, expanded faster than any other sector of industry, as the chart on this page shows. By 1940, South African factories were employing 236 000 workers, most of whom were already black (93 000 were whites).[7]

During the 1930s, the industries of blankets, clothing, footwear, canning, sweets, soap, cigarettes and tobacco had expanded. These were *light consumer* industries, producing goods which people needed to buy regularly. They were not yet very large − the average factory employed only 33 workers − but they were already beginning to change production by dividing jobs into smaller tasks, repeated many times in a shift (mass production). Machines for light industries did not require large amounts of capital for investment, so they were established more easily than the metal industries − Chapter 6 describes one of these light industries, the clothing industry, in more detail.

The World War boom

In 1939 war broke out again between Germany and Britain and France. For the second time in 25 years, the war spread across the world, and pulled in South Africa as part of the British Empire and the British economy.

During World War II, while millions of people were being killed, South African industry boomed. As in the previous war, foreign supplies were cut off, and South Africa was forced to turn to its own resources. The war was expected to drag on for many years, so it was necessary for the South African economy to become independent.

At this stage of its development, South Africa was well-placed for enormous growth: ISCOR was already producing the iron and steel needed to make machinery; coal and electric power were available and cheap; and there was enough capital from the gold boom to start all these new projects.

The government did not stop to count the costs of war, but immediately placed huge orders at good prices for war supplies with local factories. Hundreds of private investors, too, were eager to provide capital for all this new war industry, and to profit from its growth.

All these changes led to higher productivity and lower costs for the manufacturing industry. Bigger profits created more capital for investment, and massive growth resulted. In the six years between 1939 and 1945, manufacturing nearly doubled its output, from R164 million to R316 million. By 1943 it was producing more of the country's wealth than gold mining.

Cigarette makers, rolling and packing, 1934. The new factories required a new kind of worker — the semi-skilled 'operative' who needed less training because the machines required repetitive movements. The worker got less pay.

Control of labour

Increased capital and the availability of raw materials were one aspect of this 'success story' — the other was the ready supply of cheap labour. The ultra-low wages paid by the mines set a pattern which the manufacturers were happy to follow. Low wages meant bigger profits, more capital accumulation and growing factories.

The war led to more careful planning by the state. A Directorate of War Supplies was set up to study and encourage greater productivity at lower cost. It tried to fix wages and regulate disputes in terms of the War Measure of 1942. It did not succeed entirely in suppressing strikes and worker resistance, as we shall see in the next chapter.

Nevertheless, this tighter control over the workers, in the name of the war, was important in lowering the cost of production.

Conclusion

This chapter has shown how the manufacturing industry, after some early difficulties in getting started, got massive support both from the government and also from the other two main industries, mining and farming. It was thus able to grow very quickly under the favourable economic conditions of war.

This chapter has also explained how manufacturing, as it switched to mass production, needed a new kind of worker — the semi-skilled, industrial worker, black or white, who lived in the towns. During the 1930s the working population of the Rand almost doubled. It is this working population that we read about in Chapter 6.

The Birth of Afrikaner Capitalism

We have already seen that in the early years the big mining capitalists and traders had strong links with Britain. The language of big business was English, and there were few Afrikaner capitalists.

Afrikaners in those days called themselves 'Boere' — farmers — because most were in fact farmers at the time. They made a living from the land and were not familiar with the capitalist system. Later, as many Afrikaners were driven off the land, they became wage workers. As we have seen, there were also thousands of unemployed Afrikaners in the cities.

The Broederbond in business

In 1918, a group of town-based Afrikaner school teachers, clerks and ministers formed the Broederbond. Their aim was to work for Afrikaner upliftment, mainly in three ways: 1) through developing Afrikaner education and culture; 2) by helping the poor and winning over the workers to Afrikaner nationalism; and 3) by promoting Afrikaner business and farming interests.

This third aim only really got off the ground after the Pact government came into power, when the South African economy picked up after the increase in gold sales in the 1930s.

A few Afrikaner companies had already been set up in the Cape — a newspaper and publishing company,

The founders of the Broederbond, 1918. The Broederbond, a group of professional Afrikaners, aimed to uplift Afrikaners by promoting their political and economic power.

the Nasionale Pers, and the insurance companies of Sanlam and Santam. There were also a number of prosperous commercial farmers. But in the Transvaal it was mainly in the 1930s that Afrikaner businesses sprang up.

An Afrikaner investment company was started (the Federale Volksbeleggings) with the help of Sanlam and the Broederbond, and an Afrikaans chamber of commerce called the Handelsinstituut was set up, which became the watchdog of Afrikaner business interests.

'People's capitalism'

The idea of *volskapitalisme* — people's capitalism — took root. Afrikaners were urged to buy from Afrikaner shops and invest their savings in Afrikaner firms. At a *volkskongres* in 1939, Professor L J du Plessis outlined the plan for volskapitalisme:

> 'the roots of poverty lay not in capitalism as such, but in the fact that Afrikaners had been systematically excluded from the fruits of capitalism. What was needed was not the abolition of capitalism but that it be captured for the volk.'[8]

The aim of *volskapitalisme* was to help Afrikaners start small businesses as well as to organise large-scale investment.

Afrikaner companies developed during the 1930s and 1940s. By 1946 there were hundreds of small firms, set up mostly in *dorps* or small towns near the farms. Most had a single owner, with an average of twelve employees. These little industries processed food, cigarettes, leather goods and other farming products.

They were very different from the fewer, large and still-growing firms with huge investments in machinery and employing hundreds or thousands of workers. Many of these small Afrikaner manufacturers were members of the Broederbond and found their political home in the National Party. They helped to vote it into power in 1948.

In the years that followed, Afrikaner capitalism expanded more rapidly and became drawn into the system of international capital. The dream of *volskapitalisme* faded away.

The Labour Nationalist Alliance

In order to secure an alliance with the Nationalist party, the Labour party played down its socialist aims, while the Nationalists promised not to push for independence from Britain by calling for a republic.

The cabinet members of the Pact government.

But both parties promoted white supremacy and were in favour of job reservation to protect white workers. From its earliest years, the Labour party developed the idea of separation between white and black. It maintained that Africans were not an industrial people but should stay on the land. While those who were in the towns would not be 'forced' to leave white areas, a Labour government would finance Africans to move to certain reserves. Eventually these reserves would be granted limited self-government.

The result of this early form of 'separate development' was a refusal to consider blacks as part of the working class, or as permanently settled in the towns. In the 1924 elections the Labour party won 18 seats, the Nationalists 62, and the South African party (SAP) 52. During the depression, support for the Labour party dwindled, its leadership split, and a breakaway group joined the SAP. The Labour-Nationalist Pact came to an end.

'Civilised Labour' and Deskilling on the Railways

The 'civilised labour' policy

From the earliest years of the SAR (established in 1910, when the Union of South Africa was formed), the government gave preference to whites for unskilled jobs. Later, this became known as the 'civilised labour' policy. The word 'civilised' was used to mask the fact that it was a racist policy, so as not to displease the International Labour Organisation in Switzerland. The 'civilised labour' policy was mainly a political move.

- Poor whites had the vote – unlike other unskilled workers. They therefore had some influence over election results and could put pressure on the government to help them.
- The South African racial system needed to separate poor whites from blacks, to maintain order and control over labour. Most poor whites had settled in the poor areas of the Rand towns, where poor blacks were living too. This situation was a political problem for the government.

In the first place, the control of black labour might be weakened by large numbers of unemployed whites living in 'idleness' and close to blacks. The government was also concerned about the growing 'criminal' population of poor whites. For example, many whites survived by selling liquor to blacks, which was illegal. In 1914, as many as 727 whites were jailed for this offence.[9] This state of affairs, a government report said, weakened white rule:

'the European minority, occupying . . . the position of the dominant race, cannot allow a considerable number of its members to sink into [poverty] and to fall below the level of the non-European workers.'[10]

Another government report commented:

'There is no need for us to explain how important it is to the future of the white race that as many of the rising generation of [white] townsfolk as possible should become skilled workmen.'[11]

It went on to suggest a programme of education and training in industry.

Many unemployed whites had participated in the militant action of strikers in 1913, 1914 and 1918-1920, as well as demonstrations and protest campaigns during 1920 and 1921. White unemployed were also active in the biggest white strike in the country's history in 1922, when they joined the armed commandos raised by the strikers. The government saw poor and unemployed whites as a threat to the social order and felt that they needed to be moved firmly into a 'white way of life'.

When the Pact government came into power in 1924 it immediately instructed all government departments to replace 'uncivilised' with 'civilised' labour. An 'uncivilised' person, they stated, was one who could live with 'the bare needs of life as understood among

Semi-skilled machine 'operatives'. They took over more and more jobs that once required greater training. They therefore undercut the skilled artisans. In 1929, the Iron Moulders' Society, realising that they had lost control over the demarcation of jobs, invited the semi-skilled operators of moulding machines to join the union. In this way they hoped to negotiate and regulate tasks and wages in the foundries.

barbarous and undeveloped peoples'. A 'civilised' person, they said, aimed for a standard of living which a European would find acceptable. In practice, as everybody knew, this meant that whites were to get preference in jobs, at higher wages.

'Civilised labour' was not very popular in small factories because it pushed up the cost of unskilled labour. The policy was used mostly in municipal and government departments, especially on the railways. In 1925-1926, the government found jobs for 1400 whites, at the expense of black workers and at an extra cost of R354 000.[12]

The Pact government backed up the 'civilised labour' policy with the 'Colour Bar' Act, passed in 1926, which reserved certain jobs for whites only.

Deskilling

The 'civilised labour' policy brought rapid deskilling on the railways. From the beginning, the SAR made great use of semi-skilled labour – for **political reasons**, because the semi-skilled workers were whites, with the vote; and for **economic reasons**, because semi-skilled workers were cheaper than qualified craftsmen.

As early as 1910, it established a special category and wage rate for the 'skilled labourer' – in practice, white unskilled labourers. White labourers could be promoted to semi-skilled categories such as 'fitter' and 'handyman', cutting into the closed shop of the craft unions.

White labourers on the railways. The government placed them in the special wage category of 'skilled labourers'. To pay for the greater expense of employing more expensive white labour, the SAR management speeded up deskilling, which cut down on the wages of the higher-paid artisans employed on the railways.

Craft workers were quick to resist, but proved too weak for the powerful SAR management. As early as 1909, for example, railway craft workers in Natal went on strike against the introduction of piece work; yet by the following year, piece work was firmly established. Craft workers continued to protest against piece work on the railways, but they were unable to stop the practice.

Then, in 1914, the SAR introduced moulding machines. The moulders' union refused to allow its members to operate them, thinking that management would be forced to abandon the machines. Instead, management immediately gave the machine-moulding job, as well as the core-making job, to semi-skilled workers (now named 'operatives') at lower wages. Between 1928 and 1934 the SAR management introduced new kinds of moulding machines which, the Iron Moulders' Society reported, were so simple that anybody could work them.[13]

A railway ganger with his white gang, 1915. The policy of employing white labourers began with the establishment of the Union of South Africa in 1910. But when the Pact government came into power in 1924 it tried to be more systematic in promoting white labour over black.

Weak Unions

In 1929, the Iron Moulders' Society decided to invite the semi-skilled operatives to join them. The minutes of their meeting reported:

> 'Mention was made of core makers and machine moulders in the railway services and it was thought that the time had come when the society should seriously consider accepting machine moulders and core makers into the society . . . the railway administration had for some time been putting forward their 'poor white' policy and introducing the men to different trades.'[14]

As more and more machine operatives took over jobs that used to be skilled, the craftworkers began to realise their mistake. In 1921 the British National Union of Foundry Workers wrote to the South African union, warning them not to make the same mistake the British moulders had made, but to include all machine moulders in their union.

But by then semi-skilled workers were already joining the separate industrial unions that were forming. A division developed between skilled and unskilled workers on the railways. An unskilled National Union of Railway and Harbour Servants had been established during the First World War. Other unions sprang up as well, each representing workers of different grades and skills. There were also *sectional* unions – the Locomotive Enginemen's Mutual Aid Society was one, as was the Salaried Staff Association whose members were monthly-paid clerks and office workers.

There was also the Artisan Staff Association, which aimed to represent all the skilled and semi-skilled workers on the railways. The ASA argued that conditions of service were different on the railways – railway workers had privileges which made the unemployment funds and sick benefits of the craft unions unnecessary. They called for cooperation between labour and management, as opposed to the militant tradition of the craft unions.

Then in 1934, there was a breakaway of Afrikaner railway workers, mainly labourers. They formed Die Spoorbond. This split further weakened the power of the unions in the railways.

Craft unions lose power

With more and more sectional unions forming, the craft unions had little power to prevent the steady

Deskilling 'under the guise of a "civilised labour" policy', complained the Trades and Labour Council. In the railways, most of the operatives formed their own, sectional unions. Mindful that their members owed their jobs and security to the state's labour policy, these unions cooperated fully with management.

deskilling, except to protest. 'The policy of the government appears to be one of dilution of labour [deskilling] under the guise of a "civilised labour policy". The handyman is undertaking artisan's work', complained a delegate to the Trades and Labour Council in 1932.[15]

When the craft unions tried to combine with the other railway unions to resist lowering of wages and job reorganisation, they failed. The new workers benefited from deskilling and were not prepared to resist poor working conditions and wages. As an Iron Moulders' Society meeting reported in 1932:

> 'In South Africa there is too large a difference between the wages of skilled and unskilled workers . . . and as long as a difference within the [railway] workers continued, the SAR administration would be successful in having their own way.[16]

Deskilling continued steadily in the railways. During the depression years of 1931-1933, management downgraded some artisans to the level of labourer, getting skilled labour for the price of unskilled wages. Most of the losses of the craft unions through deskilling were never recovered after the depression. The result was that the craft unions' powers of the closed shop and the demarcation of tasks were broken down.

Management realised the weakness of the craft unions and was more and more inclined to ignore them. In 1931 Pretoria officials of the Iron Moulders' Society working on the railways complained that the chief SAR engineer in the Pretoria foundry had walked out of their meeting, leaving them to negotiate with a junior official.[17]

On the railways, the craft unions lost the struggle against deskilling. Their members had to work for lower wages than they could get in private industry.

Powerful employers

The SAR management were powerful employers. They had advantages that employers in private industry lacked.

- The SAR had thousands of workers under its control and was fully backed by the government.
- It was able to invest large amounts of capital in the latest machines needed for deskilling.
- The SAR did not have to conform to the Industrial Conciliation Act, which allowed the workers in other industries some bargaining rights. (See *Labour Laws of the 1920s* in Chapter 6). The railways were considered an 'essential service' and the regulations made it very difficult for workers in 'essential services' to go on strike. Their bargaining position was therefore weakened.

So the management of the SAR was able to lead the move towards deskilling with little resistance except from the weakened craft unions. The managers were able to increase the supervision of work. They employed bonus work inspectors to revise piece work rates, which the craft workers had once so angrily resisted. By 1929, the SAR management was able to report that:

> 'By the introduction of improved labour saving machinery it has been possible to speed up output in many instances. The question of setting reduced bonus work times for operations performed on such machines is being closely watched.'[18]

Painters and their apprentices employed by the railways, Pretoria.

Conclusion

The SAR management was able to impose control over its labour force. It was even able to gain the cooperation of most railway workers. It did this by combining its political policy of 'civilised labour' with the profitable programme of deskilling.

- The 'civilised labour policy' split the railway workers by speeding up deskilling.
- Deskilling made the traditional rights of the craft unions – the closed shop and the demarcation of tasks – pointless and out of date. The craft unions lost their influence. This happened on the railways long before it happened in private industry.

The new workers set up sectional unions which broke with the militant tradition of the craft unions. Most of the railway workers realised they owed their jobs to the 'civilised labour policy' and had no wish to risk losing these by clashing with their employers. Employees in the SAR were divided and weak – in return, they got job protection and security. Their unions were not organisations that had developed out of struggles between bosses and workers. As a result, railway workers stayed out of the mainstream of the labour movement.

South Africa in the Depression

World depression

The period between the end of World War I (1918) and the begining of World War II (1939) was a time when the world economy shrank. In Europe and America, capitalist growth slowed down as it does from time to time. In the early 1930s, it stopped growing altogether. For a time it seemed that the whole capitalist system was coming to an end.

There are a number of explanations for the world depression. Some say that the factories, always in search of growing profits, carried on producing more than the customers could buy. Then, when people stopped buying, factories stopped producing and closed down. Others blame the uncontrolled buying and selling of business shares on New York's Wall Street Stock Exchange in 1929. When the prices of shares suddenly dropped, shareholders panicked. A wave of selling swept over Wall Street for several days. The prices dropped to almost nothing as firms and banks went bankrupt after the withdrawal of so much capital.

Factories closed down. Millions lost their jobs. With so many unemployed unable to buy enough food for their families, farmers all over the U.S.A. went bankrupt, too. One American reported:

> 'In Oregon I saw thousands of bushels of apples rotting in the orchards. Only absolutely flawless

A scene in Europe during the Depression of the early 1930s – Austrians searching through the market rubbish for something to eat. At the same time, wheat was rotting in the fields because it could not be sold.

apples were still saleable, at 40 or 50 cents a box containing 200 apples. At the same time, there are millions of children who, on account of the poverty of their parents, will not eat one apple this winter . . . thousands of ewes were killed by the sheep raisers because they did not bring enough on the market to pay the freight [transport costs] on them. And while Oregon sheep raisers fed mutton to the buzzards [vultures], I saw men picking for meat scraps in the garbage cans of the cities of New York and Chicago . . . hence we have over-production and under-consumption at the same time and in the same country.'[19]

And so because goods were produced for profits, and not for use, people starved when food was available, and went jobless while machines lay idle in the factories.

The economic depression spread to Europe. Countries like Germany and Austria were relying on American capital to build up their industries after their defeat in World War I. Suddenly, after the Wall Street stock market 'crash', American investments stopped. The pattern repeated itself in Europe – factories closed down, people lost their jobs, there was less money to spend, farmers went bankrupt and whole economies were ruined.

The crisis spread to Britain. Capitalists investing in British money, which always seemed so steady, withdrew their investments to pay their debts at home. They demanded payment in gold. By September 1931, there was such a rush that Britain announced it was no longer able to make payments in gold. It went off the *gold standard*. The result was that British money was devalued – the British pound dropped in value. (The box on page 134 explains the meaning of these terms.)

A cartoon comments on the Depression: the world tightens its belt.

South Africa and the gold standard

How did these disasters affect South Africa? When Britain went off the gold standard and devalued her money, South Africa at first did not follow her example.

The prime minister of South Africa, Hertzog, wanted to show the world that South Africa did not have to

Shipping export grain. When Britain and more than twenty other countries went off the gold standard, their currency was devalued. South Africa, on the other hand, remained on the gold standard, so her currency remained high. The result was that South African exports dropped, because Britain could not afford South African prices.

follow whatever Britain did. He wanted South Africa to be independent. After all, South Africa was the world's greatest producer of gold and had full backing for her money. South Africa therefore did not devalue, but remained on the gold standard.

This meant that South African money was worth more than British money, because it was fully backed by gold; while Britain's money was only partly backed by gold. That sounds as though it was a good thing for South Africa, but it was not – the result was a setback for the South African economy.

Effects on South Africa

- Firstly, many South Africans began to send their money to Britain to invest there. South African money could buy a lot more than the devalued British money. By 1932, R25 million had been sent out of South Africa.
- To make things worse for South African business, people started buying more British goods (in spite of the government's protective tariff) because devaluation had made British products cheaper. This meant that South African industries were selling fewer products. Factories slowed down production – in 1932 they produced R44 million less than they had in 1929.[20]
- Commercial farmers were hit even harder. Orders from overseas countries for wool and maize dropped. To make things worse, the British payment they got for their exports was now worth less than it had been before. In other words, the price of exports fell.

So, in at least three ways, capital was draining away from South Africa. Without enough capital, some gold mines were forced to close down, and manufacturers and farmers were unable to sell all their products.

What effects did all these developments have on workers? Many of them lost their jobs – often, black workers were the first to be dismissed, as we shall see in Chapter 6.

The South African depression hit people of all classes. Powerful mine owners, farmers and manufacturers, as well as white workers began to criticise Hertzog for staying on the gold standard. They argued that if South Africa devalued her money, capital would start flowing back, and the economy would improve. Even members of Hertzog's own cabinet urged him to devalue. Unwillingly, he had to give in.

South Africa goes off the gold standard

At the end of 1932, South Africa went off the gold standard. South African money was therefore devalued and thus cheaper to buy.

The quick results surprised even the supporters of devaluation:
- Immediately, capital poured back into South Africa.
- The price of gold suddenly began to rise, and continued to go up during the rest of the 1930s.
- Manufacturing resumed full production and started expanding rapidly.

The depression came to an end in South Africa.

Women workers at Pretoria's mint in the 1930s, counting newly issued paper money.

Money, the Gold Standard and Devaluation

The uses of money

Money has two uses:

- Money is used as *a means of exchange*. It can be exchanged for anything — for example, cattle, tools, clothes, food — over and over again. For this reason, money is useful to all people.
- Secondly, it is used as *a store* of wealth. This means that it has value in itself — much human labour has gone into producing it, it cannot be easily obtained, and everybody wants it. In the past, different societies have valued different forms of money for trade. In Ancient Egypt, for example, wheat, gold, and copper were used as money; the Chinese used wheat, rice and silver. In each case they used commodities for which there was a big demand and which required human labour to produce.

Gold as money

But for many centuries gold has been the most popular form of money. What are the advantages of gold as money?

- Firstly, gold has great value in itself because it needs so much human labour to produce it. It can be bought and sold for a good price.
- Secondly, it can be stored for a long time — it does not rust, like other metals.
- Thirdly, gold can be divided up and carried around more easily than other metals — even small gold coins are valuable. (Silver, which was also much used as money, is less valuable, and therefore needs larger and heavier coins to equal the value of gold.)

Gold became even more useful with the rise of merchant and industrial capitalism, because as world trade grew, it came to be valued by all trading countries. By the end of the 19th century, all the industrialised countries held a large store of gold to use as money.

The glitter of gold — the mineral that still determines the wealth of nations.

Paper money

Nowadays, however, the money we exchange is paper money. Of course, the paper itself has no value. What makes it valuable is what is printed on it. It says:

SOUTH AFRICAN RESERVE BANK
I promise to pay the bearer on demand
TWO RAND

This means that the Reserve Bank in Pretoria has stored enough gold to **back** the paper money it prints – the Reserve Bank should be able to give gold in exchange for the paper money it prints. The gold is stored in the Reserve Bank, while paper money is used in its place. Why is this?

Paper money is more convenient to use. It is light and takes up very little space in pockets or banks, and it can be replaced when it gets worn out by too much handling through exchange. Paper money therefore makes trading easier in our busy industrial world because it is easier to handle and circulate.

But paper money takes over only **one** of the uses of money – it becomes a **means of exchange**. The second use of money – as a **store of wealth** – depends on the store of gold held in the reserve banks of countries around the world. Without this store of gold, paper money would be almost worthless.

As paper money has no value in itself, the Reserve Bank cannot print as much paper money as it likes. It has to have enough gold (or other reliable wealth) in store to back its paper money.

Iron and steel works in the 1930s. At first, most mining capitalists in South Africa opposed this development, pointing out that a huge investment would be needed to build a local iron and steel industry. Mining capital had vested interests in the British firms from which South Africa imported its requirements.

The gold standard

Because money is produced by human labour, the value of money has changed over the years. In 1930, both South Africa and Britain were on the **gold standard**. It was possible to exchange a fixed amount of paper money for its value in gold. The paper money was 'as good as gold'. It was on the gold standard, and was fully backed by gold.

Devaluation

When a country goes off the gold standard, it means the price of gold is no longer fixed. Usually, the result is that that country's money is worth less than it was before. This is what happened to Britain's money when Britain went off the gold standard in 1931, as we saw on pages 132 and 133. When money decreases its value, we say that it has become **devalued**. That is, more paper money is then required to buy the same amount of gold.

The gold standard today

Today, no country in the world is on the gold standard – but gold still provides backing to the world's currencies. Because the richer countries have a greater store of gold than the poorer countries, their money is worth more than that of the poorer countries. The United States of America has by far the greatest supply of gold in its reserve banks. For this reason the dollar (USA money) has been generally considered to be the most reliable form of paper money.

An ISCOR plant rolling the first cast of ingots (metal blocks) in 1934. The ready local supply of metal enabled South African heavy industry to develop very rapidly during World War II.

The Development of ISCOR

ISCOR illustrates an important element in the development of industry in South Africa. The government taxed the mines, then used some of that money to build an iron and steel works near Pretoria which was called ISCOR for short.

Why did the government decide to produce iron and steel? Iron is very important.

- It is used in making almost everything — from machines, weapons and railway tracks, to stoves, fridges, cars, window frames and other goods. Iron is also used in making machines for the mines.
- If a country cannot produce its own iron, it will always have to depend on other countries for iron and steel. The government wanted to be independent of other countries for these important raw materials, especially in times of war.
- The government also decided that a ready supply of steel would help local factories to grow. The engineering industry could use it to make machines. Then these machines could be used in other factories to make other goods.

The big fight

When the government first announced that they were going to build ISCOR, different people such as businessmen and politicians were against the idea. What were their arguments?

- Firstly, they said that ISCOR would not make enough profit to justify the cost of a large iron and steel works. They were worried that this would make South African steel more expensive than imported steel. Mine owners especially were worried because the price of machines might go up — until this time there were no tariffs on imported machinery — and if they paid more for machinery their profits would go down.
- Secondly, many businessmen and politicians argued that it was not the government's job to build factories. South Africa was a capitalist society, with a system of free enterprise — private, industrial capitalists should build the factories, and not have to compete against the government. The government had no business building or running factories. They argued that the government's job was to see that the system of free enterprise ran smoothly, but otherwise it should not interfere with the economy.

The government replied to these arguments. The private iron works in Newcastle and Vereeniging, they said, were not big enough to supply the country's need for steel. Factory owners did not have enough money to make them bigger. So the government built ISCOR.

Who won?

Who won the argument? Was the government right to build ISCOR? ISCOR became a success for those who planned it.

- South Africa was soon producing many important machines and goods made from iron and steel.
- Not long after ISCOR started production, World War II began. Again, Britain could not supply South Africa with steel. British steel was needed to make weapons for the war. The steel mills in Pretoria were then able to supply most of the iron and steel that South Africa needed.
- ISCOR was the start of a new period of growth for South African factories. More ISCOR iron and steel works were built in Newcastle and Vereeniging. Today, the iron, steel, and engineering industry is the largest manufacturing industry in the country. In 1973 it employed about 350 000 people.

The building of ISCOR meant that South Africa became a little less dependent on foreign capital and foreign supplies. It meant that local capital became important. Even the mine owners saw the advantages of ISCOR, and they began to build their own factories to produce machines and goods for the mines.

The Growth of a South African Factory – a Case History

The period of rapid industrial growth in South Africa provided artisans with a chance to move into the capitalist class. Many tried and failed, as we saw in Chapter 2. A few, however, were successful.

The case history below shows how one industry played its part in the development of manufacturing in general in South Africa.[21]

Backyard workshop

The story begins in 1929 when Carl Fuchs, a young artisan, opened up a plumbing and sheet metal workshop behind some old stables in Johannesburg. He raised enough money for some basic equipment. For example, he made a compressor which was operated by hand, to press steel. Then he was able to weld the pressed steel into light metal goods for special orders (known as jobbing). At first, Fuchs worked on the jobs himself, together with a black worker. One of the first orders was for shades for the new electric street lights

near the Johannesburg Library. They also made cylinders for heating water – known as 'geysers'.

With the growth of ESCOM, the electricity power supply company, more and more people were encouraged to use electricity. Business increased until Fuchs was employing four or five artisans and a number of labourers.

But depression struck South Africa in 1931 and the number of orders dropped. The staff were laid off except for one artisan and three labourers. In late

An early workshop.

December 1932, the South African government went off the gold standard. Within a few months, business picked up again.

The firm grows

Fuchs was again busy with orders, employing more workers to carry out the contracts. Profits multiplied. Fuchs bought new machinery to speed up production, including a power-driven guillotine to cut the metal sheets. Until then, cutting had to be done by hand-operated tools.

Soon, the old workshop became too small. Fuchs had new premises built – the two-storey Metal Craft House. The staff moved in in 1934, just before Fuchs's first mass-production job. Swarms of locusts had attacked the countryside that year, and thousands of spray pumps were needed in a hurry to poison them. Fuchs put the whole staff on the production line, turning out 100 pumps a day.

In 1936, the Fuchs firm had its own stand at the Empire Exhibition at Milner Park (where the Rand Easter Shows were held) and collected more big contracts.

Business grew steadily. By 1939, there were more than 100 workers in Fuchs.

Change to manufacturing

But the big turning point for Fuchs came with the outbreak of World War II. By 1940, Carl Fuchs had the capital and experience to apply for large contracts for the making of war equipment. As the orders grew, Fuchs employed up to 1 500 workers to mass-produce aeroplane parts, bomb shells and food canisters strong enough to be dropped from the air to soldiers on the battlefield. The workers worked day and night, in three daily shifts, in fast-moving production lines.

In 1943 the Fuchs business had grown so large that new premises were built in Alberton on a fifty-acre site. Business continued to thrive until the end of the war.

Then, in 1945, the contracts stopped. Workers were laid off, until only 400 workers remained.

But the profits from the war left the company with R300 000 capital. This was used to gear production to peace-time needs. Fuchs decided to switch to the production of water-heaters and steel kitchenware. The company bought a new enamelling plant to give the smooth, shiny surface that would compete with modern imported kitchen equipment.

C J Fuchs also visited the USA, where he bought leftover war stocks — two powerful metal presses that were the biggest to be introduced into South Africa and could press thick steel into any shape.

Move to machinofacture

From then on, Fuchs expanded steadily. As the economy grew, more and more people were buying stoves, refrigerators and washing machines. Fuchs manufactured these — the Fuchs workers and machines were now producing not just parts, but whole machines.

After 1948, the protectionist policy of the National Party government encouraged the South African manufacturing industry even further. As a result, foreign companies were forced to find South African industries to make and sell their goods for them. Fuchs made agreements with Westinghouse in the USA and Electrolux in Sweden to manufacture and supply their products in South Africa and Rhodesia (as Zimbabwe was then called).

By 1963, the company's capital had grown to R5½ million, and its profits were worth well over R1 million a year. Today, Fuchs has been absorbed by the Barlow-Rand group of companies with assets of more than R2 billion in 1980.[22]

Notes

1) D Innes, 'Monopoly capitalism and imperialism in South Africa: the role of the Anglo American Group', Ph D thesis, Sussex University, 1980, p.280.

2) H Houghton, *The South African Economy* (OUP, 1969), p.125.

3) However, it is important to remember that as the mines developed their machinery, they gave more and more of the skilled work to black workers, at the same low wages. This 'deskilling' and undercutting of the white workers was a major cause of the 1922 strike.

4) Cited by R H Davies, *Capital, State and White Labour in South Africa 1900-1960* (Humanities Press, New Jersey, 1979), p.84.

5) D Innes, *Anglo American and the Rise of Modern South Africa* (Ravan Press, 1984), p.131.

6) Innes, as above.

7) Houghton, as above, p.199.

8) D. Moodie, *The Rise of Afrikanerdom* (University of California Press, 1975), p.357.

9) R H Davies, as above, p.133.

10) R H Davies, as above, p.80.

11) Select Committee on European Employment and Labour Conditions, SC9, 1913.

12) J Lewis, 'Industrialisation and trade union organisation in South Africa, 1924-55', Ph D thesis, Cambridge University, 1981, p.34. This thesis has also been published in book form under the same title by Cambridge University Press, 1984.

13) E Webster, 'The labour process and forms of workplace organisation in South African foundries', Ph D thesis, University of the Witwatersrand, 1983, p.89. See, too, Webster's book based on this work: *Cast in a Racial Mould* (Ravan Press, 1985).

14) E Webster, as above, p.88.

15) J Lewis, as above, p.34.

16) E Webster, as above, p.92.

17) J Lewis, as above, p.35.

18) E Webster, as above, p.91.

19) A J P Taylor and J M Roberts, eds, *History of the Twentieth Century*, 'Crisis of Capitalism', Chapter 45 (PBC Publishing Ltd, 1968), p.1255.

20) Houghton, as above, p.116.

21) Based on information from J Shorten, *The Johannesburg Saga* (John R Shorten Publishers, 1970), pp.689-98.

22) *Barlow Rand: a symbol of strength for 75 years* (Johannesburg, 1977).

Chapter 6
New Workers, New Unions

Chapter 5 described how rapid growth in the manufacturing industry led to a change in the labour process in the factories – new machines speeded up production and jobs were split up into smaller tasks. These tasks could be repeated over and over again, and could be done by semi-skilled workers. As a result, craft workers were deskilled and many of their jobs fell away. New workers, both black and white, took over more and more of the productive work. This chapter traces the rise of the semi-skilled worker and new worker organisations.

Cheaper labour

Many of the new workers on the Rand were white women and black men. (See pages 155 and 157 for brief summaries of labour patterns in this period in the Cape and Natal.) The chart on pages 142-3 shows how the numbers of Rand workers grew between 1916 and 1930.

The new workers got jobs fairly easily because they were paid lower wage rates than craft workers. They had to accept low wages because they were weakly organised, with little bargaining power. (For example, in 1926 white women were starting on two rand a week, which was the same wage as black men in the industry were earning.)[1]

Women workers were paid a third less than white men, in line with the official Wage Board policy. The reasoning was that women did not need higher wages because they were supported by their fathers and husbands.

But this argument was false. Most white women workers at that time were Afrikaners fresh from the land. (Black women had not yet left the land in large numbers. When they did find jobs in the towns, they tended to find work as domestic workers. Black women began to enter factories as workers only during and after World War II.)

These Afrikaner women had not only to support themselves in the town, but also to send money home to help their struggling families in the countryside.

Black factory workers, too, were paid equally low wages and similar reasons were given. Employers argued that as their families lived off the land, black workers needed to be paid only enough for one person. Factory owners were using the same excuses as the mine owners had to justify the miserable wages paid to mine workers on the Rand.

But this was a false argument, too. In the first place, the removal of land through conquest and the 1913 Land Act caused growing poverty in the countryside. Land shortage was the very reason why blacks were entering the towns in search of wage labour.

In fact, most black factory workers were settling in the towns with their families. Factory owners tended to choose settled townspeople rather than migrant workers. They found that production went faster with an experienced, stable work force that would not leave after a short time. As time went by, more and more black factory workers were having to support their families in the towns from their meagre wages. As one observer noted in 1928:

> 'Much of the semi-skilled work which formed part of the skilled man's work was handed over to the native, generally without any increase in wages.'[2]

An industrial school for white apprentices in the early 1930s. Apprentices worked on three to five-year contracts for low wages. They were thus one form of cheap labour available to employers.

Young apprentices also earned low wages and employers therefore preferred them to craft workers. In the furniture industry on the Rand in 1928, for instance, there were 734 apprenticed workers compared with only 596 skilled workers.[3] Apprentices worked under a contract that lasted from five to six years. As contract workers they were not allowed to strike or join a union. Their bargaining power was therefore low – and so were their wages.

The Furniture Workers' Union saw that apprentices were being used as cheap labour, and raised the question:

> 'Is systematic apprenticeship a practical and satisfactory method today, remembering that the young worker is bound by contract from five to six years to an occupation wherein mass production and repetition work has replaced technique and skill?'[4]

As they became qualified, many apprentices were discharged and had to look for new jobs. During the 1930s, semi-skilled furniture workers demanded a change in the Apprenticeship Act, while on the other hand the old craft unions strongly supported it as protection against deskilling in the factories. However, with the growing numbers of white women and black workers available, the use of apprentices as a form of cheap labour gradually fell away.

These three groups of new workers – white women, black workers and young white apprentices – formed the deskilled, lower-paid labour base of early mass-production on the Rand.

New unions

The semi-skilled workers formed new kinds of unions. These were more suited to the new organisation of work and division of labour in the factories. Semi-skilled workers could not organise along craft lines because they did not have craft skills or traditions. Instead, they organised themselves into general or industrial unions.

In the 1920s and 1930s three kinds of unions developed.

- Firstly, there was the nation-wide *general union* of black workers – the ICU. Its history, its successes and its failures have been described in Chapter 4.

- Then there were the *whites-only unions* of South Africa's two largest employers, the mines and the railways, and later the iron and steel union, Yster en Staal. The reasons for their strict racial policies are indicated in *Afrikaner Nationalism in the Unions* on page 158. See also *'Civilised Labour' and Deskilling on the Railways* on page 127.

The members of these unions relied on the state to protect their jobs and wages, rather than on class

---

Sweetmakers in an East London factory. This was one of the industries that grew rapidly in the 1920s and 1930s, and had an active trade union.

struggle and trade union action. So, just as the labour process in the workplace was racially divided, so the organisations of the workers in these industries were formed along *racial* and not *class* lines.

- Thirdly, most of the *industrial trade unions*, registered and unregistered, developed along racially *parallel* lines. The histories of the struggles of some of these unions are described in *Black Trade Unions after the ICU* on page 161 and *The Story of the Garment Workers' Union* on page 146.

The most important trade unions to emerge on the Rand in the 1920s were the leather, clothing and furniture unions, followed a few years later by unions in the laundry, rope and canvas, chemical and sweet industries. These were the industries that employed most semi-skilled workers, whether black or white. They were also the industries which grew most rapidly. The unions in these industries were the most active in the years between the two world wars (1918-1939), as is illustrated in the chart on this page.[5]

Heavy industries, like the metal industry, were slower to introduce machines – to *mechanise* – because of the very high cost of heavy machinery. So the labour process in that industry continued to be based on craft work for a much longer time. Their unions remained craft unions until after World War II.

It was thus the change to *mass production* that led to *industrially-based trade unions*.

Industrial bargaining

The growth of the new trade unions was encouraged by the Industrial Conciliation Act – as described in *Labour Laws in the 1920s* on page 152 – because it demanded industry-by-industry bargaining.

But some labour leaders pointed out the dangers of the Act. Bill Andrews, secretary of the Trade Union Council, argued that the Industrial Conciliation Act 'made a successful legal strike almost an impossibility'.[6]

A veteran trade unionist said years later that the Act encouraged bureaucracy instead of union action:

'My personal opinion was that it [the Industrial Conciliation Act] was a means of control . . . . The Industrial Council was in a sense a retarding factor, keeping back the class consciousness of the worker – the whole system needed inspectors, district committees to monitor, and then the law courts. It cut the wings of the trade union movement. But we had strikes. Strictly speaking they were illegal. I got fined for organising illegal strikes, and I was also banned under the Riotous Assemblies Act.'[7]

Thus during the 1930s the industrial trade unions could not rely on the Industrial Council, labour laws, and the supposedly pro-labour Pact Government. They had to take militant action to further their interests.

The Changing Nature of Unions in the Trades and Labour Council

	1925	1937
CRAFT UNIONS	8	5
INDUSTRIAL UNIONS	4	25

CRAFT UNIONS IN 1925

Affiliated Plasterers' Trade Union of South Africa
Amalgamated Building Trade Union of South Africa
Amalgamated Engineering Union
Amalgamated Society of Woodworkers
South African Boilermakers' Society
Building Workers' Industrial Union
South African Typographical Union
Witwatersrand Tailors' Association

INDUSTRIAL UNIONS IN 1925

Baking Employees' Association
Johannesburg Tramwaymen's Union
Mineral Water Employees' Union
National Vehicle Builders' Union

CRAFT UNIONS IN 1937 Affiliated members

Amalgamated Engineering Union	1 600
Ironmoulders' Society of South Africa	501
South African Boilermakers' Society	666
South African Typographical Union	2 500
Tailoring Workers' Industrial Union (TVL)	100
Total	5 367

INDUSTRIAL UNIONS IN 1937

African Laundry Workers' Union	100
Brewery Employees' Union (Cape)	200
Building Workers' Industrial Union	1 500
Bloemfontein Municipal Tramway and Bus Employees' Union	20
Bloemfontein Motor Transport Workers' Union	39

Cape Stevedoring Dock Workers' Union	150
Commercial Employees' Union	120
Durban Municipal Tramway and Motor Employees' Union	280
Furniture Workers' Union (Tvl)	1 005
Garment Workers' Union (Tvl)	2 000
Hotel, Bar and Catering Trades Employees' Union	100
Johannesburg Municipal Transport Workers' Union	600
Port Elizabeth and Catering Trades Employees' Union	60
Port Elizabeth Tram and Bus Workers' Union	100
Pretoria Municipal Tramway and Bus Workers' Union	80
Reef (Native Trade) Assistants' Union	501
South African Cinematograph Operators' Union	360
South African Garment Workers' Union	120
South African Railway and Harbour Workers' Union	120
Transvaal Explosives and Chemical Workers' Union	144
Textile Workers' Industrial Union (South Africa)	300
Transvaal Leather and Allied Trades Industrial Union	50
Transvaal Retail Butchers', Blockmen's and Ordermens' Association	60
Witwatersrand Baking Employees' Association	100
Witwatersrand Liquor and Catering Trade Employees' Union	200
Total	8 309

Industrial unions had grown very rapidly in 12 years, surpassing the craft unions in numbers by 1937. At the same time, the small size of most of these trade unions shows how few organised workers there were, partly because these industries were just beginning to develop.

Racial division in the unions

The Industrial Conciliation Act had an added result. It divided workers by excluding African men from bargaining rights and from membership of registered trade unions. (See *Black Trade Unions After the ICU* on page 161). The racial separation of the workers by law encouraged a racism that already existed amongst white workers. (The South African heritage of racism is discussed further in Chapter 8 on page 199.)

Racism occurred most readily in those unions where whites relied on protected jobs, as described in *Afrikaner Nationalism in the Unions* on page 158, and also in Chapter 17 of *Gold and Workers*. The 1922 strike, for example, started by the Mine Workers' Union, made racial demands, and was mainly about keeping certain jobs for whites. One industrial union organiser recalled:

'On no occasion [during the strike] did anyone suggest that blacks should be brought in on the strike. They could have smashed this place to smithereens. But the cause of the strike was a black/white ratio.'[8]

White miners were a privileged class of workers (a 'labour aristocracy'), whereas black miners were the most exploited workers on the Rand. Afrikaner nationalists were able to play upon this division to find a base amongst white workers, as *Afrikaner Nationalism in the Unions* shows. Similarly, white workers on the railways and in the iron and steel industry turned to Afrikaner nationalism because it promised to protect their jobs as 'civilised labour'.

Non-racial cooperation in the unions

The industrial unions, by contrast, had a more open tradition which went back to the 1920s. Under conditions of mass production, the interests of black and white workers did not necessarily clash – both white and black workers were productive, and both were semi-skilled workers. There were bonds of interest especially between white women and black workers, as we have seen, because both were used as cheap labour.

The division of labour in those early years of mass production did not go according to race – for example, in the clothing industry black and white worked together. Most cleaners were white women, while the more skilled job of pressing the garments usually went to African men.[9]

An example of non-racial solidarity amongst workers was the 1928 strike at the Ideal Laundry, in Johannesburg, when all the black workers struck in support of a white woman worker who had been victimised.[10] There were a number of such examples in the late 1920s. However, there were also occasions when white workers failed to come out on strike in support of their black fellow-workers.

In spite of the conservatism of many white workers, their workplace situation made them realise that the way to improve their bargaining position was to unite with black workers. In the late 1920s, the garment, leather, furniture, and canvas unions dropped the colour-bar against Indian and 'coloured' membership. They also held joint meetings with the African unions, which in many cases they helped to organise. Black and white laundry workers went a step further and had a joint executive committee. Their unions actually merged for a short while in 1935.

In 1930, the Trade Union Council and the Cape Federation of Labour unions held a joint, multi-racial meeting to form the South African Trades and Labour Council (the TLC). The new council called for non-racial unions and demanded that racial labour laws, such as the Native Administration Act and the racial

The first Trades Union Congress held in 1925. Surprisingly, Communist Party founder-member Bill Andrews (fifth from the left in second top row) was voted in as president. Another Marxist, Fanny Klenerman, organiser of the Women Workers' Union, is one of the two women representatives in the picture, on the right of centre in the second-last row. In spite of radical leadership, the TUC itself was cautious in its relations with black unions. It was especially nervous of the ICU with its claim to 100 000 members, a figure which dwarfed the TUC federation's membership. In 1930 the TUC merged with the Cape Federation of Labour to form the Trades and Labour Council (the TLC).

clause in the Industrial Conciliation Act (excluding African men from registered unions) be abolished.

Although their actions were slower than their words, the TLC at least gave money to help establish African unions in the late 1930s. (See *Black Trade Unions After the ICU*.)

Cooperation and solidarity between the registered and unregistered unions continued after the depression. For instance, after a non-racial strike in Natal in 1935, the Transvaal Textile Workers' Union passed a resolution at their next meeting:

> 'that we organise all South African textile workers irrespective of race, colour or creed into one union.'[11]

The union remained non-racial for nearly twenty years.

In 1942 the Johannesburg Sweetworkers' Union went on strike for a sixty percent increase in wages:

> 'One of the finest features of the strike was the unity and solidarity between the Europeans and the African strikers, both determined not to return to work unless the wage demands of the other were agreed to by the bosses.'[12]

The solidarity of the two unions succeeded and both black and white workers got their wage increase. This cooperation between the registered and unregistered unions in the sweet industry continued until 1948 — African workers refused to cross the picket lines of registered union members during strikes, and the registered workers continued to push for equal wages for Africans in the industry.

Democratic organisations

As we have seen, it was the democratically organised registered unions which cooperated on a number of occasions with the black unregistered unions. This was not a coincidence. Workers in these unions had not yet become part of the system which divided them racially into productive workers (black) and supervisors (white). In unions like the Garment Workers' Union (see page 146) participation by workers was stressed. Shop stewards had to obtain mandates from the workers they represented. Although the union leaders required special skills and a good understanding of labour law, they also depended on mandates from the membership. Their decisions had to be confirmed at general meetings.

By contrast the 'whites only' unions on the mines and in government-owned industries like the railways left decisions to the union officials. (See the story of the Mineworkers' Union on page 160). These leaders were responsible to themselves rather than to the workers, and also developed close links with the employers. The underlying reason for this was that these unions relied on the policies of the state to protect their jobs, rather than on worker organisation.

Up to World War II registered unions like the GWU remained democratic and militant. They used the strike weapon as much as they used government laws to

Furniture factory, 1927. The Transvaal Furniture Workers' union, founded in 1925, stipulated in its constitution that 'all workers employed in the furniture industry shall be eligible for membership'. This definition included Indian and coloured workers, but was obliged to exclude Africans, who were not regarded as 'employees' by law. The Furniture Workers' Union was, however, supportive to African unions.

improve wages and working conditions. In the 1930s, there were strikes in the leather, garment, textile, food and canning, and sweet industries, as examples in the following pages of this chapter will show.

But during and after World War II the militancy of these unions declined. As the factories grew, the racial composition of labour in mass production changed. While white men joined the army, more and more black workers joined the factories and many white women workers took up clerical posts. And as the racial division of labour became more marked, the trade unions began to assume a more racial character, until in the early 1950s most registered and unregistered unions – pushed by the state – broke off relations completely.

Conclusion

This chapter has shown how changes in the *labour process* affected worker organisation. It has shown how racial divisions of labour in the mining and iron and steel industries, as well as on the railways, led to racially exclusive unions. On the other hand, mass production, in its early stages, led to the employment of cheap semi-skilled labour, regardless of colour. This in turn led to class-based unions which cooperated across the racial divide, as far as the law would allow.

But to argue that racial division by employers in the labour process was the *only* reason for racism in trade unions would be misleading, for we cannot separate the workplace from South African society as a whole.

For a start the government itself encouraged racial divisions.

- We have seen how, for example, the Pact Government stepped in to give aid to poor whites, and not to poor blacks. For political reasons, it encouraged capitalists to employ whites rather than blacks (where it was profitable!) As an employer itself, the government applied the 'civilised labour' policy in state industries.

- The government's labour laws, too, deliberately aimed to divide the workers racially. In the Industrial Council, even the registered industrial unions, which as we have seen were largely sympathetic to the black registered unions, tended to push their own wage demands in preference to those of black workers.

- Furthermore, in the Transvaal, the Orange Free State and Natal the state allowed only whites to vote for parliament – in the Cape, African men had the vote taken away from them in 1936. (Black women never had the vote.)

White workers – men and women – had the vote, and this gave them political and economic power. It allowed them the freedom to look for work in an open job market, while black workers had to carry passes. White workers were able to push for better housing and transport. They were able to mix with the growing white middle class socially and in public places, and most aspired to become like them.

As a result black workers were separated from white workers outside the workplace. They therefore experienced different living conditions and took part in different struggles. Racial discrimination weakened the bargaining power of black workers, kept their wages miserably low, and caused them to develop a different way of life in town.

The lives and living conditions of workers outside the workplace are discussed in the next two chapters.

White male semi-skilled workers assembling motor chassis at General Motors in 1935, before the days of the automated assembly line. The parts were imported and put together by South African workers using hand tools.

The Story of the Garment Workers' Union to 1941

The clothing or garment industry is an example of the rapid change in the 1920s from the craft work of manufacturing to the semi-skilled labour of mass production. The development of this industry illustrates the way in which the unions changed along with the changing labour process.

Garment factory in 1918. In the early days of the clothing industry, many of the workers were men who were master tailors.

Master tailors

The craft union in the clothing industry was called the Witwatersrand Tailors' Association. Its members were master craftsmen who worked in small tailoring shops, making clothing on contract for wholesale merchants.

They were the 'middle-men', who in turn employed others to help them finish the job. They used the merchants' material and were paid on a piece-work basis, called the 'cut-make-and-trim' system – that is, so much money for each garment that they made.

The tailors were mostly British, and proud of their militant, trade-union tradition. There was also a growing number of Jewish tailors newly arrived from Eastern Europe.

After World War I, the clothing industry grew and began to change. Larger workshops were set up, and workers were hired to do semi-skilled jobs such as machining trouser seams and other straight stitching.

As the numbers of the semi-skilled workers grew, the tailors began to realise that they would have to open their union to prevent undercutting, otherwise large numbers of low-paid workers would bring down the cost of producing clothes, and the tailors would get paid less for the clothes they made. To protect themselves tailors were forced to support the interests of the other workers in the industry.

By 1927, the union had two sections: the Bespoke Tailoring Section for craft tailors who made clothes to order; and the Factory Section for machine operators and semi-skilled workers, whose numbers made up two-thirds of union membership.

The new garment workers

Most of these new workers were young, unmarried Afrikaner women straight from the land. (*The Story of Two Bywoner Families* in Chapter 1 describes the background of many of these newcomers to the towns, and explains why they were forced to migrate to the cities to work for wages.)

These Afrikaners were easily exploited, both as women and as inexperienced workers. They were paid 'starvation' wages. Some girls were paid nothing at all for the first six months on the grounds that they were 'learning'.

The Factory Section of the Union, later named the Garment Workers' Union (GWU) fought long and hard through the 1930s: in the struggle to get employers to pay the legal wages to workers, and in the struggle for union recognition.

The struggle over wages

In 1927 the Pact Government introduced a Wages Act designed to encourage industrialists to employ whites. (See **Labour Laws**, page 152). The Act laid down minimum salary scales, but there were hundreds of workers – tailors as well as operatives – who were being paid wages well below these rates.

All over the Rand, there were small workshops

employing workers in miserable conditions. They worked in crowded, stuffy workshops with poor lighting and worse sanitation, without tea breaks, forced to work late at night without overtime, and sometimes made to wait for their wages because employers themselves were 'short'.

Many years later, a veteran trade unionist, Anna Swanepoel, recalled her first job as a garment worker:

> 'I started at R1 a week. The hours were from seven a.m. to six p.m. daily, with an hour for lunch, and seven a.m. to twelve noon on Saturdays. The workshop was terribly overcrowded and hot, with primus stoves going all day and the smell of paraffin filling the air.'[13]

Then in 1928 E.S. (Solly) Sachs was elected secretary of the Tailors' and Garment Workers' Union. Sachs's hard work and careful union strategies had a very important influence on the members and on the development of the union.

Sachs spent much of his time going from workshop to workshop, checking workers' wages. Often, the workers themselves would not reveal how little they were earning for fear of losing their jobs.

For example, this is how a migrant Jewish tailor described his situation:

> 'I know the union is trying its best to help us, but what can I do? I am a first-class tailor and work very hard. I know that under the agreement I am entitled to R16 a week, but I only receive half that amount.

A 'sweat shop' in the 1930s.

> 'You think I like it? I have a wife and family in the old country [in Eastern Europe]. I have to support them. In fact, I want to bring them here. I have also to support myself, and if I told you the truth and my boss got to know, I'd soon get the sack and who would give me a job then?'[14]

The answer to his question lay in the *collective power* of the union. Guided by Sachs, the union developed a strategy of using any weapons available to it to enforce the legal wages. It even mastered the tools used by the employers themselves – the Industrial Councils, the Wage Board and the law courts.

In 1929, 27 employers were prosecuted for not keeping to agreements. Twenty-five were convicted. One employer had to hand over R80 in fines as well as back pay to his workers. The employers were warned that it was illegal to victimise workers who had given evidence to the Industrial Council or in court.

But it was not always possible to prove victimisation. In one case, two workers were sacked. The union immediately called a strike and over a thousand workers demonstrated outside the shop. The workers got their jobs back, and the importance of solidarity was proved.

Police escorts during the 1932 garment workers' strike in Germiston. Although the workers were almost all Afrikaners, the Nationalist Party government mobilised large numbers of police, and scores of girls were arrested. On one occasion during the strike, mounted police rode into a crowd of pickets, badly injuring a number of strikers.

Strikes, the depression, and the recovery

There were many other strikes. Between 1928 and 1932 there were over a hundred work stoppages. The strikes of 1931 and 1932 brought the clothing industry to a standstill.

The union made full use of labour laws, but it also recognised that the laws helped the workers only to a certain extent, and that strike action, used wisely, remained the most powerful weapon of the workers.

However, strikes can only be really successful if the workers are not easy to replace. In times of mass unemployment, 'scabbing' grows, and wages remain low. The GWU lost hundreds of members during the depression of 1931-1933. Workers' wages were cut, and the Industrial Council fell away. The union was not strong enough to stand up to employers.

Union membership picked up only after the depression lifted, as described in Chapter 5, and industry began to prosper again. New capital flowed into South Africa and modern factories were built, needing more staff. By 1934, the GWU had a membership of 3 000 –

over 90 percent of the semi-skilled workers in the clothing industry in the Transvaal. The union managed to negotiate a small wage increase.

Union recognition

In general, the new, more up-to-date factories had employers who were prepared to recognise the union. As modern capitalists, they felt that disputes and strikes were wasteful of labour and therefore expensive, especially at a time when business was growing.

When employers saw that most of the workers were union members, they began to make more agreements with the union. The Industrial Council was prepared to enforce these agreements because employers realised that low wages led to undercutting amongst the capitalists themselves.

Some employers even put advertisements in the union magazine, *The Garment Worker/Die Klere-werker* describing the good working conditions in their factories.

One of the larger clothing factories in the late 1930s. As the GWU grew in strength it was able to challenge the small under-capitalised factories that relied on 'sweated' labour, leaving the larger and more efficient factories to control the industry.

Union strength

The GWU grew in strength, and eventually was powerful enough to change the clothing industry itself – the GWU hunted down many of the small, under-capitalised factories that relied solely on paying workers less than the minimum wage. Many of these factories had to close down, leaving the larger and more efficient factories to control the industry.

By 1936 the GWU was able to enforce a closed shop – the employers agreed not to employ anyone who did not belong to the union. Employers even agreed to collect *stop-orders* for the union by deducting members' subscriptions from their wages and paying these straight to the union.

The union also campaigned for – and got – paid holidays, a shorter working day, crèches, maternity and sick leave, and even special hostel accommodation for women workers in the municipalities of Johannesburg and Germiston.

By 1941, when the South African economy began to expand even more rapidly, the GWU was firmly established.

Democratic organisation

The union won more than higher wages, better conditions and shorter hours. The democratic nature of the union's organisation was as important a victory.

From the beginning, the Factory Section of the union held many meetings. The general meetings attracted three to four thousand members. There were also weekly meetings of the 32 members of the central committee. At these meetings, members were active

---

HOLIDAY LEAVE FOR GARMENT WORKERS

In terms of Clause 13 of the Agreement for the Clothing Industry, all employees in the Clothing Industry, Transvaal, are entitled to Holiday Leave which must be granted to them by their employers between December 1st, 1936, and January 22nd, 1937, as follows:

(1) Employees who have started work for their present employer before 25th May, 1936: ONE WEEK'S HOLIDAY ON FULL PAY.

(2) Employees who have started work for their present employer after the 25th May, 1936, and have worked for not less than eight weeks: Two per cent. of the Total Wages (1/- for every 50/-) which they have earned from the time they started until the Factory closes for the Xmas period.

(3) Employees who have left their work before the 1st of December, 1936, and have been employed for not less than eight weeks by the same employer; Two per cent. of the total Wages earned by them as from the 1st January, 1936, or from the time they started their employment.

Announcement in *Garment Worker*, November 1936.

and exercised their skills as public speakers.

The shop stewards, elected in all the factories, were the 'live wires' who kept democracy going. They were in daily contact with the workers on the shop floor, and also called regular meetings where practical problems and ideas could be discussed.

Union members were therefore in close touch with their representatives and took a close interest in the decisions of the union. Complaints were taken up quickly and efficiently.

Solidarity

Democratic organisation also meant educating workers on the importance of solidarity. The GWU worked hard at spreading organisation to other centres where garment workers were employed. They set up branches in Port Elizabeth, East London, King William's Town, Kroonstad and Bloemfontein, and also battled to establish themselves in Cape Town. In all these places, the wages of garment workers were lower than on the Rand. (See *The Labour Movement in the Cape and Natal* on page 155.)

The GWU also believed that workers in all industries needed their own organisations. They helped workers in the textile, sweet, tobacco and hat industries to form unions, and gave money to strike funds.

Ten years in the GWU

'Ten years ago the bosses paid us any wages they liked, we had only two paid holidays, no rest intervals. In some factories workers had to work day and night. When we were sick or unemployed we got no help. Today we have fixed wages by agreements between our union and our employers. Women workers start at £1 [two rand] per week, get periodical increases and after three years 35/-[R3,50] per week. We get ten days' holiday per year instead of two. We work regular hours, get rest intervals, and when we are sick or unemployed we are looked after.' (From *Garment Worker*, February 1939.)

Race and the GWU

The GWU is an example of an industrial union which was not a whites-only union. From 1926 onwards, it accepted black operatives as members.

However, African men, defined as 'pass-bearing Natives' by law, were not allowed to join registered unions. (See *Black Trade Unions after the ICU*.) Black members in the GWU included coloured and Indian operatives, as well as African women after they began to enter the clothing industry in the Transvaal during and after World War II. (As African women did not have to carry passes at the time, they were able to join registered unions.)

The GWU worked closely with the black SA Clothing Workers' Union. As a registered union, the GWU made many representations on behalf of the unregistered union to the Industrial Council to extend wage agreements to African workers. They never succeeded, however, and the wages of African clothing workers remained low. The GWU also helped sometimes with strike funds, although it never went out on strike to support the Clothing Workers' demands. The clothing workers, on the other hand, joined several strikes of the GWU.

The GWU allowed black operatives as members, but some white workers did not treat them as equals, even though they worked side by side on the factory floor. Perhaps this was not surprising, as many of the menfolk of the garment workers were working on the railways, or in the mines, where white workers were threatened by black workers undercutting them. Although many of the white women workers were loyal to the union and had a strong class consciousness, they were influenced by the prejudices of their society.

Race prejudice increased especially after the rise of Afrikaner nationalism in the unions, because its policy was to separate Afrikaners from other workers. (See *Afrikaner Nationalism in the Unions*.) When World War II started, the garment industry expanded rapidly, and a shortage of labour developed. More and more coloured women workers entered the industry. Although the union leaders tried to persuade the members to form one big non-racial union, most of the members were in favour of two separate branches.

The result was that two branches of the GWU were formed – a 'Number 1 Branch' for white members, and a 'Number 2 Branch' for coloured, Indian and African women workers. The 'Number 2 Branch' did not send representatives to the Central Executive nor to the Industrial Council. There was a distinct feeling that 'No. 2' also meant 'second class'!

The division into two branches went against the ideals of trade unionism, for the union was now divided not by skill, as it was in the 1920s with the 'Bespoke' and 'Factory' sections, but by race. However, the GWU was able to improve the wages and working conditions of the 'Number 2 Branch', and its members were active and interested.

Nevertheless, the separation of the workers gave the leaders more power, as they were the only ones who met both groups of workers, with the result that ultimately there was less democracy in the union.

Conclusion

The first fifteen years of the 'Factory Section' saw great gains. The wages of operatives more than doubled during that time, and many other benefits were introduced. The successes of the union also gave its members confidence in themselves as women workers.

After 1934, when the GWU formed its own organisation, separate from the tailors, the women had a greater chance to develop their own union and leadership skills. They learnt to demand their rights as workers — they were not just 'factory servant girls' — *'maar 'n klomp factory meide'* as one policeman scornfully called them.[15] They did not need to apologise to anyone, and they learnt how to demand respect from foremen and managers.

Solidarity Forever

(This is a union song popular with industrial workers in South Africa and the world over. The words were composed by a union organiser, journalist and poet — Ralph Chaplin — during the great 1915 coal miners' strike in the state of Virginia, USA.)

When the Union's inspiration through the
    workers' blood shall run,
There can be no power greater anywhere
    beneath the sun.
Yet what force on earth is weaker than the
    feeble strength of one?
But the Union makes us strong.

Chorus
Solidarity forever
Solidarity forever
Solidarity forever
For the Union makes us strong.

In the years after 1941, the GWU was to grow faster than ever, and union members faced greater challenges. Would they realise that white workers could strengthen their position as workers only if they shared the benefits they gained with *all* workers, black and white?

Organising in a Country Town

'I was going to hold a meeting at 5 p.m. Well, the manager let the girls out at 4.30 p.m., so I missed a lot of them. But still the meeting was not so bad. I called upon the girls to enrol, and the manager came forward and said,

"Girls, I know you like to think things over. You already pay sixpence (five cents) a week to the doctor and now it means another sixpence for you people to pay the union. If anyone makes trouble here we make trouble

for them. If any girls want to fill in forms, Miss du Toit will give the forms to me and I will see that you fill them in and pass them on to her."
I asked the girls if one of them would come forward. After a bit one little girl offered to take the forms. Just as I was leaving I went to the manager's office and saw him talking to this girl.'[16]

The writer of this report, Bettie du Toit, was a nineteen-year-old textile union organiser who had already started a non-racial textile union in Cape Town, which had won some important victories. Excited by this success, the union then sent her to the small Cape village (or *dorp*) of Huguenot to organise the workers of a blanket factory there. There were both white and black workers in the factory, but the union decided to start with the white workers first.

Early success

The owner of the textile factory was Jewish, and although he was wary of his workers joining a union, he was also disturbed at the growing influence of Nazism in South Africa. (See also page 225.) When he realised that Bettie du Toit was anti-Nazi and non-racial, he not only allowed her to organise his workers but also offered her a job in the factory as a weaver.

Textile workers on strike, 1930.

Bettie accepted the offer, and soon learnt to work the looms, determined to weave as expertly and as fast as the other girls, and so win their respect. With the low wages of a textile worker, she could only afford to move into the women's hostel. This had been established by the Dutch Reformed Church's *Armesorg* (poor relief) Committee, which tried to place whites in employment in rural areas, and also kept a watch over the morals of the young workers. Bettie du Toit was pleased to have the chance to be among her fellow-workers, working with them, living with them, and sharing their sparse meals.

At first the union grew rapidly. Bettie du Toit had no trouble enrolling nearly every white worker in the factory. Excited meetings were held, and in homes, cafes and cinemas there was a buzz about what the new union could do for the workers.

Rejection

But one Sunday evening, after Bettie returned from a weekend in Cape Town during which she reported to her union, she found posters in the streets of Huguenot, denouncing her as a communist. Throughout the next morning, girls came up to her loom, tore up their union cards, and threw the pieces in her face. When she got home to her bed that evening, she found that her suitcase had been searched and a letter from a black fellow organiser was being shown around as proof of the 'immoral' life she was leading. She was asked to leave the hostel. No one else in the village would give her accommodation. She was 'sent to Coventry' – that is, no one would speak to her; and when she walked along the pavement, people would cross to the other side. Those who sympathised with her were too afraid to show their support openly.

Hurt and disappointed, Bettie went back to Cape Town. There she learnt that the Dutch Reformed Church, together with other supporters of the Afrikaner Nationalist movement, were planning to hold a meeting in the Paarl town hall to warn workers against the communist organiser. They were unhappy about the growing class consciousness amongst Afrikaner workers and were determined to block it. (Bettie du Toit was, in fact, a member of the South African Communist Party – see *The Communist Party and Black Workers* on page 166 and *Afrikaner Nationalism in the Unions* on page 158.)

Bettie was encouraged by other trade unionists to attend the meeting and defend herself from the floor. A young Afrikaner waitress and organiser, Joey Fourie, went with her to give moral support. During the meeting, speaker after speaker denounced the communist in their midst and warned workers of the dangers of associating with such a person. Then a farmer, sitting near her, spoke up in a loud voice:

'Man, waar is hierdie vreeslike kommunis?' – 'Where is this terrible communist?'

Bettie nervously stood up and said in a small voice:

'Dis ek, meneer' – 'It's me, sir.'

The farmer turned to look at her and exclaimed:

'Maar jy's blerrie mooi!' – 'But you're bloody pretty!'

The audience all laughed, and the hostility against her melted away. Bettie then spoke about the aims of the union and the need for workers to organise. At the end of her speech, she got as much applause as the other speakers, and when she left the hall she was not beaten up by the young Greyshirts (a Nazi-like youth group) who had followed her into the meeting.

The people of Huguenot and Paarl proved their humanity and warmth by giving Bettie du Toit a hearing, but the union abandoned its activities in that area. When the Cape Town branch tried again a few years later to organise a textile union in Huguenot, it again failed in the same way – after a successful start, the *predikant* (church minister) would visit new members' parents, or threaten to have them evicted from the hostel, and the young workers would resign from the union. There were similar experiences in other rural towns in those years.

The difficulties

Organising workers in the countryside was even more difficult than forming unions in the towns. In all small communities there is great pressure for people to conform – to comply with everyone else, and not behave differently. In the typical South African *dorp* of Huguenot, there was the deeply-rooted tradition of inequality between black and white. Added to this, trade unionism (and the Communist Party) preached *class consciousness*, which cut across the aims of the Afrikaner nationalist movement of bringing all the *volk* together – workers, professionals, farmers and capitalists alike.

Afrikaner workers were therefore torn between two different movements:

- one which called on them to overcome their prejudices and organise *as workers* together with other workers, for a better life over which they could have more control;
- and the other which called on them to keep themselves separate from 'foreign' influences, and remain loyal to the Boer culture of pre-industrial society. In the country *dorps*, Afrikaner workers came from farming stock and although many of them wanted to develop their rights as workers, they were unable or unwilling to break from their own people, their church and their traditions.

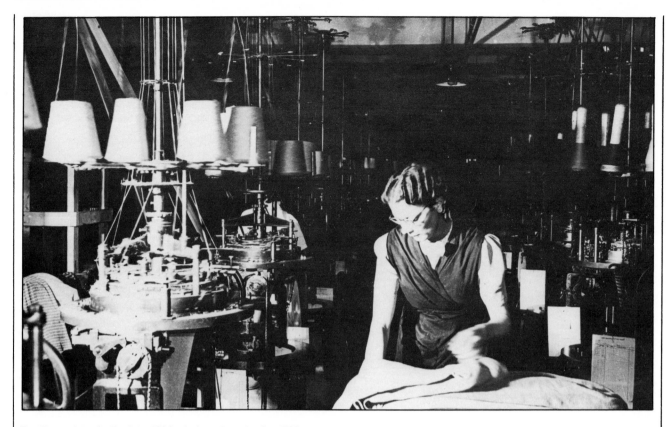

Textile workers in the late 1930s. Labour laws in the 1920s aimed to control conflict between workers and employers and to regulate white worker organisations.

Furthermore, the trade union movement itself had not developed enough solidarity to come out in support of small, struggling unions such as the textile union branch in Huguenot. The strong craft unions, represented by the well-established Trades and Labour Council, passed fine resolutions condemning racism, but their support stopped there. Unions in the rural areas did not take root.

Labour Laws of the 1920s

Laws on labour passed by the two South African governments in power in the 1920s — Smuts's South African Party and the National-Labour Pact Government — had certain aims in common. They were intended to *control conflict* between workers and their employers, and to *regulate* worker organisations.

The Industrial Conciliation Act, 1924

This important law, passed by the South African Party, followed the 1922 strike, the biggest and most violent strike by white workers in South African history. Although the mine owners and government defeated the strike, they were shaken by the strength and bitterness of the workers, and they realised that trade unions would have to be recognised in order to be regulated.

The Industrial Conciliation Act was a safe way of regulating disputes between workers and their bosses so that strikes would not be necessary.

- The law allowed for joint boards, or *industrial councils* to be formed, on which registered trade unions and employers in a particular industry were represented. These councils could make agreements on wages, working hours, working conditions, and leave. Once an agreement was made, all workers and bosses in the industry had to follow it, otherwise they could be prosecuted.
- No strikes or lock-outs were allowed while the councils were discussing an agreement. This meant that there was very little chance of legal strikes taking place.
- However, many workers could not take part in the industrial council machinery. The government left out all employees of the government and municipalities, all farm workers, all domestic workers, and all contract workers in its definition of 'employee' — and only employees could sit on industrial councils. In addition, the law stated that any 'worker whose contract of service or labour is regulated by any Native Pass Laws and Regulations' was not to be considered an 'employee'.

Workers were therefore divided by the Industrial Conciliation Act. Government employees had separate agreements (see *'Civilised Labour' and Deskilling*

Farm workers in the Cape. The terms of the Industrial Conciliation Act of 1924 excluded farm workers, domestic workers, contract workers, municipal and government employees, and pass-bearing Africans.

on the Railways), while black workers had no legal way of bargaining at all. The Industrial Conciliation Act, therefore, was a settlement between organised business and organised labour.

The Pact government's labour laws

The labour policy of the Pact government was to protect unskilled whites against the cheaper labour of unskilled black workers, and skilled whites against undercutting by black artisans.

But as we have seen in Chapter 5, the Pact government also wanted to develop South African capital by encouraging South African industries.

Clearly the interests of the white workers and the growing number of factory owners were bound to clash. The job of the Pact government, therefore, was to find a way of satisfying white workers without upsetting the development of the new manufacturing economy.

A brief summary of the main labour laws passed by this government gives an idea of how it tried to settle the different interests of white workers and manufacturing capital.

The Wage Act, 1925

This law provided a single national board (the **Wage Board**) to recommend minimum wages and conditions of unorganised or unregistered groups of workers in all industries. The act aimed to raise the wages of semi-skilled workers to a 'civilised' level. Ironically, the government recognised that there was a need to fix a minimum for black workers in order to protect the white workers' wages against undercutting. A government minister put it this way:

> 'What we are not prepared at the moment to do is allow the natives to organise and function under the Industrial Conciliation Act, the same as carpenters, joiners and other organised trades which have had many years in trade unionism, and which can be calculated to hold their own with employers. The time will come, possibly, when the natives will reach that stage of advancement, and something on these lines will have to be done; but that time has not yet arrived.'[17]

The government hoped that the act would tend to price black workers out of jobs. For example, the Minister of Posts and Telegraphs said that he was confident that the Wage Act would help especially those white workers in Natal who were losing jobs in many trades because of 'unfair competition' from Indians, who were efficient and cheap. Under the new laws, he said, employers were forced to pay everyone the same wages, and then they would prefer to employ the more experienced white workers.[18]

The Wage Act was not entirely successful. It did not

Railway workers. The Pact Government's labour laws aimed to protect the jobs of unskilled white workers against the cheaper labour of black workers. In spite of the law, this 'civilised labour' policy succeeded mainly in government industries, where profit was not as important as in private industry.

always suit employers. They often argued that their businesses would go bankrupt if they paid 'civilised' wages, and managed to persuade the Wage Board to fix wages at lower rates. Wages for white workers really improved only with militant bargaining by their unions, combined with the upswing in the economy at the end of the depression in 1933. A number of black unions, on the other hand, were able to make some gains through the Wage Board. (See *Black Trade Unions after the ICU*.)

The Mines and Works Act, 1926

The 1926 Mines and Works Act must be seen against the background of the wage and job colour bars in South Africa. The 1911 Act, mentioned earlier, reserved skilled work for whites only. But in spite of this law, mine owners continued to deskill jobs and give more and more work to black miners to save labour costs. (The wages of black mine workers remained the same no matter what work they were doing – they earned about a tenth of the wages of a skilled white worker.) The 1922 strike was caused by the mine owners' attempt to replace a number of white workers with lower-paid black workers.

Just one year after the strike, a court of law ruled that race discrimination in jobs was not allowed. Immediately there was a storm of protest from white

The South African Employer

Exploiter and Exploited

In 1937 a black American sociologist, Ralphe Bunche, made a study tour of South Africa. The following is an extract from his notes.

'The other day Robertson, the Cape Town University economist, interrupted me to state that not only does the employer exploit the racial conflict situation, but the situation also exploits the employer. This stumped me until Sachs and I figured out last night what he meant. This was true in South Africa only, where government protection of white workers makes employers pay higher wages than he would have to in a free market. But, I answered, this is really insurance against the ultimate labour unity trouble for the employer and therefore a good investment.'[19]

workers. They felt it was only a matter of time before all their jobs would go to lower-paid black workers. Soon after the Pact government came into power, the old Mines and Works Act was revived. The government recognised that the system of labour control could also work against the white worker. Therefore the aim of the new Mines and Works Act, said the Minister of Mines and Industries, was to protect white workers against

'the advantages in favour of the native . . . which make him more attractive to the employer as a source of labour . . . . The whole system is all through the colour bar. The native is kept under control, but not the white man . . . . The native is preferred by the mining companies owing to the compound system, pass laws, right of prosecution for desertion [the contract system] and so on.'[20]

Over the next few years, more regulations were added to the law, extending the colour bar even further in order to protect skilled and unskilled white workers from being undercut by the cheap labour of black workers.

The Leather Worker in Mass Production

'A pounder is a machine that beats the edges of the upper [shoe] after the shoe has been lasted.

Operating it is heavy work. The shoe is held tightly against a vibrating piece of steel, while every muscle and nerve in the operator's arm shakes in a frenzy of movement. It has turned men into nervous wrecks.

In 1937 the labour cost of a pair of shoes was

Mass-produced boots.

3s10d (76 cents). In 1933 it was 2s (20 cents). In the speed-up factories today men are driven to make this figure even lower.

For every minute of the eight and three-quarter hour day a pounder stands before his machine, he puts through one pair of shoes.

At five o'clock, his arms still twitching, he is released, too tired to read, too tired to talk much. And besides, there are 525 pairs to be put through tomorrow.'[21]

'Rumour hath it'

'Rumour hath it that the Automatic edge-setting machine which has recently been introduced is causing a good deal of unemployment as each of these machines does the work of two men, and that the Union's Executive is to be congratulated on demanding the highest possible wage rate for this new machine.'[22]

The Labour Movement in the Cape and Natal

Labour conditions at the coast were very different from those in the heavily industrialised Transvaal. There were fewer factories in Durban, East London, Port Elizabeth and Cape Town, and the workers were paid much lower wages. Employers argued that their profits were lower than those of the Transvaal industries, and therefore they could not compete with the Transvaal's higher wages.

The result was that, unless there was organisation and solidarity, the coastal workers could *undercut* the Transvaal workers. It was therefore important that the trade unions should be able to organise on a national scale.

What follows is a brief outline of worker organisation in the two coastal provinces — the Cape and Natal. Each province had its own tradition of organisation and resistance. An example is given of the early labour experiences in each of these areas to show how they differed from each other and from the Transvaal.

Industrial unions in the Cape

From the earliest days of industrialisation in the Cape, a large proportion of workers were coloured. They were not excluded from joining registered trade unions, as African men were, by the 1924 Industrial Conciliation Act. The Cape unions were therefore non-racial in membership, unlike the Transvaal.

Nevertheless, the industrial unions, and also their federation, the *Cape Federation of Labour Unions* (the CFLU) were dominated by white leaders with racist ideas. The CFLU had, in fact, grown 'from the top' — after the passing of the Industrial Conciliation Act and the Wage Act, most industrial unions were formed through contact between craft union leaders and employers, leading to agreements and union recognition.

The craft unions saw the need for industrial unions. The employers, too, supported industrial unions — but for a different reason. They were confident that they could control wage levels through Industrial Councils if workers were unionised. The price of union cooperation with employers was that the industrial unions did not grow out of the struggles or actions of the members themselves. The trade unions remained weak, and the wages were fixed at a rate 25 percent below the wages of Transvaal workers.

Garment workers in the Cape

In the clothing industry, for example, the Garment Workers' Union of the Cape Province (the GWU CP) became a 'paper union' less than two years after the agreement with the employers in 1926 — there were no active members, no meetings, no union officials who had ever been garment workers, no democratic elections. Nor was there any attempt to enforce the official wage rate — low as it was. Yet, in spite of all these faults, the GWU CP was the officially recognised union for workers in the clothing industry.

The sharp difference in wages between the north and the south affected the Transvaal GWU. As a GWU leader recalled:

'By 1930 our union realised that unless the workers of the coastal area were organised, their conditions would remain deplorable, and our conditions would ultimately sink to theirs.'[23]

In that year, the Transvaal started a new clothing workers' union in the Cape, with Johnny Gomas and Jimmy La Guma as organisers. Immediately, the official GWU CP got the employers to put up notices in

155

Canning factory in the Cape. The non-racial Food and Canning Workers' Union was formed in 1941 in Cape Town.

Candle factory, Cape, 1934.

the factories to say that the employers

'had no objection to their employees being members of the trade union, and that it would be advantageous for them to join.'[24]

Then, in 1931, as the depression hit South Africa, several garment workers were dismissed. The new union called for a strike. But in that poor economic situation, the workers' bargaining power was very weak and the timing for a strike was wrong. As management itself declared:

'The strike could not have taken place at a more convenient time as far as they [management] were personally concerned.'[25]

Many garment workers seemed to agree, because two thirds did not strike. The strike failed, and the new union collapsed.

Militant organisers in better times

Then, in the mid-1930s, after the economy picked up again, a new crop of militant organisers — mostly members of the Communist Party — began to organise in the Cape. (See *The Communist Party and Black Workers*.) Eli Weinberg, La Guma, Gomas, and Ray Alexander successfully formed the African Garment Workers' Union. The leather, rope, milling, and chemical industries soon followed, as well as the Commercial Workers' Union.

In February 1941, Ray Alexander organised the Food and Canning Workers' Union (FWCU), a non-racial union which continued militant action for many years, and which in 1986 was still active and growing.

Indian workers in a match factory, Durban 1913.

The labour movement in Natal

In Natal, cheap labour in the early years consisted mainly of Indian *indentured labour* – that is, contract workers from India, who worked on the sugar plantations, the Natal Government Railways, or in the Natal coal mines, under conditions close to slavery. (Other Indians, mainly Moslems, had paid their own way to South Africa and set themselves up as traders. Their resistance against discrimination is described in *The Indian Resistance of 1913* in Chapter 4.)

As their contracts expired, a few Indians were able to make their own way in the Natal economy by hawking – selling fruit, vegetables and flowers in the streets from carts – or by setting up small shops. A few also obtained 'white collar' jobs in the civil service. But most of the 'freed' Indians could only survive through wage labour – they had no land, and being new workers, they had not been trained in industrial skills.

Labour through taxation

The Natal government used taxes to force people into wage labour. (See *Msilana Refuses* in Chapter 1.) Zulu resistance resulted in a shortage of labour for Natal employers for many years.

The tax method of encouraging wage labour was also used on Indians whose indentures or contracts had expired. All 'free' Indians were forced to pay a six rand tax every year because they were not working under contract. For poor people, this was a heavy burden, and the result was that thousands of destitute families were forced back into indentured labour.

By 1913, more than 62 percent of the entire indentured Indian workforce were still working on the sugar plantations under harsh working conditions, because they could not find other jobs. In that same year, Indian workers took part in a massive strike to protest against this labour tax, as we saw in Chapter 4.

Early trade union activity

As early as 1917 and 1918, skilled Indian workers formed printing, garment, furniture, tobacco, leather, liquor and catering unions. In the 1920s, the African-based ICU became very popular under Champion as the Natal secretary. (See *The Rise and Fall of the ICU* in Chapter 4.) The result of these racially grouped or *ethnic* unions was a divided workforce in Natal for many years. At the same time, Natal was always an active area for worker and community protest.

In 1930, the Communist Party organised an anti-pass campaign. The campaign did not succeed so well in other parts of the country, but in Durban it drew a great response. It was during an anti-pass meeting in Durban that the police battered to death the popular trade union leader and young communist, Johannes Nkosi, the first martyr of the Communist Party. The government then banned a number of trade unionists from Natal, including Champion of the ICU and Gana Makabeni of CNETU. (See *Black Trade Unions After the ICU* on page 161.)

Other labour leaders stepped forward, in particular two Indian organisers who worked very hard to overcome rivalry between African and Indian workers for jobs, and to promote non-racial unionism amongst Indian workers. They were George Ponen and H A Naidoo, supported by trade unionist Errol Shanley and Communist Party organiser Eddie Roux, as well as A Wanless of the Labour Party.

Natal trade unionists in the 1930s. Errol Shanley, D Naidoo, H A Naidoo, P M Harry, George Ponen.

As in the Cape, the unions were led by whites with racist ideas. For example, a number of trade unions were controlled by J C Bolton. Although he did much to build up labour organisation, he believed that African and Indian artisans were inferior to white skilled workers. As one trade union organiser from the Transvaal recalled:

> 'In Natal there were lots of Indian and African craftsmen working in backyard premises – upholsterers, furniture-makers and leather workers. They had learned their trade in the mission schools or through experience . . . . Bolton wouldn't recognise them.'[26]

Solidarity and strikes

But, rather than form separate unions, Ponen and Naidoo encouraged black workers to challenge the existing unions. In 1934, black and white garment workers united to come out on strike against a factory boss who had drilled peep-holes in the doors of toilets used by the black workers to see if they were concealing stolen articles in their clothing. The strike was successful, although Bolton helped to get evidence against Ponen and Naidoo when they were charged for organising an illegal strike. They were each fined four rand. Workers paid the fine.[27]

There were other successful strikes across the colour and ethnic lines. When the newly-formed Iron and Steel Workers' Union (Natal) downed tools after their chairman was victimised, there was resistance from Champion of the ICU yase Natal, as well as the white craft unions, against the bosses and the police. The strike lasted for thirteen weeks. During this time the middle-class Natal Indian Congress supported the strikers with food and strike funds. At last, the strike was settled, with shorter working hours and wage increases for the workers.

The success of the iron and steel workers resulted in the rapid growth of unions – between 1936 and 1945, 27 new trade unions were formed.[28]

In most of these, membership included both Indian and African workers.

Many of the new unions were also involved in fighting against racism in South Africa and the growing influence of fascism and Nazism that was spreading throughout Europe in the 1930s. In 1935, for example, Durban, Cape Town and Port Elizabeth dock workers refused to offload Italian ships – Mussolini's fascist government in Italy had invaded Abyssinia, one of Africa's few independent countries at that time. From the mid-1930s, the industrial unions had to struggle against the attack by Afrikaner Nationalism on non-racial unions. The story of the Cape organiser in *Organising in a Country Town* gives an idea of some of the difficulties that faced non-racial union organisers at the time.

Similarities and differences

The struggles of workers against their employers for better wages and working conditions was a country-wide struggle. The differences in each province arose out of regional situations. In the Cape and Natal, industry was less developed and there was less capital available. The squeeze on the workers was therefore even tighter in these two provinces, and the struggle for union recognition was long and hard.

In the Cape racism was less evident than in the Transvaal and Natal. It was the CFLU that organised the first non-racial conference of trade unions, registered and unregistered, held in Cape Town in 1930. Out of the 86 Cape delegates, about half were black.[29] The Transvaal, by contrast, managed to bring only one black delegate, John Gomas, a Cape tailor who had joined the GWU on the Rand.

Out of this conference, the SA Trades and Labour Council emerged. It agreed that 'equal opportunities and equal remuneration' – that is equal pay for equal work – were the best defence against racial exploitation. It promised to admit 'all **bona fide** trades and labour unions' and aimed to 'promote the interests of all organised workers'.[30] For the first time, the Transvaal unions agreed to admit black unions into their federation, and three blacks out of eighteen representatives were elected to the council.

These were small gains, but they were an important start. For they contained the recognition that class, not race, was the key to strong workers' organisations.

May Day demonstration in Cape Town, 1937. The placards read: 'No Colour Bar in the Trade Unions!' and 'Down with the Personal Tax! Make the Rich Pay!' In the western Cape, racism was less evident than in the Transvaal and Natal labour movements.

Afrikaner Nationalism in the Unions

Afrikaners founded the Nationalist Party in 1912. Only twelve years later, in 1924, it was voted into power. But it had to share the government with the Labour Party, because it did not have enough votes to govern on its own.

Afrikaner nationalism was therefore allied to a workers' movement. Its leader, General J M B Hertzog, even sympathised briefly with the black workers' ICU. (See *The Rise and Fall of the ICU* in Chapter 4.) However, we have also seen in Chapter 5 how the Pact Government passed laws favouring white workers and put forward a 'civilised labour' policy, and how it encouraged the growth of South African capitalism.

Nevertheless, although Afrikaner nationalists had political power, the economy was still controlled by English-speaking capitalists. The English also held top civil service and government posts as well as the top positions in the army and the police force. South Africa's middle class was almost entirely English. Even in the white working class, the English controlled the influential craft unions and their federation, the Trades and Labour Council.

But there was a small group of Afrikaner professionals − teachers, church ministers, and lawyers − who wanted to change all this. As described in *The Birth of Afrikaner Capitalism* in Chapter 5, they formed a society called the *Broederbond*, which aimed to uplift and unite all Afrikaners, so that one day they could take over full political and economic control of South Africa. After Hertzog's Nationalist Party united with the South African Party led by Jan Smuts in 1933, the Broederbond renewed its efforts to prevent Afrikaners from getting 'lost' in an English way of life.

Attack on the trade unions

To unite the Afrikaners, Afrikaner Nationalists had to separate them from other groups − from other whites, and from other workers. The Broederbond was especially worried about the power of the trade unions, which preached the unity of the white working class. (The socialists and communists in the trade unions went even further and included black workers in the labour movement.) The Broederbond preached that there were no class differences amongst Afrikaners − they were one people, one *volk*. Their plan was:

'to make the Afrikaner labourer part and parcel of the national life and to prevent the Afrikaner workers developing as a class distinct from other classes in the Afrikaner national life.'[31]

In their labour policy, Afrikaner Nationalists were opposed to free collective bargaining − as a future Nationalist party Minister of Labour said in 1942:

'Firstly, we contend that wage control and wage fixation should be entirely in the hands of the state . . . . Secondly, and this is much the most important principle, self-government in industry must be eliminated . . . self-government in industry and collective bargaining are things of the past.'[32]

From about 1934, the Broederbond began a campaign to promote Afrikaner trade unions. They decided

A Bob Connolly cartoon in the late 1930s.

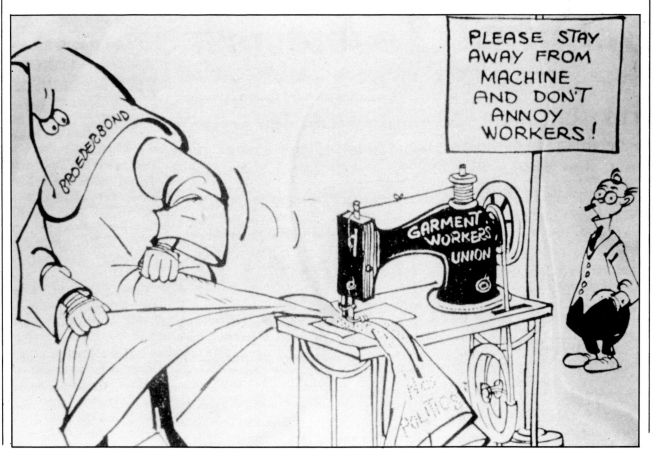

Afrikaners or Workers ?

'We Afrikaners acknowledge no "classes" as you and your satellites are trying to introduce – therefore, we do want the garment workers as a "class" to participate in the [voortrekker] celebrations, but all together with us as Boers – the factory girl together with the professor's wife.'
(Extract from letter to Solly Sachs from D.B.H. Grobbelaar, a 'Reformer'.)

to attack the leadership of trade unions which had the most Afrikaner members. The unions they concentrated on were in the mining, building, iron and steel, railway, clothing, and leather industries. (See *The Story of the Garment Workers' Union to 1941*.)

The railway workers' Spoorbond

The Spoorbond was formed in 1934 by the founder of the Broederbond. It was originally a salaried staff association formed to combat discrimination against Afrikaner office workers on the railways.

Later, membership was extended to the Afrikaner workers, and then its policy was developed to replace all black workers on the railways with Afrikaner workers. (The relationship between the Spoorbond and the government's 'civilised labour' policy is discussed in Chapter 4.) By 1937, the Spoorbond was able to claim 16 000 members. Its rival union, the National Union of Railways and Harbours (NURAHS), had been forced to close down.

Why was the Spoorbond so successful? The answer lies partly in the failure of NURAHS to organise the many new workers who joined the railways in the 1930s – by 1939, every eleventh Afrikaner was a railway worker.[33] Yet NURAHS did not bother to recruit these largely unskilled white labourers.

Spoorbond was able to take advantage of this neglect of Afrikaner workers and appeal directly to their sense of nationalism. At the same time, Spoorbond rejected class divisions and strikes – it encouraged members to follow the Spoorbond motto of 'Conquer Through Service', and to give loyal service to their employers.

In 1942 the railway administration finally recognised the Spoorbond's right to speak for all grades of railway workers. By then it had a membership of 29 000 out 77 000 railway workers. By 1946, the Spoorbond had its own bank consisting of its members' savings, with a capital of R340 000.[34]

The white miners

The struggle for control of the white Mine Workers' Union was a very important one for three reasons:

- Firstly, the mining industry was the biggest industry in South Africa. Its labour policies had an important influence on other industries.
- Secondly, after the railways, the mines employed the greatest number of Afrikaners and the Mine Workers' Union (the MWU) in the 1930s was the biggest union in the country.
- Thirdly, the MWU was a whites-only union. White miners were the highest paid white workers in the country, and their wage rates depended directly on how much production they could extract from the African workers they supervised. There was little chance that they would cooperate with black workers to form unions or other worker organisations.

In 1937, Afrikaner nationalist leaders formed an alternative white miners' union – Die Afrikanerbond van Mynwerkers (The Afrikaner Mineworkers' Union). But as soon as this happened, the leaders of the MWU made a closed shop agreement with the Chamber of Mines. The Afrikanerbond had to close down. Instead, they formed an active group known as the Reformers and agitated for change within the union.

As had happened in the struggle between the Spoorbond and NURAHS, the Reformers exploited the weaknesses of the existing union. The leadership of the MWU had become very sure of itself and undemocratic. It had also become corrupt. To keep the Reformers out, it held false elections and changed the minutes of meetings. During the war years, it stopped elections altogether.

In the closed shop agreement, the MWU leaders promised to 'discourage and prevent any actions of their officials and members which may have the effect of causing unrest and undermining discipline'.[35] The union leaders had done a deal with the bosses. They carried out their promise – members who challenged union policy were beaten up and expelled from the union. Once workers lost union membership, they also lost their jobs under the closed shop agreement.

In 1939, the secretary of the MWU was shot dead by a Reformer. The struggle for control continued. In 1942 a group of mine workers complained that their real wages (that is, the buying power of their wages) had dropped, but the MWU had done nothing about it. The Reformers began to make demands that the MWU should have made – they pushed for health and safety in the workplace, for workmen's compensation, phthisis benefits and improvements in pensions.

During the war, the Trades and Labour Council, as well as the Labour Party, criticised the Reformers' racism. Unfortunately, however, they continued to support the corrupt leaders of the Mine Workers' Union, seeing them as allies fighting fascism in the labour movement just as South African soldiers were defending democracy in Europe. More and more miners became frustrated with the MWU. In the 1948 elections, most white miners voted for the Nationalist Party.

The funeral of Charlie Harris, secretary of the Mine Workers' Union, who was shot dead outside the union offices by a Reformer.

The industrial unions

Afrikaner nationalism was not as successful in the industrial unions, however. While there were many Afrikaner workers in the textile, clothing and leather industries, these workers were different from the miners and railway workers.

In the first place, most of these Afrikaner workers were women, and had experienced greater exploitation as 'cheap labour'. They had also successfully struggled through their unions for higher wages and better working conditions, as *The Story of the Garment Workers' Union* shows. They therefore valued their unions, and also the way the unions were organised. Their leaders were democratically elected, and most were loyal to them.

There was also another important difference. The garment, textile and leather workers were direct producers in the factory, and not supervisors, like the miners. Nor did they rely on government protection for their jobs, like white railway workers. They worked side by side with black workers, taking part in the same labour process on the shop floor. So although many of these workers were not free from racial prejudice, they recognised the value of class solidarity.

The following story is a typical example of cooperation amongst workers in the 1930s, told by the secretary of the Leather Workers' Union:

'In about 1936 I went to a lunch hour meeting to recruit Afrikaner workers in the tanning industry — I remember the firm was called 'Gibson and Gibeau'. They said, "What about the black workers? We can't do anything without them", and this was in the days of the Blanke Werkers se Beskermingsbond [White Workers' Protection League, a miltant right-wing group].'[36]

Song of Workers

'We pledge ourselves tonight!
All people of this land,
Be white their colour or be they dark,
Have got to live a decent life!
And it's our bounden duty to help them all!
So, workers, join the ranks of unity!
Join the ranks of strength!
Join the ranks of struggle for a better life for all!'

(Sung at the Pageant of the Trade Union Movement, at Port Elizabeth's Feather Market Hall, 29 June 1939.)

Black Trade Unions after the ICU

The first African industrial unions were started in 1927, the year after the ICU expelled communist organisers. (See *The Rise and Fall of the ICU* in Chapter 4.) It had become clear to many organisers that the general union of the ICU had been too clumsy to be effective. There seemed to them to be a need for unions organised in specific industries. Many of these organisers therefore went on to start small unions in the towns on the Rand.

Black workers bottling minerals in a beverage factory, 1936.

FNETU is formed

Two communists, T W Thibedi and B Weinbren, were successful in building up a number of African unions. Weinbren had already organised the white workers' laundry union. He had a laundry van, in which he and Thibedi drove from one work place to another, recruiting members. They concentrated on light or service industries, where it was easier to recruit workers than in the large, well-controlled primary industries of mining and farming.

The Native Laundry Workers' Union was the first to be organised. Other unions followed – the Native Bakers' Union, the Native Clothing Workers' Union, and the Motor Workers' Union.

In 1928 these unions were organised into a federation of unions called the Non-European Trade Union Federation (later known as FNETU), with a total of 10 000 members. Jimmy La Guma, another communist expelled from the ICU, came up from the Cape to serve as secretary. In 1929 more unions joined FNETU – among them the dairy, meat, canvas, transport and engineering unions.

Some of these unions were 'parallel' unions to white unions, like the clothing and laundry unions, and sometimes worked with them. (For example, the black clothing union in Germiston, which boasted a 100 per-cent membership, came out on strike in support of three sacked white women workers. Their strike forced the employers to re-instate the workers.)[37] Other unions soon made gains for their members by making use of the Wage Act. (See *Labour Laws of the 1920s*.) Their secretaries held meetings with the Wage Board to negotiate for minimum wages in each industry. Once the Wage Board fixed a minimum wage, all employers in that industry had to pay that wage to their workers.

Strikes

But sometimes employers would not pay the legal wages, and strikes followed. There were also strikes for holiday and overtime pay. For example, in May 1928, black clothing workers went on strike and demanded pay for Good Friday. After they had been out for only half a day, the pay was granted. At a large laundry firm, there was a dispute about overtime pay. A worker was dismissed and the other workers went on strike. Eventually the worker was re-employed.

In September 1928 black workers of the Transvaal Mattress Company went on strike to force their employers to pay them the legal minimum wage. In the following month furniture workers did the same. Both strikes were successful.

Trade unions in the towns stood a better chance of winning negotiations. Many black workers who were classified as 'unskilled' labourers were in fact experienced workers who had stayed in one job for a long time. They were not so easy to replace. They were the new, town-based black workers – many of whom had settled in the townships and brought their families to live with them. Their ties with the land were getting looser, and it was easier to recruit them into the unions. In the words of an organiser:

> 'In contrast to the more shifting and semi-peasant miners, building labourers and railway construction workers, here today and gone tomorrow, always preoccupied with cows and land, these urban workers were comparatively quick to grasp the idea of trade union organisation.'[38]

The decline of FNETU

Not all strikes were successful. As the story of the ICU shows, black workers in the towns were still in the minority – there were far more white workers, who

Table of Strikes by Black Workers and Membership of Unions, 1933-1939.		
	Strikes	**Number Unionised**
1933	300	31 100
1934	800	37 400
1935	1 400	29 200
1936	1 600	35 100
1937	4 800	35 200
1938	3 700	37 500
1939	4 800	36 600

Source: R. Davies, *Capital, State and White Labour in South Africa 1900-1960* (Humanities Press, New Jersey, 1979), p.262.

Black and white speakers during the March of the Unemployed on May Day 1930. Issy Diamond (the white speaker) was arrested later that day and sentenced to twelve months' hard labour.

enjoyed the advantages of skills or job protection. Most employers refused to recognise or negotiate with black unions, and often called the police to stop a strike.

When the depression of 1930 to 1933 came (described in Chapter 5), black workers were the last to be hired, the first to be fired. The pass system forced unemployed Africans to leave the towns unless they found another job within six days. They were therefore pushed back into the reserves. Nevertheless, there were ways of escaping the pass 'net', and at the beginning of 1932 there were as many as 14 000 Africans looking for work in Johannesburg. With labour in good supply, the bargaining power of black workers dropped.

To add to FNETU's problems, there were disputes in the Communist Party, which was very closely linked to FNETU. Key organisers, like Thibedi and Weinbren, as well as Gana Makabeni from the Native Clothing Workers' Union, and Solly Sachs from the Garment Workers' Union, were expelled for not following strictly enough the 'party line'. (See *The Communist Party and Black Workers*.) The remaining communists began to organise other unions and form their own federation.

In the face of all these difficulties, FNETU gradually collapsed.

The African Federation of Trade Unions

In the meantime, the communist organisers formed the African Federation of Trade Unions (AFTU). They battled during the depression to keep small unions going in the tailoring, engineering and leather industries.

A union which attracted a lot of attention at the time was the union of the unemployed. On May Day 1930, there was a huge demonstration of both whites and blacks without jobs. They marched in the streets outside the two places popular with the rich – the Carlton Hotel and the Rand Club. They held placards and

shouted the slogans, *'We want bread!'* and *'Work or wages!'* and tried to push their way into these buildings. They were stopped by the police and their organiser, Issy Diamond, was arrested and later sentenced to a year's imprisonment.

The unemployed of all races cooperated again on Christmas Eve in 1932. This time over a hundred jobless, led by a communist, marched through the Johannesburg streets collecting food from bakers, butchers, and grocers and putting it all in a wagon they were pulling. At the end of the march, the food was shared amongst all those who had gone along.

Many people were alarmed at this cooperation between whites and blacks, especially as the demonstrations were organised by communists. The government responded by laying on more pass raids and encouraging white organisations to help the white unemployed separately.

When the depression lifted, AFTU decided to concentrate on organising strong African unions. Once they were in a position of strength, argued AFTU, they would be better able to work in solidarity with registered unions. The pattern of the 1930s, then, was to form registered unions of white, Indian and coloured workers as laid down by the Industrial Conciliation Act (see *Labour Laws of the 1920s*) and parallel, unregistered unions of African workers. But progress was slow, and membership numbers remained low.

New federations

After the depression, industries began to grow again, and called for more labour. The number of Africans on the Rand grew from 36 000 to 80 722 between 1932/3 and 1936/7.[39] Old, declining unions slowly began to pick up again in strength, and a number of new unions were formed.

Beside the communist unions, there were the unions

led by Gana Makabeni and other black organisers — these were the African Clothing Workers' Union as well as the Broom and Brush, the Sweet, the Tobacco, the Rope and Canvas, the Tin, the Metal and Iron and other unions. In 1940, these unions formed themselves into a Co-ordinating Committee of African Trade Unions which excluded whites and communists.

Then there were the unions largely organised by a white socialist called Max Gordon. He was a young chemist who gave up his job in 1935 and set about reviving the Laundry Workers' Union. Within a year, the laundry workers went out on strike for higher wages and better working conditions. They were successful.

In the next few years, more than twenty industries were organised into unions, including the Commercial and Distributive Workers' Union, the Bakers', the Printers' and the General Workers' unions. By 1939, eleven unions with 20 000 members formed a federation called the Joint Committee, with Gordon as the secretary.

Organising unions

After the depression, the unions made good gains, mainly by working through the wage boards. For instance, in 1938 alone, unions gained over R50 000 from employers who were underpaying their black workers. These successes encouraged many workers to join the unions.

But there were also difficulties. Unions could not always produce wage gains for the members. Besides, there was the organisational groundwork without which wage campaigns could not be successful. There were practical problems that organisers had to tackle.

Firstly, they had to recruit enough members to pay for the organisers' salaries, small as they were. They had to persuade poorly paid workers that it was worth their while to give up five cents a week to the union. This was at a time when the average male worker earned two rand a week, which was much less than he needed for his family to live. Every five cents had to be spent very carefully.[40]

Then, organisers had to find rooms for offices — not easy for black unions, even in Johannesburg, especially if the organisers themselves were black.

In addition, secretaries had to have the skills to help workers to check whether they were getting the right pay. They had to be able to work out overtime pay, sick leave pay, workmen's compensation, and very often back pay from employers who had not paid the fixed wages.

Some unions, especially the Joint Committee unions, also offered other benefits to attract members. They offered to find jobs for the unemployed, legal help for the many blacks who got into trouble with the law, and sometimes medical help, too.

Most union offices also offered classes in reading,

Gana Makabeni, secretary of the African Clothing Workers' Union, which he first started in 1927 as the Native Workers' Clothing Union. Also an important leader in CNETU, Makabeni's active involvement in labour spans a remarkably long period, from the mid-twenties to his death in 1955.

arithmetic, book-keeping and history. The communist organisers were the most successful in organising *night schools*, and many of their brightest students were recruited into the Communist Party — leaders like Albert Nzula, Johannes Nkosi and Moses Kotane had been students in the night schools.

A very important skill that was needed was to be able to prepare applications and evidence for raising workers' wages at the all-white wage boards. Union officials had to represent their organisations in person at the wage board sittings.

Recruiting organisers

It is not surprising that many of the unions were run by whites. They had the skills, the trade union experience and a knowledge of how the system worked — in short, it was easier for them to get the unions started and keep them going.

Nevertheless, there were many black organisers. Some, like the communists, worked with whites. Others worked independently, like the Coordinating

A night school in the late 1930s. Night schools were first started when the Communist Party, under the general direction of T W Thibedi, decided in 1924 to 'turn to the masses' and organise black workers. The ICU and, later, the unions associated with Max Gordon, also ran night schools for workers. The schools offered workers classes in literacy, numeracy and trade union theory, and attracted many students who later became well-known labour and community leaders. By the late 1930s liberal groups had also established night schools. In 1938, anti-fascist students from the University of the Witwatersrand started the African College, and in 1940 this was followed by the 'Mayibuye School'. Most of these schools offered adults skills designed to enable them to get on as individuals in the existing system, rather than introducing them to the collective organisation emphasised by the unions.

Committee of African Unions, led by Gana Makabeni, although they were prepared to ask for help from some white organisers, such as Solly Sachs of the Garment Workers' Union. (See *The Story of the Garment Workers' Union*.)

When Max Gordon was detained during the first years of the Second World War, Daniel Koza took over some of the Joint Committee unions and achieved the biggest pay rise for the dairy workers.

In the smaller towns outside Johannesburg, there were many unpaid organisers whose names are lost to history. Just one example is a report from Gordon in 1938 on the progress of the Pretoria branch of the Laundry Union:

'During the beginning of this year a branch of the union was established in Pretoria and has a membership of two hundred. The chairwoman deserves particular mention for the capable way in which she has attended to the complaints of our members in Pretoria.'[41]

We do not know who this active member was. But committee members like this lady, as well as the thousands of workers who joined the unions, formed the very basis of a successful trade union movement. Without their active interest, the successes at the Wage Board level could not lead to a democratic workers' movement.

The birth of the Council for Non-European Trade Unions

Until about 1940, black trade unions remained small, weak and divided. Their gains through favourable Wage Board decisions were also a loss — because leadership in these unions began to rely more on Wage Board meetings than on the bargaining power of organised members. The unions were also divided. We have seen that there were three different federations — the JCATU, the CCATU and the AFTU. Unity talks in 1938 between the two bigger federations, the JCATU and the CCATU, had failed. But major change was soon to come. World War II was to bring thousands more blacks into the factories and service industries, creating a new movement from within a growing working class.

In the first years of the war, most of the established unions grew rapidly. New unions were started by organisers from the Communist Party and the Joint Committee, helped by members of the ANC interested in labour. An African Mineworkers' Union was established and began to grow.

Organisers of all unions were greatly encouraged by this progress. In 1941, there were successful talks on unity, and in November of that year, the Council of Non-European Trade Unions (CNETU) was formed. Gana Makabeni was elected president and Dan Tloome of the ANC became vice-president.

CNETU became a nation-wide federation with affiliated unions in Port Elizabeth, East London, Cape Town, Bloemfontein, Kimberley, and Pretoria, and a central office in Johannesburg. By the end of the war (1945) there were 119 unions in CNETU, which claimed a 150 000 membership. Volume 3 of *A People's History of South Africa* will take up their story.

Clothing factory. African workers in this industry belonged to a separate union, the African Clothing Workers' Union, formed in the mid-1930s by Gana Makabeni. In the 1940s it was to become one of the major unions in CNETU — the Council for Non-European Trade Unions.

J T Gumede, President of the ANC and editor of *Ilange Lase Natal*, whose radical speech alarmed many delegates to the Congress in 1927.

Chief Moshoeshoe of Matatiele, who was alarmed at the influence of the Communist Party on the ANC.

The Communist Party and Black Workers

'The Communist Party alone has stood by us and protested when we have been shot down. Others are persuaded to be communists. The African has been a Communist from time immemorial. I have seen the new world come [in the USSR] where it has already begun. I have been to the new Jerusalem.' – J T Gumede, President of the ANC, 1927.[42]

'The Communist Party has brought Russia to the stage it is now. The Tsar was a great man in his country, of royal blood like us chiefs, and where is he now? . . . It will be a sad day for me when I am ruled by the man who milks my cow or ploughs my fields.' – Chief Joseph Moshoeshoe of Matatiele, 1928.[43]

The two quotations above capture the range of responses to communism amongst blacks. Although its membership was small, the Communist Party of South Africa played an important role in the 1920s and 1930s in both the black national and labour movements. Communism, also known as 'scientific socialism', is a world-wide movement today and still influences politics in Africa.

Colonialism

Chapter 4 has described how the racism of the white workers in the 1922 strike led to a 're-think' by the CPSA (until 1950, a legal party). Some of its leaders began to argue that it was inadequate to analyse South Africa as a simple class struggle between capitalists and workers. From 1924, the party began to take up the issues of race and nationalism more seriously. Seeing that South Africa was a colonial state, argued some of its leaders, revolution was more likely to be carried out by the *colonised* black than the *colonising* white worker. The Party then launched a programme of recruiting African members.

The new policy was almost immediately successful, for a number of black workers and intellectuals responded to the Marxist analysis of society. A good half-dozen soon became organisers in the ICU until they were expelled (as described on page 111). The CPSA also won many black members by its opposition to the discriminatory laws and practices of the state. (See, for example, *Potchefstroom's Story of Resistance* in Chapter 7 and *Politics and Protest* in Chapter 8). Their anti-pass campaign in 1930 resulted in the death in Durban of one of their most promising and committed young activists, Johannes Nkosi, and convinced many blacks of the genuine concern of the party for the oppression of blacks. In 1932, the CPSA put forward a black communist, J.B. Marks, to contest the elections in Germiston. Needless to say, as he was black he was not entitled to the vote, and his election speeches provoked many angry fights. But the black residents of Germiston were impressed by his courage and his message to black workers.

During the late 1920s and early 1930s the CPSA was active in the encouragement of black trade unions (see *Black Trade Unions after the ICU*). Their members, both black and white, were noted for their role as organisers. A one-time union organiser and member of the CPSA during the 1920s and 1930s recalls the party's approach to black workers through his own speeches to workers:

'Your struggle is a two-fold one. You struggle for better wages and also because you are not free. But it is important to build up a union because your power lies in this factory, and in the other factories. If you paralysed industry, the strike would eventually become political.'[44]

Internal conflicts

However, the 1930s were years of struggle for ideological control, with the result that the CPSA was weakened by the splits and conflicts within the organisation itself. In 1928 the sixth congress of the Comintern (the Communist International) met in the USSR. Advised by some members of the CPSA, the congress decided to formulate a black Republic slogan for South Africa:

'An independent Native Republic of Workers and Peasants.'

This slogan was to lead to intense debate inside the party. Traditionalists such as Sidney Bunting, who had led the Africanisation policy, believed that by emphasising black nationalism, the party was substituting a race war for class war. They feared that the party would lose support among white workers.

Others, influenced by the Comintern and Lenin's successor, Stalin, insisted on following the strategy of national liberation. The new slogan was adopted. Over the next few years the traditionalists, including organisers of white trade unions, such as Bill Andrews (one of the founders of the party), Solly Sachs of the Garment Workers' Union (see page 146), C B Tyler of the Building Workers' Union, Fanny Klenerman of the Women Workers' Union as well as B Weinbren, founder of the Non-European Trade Unions Federation (FNETU), and Issy Diamond (of the March of the Unemployed – see picture on page 163) were expelled and labelled reactionaries. Some black members, for example Gana Makabeni, Secretary for the African Clothing Workers' Union, and T W Thibedi of the Laundry Workers' Union were also eventually expelled for not observing party discipline.

The expulsion of so many key members damaged the party's leadership, its unions and also its grassroots support. In 1932, AFTU's membership declined from 4 000 to 851 in four months as a result of the expulsions. Furthermore, critics accused the CPSA of being too dependent on the Comintern in Moscow. An example given by Eddie Roux (also expelled from the CPSA) was the sudden ending of the League of African Rights on the instructions of the Comintern. The League was a popular organisation which aimed to link militant ICU, ANC and CPSA members to combat the pass system and other oppressive measures and to support the Black Republic slogan.[45] By 1940, the membership of the CPSA had dwindled to 280.[46]

However, the fortunes of the CPSA were to pick up again in the 1940s. When the Nazis attacked the USSR in 1941, the CPSA along with socialists the world over began to work more closely with other anti-Nazi groups in a Popular Front until the end of World War II.

Albert Nzula, a school teacher and one of the Communist Party's outstanding leaders. Nzula had a keen intellect and was a gifted public speaker, 'whose talents were used not only in location meetings among Africans, but also in our Sunday meetings on the City Hall steps where he impressed white audiences.'[47] Only twenty-six at the time this photograph was taken, Nzula was general secretary of the South African Communist Party (the first black to hold the position), acting editor of the CPSA newspaper *Umsebenzi* and joint secretary of the League of African Rights. He was also a member of the ANC. With a number of other delegates, he tried to radicalise the ANC at the 1930 congress, but the conservatives were voted into power. In 1931 he went for further study to Moscow, where he co-authored a book on forced labour in colonial Africa. Tragically, shortly before Nzula was due to return to South Africa he died suddenly, reportedly of pneumonia.[48]

Class and nationalism

The Black Republic slogan was a serious attempt to confront the problems of class and nationalism in a racially divided society, and in later years the CPSA tried to develop this theme further. However, the issues of race and class were not resolved – they continue to be debated by Marxists and national liberationists to this day.

Notes

1) E S Sachs, 'Conditions of Garment Workers in South Africa', *Garment Worker*, October 1936.

2) *The Social and Industrial Review*, 30.6.1928. Quoted by J Lewis, *Industrialisation and Trade Union Organisation in South Africa, 1924-25* (Cambridge University Press), p.53.

3) J Lewis, as above, p.55.

4) Minutes of the Trade Union Congress, 1930, cited by J Lewis, as above, p.55.

5) Compiled from J Lewis, as above, Appendices A-D.

6) W H Andrews, *Class Struggle in South Africa*, p.37.

7) Interview, 24.6.1983.

8) Interview, 28.8.1983.

9) J Lewis, as above, p.64.

10) *Ibid*.

11) S A Textile Workers' Union, documents, 1935.

12) *Inkululeko*, November 1942, cited by J Lewis, as above, pp.66-67.

13) Cited in E S Sachs, *Garment Workers in Action*, p.33.

14) E S Sachs, as above, p.46.

15) Cited by E Brink, '"Maar 'n klomp factorie meide": The role of the female garment workers in the clothing industry, Afrikaner family and community on the Witwatersrand during the 1920s'. Paper presented to the University of the Witwatersrand History Workshop, February 1984.

16) B du Toit, *Ukubamba Amadolo* (Onyx Press, London, 1978), p.41.

17) J Lever, 'Capital and labour in South Africa: the passage of the Industrial Conciliation Act, 1924', in ed. E. Webster, *Essays in Southern African Labour History* (Ravan Press, Johannesburg, 1978), p.102.

18) H J and R E Simons, *Class and Colour in South Africa 1850-1950* (Penguin, Harmondsworth, 1969), p.338.

19) Unpublished diary of Ralphe Bunche, 1937.

20) House of Assembly Debates, 4/5/25, C267.

21) *The Leather Worker*, Transvaal Leather Workers' Union, Johannesburg, October 1938.

22) *The South African Leather Worker, being a Private Publication Catering for the Workers in the Boot and Shoe, Tanning and General Leather Goods*, edited, published and printed by W H Jones, Port Elizabeth, August 1934, p.12.

23) M Nicol, '"Johburg Hotheads" and "Gullible Children of Cape Town" – the Transvaal Garment Workers' Union's assault on low wages in the Cape Town clothing industry'. Paper presented to the University of the Witwatersrand History Workshop, February 1984, p.5. This section on the GWU CP is largely drawn from Nicol's paper.

24) M Nicol, as above, p.8.

25) M Nicol, as above, p.16.

26) Interview, 24.6.1983.

27) Luckhardt and Wall, *Organise . . . or Starve!* (Lawrence and Wishart, London, 1980).

28) Luckhardt and Wall, as above, p.57.

29) J and R E Simons, *Class and Colour in South Africa, 1850-1950* (Penguin African Library, Harmondsworth, 1969), p.383.

30) J and R E Simons, as above, p.384.

31) J Lewis, as above, p.70.

32) B J Schoeman, from *Trade Union in Travail* by A Hepple, quoted by J Lewis, as above, p.70.

33) D O'Meara, *Volkskapitalisme: Class, Capital and Ideology in the Development of Afrikaner Nationalism 1934-1940* (Ravan Press, Johannesburg, 1983), p.90.

34) D O'Meara, as above, p.91.

35) D O'Meara, as above, p.92.

36) Interview, 24.6.1983. Solly Sachs, secretary of the Garment Workers' Union, and Betty du Toit of the Textile Workers' Union were able to relate similar examples of racial cooperation at the height of the Afrikaner nationalist assault on their unions.

37) J Lewis, as above, p.126.

38) E Roux, *Time Longer Than Rope*, p.207.

39) S van der Horst, *Native Labour in South Africa*, p.263.

40) R Phillips, *The Bantu in the City*, p.31.

41) Cited by Hirson, 'The reorganisation of African trade unions in Johannesburg, 1936-1942' in *Societies of Southern Africa in the 19th and 20th Centuries* Vol. 7 (University of London Institute of Commonwealth Studies, 1976), p.187. I am indebted to this paper for much of the information in this section.

42 *S.A. Worker*, 22.4.1927.

43 Quoted by J. and R. Simons, *Class and Colour in South Africa* (Penguin, Harmondsworth, 1969), p.402.

44 Interview, 18 June 1983. (Interviewee wishes to remain anonymous.)

45 See Eddie Roux, *Time Longer Than Rope* (University of Wisconsin Press, Madison, 1964).

46 J. Burger, *The Black Man's Burden* (Gollancz, 1943), p.244.

47 Eddie and Win Roux, *Rebel Pity* (Penguin Books, Harmondsworth, 1972), p.81.

48 Roux described Nzula's death as follows: 'Brilliant but unreliable in his personal life, he was addicted to drink, and vodka was to prove the cause of his death. He fell down one night in a frozen street and there lay for some hours. He died of pneumonia.'

Chapter 7
'Locations' for Labour

The last two chapters dealt with the development of the manufacturing industry and the changing nature of production in the factories. We have seen how altered conditions gave rise to a new kind of worker. In turn, these new workers developed new unions.

As the industries grew on the Rand, so did the number of workers. These workers had to find their own accommodation. Usually they tried to live near their place of work to cut the cost of transport. Chapter 3 has shown how the inner city areas became crowded, and how in the early years the housing of the poor was more or less unplanned, and racially mixed. This chapter will describe how the state — both the government and the town councils — came to realise the importance of planning the housing of workers, how they did it, and why.

Orlando, hailed as 'the future great city of Bantudom', about 1935.

'It is in the towns that the native question of the future will in an ever-increasing complexity have to be faced.'

(Government Report UG 1919, p.17.)

The Urban Areas Act

The first major response by the South African government to the housing of the poor came with the upheaval and protest of both black townspeople and white workers after World War I, as described in Chapter 4.

The government could not ignore the militant collective action of that period. The prime minister appointed a commission of enquiry which resulted in a small increase of wages for unskilled workers in the towns (but not on the mines). The government also appointed the Stallard Commission to look into the position of black workers living in the towns, and consulted black ministers of religion and professional people for their opinions on housing. Then the government passed a law, the Natives (Urban Areas) Act, 1923, spelling out government policy towards blacks in the urban areas.

Significance of the Act

The Natives (Urban Areas) Act was at first simply a guide line for municipalities to follow if they so wished. But it was an important law because in time it came to be adopted by all the towns in South Africa. It played a major part in establishing the policy of urban segregation which was to be implemented by successive governments. The comments by various government officials quoted below illustrate one aspect of the influence of the Act.

An urban labour supply

The Act recognised the need for African accommodation in the urban areas. In the eyes of the government, however, black residents were in the towns for one purpose only: to work. Their lives thus had to be regulated to service the system of racial capitalism that was developing in industrialised South Africa. Together with influx control through the pass laws, the Native (Urban Areas) Act would help to achieve this aim.

In the words of Colonel Stallard, who headed the government's Transvaal commission of enquiry, blacks were not welcome in the towns except as workers; at the same time it suited the industries of the Rand to have a settled black population living in the towns to serve as a ready supply of labour. As a 'location' superintendent commented:

> 'the traditional policy of treating urban native locations and villages as reservoirs of labour to supply the demands of European employers reflects a large volume of European opinion'.[1]

A self-made house on the outskirts of the city. Surrounding the major towns were hundreds of smallholdings called 'plots' owned by white workers (often bought with compensation money by phthisis victims). Black workers were usually made welcome on these plots as their wives could provide labour as domestics. For the blacks, living on the plots was rent-free and it subjected them to less control than the locations.

A supply of surplus labour would prevent a shortage of people looking for work, and thus keep the wages down. The Act therefore recognised that, in addition to the working population, a sufficient number of unemployed blacks was necessary to the system of cheap labour in the industrial areas.

The cost

The Act made it clear that the responsibility of housing workers lay with the municipalities. The effect of this was that municipalities tried to use the pass system to control the number of Africans entering the towns. 'The first thing that is necessary to do is to control or restrict the influx of families into the towns', said the manager of Johannesburg's Native Affairs Department.

> 'The kraal native who comes to town to work and is required there is no difficulty to us at all, but when the native brings his family there, as he is doing today, you have got an entirely different state of affairs. The native is not in the economic position of being able to house himself and someone else has to do it.'[2]

Clearly, the municipalities were reluctant to foot the bill of housing the poorest-paid workers.

Yet officials could not ignore the thousands of blacks settled permanently in the towns. In 1922 the Unemployment Commission reported:

> 'There is now a considerable population of pure bred natives permanently resident in the towns of the Union. These people have no other home and many of their children were born in the town and have grown ignorant of tribal life. Some of these live in locations but in Johannesburg they live scattered through the poorer parts of town side by side with the whites.'[3]

The Act suggested ways in which the municipalities could get black workers to pay for their own housing – through rents, beer-hall profits, and fines that would go into the special 'Native Revenue Account'. It recognised that black workers earned too little to provide for even the simplest accommodation for their families, and recommended that it would be more efficient and cheaper to provide low-cost housing officially and then get the money back in a number of ways from the tenants themselves.

Control

The segregated ghettoes or 'locations' became a means of controlling the town-based workers, just as the compound system controlled black miners. It was easier for police and other officials to keep a check on the

A Johannesburg scene in the 1920s. Already, there was a sizeable black population of settled townspeople with children who had never known life on the land.

movements of black workers, on their passes and labour contracts, if they lived in one place – the location.

In 1930, the Act was amended to tighten control over the movements of Africans further. For example, they could be removed from one area to another, and the amendment attempted to control the movements of African women into town.[4] As one councillor said:

> 'My council is sympathetically disposed towards the natives. We do not want to hinder them at every turn. *But we must have absolute control.* We have to see that law and order is maintained, and if we don't we are failing in our duty to those whom we represent.'[5]

In 1937 the Native Laws Amendment Act implemented even stricter controls, partly to help commercial farmers to hold on to their labour – by 1936 nearly half of the black workers in the towns had come directly from the white farms.[6] (See the sharecropper's story in *Alexandra Township* on page 186.)

Gradual results

The application of the Natives (Urban Areas) Act was gradual and uneven. Most towns did not carry out the terms of the Act for many years – the law was, as we have said, a guideline at first, and each municipality could decide whether it wanted to proclaim itself a 'whites only' area, according to the Act.

Johannesburg, for example, asked to be proclaimed a white area in 1924, whereas Port Elizabeth followed suit only in 1935. It was only in 1937, with the amend-

The once grand Empress Victoria Hotel in Ferreirastown. By the 1920s it had become a seedy, inner-city tenement, housing scores of poor families, both black and white.

ment to the Act, that all towns outside the reserves automatically became restricted areas.

There were other reasons, too, for the slow application of the Act.

- For one thing, there was the high cost of change. In 1926, after Johannesburg began a 'drive' to remove all Africans without permits from the 'yards' in the inner city area, a Doornfontein resident contested the removals in court. The magistrate then ruled that the municipality could not evict people from their homes unless there was alternative accommodation for them. The town council then had to start building houses and compounds to house the people removed from the town, which delayed the planned removals by two years.
- The municipalities also ran into resistance from slum landlords and traders (such as the owners of black 'eating houses') who wanted their black customers to remain in town. A government commission exposed several cases in Johannesburg alone of town councillors who were bribed to postpone slum clearance.[7]
- The cost of housing created division in the white ruling group. While industrialists wanted a 'reserve army' of labour living in the towns, the white workers were threatened by the constant presence of cheap black labour. Through the Labour and the Nationalist parties, they tried to discourage the establishment of a black urban working class. Furthermore, as ratepayers, many white working-

class home owners resented paying for 'the cost of housing . . . that helps the employer to have native labour at a cheaper rate'.[8]

The municipality was forced to rely on its ratepayers – that is, the owners of property, mostly homes, in the city – to foot the bill for black housing. This was because the mining companies were powerful enough to evade paying municipal rates for the vast tracts of land that they owned in the city – one third of Johannesburg's land, including some suburbs. The mine owners, unlike the industrialists, did not require a resident working class, since they relied on migrant labour housed in hostels. In addition, the central government collected all the pass fees from employers and African workers, but did not pass this revenue on to the municipalities.

These divisions, together with different forms of resistance from the black population, delayed the implementation of the housing policy in Johannesburg for many years.

Black resistance

Resistance came from the blacks themselves. Black home owners in Sophiatown, Newclare and Martindale had formed the Non-European Ratepayers' Association in Johannesburg in 1926. In 1932 the Johannesburg Council applied for the whole city to become a restricted area. This meant blacks who had their own homes in the freehold townships would no longer be allowed licences to keep tenants. As most black home owners had borrowed money to buy their property and earned very little, they relied on their tenants to help them to pay back the mortgages on their properties.

The backyard of a house in the freehold suburb of Sophiatown, with tenants in the outbuildings, about 1933.

The residents of these townships also foresaw the stepping up of pass raids and police harassment.

The result was a storm of protest from the Non-European Ratepayers' Association, which gave the following evidence to the Native Economic Commission:

> 'The historical records of this country abound with the evidence of the inevitable reactionary consequences of laws . . . for the purpose of keeping wages at the lowest possible level. The Industrial Conciliation Act and the Wage Act seek to entrench the policy of 'white-ism' and to disregard the interests of non-white workers; while the pass laws, Masters and Servants Act, Native Regulation Act and the Natives (Urban Areas) Act all seek to perpetuate a policy of top-doggism to entrench a system of cheap labour.'[9]

They also sent their lawyer to put their case to the Minister of Native Affairs. After months of negotiations, the minister agreed that the Johannesburg municipality could not provide enough accommodation for black workers. Finally, in 1933, the municipality of Johannesburg was proclaimed a restricted area except for the freehold areas of Sophiatown, Martindale and Newclare. These townships were proclaimed separately and allowed to apply for licences to keep black tenants.

Many black workers were thus able to avoid the municipal hostels and locations for many years by finding homes in the freehold areas of Johannesburg. (See *Alexandra Township*, page 186, and *Sophiatown*, page 179.)

The influx continues

Meanwhile, the Rand towns continued to grow steadily. Between 1921 and 1936 the number of urban Africans increased from about half a million to just over one and a half million – that is, it trebled in the short space of fifteen years.[10]

After 1933, with the rise in the price of gold, the industrial economy picked up and manufacturers and businesses called for more labour. Large numbers of young people left the commercial farms, where they were often expected to work *'vir kos en slaapplek'* rather than for wages, and went to join the cash economy in the towns.

By this time many of the reserves were becoming more crowded and less able to support their populations. For example, the Native Economic Commission reported on the Ciskei in 1932:

> These two areas [the Herschel and Glen Grey districts], with fertile valleys containing great depth of soil, show some of the worst *donga* erosions in the Union. The difference between these and other areas is one of degree only . . . . Actual desert conditions have in twenty years been created where once good grazing existed.'[11]

The same commission heard Dr Xuma, a leader of the ANC, say:

> Young men are coming of age every year but there is no land allotted to them. Most of these landless

A domestic worker sweeps the yard, about 1934. After the mines and the farms, white households employed the largest number of black male workers. Most of them were migrants from the rural areas.

173

youths marry and have to squat on their fathers' four morgen plots and under the present conditions of agriculture with repeated droughts, these plots hardly yield the needs of one family. These people are poverty-stricken and destitute. What must they do? Where must they go? Naturally to the industrial centres.'[12]

Not only men, but women too started to look for a living in the towns. In 1927, there had been only one African woman to every six men in Johannesburg. By 1939 the proportion was one to three – in twelve years, the number of urban women had more than doubled.[13] This made for a more settled population, more families and the need for more homes.

So, in spite of the building programmes in the new locations, the Rand towns could not keep up with the needs of the fast-growing black working class. And as fast as people were removed from the yards and other inner city areas, as fast did more people move into them. Despite the pass system, people continued to enter the towns because the industries needed them. After the depression had ended, more jobs were available for newcomers. In Johannesburg the manager of the Native Affairs Department reported in 1937:

'It is pleasing to record once again that there is virtually no unemployment amongst able-bodied natives willing to work.'[14]

In the same report he also noted that as the industries grew, so did the black working population; and that this had slowed down the programme of slum clearance and segregation into municipal locations.

Locations for industry's labour needs

Nevertheless, separate black locations were developed, slowly and irregularly, according to the labour needs of industry. Once Johannesburg established a Native

Affairs Department in 1927, it began to extend Klipspruit, Western Native Township and Eastern Native Township. A total of 2 625 houses had been built by 1930.

In 1930, too, the council bought a further portion of the Klipspruit farm and began to build houses there. The new township was named Orlando, after one of the councillors. Orlando, the 'future great city of Bantudom' and birthplace of Soweto, might be seen as the blueprint for a black workers' location in a modern industrial city. It became an example of cheap housing to other growing industrial towns in future years.

In 1933, the Johannesburg City Engineer set out the basic aims in establishing black townships. What he said is interesting because it clearly illustrates the use of the location in the eyes of the ruling class.

'The location', he said, 'is practically a satellite town and is best planned as such.'[15] In other words, it could not ever become an independent town, but existed only for the convenience of industry and the white population.

About the site of the township, the City Engineeer went on to say:

'The area selected should not be such that the natural development of the European area of the town is interfered with in any way . . . . The site should be near as possible to the industrial area, or to where the majority of natives are employed.'

The cost of transport should be reduced by having workers' housing as near as possible to the place of work. The function of a location, therefore, was to maintain an orderly labour supply – at the cheapest possible rate.

___

Workers being transported in cattle trucks. Employers were concerned to keep the cost of maintaining black workers as low as possible. The new locations were further away from the work-place. The cost of transport had to be added to the wage, and thus the employers tried to keep it to a minimum.

Cutting costs

For management, the most important purpose of the location was to provide a place where labour could be maintained cheaply – a place where workers could be fed and sheltered, so that they could present themselves for productive work at the start of the next working day or shift.

This aim of maintaining the worker had to be achieved, but at the same time the worker and his or her family had to survive on the lowest possible wages. Housing and services, therefore, had to be as cheap as possible.

The City Engineer warned that an increase in rent and transport 'will put up [the black worker's] cost of living and ultimately his wages. It should be realised that an increase in wages or a loss of energy will result in putting up production costs and react to the detriment of the industries and commercial activities in that area.'

So, for the sake of productivity, profits, and industrial development, the black worker had to be provided with housing and services – but at a minimum level, because he was being paid a minimum wage.

In the new location of Orlando, the system of building large numbers of low-cost – or 'sub-economic' – houses enabled the municipality to save costs. The houses had a simple plan: two rooms, one entrance door (no back door), no door between rooms, no floors, no ceilings. As the City Engineer pointed out:

> 'Ceilings were omitted on account of the extra expense entailed' – as well as, 'to give additional air space in the buildings'.

A location outside a small town. The buckets on the side of the road are for water. Locations throughout the country lacked a ready water supply and other essential services.

Building houses on a large scale reduced costs.

'A great reduction has been made in the capital cost in connection with housing native families as far as Orlando is concerned compared with the Western and Eastern Native Townships', reported the Manager of the Non-European Housing and Native Affairs Department.

He went on to give the following figures: the average three-roomed house in Western Township cost R270; the average three-roomed house in Eastern Township cost R240; and the average house in Orlando cost only R226, though it was larger and of a better quality.[16]

The neglect of services

To keep the costs low, few services were provided. As the Johannesburg Engineer recommended:

> 'The most suitable method of water supply is by means of public standpipes in the street.'[17]

But this was false economy. Chapter 3 showed how basic needs – such as warm and dry shelter, fresh water, sewerage and rubbish disposal – were essential to health and life, otherwise disease could take hold of impoverished people and spread through the whole town. The cost of disease could be crippling to the community as a whole. (See *Some Facts and Figures* on page 188.)

Housing alone was therefore not enough to maintain people in the city. Water supplies, disposal of refuse, transport, health services, education, and recreation facilities could not be provided by individuals alone but needed to be provided collectively. The municipalities and industry ducked this responsibility. To some extent, the churches tried bravely to supply some clinics, schools and feeding schemes for the poor, but their resources did not begin to meet the need. Inadequate basic facilities in the townships remain

an issue in the struggle of black workers right up to the present day.

The beer monopoly

In the meantime, as private industry refused to pay the costs of housing their workers, or to raise their wages, the municipalities had to find ways of raising money for the building of cheap houses. The 1923 Urban Areas Act suggested one way: it encouraged municipalities to give themselves the monopoly of selling traditionally brewed beer in the locations.

Brewing and drinking liquor were illegal activities for Africans in most towns. Ministers of religion were concerned about the effects of drunkenness, which they felt led to violence and wasted lives. Medical officers worried about the health of drinkers. Employers, including mine managers, complained that drunkenness resulted in fewer working days and loss of production. The police had therefore made constant raids on the yards and the townships for hidden liquor.

While the Johannesburg Town Council debated whether it should introduce beer halls for profit, the government took the initiative. In its 1937 amendment to the Urban Areas Act it insisted that municipalities either introduce beer monopolies or allow licensed brewers to supply beer. Johannesburg then declared a municipal monopoly for itself, and the manager of the Native Affairs Department announced:

'With effect from 1 January 1938, the City Council has exercised a municipal monopoly from the sale of beer. The municipal monopoly promises to be lucrative and it may be remarked that any profits accruing from the sale of kaffir beer must be paid into the Native Revenue Account.'[18]

The profits were indeed great. In the year after beer halls were opened, the Johannesburg City Council made a profit of over R65 000, and in the following year the profit amounted to R127 502, as compared with the R84 000 received from rents in Orlando.[19] The City Council built more beer halls. Often they were the largest and most solid buildings in the locations.

Moral objections to drinking were overlooked as long as the drinking took place in the beer halls and the beverage consumed was the traditional brew. Doctors began to allow that beer was

'good for the consumer from a dietetic point of view and contains a high food value.'[20]

Supporters of the system argued that municipal beer halls provided men (but not women) with a legal place to relax and enjoy their beer without fear of raids, and that the customers were protected from the poisonous brews often found in the shebeens. At the same time, the more drinking took place in the beer halls, the less the municipalities would have to pay for the cost of the locations, and the more the poorest section of the population financed their own housing.

The beer hall profits, rents, licences, and fines paid for the housing schemes of the municipalities. In this way they were able to finance the programme of removing black workers from the inner city to the segregated locations.

Customers at the new municipal beerhall in Orlando, 1939.

The new township of Orlando. After the overcrowding of the inner-city 'yards', the new houses were spacious and offered fresh air, sunshine and gardens. But black residents were now under the firm control of the location superintendents.

Removals and resistance

For political reasons, too, 'slum' removals became necessary. Chapter 5 described the welfare policies for white workers of the Pact government. The central government embarked on a drive to provide sub-economic housing for the white working class (see page 185.)

Meanwhile, as the municipal programme speeded up, more people were removed from the yards, which were then demolished. In spite of the advantages of the locations, they were usually the last place where people would choose to live. They had the example of Nancefield (whose 1919 stayaway is described in Chapter 4) and other locations before them, and were not unaware of the 'grand plan' of segregation that was unfolding. In the words of ANC President John Dube:

> 'it seems to us Natives that you want our labour, but as soon as you have finished with us you want us removed so far away from you that you do not want to see us until certain hours when you again want our labour. We are just so many horses that have to be stabled after they have been working – just as though we were not human beings'.[21]

Others noted that the locations were intended to control the workers living in them. Union leaders Henry Tyamzashe and Thomas Mbeki asked:

> 'Why is it necessary to deliberately herd something like 13 000 people into a location with only two gates, one of which is usually kept closed?'[22]

So while the new Orlando houses had more space than the slum yards, with fresh air and gardens for the children to play in, many houses remained empty at the time of the removals. Thousands preferred to move to the freehold areas such as Sophiatown and Alexandra to escape the controls of the locations.

In her study of 'Rooiyard' in 1935 (see *Doornfontein's Yards* on page 181) Dr E Hellman noted how much people disliked the locations. Brewers worried that their trade would drop, because the 'locations' were so far from the mine and municipal compounds where most of their customers lived. Everyone realised that the cost of living would go up because of transport expenses. They would be under the controlling eye of the superintendent, who would note their doings and movements and subject people to the regulations. If they failed to pay their rents on time, their furniture and household possessions might be seized – a common event, as described in *Potchefstroom's Story of Resistance* on page 190. An unmarried woman could only get a location house if she could produce the pass of a male relative. In short, people had a strong 'dislike of living inside a fence'.[23]

Sophiatown, Martindale, Newclare and Alexandra thus became swollen with new tenants. But as more and more people came to the city, Orlando began to fill up. By 1937, the manager of the Native Affairs Department was pleased to report:

> 'The resistance of the natives to the slum clearance process has almost disappeared. Four years ago not more than twelve percent of those evacuated from the slum areas actually took up residence in locations and hostels. This figure is now over ninety percent, and in the present abnormal conditions obtaining [the desperate housing shortage], the demand is so keen that all sorts of subterfuge is employed by natives from other areas to secure municipal accommodation.'[24]

A scene during the slum removals drive of the late 1930s. Although hundreds of families settled in the new location, many others tried to find alternative accommodation.

Future struggles

However, this moment of official satisfaction was not to last, for the problems of trying to house black workers at the lowest possible cost were to be multiplied many times over in the future.

The Johannesburg municipality had made very slow, small gains in trying to provide urban workers with minimum living standards, financed by the people themselves, in order to spare industry the cost of higher wages to pay for higher rents.

But soon after the start of World War II came the rapid development of the economy and a demand for more labour. There followed a dramatic rise in the population of the Rand in the 1940s. Desperate housing shortages followed, with large squatter camps sprawling on the outskirts of Johannesburg, and the existing townships packed to bursting point. Volume 3 of *A People's History of South Africa* will take up this story.

We have seen how closely related the housing of workers is to the labour needs of capital. In the urban areas, black housing took three forms:

- compounds for the larger monopoly industries employing migrant workers – the mines, the municipalities and state industries;
- backyard shacks for the thousands of domestic workers, called on to service white homes of all classes;
- closely settled townships to house the workers, and the families of workers, in the manufacturing industry and commerce.

It is these townships – the 'squatter camps' the 'slums' and 'locations' – that were to witness in future years the major struggles for freedom from oppressive restrictions, for basic living conditions, and higher wages.

A hostel, 1935 – bachelor quarters for married men.

Topics

Sophiatown

Sophiatown was never a 'location'. The Johannesburg municipality never owned the land, nor the houses. Sophiatown never had the rows and rows of tiny, two-roomed 'matchbox' houses found in the municipal locations. Like Martindale and Newclare, Sophiatown was a freehold township, where blacks could buy stands and build their own homes.

There were therefore differences in the style, size and quality of the houses. Some were solid, brick buildings of four or more rooms, some were similar in style to the homes on the land (although mud and reed walls were forbidden in the Johannesburg municipality), while others were single-room shacks patched together from scrap sheet metal.

At first the population of Sophiatown was mixed. (Martindale and Newclare were from the beginning set aside as suburbs for blacks.) Whites and blacks (including coloureds, Indians and Chinese) lived there. But gradually, more and more whites moved out until only the poorest were left in the township. In later years, people remembered the liveliness and the greater freedom of Sophiatown with great love, and with sorrow at its passing. The removals of the mid-1950s destroyed the place Can Themba called the 'little Paris of the Transvaal', where 'you have the right to listen to the latest jazz records at Ah Sing's over the road. You can walk a coloured girl of an evening down to the Odin Cinema, and no questions asked. You can try out Rhugubar's curry with your bare fingers without embarrassment.'[25]

But Sophiatown had its harsh side, too, as the following brief history will show.

Early Sophiatown

Sophiatown was named after the wife of a businessman, H Tobiansky, who bought part of the farm Waterval 79 in 1897. After leasing the land to the government for a few years, Tobiansky planned to build a township, and roads were pegged, some of them named after the Tobiansky children – Edith, Gerty, Bertha, Toby, Sol.

The stands were small – 50 by 100 feet, or 50 by 50

A Sophiatown street in the 1930s. Owners paid rates for their property in this freehold suburb, yet very few services were provided by the municipality.

feet — and at first were bought by whites. By 1910, however, the town clerk was reporting that the township owners were selling the stands to anyone, so that a mixed population was growing in Sophiatown. In 1912 a Johannesburg Town Council report observed:

> 'There are in Johannesburg suburbs, some of the stands of which were originally sold to white men, and where natives can now obtain ownership of stands on very reasonable terms. In Sophiatown, for example, we have a mixed population of white and black owners.'[26]

But by the end of World War I, with the influx of many more black workers, it seems that very few whites were left in Sophiatown. The township was close to the open sewage farm of Newlands, and whites had the choice of moving to other suburbs like Vrededorp, Brixton, and Mayfair.

In the three freehold townships, about two fifths of the stands were owned by blacks, and they paid rates for their property. However, they got very little service for their money. Even by the 1930s, the roads were mere dirt tracks, muddy channels in the summer and dust bowls in the winter. There was no street lighting, and water supplies were drawn from wells dug by the people themselves. These wells were open. Refuse and drowned animals often infected them, and this spread disease. Sewerage buckets were not collected regularly — after 1935, three times a week at most. The municipality claimed that the rates paid by the residents were not enough to cover the high costs of installing a proper water and electricity supply to service the crowded townships.

One reason why these areas were so thickly populated was that many black residents were poor, although they were home owners. In order to pay back the mortgages on their properties, they had to take in paying tenants. By the 1920s, most of the people living in the three townships were not ratepayers, but tenants.

Other basic services, like education and clinics, it was left to the churches to provide. In 1923, for example, the Anglican Church started the St Joseph's Home for Coloured Children in Sophiatown and in 1927 it began to run a daily clinic.[27] Nevertheless, in 1929, the estimated number of deaths of babies under a year was a horrifying 750 for every 1 000 births.

As the black working class grew in Johannesburg, the population of the freehold townships expanded. The following figures tell the story:

- In 1928, there were 12 000 people living in the three townships;
- By 1931, the population had jumped by 5 000 to 17 000;
- At the end of 1934, 26 000 were living there.

Naturally Sophiatown, Martindale and Newclare became overcrowded.

The effects of the removals

As more and more people were squeezed out of the 'yards' in the inner city areas, the freehold areas became more crowded still. These were the only areas where Africans could live without a permit. The manager of the Non-European and Native Affairs Department, who wanted to speed up the removals, was well aware of this.

'The Health Department need not curtail its programme re closure of insanitary properties', he argued in 1930. 'In fact the Health Department can proceed with an intensive policy of closures, and need not concern itself with the problem of where the tenants have to reside, as the native has the choice of removing to such areas as Sophiatown, Newclare, and Prospect Township.'[28]

The result was, in the same man's words four years later, that 'it is an invariable practice to let one room to a family, with the result that in some cases where there are 16 rooms on a stand of 50 by 100 feet, there are often as many as 80 or more persons living on the stand.'[29]

With the growing shortage of housing in these areas, the rents jumped up too. As in the yards, profiteers moved in. Most of the stands were still owned by whites in the 1930s (although they did not live there) with about one fifth belonging to Africans and another fifth belonging to coloureds and Asians.

In the newspapers of the time we read of complaints, by both whites and blacks, about the landlords who built 'barracks' on the stands and charged high prices. In the *Bantu World*, for example, many articles and letters were published complaining of overcrowding, high rents and increased crime and violence.

Sophiatown, Martindale and Newclare thus became the dumping place for those who had nowhere else to go as a result of the removals. The municipality did not destroy the slums created by industrial society — it simply moved them further out of town.

Moving to Sophiatown. During the slum removals, many people poured into the freehold black areas, preferring a shack there to the new municipal housing provided in Orlando.

Doornfontein in its grander days at the turn of the century.

Doornfontein's Yards

Doornfontein started off in 1887 as a fashionable suburb for the well-to-do. Most of the stands were sold for as much as R1 000 each. Mine owners built fine houses in Doornfontein, importing most of the materials from Britain.

Decline

However, this elite suburb was not to last. Before the end of the century, most of the upper class had moved out to Parktown, which had beautiful views. This new elite suburb was also warmer in winter because it lay north of the ridge, which prevented the cold south winds from blowing the fine dust from the mine dumps into the northern suburbs. It was not many years, therefore, before Doornfontein was left to the lower classes. The large stands were divided up and sold.

Many of these stands were bought by speculators who wanted to make profits from their property. Since there was a growing housing shortage for both white and black, profits were easily made. The most profitable arrangement was to pack the stands with cheap tin shacks and let them to the poor. These became the 'yards' of Doornfontein.

According to Modikwe Dikobe, author of *The Marabi Dance*, there were six main yards in Doornfontein — Rooiyard, Makapan yard, Molefe yard, Mveyane yard, Magonyanye yard, and Brown yard.

The plan of a large Doornfontein yard — Rooiyard — shows how 376 people (plus their visitors) were crowded into 105 rooms on five stands. The rooms brought the owner over R150 per month in rent. As he was said to have paid R1 200 for the property, he was able to get a return on his investment in little over a year. (This owner had also bought several other properties at the same time.)

Rooiyard

In the years 1933 to 1934, a study was made of the life in Rooiyard.[30] A description of conditions in the yard gives us some idea of what life must have been like for the people living there.

The yards were crowded with boxes, bins and pails that did not fit into the small rooms. All the cooking was done outside, and there were always large packing cases piled next to the braziers for use as firewood.

Two garbage tins served all the people — but after the landlord was fined for neglecting the property, he built two cement bins. These bins were constantly overflowing, attracting many flies.

The unhealthy surroundings were made worse by the fact that there were only six lavatories — three for men and three for women — to serve the whole yard. These were so neglected and overused that the children avoided them and used the alley-way instead.

The so-called 'washing room' was a tin hut with two taps, one of which was never working. There was almost always a long queue of women waiting to fill large tins with water.

Striking contrast

On the other hand, wrote the author of the study,

> 'The interiors of the greater number of rooms presented a striking contrast to the unsavoury disorderliness of the yard. Although the ceilings are often covered with cobwebs, the floors are well scrubbed and the belongings of the family tidily arranged. That this cleanliness is achieved only by the tireless expenditure of energy and labour is conclusively proved by the constant preoccupation of the Rooiyard woman with her washing, scrubbing, polishing and dusting. It is no mean feat on the part of the Native woman to keep the small and congested abode of her family in such good order, for the Rooiyard does not offer any stimulus towards greater effort.'[31]

In 1933, the Johannesburg Town Council declared the Johannesburg municipality to be a white area. This meant that all blacks without special permission would have to move out of town and into municipal hostels or 'locations'. Then the 1934 Slum Act gave the power to the council to demolish condemned slums. As yards in other suburbs (like Bertrams, nearby) were pulled down, more and more people began to ask for rooms in Rooiyard. The landlord put up the rents for the newcomers. But in 1935, the police moved in to evict the people living in the Doornfontein yards, too. They destroyed the buildings to forestall further occupation.

Where did the Rooiyard people go? Out of 30 families, 4 found rooms in other yards in Johannesburg; 6 went to rooms in Sophiatown and Alexandra; 5 went back to the land; 7 wives and their children also went home, leaving their husbands behind to work in town; and 8 families unwillingly moved into the locations, up to 20 kilometres away.

From Modikwe Dikobe's
The Marabi Dance[32]

'The Molefe Yard, where Martha lived, was also home to more than twenty other people. It served a row of five rooms, each about fourteen by twelve feet in size.

A Doornfontein 'yard', 1934.

When it rained, the yard was as muddy as a cattle kraal, and the smell of beer, thrown out by the police on their raids, combined with the stench of the lavatories, was nauseating.

Martha's father, guided by the carbide light of his cycle, splashed through the yard and waded his way ankle-deep through the pool of muddy water. It took him all his strength to pull his feet and boots out of the slush. One of the lavatories had overflowed and the excrement and urine mixed freely with the mud and water. The stench polluted the air which had been purified by the rain. A tin of skokiaan which had been dug into the ground, to conceal it from the police, lay uncovered and threw a yellow circle of colour, and the whole yard smelled of bread and yeast.

Mabongo stumbled further until he reached the gate. "Morena![33] If this is how we live, then, God, suffer us all to die."'

'Doornfontein is in two. It is bounded by a rail line from Jeppe to Doornfontein station. South was despicably called *Leswatheng*. A name meaning dirty, overcrowded mess, filthy, and all adjectives describing filthiness. Brown yard had a population of over 500 souls; Magonyane, which stretched from Staib Street to Charles Street, had more than a hundred. A cottage barely accommodable to a family of five was twice five. An only yard which fell not in Leswatheng was Mveyane yard in Loneer Street, in Zulu Congregational Church.' (From Modikwe Dikobe's unpublished notes.)

White Worker Accommodation

Extracts from
'The Life of a Garment Worker',[34]
by Hester Cornelius

'It was in the year 1932. The conditions of workers were very bad, just after our strike. We were four garment workers, who had to live together in Vrededorp. All four of us were earning very little because the wages were R1.75 a week. Many of us had to work for months without a rise — if we dared to open our mouths we would be chased away.

Our little room was in a backyard and was so small that we could not move. All the furnishing that we had was a single bed, a small table and a few soap boxes for chairs.

We had to pay R2 a month rent, so you will understand why we still had to pay off our bed and table. We worked out a plan for bedclothes. One of the four had a cushion and we took turns to sleep on it. We had two blankets which we had brought with us from the farm. Our sheets were made from mielie bags which we joined together, and which we washed every Saturday . . . . There was no window in the room but there was glass in the door, so we joined more mielie bags together to make a curtain.

You will surely be wondering, how could four sleep on a single bed? But again we worked out a plan. We put the mattress on the floor, and one of us slept on coats. And so we struggled on for nine months . . . .

Saturday was our busiest time. We scrubbed our little room, washed our clothes and it was also baking day. We could not afford to buy bread, so we bought flour and kneaded a big loaf of bread, then sent it to the bakery oven to bake.

The hardest time was in winter. Each of us had to have a coat, so we had to cut down on our food. For months we ate only bread and jam . . . .

So it continued until one of us became seriously ill. The doctor diagnosed malnutrition and wrote out a prescription; of course we couldn't afford it, so the

Whites also lived in back yards.

remaining three of us had to go without food to buy better food for the sick one; a month later a second one of us became seriously ill . . . .

We were forced to split up so that we would not get worse, and had to look for lodgings with other people. We could only pay a few shillings a month, so we had to work for the people [to pay for the accommodation].

Early in the morning, before we went to work, we had to polish the stoep, the side room and clean a few things. In the evenings after work, we had to do the washing, ironing and mending. We were not the only ones.'

After the depression lifted in 1932-33, middle-class white surburbs grew rapidly. Working-class housing, which was not profitable, lagged behind.

'Why do we workers live in backyards?'— 1938

(From *Die Klerewerker*, September 1938, by Hester Cornelius, Garment Workers' Union organiser.)

'One of the saddest, most deplorable difficulties that we workers on the Rand, especially in Germiston, have to face is the living conditions . . . .

I do not exaggerate when I say that five or six workers (*plaaskindjies* —little girls from the farms) have to sleep in one room. Very few boarding houses that the workers can afford here in Germiston are built with bathrooms with hot and cold water. And anyone with experience of factory life knows what an important need it is in the community of such a worker.

The people who take them in as boarders are workers themselves. The man does not earn enough to maintain his family unless they take in boarders. Rents are so high and they have to pay so much for food that it is impossible to give the workers (the boarders) the food they need. The young worker's constitution must be built up so that she can become a healthy and happy mother in our land one day; she is underfed; grows up as an unhappy wreck in our society.

We as residents of Germiston, workers and house-wives, must fight together against this terrible problem. We are honest workers whose labour is building up our country and our people. Why should we be cast aside without decent lives and pleasant homes?

Two years ago we got promises from the government that a hostel for garment workers would be built in Germiston. But in the meantime, the health of our workers is suffering – or was the building just a happy dream castle of yesterday, that today lies in ruins?'

Housing white workers

As with black housing, homes for white workers owed a great deal to the labour needs of industry. Although the Pact government introduced a scheme in 1930 for building low-cost housing for 'poor whites' at a very low interest rate, few municipalities took advantage of the offer – the Depression hit the incomes of most towns hard.

Until the latter part of the 1930s, housing was left to private enterprise on the Rand, although government employees like railway workers received housing.

After the Depression ended in the mid-1930s, the Johannesburg municipality launched on the slum removal scheme and the moving of inner city blacks to the new location of Orlando. There were also hundreds of white families living in slums. For them, sub-economic houses – like those in the Jan Hofmeyr township shown on this page – were built on the demolished sites of the old inner-city slums to a somewhat higher standard than the houses provided for the blacks. Because the white poor were fewer in number, it was easier to bring about an improvement in their living conditions. In Johannesburg two hostels for white women workers were finally established in the early 1940s.

Nevertheless, poverty amongst whites remained, and the demand for cheap but decent accommodation continued.

It was only in the boom years during and after World

A new house in Jan Hofmeyr, part of the municipal sub-economic housing scheme for whites that was introduced from the late 1930s.

War II that many more whites were absorbed by the economy and given improved wages. Only then were they able to afford better housing.

A Vrededorp yard

'Where do I wash, Ma?'

'Downstairs.'

I got the soap and the towel and went down the stairs. The stairs were steep, narrow and short. In places a stair was broken and had been covered with a thin plank that sagged as my weight came down on it. Once I nearly slipped. I grabbed the bannister. It moved outward, dangerously. At the bottom of the stairs I turned left into a dark little passage. I fumbled in the dark till I found the door. I jerked it open: daylight rushed in.

The yard was tiny: no more than six yards wide, and just as long. And in it, taking up half the space, was a high pile of junk: twisted bicycle wheels, old tyres, a bicycle frame, broken chairs, part of an iron bed, brown with rust; pots and pans and pieces of broken crockery; rags and bones; and much other rubbish beyond recognition. Three short steps led down into the yard and the tap was near the door. The lavatory was beside the tap. I leaped across the three steps and landed near the tap. I tucked the towel into my shirt collar and washed.

Going back, I bumped into an old Indian in the dark passage. He spoke to me in English. I couldn't understand and fled up the stairs.'

From *Tell Freedom* by Peter Abrahams (Faber and Faber, London, 1954), pages 56-7.

185

Scene from a Vrededorp yard.

Alexandra Township

'Alexandra was a very good place for poor people. We used to love it for that. When a youngster from our village wanted to work in Johannesburg it was usual to find him going to Alexandra to get himself a pass. It was very simple to get a pass. All we had to do was to go with the boy to the Health Committee offices in Alexandra. Then we had to introduce him to the committee which gave him a pass without any fuss. It was very easy. The only document I had to take along to the office was the receipt I was issued with when paying rent. With that receipt, one was eligible for a pass.'

(Interview with Mrs N.S., who lived in Alexandra Township from about 1929 to 1962.)[35]

Early residents

Alexandra was a freehold township outside Johannesburg, on the main road to Pretoria. Its main attraction for blacks was that it was not subject to the controls of the Johannesburg municipality, and many people who had a little money bought a piece of land and settled there.

Stands were first offered for sale in 1913. The plots were larger than those offered in Sophiatown, and the average price in 1922 was R130.[36] The first settlers therefore tended to be better off than the early residents of Sophiatown, Martindale and Newclare.

In the following story a man who had once been a sharecropper with some stock explained why he settled in Alexandra.

'I lived on the farm Sterkspruit for eleven years; I was well treated by my master; he gave me enough land to plough and gave me as many head of cattle as I could run. He allowed me to breed horses and sheep. In 1928, I noticed a great change in the treatment of my master. My boss complained of the number of cattle I had – and said there was not sufficient grazing. Consequently he asked me to reduce my livestock. I was unwilling to do this but he pressed on me, saying his cattle were not getting enough grass because of mine. So I tried to sell my livestock, but could not get a good price. Finally, I decided to buy a plot of ground at Alexandra township, so I left the farm and settled out here.'[37]

Work

There were no trains to Johannesburg from Alexandra, so few at first had jobs in town. Many were market gardeners in the early years – about 1 200 plots in the southern part of the township were leased for market gardening. Most of the residents also kept fowls.

Alexandra Township, 1913.

But crops and stock could only be farmed on a very small scale, for as more people settled in Alexandra, space became more valuable for accommodating people. By about 1930, when the sharecropper from Sterkspruit farm arrived in the township, there was not enough land for grazing:

> 'At Alexandra I was met with the difficulty in regard to grazing land. I asked the boss of the adjoining farm to allow me to graze my cattle on his farm; this he did, but charged me twenty cents per head of cattle a month. As this was impossible, I sold some of my cattle to a butcher and the rest died through lack of feeding. Two of my horses died; now I have got two horses, one wagon which I cannot use, and a trap. I have got to buy food for the horses and they are a trouble to me.'

Alexandra was developing fast, and its economy had to change to meet the needs of town life. While many of the women were busy building houses in the traditional style, they earned a living by brewing and selling beer. There were also traders in the township, who bought their stock from wholesale suppliers.

As Johannesburg expanded, the white northern suburbs grew steadily in the direction of Alexandra, and more and more women took in washing to add to their income. Mrs N.S. was one of these washerwomen.

> 'I used to go twice a week there, to Rosebank, near Dunkeld . . . . My washing days were Monday, Tuesday and Wednesday, therefore I was free to go

Room to let in Alexandra. After Johannesburg's slum removals, and boosted by the Rand's economic development from the mid-1930s onwards, Alexandra's population expanded even more rapidly. Rents for even the smallest rooms rocketed.

to town to sell apples on Thursday, Friday and sometimes on Saturday'.[38]

More and more people found work in Johannesburg. But in order to do this, they had to get a certificate saying they were plot holders in Alexandra. They were then given a travelling pass to get to work. (Transport remained a problem throughout the years and residents had to make their own arrangements. The struggle over transport in Alexandra has a history of its own.)

Services for the people

Alexandra township was lucky to have enough water. The Jukskei River ran through part of the township and there were three dams and a few springs, too. Residents could get fresh water from wells. They could dump their refuse on the eastern side of the river.

These service arrangements worked well enough in the early years, when the population was small and there was plenty of space. Alexandra had enough land for an estimated 20 000 people, and it was some years before that figure was reached. From 900 in 1916, the population grew slowly and steadily to about 3 500 in 1922.

Rapid growth

Eight years later, it had doubled. But the biggest increase took place in the 1930s. By 1935 numbers had swelled to the maximum capacity of the township, 20 000 people. In the following five years another 20 000 people were crammed into the original houses, plus shacks, 'barracks', 'zincs' and any other home-made shelters people could construct. In 1938, officials took a population census of Alexandra that gave a figure of 21 843 residents. Yet, in the same year, during a small-pox epidemic, Alex clinics vaccinated a far greater number of people.[39]

Why was there this dramatic increase in the number of people in Alex? There were two main reasons.

Firstly, hundreds of families had been evicted from inner-city Johannesburg in the mid-1930s. In spite of the distance, they preferred the freedom of Alexandra to the control of the location superintendent and the sense of imprisonment inside a location fence. It also had a more sympathetic Health Committee (mentioned by Mrs N S above).

Secondly, the 1930s saw a massive influx of people from the white-owned commercial farms and the reserves to the growing industrial towns, especially Johannesburg. Many thousands of these newcomers settled in Alex.

By the end of the 1930s, then, Alexandra was a major township. Its future was to be closely bound up with the struggles of the black working class.

Some Facts and Figures

The following are some figures taken from the report of the manager of the Johannesburg Native Affairs Department in 1940:[40]

	Pimville (Klipspruit)	Western Township	Orlando
Official population	15 000	15 000	35 000
No of drains	36	2 295	117 per 15000
Bins	230	220	204 per 15000
Taps	63	2 322	204 per 15000
Houses	2 392	2 322	2 524 per 15000
Average no per house	16	15.5	16.7
Deaths under 5 years old	210	68	117 per 15000

Few services

Johannesburg's municipal townships for blacks were very poorly serviced. According to the official figures shown in the table above, all the houses were badly overcrowded, dozens of families had to share the same refuse bin, and most houses had not a single tap. Only in Western Township was one tap provided for each house with an average of sixteen people. The residents of Pimville had the fewest services of all the black townships of Johannesburg. They had only 36 drains to carry away dirty water, 230 bins in which to deposit their rubbish, and 63 taps to be shared amongst 2 392 houses. The official population was 15 000 – in reality, the population was much higher.

High death rates

As the table also shows, 210 Pimville babies died before they were a year old. In that year, there were 229 registered births (although the true number of births was probably higher, for not all parents registered their babies). If that figure had been accurate, it would have meant that out of a possible 229 babies, 19 might live to see their first birthday.

The main causes of infant deaths were pneumonia (associated with lack of adequate shelter and heating) enteritis or diarrhoea (caused by an unclean environment and not enough fresh running water), and T.B. (often resulting from overcrowding and malnourishment). *The Diseases of Poverty* in Chapter 3 described the relation of poverty to disease and death in earlier years. Twenty years later, not much had changed.

A scene in Pimville, where in 1940 more than one in every five children died before the fifth birthday.

Western Township, 1935. Although the township was poor and crowded, every house had a tap, and nearly every house a drain. The child death rate was three times lower than that of Pimville.

Comparisons

We have seen a close link between the few services provided in Pimville and the high death rate of babies. A comparison can be made with Western Township, which had roughly the same population and the best (or least bad) supply of drains and taps in the Johannesburg municipal townships — 2 295 drains (compared with Pimville's 36) and 2 322 taps (compared with Pimville's 63).

Was it a coincidence that more than three times as many babies died in Pimville as in Western Township? (210 as compared with 68 per 15 000 people.)

One further fact: white South African children, most of whom (but not all) lived in homes with taps of their own, with refuse and sewerage collection, and whose government had provided free health clinics and hospitals in the cities, had one of the lowest death rates in the world.[41]

189

Potchefstroom's Story of Resistance

The following story of resistance in the Potchefstroom location centres around the attempts of the authorities to control the residents and extract extra revenue from them. The location had a history of protest right from its beginnings in 1904. The most militant residents were the women, most of whom had migrated to the town from nearby farms at the same time as their husbands.[42]

Lodgers' permits

In the late 1920s, the residents began a series of campaigns against the new lodgers' permits. From January 1928, the Potchefstroom Town Council introduced a permit and a tax for every location family that housed lodgers – and the municipality regarded all children over the age of eighteen as 'lodgers'.

The permits were a way of controlling the growing population, and also a means of raising money for improvements. The residents, however, saw them as a direct attack on family life. In any case, actual lodgers (as opposed to children whom the municipality treated as lodgers) were also important. They helped to pay the rent, besides providing brewers with more customers.

As soon as these permits were introduced, the residents began their protest campaign. Many joined the Communist Party. The Potchefstroom Town Council became alarmed and decided to tighten its control even further. It declared that people falling behind with their rents would have their houses taken away from them and sold. Two Communist Party officials were refused permits. In protest they began to sleep out in the veld. Eventually, they were given permits to stay in the location.

A war began between the residents and the town council. The residents developed a method of resistance – as soon as a family was evicted and the furniture removed from the house, women would move it back into the house. When the head of the household was jailed for disobeying the law, the family would be taken in by other women, who would then be jailed for housing people without permits.

The Communist Party gained in popularity. It successfully defended key permit cases in court. Then, on 16 December 1929, it held a well-attended meeting as part of its anti-pass campaign. The meeting was disrupted by white bystanders, some of whom were carrying guns. An argument developed, people were pushed around, and five blacks were shot. One of them was later to die.

The attacks caused great bitterness:

'For hooligans to shoot a Native, is to break a black bottle and then congratulate themselves on being such good marksmen', remarked Josie Palmer (Mpama), the secretary of the Communist Party in Potchefstroom.

The strike

The women decided to call for a general strike. They organised pickets, and on the day of the strike no one was allowed to pass. When two men tried to go to work past the pickets, they were knocked down by the women and forced to go back. One woman called them 'dogs'. Another replied:

'But at least dogs can bark.'

The strike was one hundred percent successful. Five hundred men and women marched four abreast to the court house to make their demands: 'to protest against lodgers' permits – nothing more and nothing less'.

Josie Mpama recalled:

'By this time, the townspeople were going wild – their servants hadn't shown up for work, and neither had anyone else. And now all the residents of the location were marching on the town en masse.'.

Edwin Mofutsanyana, who together with his wife-to-be, Josie Mpama, led the resistance in Potchefstroom against lodgers' permits.

Potchefstroom's main street.

When they arrived at the court house, the marchers handed a written statement to the magistrate. It said that residents could not afford to pay for lodgers' permits, and that employers had ignored all demands for higher wages. They pointed out that people were actually starving in the location. The magistrate promised to write to the Native Affairs Department and ask for a commission to investigate the case. The people then formed themselves into columns of four and marched back to the location.

But when they returned home that evening, people at a meeting pointed out that perhaps they had been tricked, and that nothing would come of the protest. Angrily, they began to demand that the location superintendent be sacked. At that point, a town councillor was called, and he assured the meeting that the magistrate had already written to the department.

The next morning he hastily called a meeting of the town council, who agreed to suspend all permit prosecutions until the commissioner investigated and reported his findings. On that same day, a commissioner arrived and heard the complaints of the residents. Two weeks later his recommendations arrived. He advised that grown-up children of parents should no longer be considered 'lodgers'. The town council, however, were unhappy about this recommendation. Where were they to find enough funds to run the location, they asked — and decided to ignore the recommendation.

Passive resistance

A passive resistance campaign followed. The people refused to pay up. They preferred to go to jail instead. Beer brewers encouraged passive resisters by giving free beer to those who had gone to jail for refusing to carry lodgers' permits. Eventually, after months of resistance, the magistrate himself began to object. The much-hated location superintendent complained:

> 'The magistrate has shown his reluctance to punish offenders under Section 11 and in some cases has made me look a fool in the presence of the natives . . . . He considers prosecution under the lodgers' tax as trivial and stated in court yesterday that he was requested by the government not to send natives to gaol for trivial offences.'

On 31 March, the superintendent withdrew all prosecutions for lodgers' permits.

Conclusion

Of course, this was not the end of the residents' problems. Low wages, beer raids, and superintendent control continued. Also, the superintendent was gradually able to get rid of some of the 'troublemakers' — quietly, one by one. He was helped by the fact that two of the location's most militant leaders were posted to Durban — Communist Party member, Mofutsanyana, and his wife-to-be, Josie Mpama.

However, this campaign was yet another example of collective response to the harassment which was a part of the daily life of every black person.

Notes

1) 'The urban native problem', cited by Edward Koch, 'Doornfontein and its working class, 1914 to 1945: a study of popular culture in Johannesburg', MA dissertation, University of the Witwatersrand, 1983, p.188.

2) Cited by A Proctor, 'Class struggle, segregation and the city: a history of Sophiatown, 1905-1940', in B Bozzoli (ed), *Labour, Townships and Protest* (Ravan Press, Johannesburg, 1979).

3) Cited by Koch, as above, p.42.

4) Koch, as above, pp.203, 205, 208.

5) J D Mitchell, *Bantu World*, 24 October 1936. My emphasis.

6) M Morris, 'State and capitalism', cited in Koch, p.201.

7) J R Maud, *City Government, The Johannesburg Experiment* (Clarendon Press, Oxford, 1938), pp.269, 266-67.

8) Cited by Koch, as above, p.188.

9) Cited by M Lacey, *Working for Boroko* (Ravan Press, Johannesburg, 1981), p.245.

10) R Bloch, 'The state in the townships: state, popular struggle and urban crisis in South Africa 1970-80', Honours dissertation, University of the Witwatersrand, 1981, p.21.

11) Native Economic Commission, 1930-32, para 72, p.11.

12) Cited by M Lacey, as above, p.37.

13) J Lewis, *Industrialisation and Trade Union Organisation in South Africa, 1924-55* (Cambridge University Press, 1984), p.32.

14) Minutes of the Mayor, Annual Report by Manager of Native Affairs Department, July 1937.

15) E J Hamlin, City Engineer, 'The municipal engineer in relation to the establishment of native townships', unpublished report, 28 August 1933.

16) Minutes of the Mayor, as above, July 1938.

17) Hamlin, as above.

18) Minutes of the Mayor, July 1938.

19) Women's Christian Temperance Union, pamphlet, 1940.

20) As above.

21) M Lacey, as above, p.271.

22) Cited by Lacey, as above, p.258.

23) E Hellman, *Rooiyard* (Livingstone, 1948), p.21.

24) Cited by Koch, as above, page 210.

25) Cited by Proctor, as above, page 1.

26) Proctor, as above, page 2.

27) Noreen Kagan, 'African settlements in the Johannesburg area, 1903-1923', MA dissertation, University of the Witwatersrand, 1978, p.88.

28) Proctor, as above, p.4.

29) Proctor, as above, p.8.

30) E Hellman, as above.

31) E Hellman, as above, p.9.

32) Modikwe Dikobe, *The Marabi Dance* (Heinemann Educational Books, London, 1973), pp.1, 32.

33) *Morena*: 'Lord' in South Sotho.

34) Hester Cornelius, *Die Klerewerker*, November 1936. My translation.

35) African Studies Institute, Oral History Documentation Project, University of the Witwatersrand, interviews by Mmantho Nkotsoe with Mrs N S, 24-11-1982 and 1-3-1982, p.10. These interviews are part of the Women in the Countryside Project, funded by the HSRC.

36) Kagan, as above, pp.89-90.

37) Evidence to a survey undertaken by the Church of the Province and given to the Native Economic Commission, cited by Lacey, as above, pp.137-38.

38) As above, p.11.

39) Minutes of the Mayor, annual report of the Manager of the Native Affairs Department, 1939, p.239.

40) This table has been calculated from information in the Minutes of the Mayor, Johannesburg, year-ending 30 June 1940, pp.103-211.

41) R Phillips, *The Bantu in the City* (Lovedale, 1938), p.112, and E Hellman (ed) *Handbook of Race Relations in South Africa* (Cape Town, 1949), p.410.

42) This case study is drawn from Julie Wells's 'The day the town stood still: women in resistance in Potchefstroom, 1912-1930' in B Bozzoli (ed), *Town and Countryside in the Transvaal* (Ravan Press, Johannesburg, 1983).

(a)
Opposite top: A scene at the Workers' Festival, Germiston, 1940.

(b)
Bottom: Hawkers in a Johannesburg Street, 1927.

Chapter 8
The World the Workers Made

So far, this book has described how the development of a racial capitalist society affected the lives of working people in the factories and at home. This chapter looks at how these first generation workers acted to change the world they found themselves in. We shall see how they coped with grinding poverty in those years and how, day by day and year by year, they created a way of life – a culture – through which they survived in the strange and hostile world of the city.[1]

The shock of the city

'Fifty years I have lived in the city . . . . In the city I found people very unkind and unsociable. I sneaked unconsciously into it. I became one of it.'[2]

For most new workers fresh from the land, the noisy, pushy city came as a deep shock. People were crowded together in large numbers, yet they were strangers to each other. A newcomer could pass hundreds of people in the street and not one would give a greeting or even a smile. The city was a cold place, and no-one seemed at all interested in the problems of a lonely and homesick person.

The support and family care of the homestead in the countryside were gone. In the city, newcomers had no homes. They lived in rented rooms, and even slept in rented beds. All comforts, entertainments, even rest itself, became items to be paid for with money – and for workers, there was very little of that. In the work-place too, supervisors and managers seemed to care very little for the feelings of workers – production and profit were the aim, with as little reward for the worker as possible.

The new worker was forced to live a new and strange way of life, suited to the new form of production introduced by the industrial capitalist system. The newcomer had to learn to value new ways, and to drop some of the old ways that did not help people to survive in the city.

Exactly how did workers live their lives away from the work-place – the hours when they had to renew and prepare themselves for another working day in between working shifts?

In this respect the labour of women was very important – for women traditionally maintain the homes where workers find shelter, food, rest and relaxation.

The arrival of women

The first chapter in this book described how workers came at different times and for different reasons to find work in the towns. For example, amongst whites, the women tended to leave the rural areas first to seek work in the towns, as described in Chapter 6. Black women, on the other hand, tended to come later – their labour was needed for the homesteads to continue. For many years, therefore, black workers in the towns were mostly men, and they had to develop a male way of life – hard and unnatural, because they were deprived of the company of women and children.

But in the 1920s and 1930s many black women, especially young women, began to arrive on the Rand in larger numbers. Many black people of both sexes were forced to make their way to the towns at that time. The move to the towns was accelerated by the removal of many black farmers from the white-owned farms after the 1913 Land Act and the droughts and cattle-diseases of that time, as well as the rapid development of industries on the Rand during World War I. Soon after the women, came children and homes. A more normal living pattern began to develop amongst the new workers on the Rand.

Around the porridge pot: children in the reserves.

Life in the city: shopping for basic needs.

Economic conditions of workers

But in order to understand the culture of workers and how they lived at that time it is important to look at their economic situation. Chapter 4 has described the growing hardships for black workers in the towns during and after World War I. We have also seen how the higher wages and privileges of the established craft workers in South Africa separated them in many ways from the low-paid industrial workers, especially black workers.

The new unskilled workers made up the cheap labour force, and poverty dominated their way of life. The chart in *The Struggle for Survival* (page 202) shows how inadequate the average black worker's wage was if he was lucky enough to be constantly employed. And for African workers, the 'Laws for Non-Europeans Only' made town life more expensive and dangerous (see page 212). African workers lived in a nightmare world of passes, curfews and controls, in which it was easy to be flung in jail or lose a job and hard to find a new one. Hardship was also the lot of thousands of early white women workers on the Rand, as *A Garment Worker's Budget* on page 204 shows.

Adding to the wage

For black workers in particular the wage was nowhere near enough to live on. How then did they manage to survive? There are different answers to this question – the first is that many did *not* survive, especially the children, as Chapters 3 and 7 show. (See also Epsie Zondo's story on page 245.) Death came from poverty – undernourishment, poor water supplies and crowded, unhealthy living conditions. It came from inadequate medical care, from danger at the work-place, from violence in the night.

Another answer was the *support of the reserves*. As described in *Children of the Ghetto* on page 231,

more than half of the children born to black town women were sent home, to the land. There they could get moral training and live in more healthy surroundings. The economy of the reserves therefore continued to support the children of many women working in the towns.

A third explanation is that workers and their families found extra ways of adding to, or *supplementing*, their meagre wages. The supplementary wage was provided mainly by the women – the wives and daughters of workers. White women, as we have seen, were employed in the 1920s and 1930s at low wages in the factories. Black women were able to make some extra money taking in washing or as full-time domestic workers.

The informal economy

But mostly workers supplemented their income in *informal* ways – that is, they found other ways than wage labour of making extra money. To do this they often had to break the laws, as *Crime and Punishment* and *Brewers in the Towns* on pages 209 and 206 show. A great deal of this informal income was earned by women.

The long ride home: a worker taking his small child back to the countryside, 1936. At the point that this photograph was taken, he had already cycled 150 kilometres.

A miner repairing the shoes of fellow-workers to earn some extra money.

In the homesteads of the countryside women were a very important part of the economy – in the town they were no different. A woman's earnings often made the difference between survival and starvation. In those early years, most black women were newly arrived from the countryside – few spoke English, the language of the ruling class in the towns – and they had little knowledge of the ways of whites. Their economic activity was directed mainly towards their own people. Often they used the skills they had learnt at home to make things and then sold their products to neighbours or fellow black workers.

Some women sewed, others hawked in the streets or outside the compounds, as the pictures in this chapter show. In addition, a great many women brewed beer which was profitable but illegal (see page 206). Many women, white as well as black, got extra income from prostitution – a natural result of poverty in town, where men outnumbered women. (See *White Working-Class Culture* on page 218).

Children were part of the informal economy too. *Children of the Ghettoes* describes how children helped their mothers in the home; they also delivered washing, earned tips carrying goods at the market, collected and washed bottles, sold newspapers, caddied on golf courses, and begged – or stole.

A number of men, too, were able to supplement their wages in the informal economy, slipping in and out of wage labour, or earning extra money part-time – for instance, as cobblers repairing shoes for people in the neighbourhood. A few were able to survive without entering the formal economic system at all.

There were, for instance, full-time musicians who earned a living playing for parties and concerts in the townships (see *Making Music* on page 213.) There were also some church ministers and diviners who managed to survive by offering their services to their own people – see *Christianity and the Ancestors* on page 227. *Crime and Punishment* deals with those who turned to a life of organised crime. Others produced goods at home, such as furniture, which they were able to sell to dealers or directly to people in their rooms and houses.

But in general, these activities were not profitable enough to earn them a full-time living and most black families lived in gross poverty.

Changing jobs

In the 1920s and 1930s even black school teachers and other professional people suffered from miserably low wages. Furthermore, their jobs were not always secure and many were obliged to join the working class, or the ranks of the unemployed, at least part of the time.

For example, author Modikwe Dikobe started his working life in the 1930s as a newspaper-seller for the Central News Agency (CNA), often sleeping in the CNA compound. Then he became a hawker, selling religious pictures:

The self-employed rag-and-bottle man doing business in a white working-class suburb.

'My stock consisted of best-selling pictures: Elijah, Crucifixion, Moses on Mount Sinai and a dozen others.'

As a hawker he did not consider himself a worker,

'I was of another class. I couldn't have the same sympathy as a worker [who] wakes up and complains of small wages and so on. I had to complain to myself that business was bad, like any other businessman who says "business is bad."'[3]

In 1942, during his time as a hawker, Dikobe also became the secretary of the Alexandra squatters' resistance movement. His hawking business was neglected and failed. Dikobe then took employment as a clerk in a furniture factory. In later years, he was by turns a domestic servant, a nightwatchman and a municipal clerk. Dikobe, like thousands of others, weaved in and out of self-employment, white-collar jobs (such as office work and teaching) and the lowest-paid workers' jobs — anything which would keep him and his family going.

The 'melting pot'

The crowded working-class areas became 'melting pots' of humanity — they were places where people from all over the country and even other parts of the world came together, pulled by the industrial revolution created by the mines. The newcomers worked in the same shops and factories and they lived in the same housing districts. As described in Chapters 3 and 7, working-class districts such as Vrededorp and Doornfontein housed both black and white workers, as well as those looking for work, the self-employed, and the workless of all nationalities. (See, too, *Memories of a Poor White Childhood* on page 234.)

In addition different *black* classes lived together — black workers, the unemployed, traders and professional people were all squashed together in one suburb or township because of the desperate shortage of black housing. And as we saw in Chapter 7, the 1923 Urban Areas Act, which discriminated against blacks, made the housing problem worse.

In the towns Africans from many different chiefdoms were brought together, especially on the Rand. Whether they liked it or not, they were forced to mix, and in time many traditional customs of particular chiefdoms fell away or merged as men and women from different parts of the country set up home together and raised families in town. As early as 1933, for example, a study of a yard in Doornfontein showed that more than half of the hundred couples living there were 'mixed' unions.[4] (On the other hand, divisions amongst blacks did not disappear. Indeed, in many cases, their differences were actually *exploited* by both state and management. These differences are discussed later in this chapter.)

The problems of people caught between the customs

197

of country life and the needs of the city are described powerfully in Modikwe Dikobe's *The Marabi Dance*. Extracts from the book on page 243 illustrate the changing patterns of marriage and the family in the town.

The changing family pattern

In the towns, smaller families became common. Often the family unit did not include grandparents and other relatives. Sometimes there was only one parent. And as we noted earlier, many children lived in the rural areas away from their parents. Few black town men had more than one wife in the same household – the housing shortage, lack of space and women's resistance prevented that. On the other hand, there were many desertions by the men. Fewer couples were married traditionally – a town couple would often decide to live together, but without *lobola* women were without protection. Modikwe Dikobe has described the new living patterns:

'Men and women were just living together because of their offspring . . . . Many such marriages occurred in Prospect Township, Pimville, Doornfontein, Vrededorp and Sophiatown in Johannesburg and Marabastad in Pretoria. In Pretoria it was known as *saambly*, in Johannesburg *vat en sit*. One does not find *saamblys* in country life. There every home is out of *bogadi*.'[5]

Usually there were economic reasons for *vat en sit*. A man and woman would have to pool their money together to survive. Dispossessed of land and cattle they could seldom afford to save up for a *lobola* marriage. But these unofficial living arrangements were unsettling for the children:

'The upbringing of children whose parents lived an unmarried life was disturbing. They [the children] regarded themselves as fatherless . . . . Their education was retarded. They lived in two worlds: city and country. They were misfits in both.'[6]

With the upheaval of the removals from the slumyards to the ghettoes or locations, many more families split up. In just one yard for example, 23 out of 43 families were separated. In most cases, the men went to live in hostels, while the women and children went home to their mothers. Other families sent the children home, while the mother and father found separate live-in jobs such as domestic or municipal work. Modikwe Dikobe remembered the hard decisions that had to be made:

'In bed a woman and husband squabbled. *Bogadi* [*lobola*] was not paid. The children were not the man's. Next door a compromise was reached: "Pay by instalment, marry by native commissioner and forge a *bogadi* receipt." In the third door mutual agreement is completely broken. The woman goes back to her old missus, the man to Wemmer Barracks.'[7]

In the rural areas, too, many families were abandoned by migrant worker fathers who set up new households in the towns and forgot their duties to their families at home. There were many family tragedies and heartaches as a result of industrialisation and the migrant labour system.

Resistance to town life

But there were also many migrant workers who valued their traditional way of life as laid down by their ancestors, and tried to protect it. They resisted the town way of life. These migrant workers saw migrant labour as necessary to help build up the *umzi* – the homestead. Wage labour was a time away from home, like military service – but men should return home as soon as it was over, while women should avoid leaving the homestead at all.

In town, these men preferred to live in hostels and mix only with their own group – their own network of 'home boys'. In their spare time they went drinking to the shebeen of a woman from their own chiefdom. They tried not to get tied up with town women. Town was the place of the white man, they believed.[8] They tried not to give in to *ukurumsha* (speaking English and adopting white ways and customs).

Men preparing their own meals in the newly-built hostel at Wemmer Pan, 1937. Some migrant workers were not drawn into city life, remaining isolated in temporary bachelor accommodation.

'There is nothing I like about whites or their way of life', said one such migrant. And another declared: 'I am not one of those Xhosa who try to ape the white man; I only want to appear what I am: a real Xhosa.'[9]

Usually this feeling was strongest in migrants from reasonably well-off homesteads who were still living in

Male domestic workers, 1931. Most were migrant workers from the rural areas. Often they were recruited by 'homeboys' – friends from the same village – so that an entire area or suburb might be serviced by people of the same clan.

their chiefdoms with enough land and cattle to continue that way of life. They were independent enough to resist industrialisation.

But gradually, as the land became steadily more overcrowded, more and more people – women as well as men – were pushed to the towns in search of a way of supplementing their subsistence in the rural areas. In the 1920s and 1930s, many settled townspeople still had very close ties with the land – for as we have seen, the reserves were helping to support them. Nevertheless the making of an urban people, dispossessed and cut off from the land, had already begun. By 1936 nearly half of the town workers had deserted the white farms, and so had no land of their own anyway, while another 29 percent were permanently settled in the towns.[10]

A racially divided society

In this book we have noted a number of times that South Africa was a racially defined society in which people were judged by the colour of their skin. This attitude was a legacy of colonial times, when white settlers had to justify their taking of the land by claiming to bring civilisation and Christianity to an ignorant and backward black people. Racism continued to flourish in industrial times – indeed capitalism profited from racism by cultivating a massive cheap black labour force, as described in Chapter 17 of *Gold and Workers*.

Racism was deep in the consciousness of nearly every South African. In the writings and sayings of both blacks and whites at that time we find constant references to different race and language groups. Black writers would sometimes write in a belittling way about coloureds, Indians, and Chinese – and bitterly against whites; while even the most liberal whites were riddled with race prejudice.

Amongst the whites themselves prejudices against other white groups flourished as *White Working Class Culture* shows – the English looked down on the Afrikaners and most immigrants, while many Afrikaners resented the high-handed behaviour of the English, and as workers were threatened by cheap black labour. And in the 1930s, anti-Semitism or anti-Jewish attitudes reached their peak in South Africa with the rise of German Nazism, which had a significant influence on the development of Afrikaner nationalism at the time.

Amongst blacks themselves divisions continued, as we have already noted. Arriving on the Rand at different times, from different regions, and for different reasons, different groups of blacks had different working and living experiences. For example, Chapter 2 described how some arrived in the early years of Johannesburg to find a place reserved for them by a kinsman as a member of the *amawasha*. Others, through their 'home-boy' networks, entered domestic service, worked for the municipality as construction labourers, or entered some other occupation monopolised by a particular group. Some arrived later than others – perhaps because the dispossession of their land (or the decline of their means of living off the land) took place at a later stage, or because they were women. Some town communities were at first comprised of groups from particular regions or chief-doms, while new 'layers' of people would move in as tenants, without having homes of their own.

Those who had left the white-owned farms settled into urban life quite quickly, for they had little to go back to; others went to town as migrant workers who intended to return to the countryside, and tried to hold themselves aloof from urban life styles.

Black society, although largely poor, did not therefore consist of a uniform mass of people. There were many and complex differences amongst blacks because of their different origins, as well as their different experiences and jobs in town. These differences affected the ways of life they adopted.

Race and class

Racism and division were a part of everyday life. The society – encouraged by the state, the schools, the press, the church, and employers – had created a racial world in which people were expected to behave according to the colour of their skin as well as the class they belonged to. Race therefore cut across class lines – most workers thought of themselves first as *blacks* or *whites*, and not foremost as *workers*.

Nevertheless, as this book has also shown, there were times in the 1920s and 1930s when blacks and whites were able to overcome some of their differences and their racial consciousness. Chapter 6 has shown how they sometimes cooperated as productive workers labouring side by side in the factories and living in the same neighbourhoods. (See, too, *Memories of a Poor White Childhood* on page 234, where the little white child and, to a certain extent, his parents, identified with the black community in which they lived.)

But as the standards of the white workers improved rapidly through the government's welfare policies of education, housing and protected jobs, more and more whites turned away from organised cooperation with black workers and identified with the culture of the white middle-class which they hoped to join. During

and after World War II thousands of whites moved upwards to become 'labour aristocrats' and supervisors. Most of them left the world of poverty and resistance behind.

Ruling and leading

Where before, as in 1922, the government had imposed its rule on white workers by force, by the late 1930s white political parties, the press, the radio, the church and the schools led the way in shaping the attitudes of the white working class. Social workers and the welfare system kept a watchful eye on those who fell by the wayside. As the standard of living of white workers improved they began to feel they had more control over their lives. They tended to see their new-found security as the proof and reward of their racial 'superiority' as whites.

The voices of the black working population, on the other hand, went largely unheard. *Politics and Protest* on page 238 shows that thousands of black workers never accepted the white ruling-class view of society. But they lacked the power to resist successfully the low wages and poverty, the racist laws, the overcrowding and control to which they were subjected in slumyard and location.

Nevertheless, out of this world black workers created a new and thriving culture. The newcomers were not completely controlled by the new industrial society. They were able to respond in creative and vigorous ways which surprised both the employers and the authorities. The workers had their own needs and developed their own way of life.

Black industrial life was born out of necessity. In the hostile world blacks lived in, protest and resistance also became necessities for survival. Black townspeople had to struggle for a roof over their heads, for food, for education, for rest and relaxation. All these activities became issues, or *sites of struggle*.

The culture of survival

In those first years of town life, most people developed a *culture of survival*. Just managing to live took all their time and energy, and it was only later that they began to organise and demand fair wages and decent living conditions. The black workers' culture of survival – the informal economy, crime (sometimes against the community), the sharing of resources through *stokvel* groups, the making of money from selling drink to black workers – *subsidised* the wage of the black worker.

The culture of survival therefore had *contradictions* – that is, effects which went against its aims. The very success of the workers in finding other ways of supplementing their tiny incomes enabled employers to carry on paying starvation wages. Employers knew that

A railway ganger and his family, 1934. As the economy began to recover after the Depression, the standard of living of many white workers slowly began to improve. They also enjoyed the benefit of the state policy of job protection.

somehow black workers were surviving, and that their labour would thus continue to be available. So, although the employers decried the way of life of the lowest-paid workers and the poor, and although middle-class liberals expressed their concern about the conditions prevailing, the culture of survival enabled employers to hold onto greater profits and build up their business enterprises.

Changing culture

In the course of these struggles, however, workers' culture was constantly in the making, always changing, shifting according to the situations in which working-class and middle-class people found themselves.

For example the early white working-class literature described on page 222 did not develop. It gradually became lost and forgotten as white workers became supervisors with the reorganisation of production after World War II. Instead of the literature of workers, their school-going children were taught the poetry, plays, novels and history of the middle class. It was as if whites had never been members of a struggling and underpaid working class. That period was like a bad dream — it was embarrassing and best forgotten.

As for black workers, they were only just beginning to form political and worker organisations to fight for more control over their lives — and at first only a tiny

minority belonged to organisations. But in the years to come many changes would take place — for employers, the manufacturing industry was to grow and reorganise its production; for black rural families the reserves were able to supply less and less subsistence. As a result of both of these developments, the number of black workers was to grow rapidly in the towns and more organised forms of resistance would develop — both in the crowded townships and ghettoes, and in the factories.

The culture of working people depended on the conditions they found themselves in, but also on the people themselves. It depended on political factors, on the economy, and on the society as a whole. But it also depended on the way people used their own experience, their creativity and their wits to respond to this society. In the years to come, there were to be increased struggles and hardships, but out of these a richer and constantly growing culture would take shape.

Trying to create order out of poverty — newly-arrived country-women in a location 'shanty town'.

The Struggle for Survival

In Chapter 6 we saw that the poorest-paid industrial workers in the 1920s and 1930s were white women and black men. The reason employers gave for low wages was that both these groups of workers were supported either by other wage earners (white male workers in the case of the women) or by the land economy (in the case of the black workers). But this reasoning was largely false. White women workers and the great majority of black townspeople were desperately poor. The following pages describe the hardships faced by both these groups of workers as they tried to survive.

Black workers' wages

In paying black workers ultra-low wages, employers were following the example of the mining industry (see *Gold and Workers*). Domestic workers and those workers living in compounds and hostels were the lowest paid. The excuse was that their employers were pro-

viding a roof over their heads, and, in some cases, food.

In 1936, the average cash wage paid to municipal workers (most of whom lived in compounds) was R65 a year, compared with the R63,25 paid to mine workers. Out of this low wage, most workers had to supply their working clothes and shoes, food, drink, and entertainment as well as the train fare to and from their homesteads (in 1939 this was an average expense of more than R4 per month for every return trip).

For domestic workers no minimum rate was laid down, but a 1941 survey showed that domestic servants' wages ranged between R48 and R70 a year in Johannesburg, and between R46 and R48 a year in Pretoria.[11]

Industrial workers were paid a little more. Most had found rooms in the working class areas and many were living with their families. As a result of union organisation, they were able to negotiate higher wages through the Wage Board (see Chapter 6). Nevertheless, even the wages of industrial workers were very low, as the following table shows:

Wages of Black Workers in Johannesburg[12]

	1917	1927	1937	1944
Average monthly wage	R7,50	R8,00	R8,50	R15,50
Poverty Datum Line	R8,00	R13,00	R13,50	R25,85

Scene in a rented room, 1940.

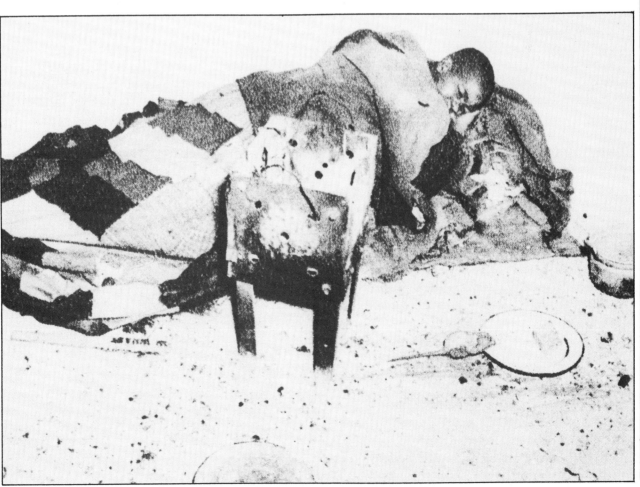

Survival

The Poverty Datum Line was the amount that was needed every month to support the poorest family (see box on this page). Yet, the average worker's wage was well below even the miserable amount allowed by the PDL for survival.

Black families had to add to their incomes with the help of the women and children. The sections on *Brewers in the Towns, Crime and Punishment* and *Children of the Ghetto* describe some of the many ways, both legal and illegal, in which extra money was earned. The 'average family income' from legal activities in Johannesburg in 1943 was as follows:[13]

Man's average wage	R15,50
Wife's contribution	R3,05
Children's contribution	R1,50
Total	R20,05

Even with this extra income, the 'average black family' still got far less than the required amount for survival (R25,85 in 1944). The family therefore resorted to brewing or other *informal* (and often illegal) economic activities. Brewing, especially, was a very important stand-by for most families, and often, in the hard times of unemployment, it was the main income for a family. In the words of one Doornfontein yard brewer, 'we eat from beer'. Studies made of that yard showed that brewers made anything between R3 and R16 a month profit.[14]

In really desperate times, the black town family would turn to relatives for help, or it would send some of the children to the rural areas for at least part of the time. And in times of crisis, the families would split up — the father might look for a job in another town, living perhaps in a compound, while the mother might take up full-time domestic service or go home to the rural areas with her children for a while. The working-class poor moved many times between town and country, from town to town, room to room, and job to job, in search of survival.

The Poverty Datum Line

From time to time, economists would draw up a *Poverty Datum Line* or *PDL* to estimate the minimum amount of money needed for an average family to survive in the towns. The PDLs were drawn up by different people with different ideas of what was necessary for survival. The 1927 PDL, for example, was drawn up by the Johannesburg Joint Council of Europeans and Africans. It allowed for rent, transport, taxes, burial society fees, heating, candles, and school and church fees.[15] On the other hand, the 1937 PDL left out heating, candles,

school and church fees, not to mention clothing, medical fees, furniture, entertainment (including drink) and newspapers.[16]

In practice the Poverty Datum Line had many faults. It was usually drawn up by middle-class, white professional people. Although they were usually sincere and well-meaning, they had very little understanding of how black workers lived, or what their needs were. In 1935, the Motor Transport Workers' Union claimed that a survival wage for a small white family of three was not less than R35,30 a month (compared with the PDL of R13,50 a month for black workers). The designers of the PDLs were too ready to assume that black food was cheaper, and that the rents were lower. (The rents in the 'slum yards' and the 'locations' *were* lower — but a number of white workers were living in these slums, too.)

Another problem was the idea these 'experts' had of the 'average family'. As time went by, more and more black children in the towns did not live with their fathers. Besides, the size of black town families shifted constantly. For example, if relatives arrived from home to look for work, most black families would support these people without question for as long as necessary. A worker's wage had to be stretched to support the **unemployed** members of his or her clan. 'The boarding of relatives is a constant drain on meagre resources. But not once did I hear any woman complain of the increased burden thus placed on her and her husband', reported a study of life in a black yard in Doornfontein in 1935.[17]

Then again, most black workers were also sending money home to parents and children in the rural areas, as well as helping other needy relatives there. These extra burdens the PDL 'experts' ignored.

A shop for the poor, where most prices were higher than in downtown stores.

Another very real problem was the fact that black workers could — and did — lose their jobs for all sorts of reasons. As *Laws for 'Non-Europeans Only'* shows on page 212, they did not have much job protection, and black workers could easily be jailed for a number of offences, and so get fired. And even if they were not jailed, offenders usually had to find the money to pay a hefty fine.

The 'experts' themselves realised the shortcomings of the PDL. As one report pointed out:

'The Poverty Datum Line is perhaps more remarkable for what it omits [leaves out] than for what it includes. It does not allow a penny for amusements, for sport, for medicine, for education, for saving, for hire purchase, for holidays etc . . . . It is not a "human" standard of living.'[18]

A garment worker's budget

The following is an extract from the life of Katie Viljoen, Port Elizabeth Branch Secretary of the Garment Workers' Union. The daughter of a poor Free State farmer, she had left school at the age of fifteen to work in order to help her parents. She arrived in Johannesburg in 1932. Like newly arrived black workers from the country, she got some help from workers who came from her district.

'Like thousands of other workers, I found the city of gold unfriendly and frightening. As I could not afford the tram fares at R2 a week, I walked home from work with my friend Lena [from her home district] who, though she lived in an entirely different suburb, acted as my guide. To make sure that I would not lose my way, I took a piece of white chalk with me and made various marks on the route from the factory to my lodgings. Next morning, I left the house at 5.30 a.m. as I had to walk a distance of about four miles and work started early.

For a month I walked to and from work every day, but then these long journeys became unbearable. The work was really slave-driving. We started at seven a.m. and finished at six p.m. I could not send anything home to my parents, as my total earnings just covered my board and lodging.

At the end of my first month, I went to see my friend Lena again, and she found me a job at the Awlwear Overall Factory. I started as a machinist at R3 a week. Most beginners started at R1,50 a week, but when Lena told the manager my sad story, he agreed to raise the wage. I was very anxious to send some money to my parents, and I needed new shoes and clothes as the old ones were wearing out. I did not know the town, but I went from building to building enquiring about cheap accommodation and at last, after a great deal of walking, found a room to share with another young girl, a sweet worker, for which I had to pay R1,75 a week.

My budget was made up as follows:

Rent:	R1,75	per week
Saving up for new clothes:	75c	per week
I sent R1 to my parents which worked out to:	25c	per week
Total	R2,75	per week

The balance of 25 cents a week had to be sufficient for food.

The interior of a poorly-paid white worker's home, 1939.

Once a week I used to buy a loaf of bread for 5 cents, and a pound of butter at 18 cents. I lived on bread and butter the whole week and still had 2 cents left over at the end. Deeply religious, I used to pray every night for enough strength to carry on with my work. I was a very healthy girl, strongly built, weighing about a hundred and fifty pounds [about 68 kilos]. I kept my health, but in a short space of time my weight dropped to a hundred and seventeen pounds (just over 50 kilos). My parents never knew the hardships I had to endure.'[19]

'Children Starving in the Midst of Plenty'

In 1938 the *Rand Daily Mail* ran a series of articles alerting the public to the extent of malnutrition amongst white children. The issue was taken up by the City Council, and members made an inspection tour of the poorer areas in Johannesburg.

'Children of six, seven and eight years of age, many of them barefooted, but otherwise clad in clothes sent to them from other schools, were brought out to see the visitors. Pinched cheeks, thin legs and arms, and shortness of stature for their age told their own tale. These children are being kept alive mainly on what the school authorities can provide for them out of the Provincial allowance of a cent per child per day.'[20]

The series provoked a militantly angry reply by 'A Working Woman' in *Garment Worker*, the most vigorous trade union publication at the time.

'Keep your charity, we want a living wage'

In an article sub-titled 'Keep your charity, we want a living wage' it asked:

'Who is to blame? In all the press articles and speeches of our Social Welfare officers hardly a word is mentioned about the real cause of the prevalence of starvation amongst kids (they call it malnutrition, it sounds more pleasant).

Some ladies and gentlemen blame the "ignorant mothers" who "spend their money" on articles of food which contain little nutritional value. Others attribute the cause to laziness on the part of the mothers.

No, rich ladies and gentlemen, we whose children are starving are not ignorant and lazy. We love our children perhaps even more than you do. We are not unmindful of our kids, but we have not the means wherewith to buy nutritious food. Nor have we the time very often to attend to our little mites. You see, rich ladies, we have to get up at five or six o'clock in the morning to be at work in time. We stay far out of town because our breadwinners are either unemployed or

working for starvation wages. When we come home we feel tired, very tired, and we cannot devote to our children the attention we should give them.

We cannot afford to engage servants and nurses, as you do, for we have not enough to live ourselves. At the end of the week when we get our pay envelopes there is not enough to enable us to buy the food which we desire and need for ourselves and our little ones . . . .

We and our children are forced to starve, so that you may enjoy life. You know what food to buy because you have got the money with which to buy it. But if you would have to come out on the miserable pittance which we and our husbands get in wages, you would probably prove to be more ignorant than we are. Try and sit at the machine or stand at the loom for a whole day and see how energetic you will feel at the end of the day.

The mayoress of Johannesburg dispensing milk to the children of the poor, 1937.

The remedy - 'a living wage'

Farm schools and a free meal per day will not solve the problem. Besides, there is little provided by the Government for the first, and still less for the second.

We don't want your charity, ladies and gentlemen.

We are quite unmoved by the heartrending appeals of Mrs Bertha Solomon, MP for Jeppe, for oranges and apples, potatoes and onions. We do not want your charity . . . .

We will give you a solution. Give us or help us to get a living wage, a living wage for our husbands or other breadwinners, a living wage for ourselves, and then our children will not starve, and your conscience will not worry you . . . .

Let the government spend money on building houses instead of prisons, let them spend money on crèches, parks and playgrounds instead of wasting money on war preparations.

Let the government stop the landlords and food racketeers from squeezing the last drop of blood out of us, then our children will not starve.

We thank you for your sympathy and for your pathetic appeals . . . . We do not need them. Your charity only perpetuates our poverty. We want a living wage, leisure, houses, and if we do not get them remember one day we shall get tired of our intolerable existence, and we shall take more – we shall take all we produce.'[21]

Brewers in the Towns

The economic value of women's labour

In the homesteads women performed essential tasks. They were a vital part of the economy. A man without women in his household was a poor man indeed. A man with many women was wealthy and respected, for women produced food, clothing and household goods; they also maintained the home and family.

In the towns women continued to make a vital contribution to the economy of their new homes. In the 1920s and 1930s, most women in the towns were newcomers who had been born in the countryside. They had been trained to serve their families, and to produce, in the environment of the homestead. When they first arrived in the towns, African women continued as much as possible to carry on production from the home, where they could be with their children and cook and clean for the family.

But in the towns the products of labour had to be turned into *commodities* – that is, goods which could be bought and sold. They therefore had to find ways of turning their skills towards making products that customers would want to buy.

Some women took up hand sewing – most did not have access to sewing machines. (In the early years commercial sewing was mainly done by men.) Others took up hawking and built up a regular trade. But this activity took women away from home. For most women, it was easier and cheaper to turn another skill into a commodity – the African woman's traditional skill of brewing.

The changing role of brewing

In the homesteads, it was customary for every wife to make beer for her husband. Traditional beer had a low alcohol content, and was relaxing and refreshing. It was usually a seasonal drink, brewed for the many celebrations which lightened the labours of country people – for harvesting and other seasonal festivals, as well as for births, weddings, and initiation ceremonies. Beer was part of religious ceremony, and it was always offered to the ancestors first.

In the towns, however, there were far fewer African women than men in the 1920s and 1930s, and beer could not be had as a gift. The many hundreds of male workers living under constant control in the compounds, hostels, and "servants' rooms" of white houses had to go to nearby yards, locations and townships to pay for drink, company and relaxation.

Town beer soon began to change its nature. In the towns, the shift, and not the seasons, controlled working times. For some workers, the weekend was the only time for relaxation. So brewers had to have their beer ready to fit in with the rhythms of industrial society.

Beer also became a stronger and stronger brew, for brewers found that they could charge more for a drink with a 'kick' in it. Stronger liquor was also quicker to prepare, which lessened the chance that it would be discovered by the police. In the words of A B Xuma, medical doctor in Sophiatown and a leader of the ANC:

'The fact is that the women who sell liquor cannot risk preparing their beer on Wednesday so that it will be ready for consumption on Saturday or Sunday because the police are likely to come, raid and destroy the liquor and arrest the possessor, who must either pay a fine or serve a term of imprisonment. Now, in order to get the kaffir beer ready for use on Saturday afternoon, something like methylated spirits must be put into it to give it a kick a few hours before men come from work on Saturday and Sunday. The usual process requires three or four days, which is too long and risky. The concoctions are added to make a get-ready-quick sort of drink in intervals between the police raids.'[22]

By the 1930s, brewers were making *skomfana* or *skokiaan*, which had a higher alcohol content, and was made from a basic recipe of sugar, yeast and warm water. Other strong brews were *isiqataviku* ("kill-me-quick"), *babaton*, and *chechisa* ("hurry-up"), or *isishimeyane*, made from sugar-cane, yeast, cooked potatoes and brandy. The brewer might add extra, secret ingredients such as pineapple skin, whisky or carbide to make it her own special recipe.

As a commodity, liquor soon lost its religious and social value. It was no longer a drink to be enjoyed slowly, at leisure, as an aid to good conversation and relaxation. It became instead a form of escape, and a way of getting drunk as quickly as possible before the next shift or the coming week's work.

In the poor communities of the yards and locations, even parties had to be paid for, and few women set aside the first can of beer for the ancestors – it was too expensive, and they could not afford to allow beer to stand in case the police should surprise them in a raid.

The dangers of brewing

Preparing for Saturday night — brewers pour beer into individual bottles.

In the towns, brewers and their customers were automatically criminals — it was against the law for Africans to brew or drink beer.[23] (Whites, of course, were allowed any alcoholic drinks on the market.) Beer brewers. therefore, had to be continually on the look-out for the police who would search their premises and probe the ground with poles and crowbars for buried tins of beer.

Women's homes were raided constantly, and a great part of their energy was spent avoiding the police. In addition to a very high fine or jail if they were caught, brewers also lost the product of their work. For example, in 1933, in just one Doornfontein yard, nearly 4 000 gallons of beer were found and destroyed by the police.[24] Brewers therefore developed careful and complicated methods of hiding their brew, as shown in the sketches on the next page.

The labour of brewing

Under normal conditions, beer brewing was a lengthy task. Traditional beer could take up to two weeks to mature. It was made from a mixture of sprouted millet (*imithombo*), mealie meal and water, which was left to stand for eight to twelve hours until it went sour. Next it had to be boiled for an hour and spread out on corrugated iron boards to cool, then mixed again with fresh *imithombo* and left to ferment for another four to five hours. Then, after it was strained, it would be ready to drink.

But the lengthy preparation of traditional beer was dangerous because it had to be prepared outside, in full view of the neighbours. As we have seen, the stronger town drinks which took half the time to prepare were therefore preferred by the brewers. The hardest part of brewing was the work needed to hide the drink from the police. The large tin container had to be buried a metre or two under the ground, covered

The police discover a drum of 'shimyana', 1937.

207

with a lid and then with earth. A smaller container might be placed on top, to fool the police. The earth on the surface had to be firmly and carefully plastered down so that the police would not notice any unevenness. All this had to be done quickly and with great skill, with children or other guards ready to warn the brewers of any danger. Digging up the tins needed an equal amount of work and watchfulness.

Beer had to be made regularly, so that there was always a supply for customers. Usually it was brewed twice a week, but often it was discovered and destroyed by the police, and then a fresh supply had to be made.

The weekend way of life

Town brewing, with its dangers, its pleasures and its profits, helped to create a new black culture or way of life, especially at weekends. On workers' nights off, women's houses were turned into bars or **shebeens**. Their small rooms were cleared of all furniture, except for rows of benches against the walls.

Often a band of guitar players, or even a pianist, was hired to provide music, and there was dancing and singing to attract customers. Stocks of beer and cigarettes would be ready, and a large pot of stew prepared. Often there was an entrance fee of five cents. Usually a brewer had her special customers. Sometimes they were workers from her home area, or else they were people who preferred her drinks or the entertainment she provided. If the brewer could not afford expensive entertainment, she could hire a choir to sing, or a troupe of dancers, in return for beer until the early hours of the morning.

The parties were often all-night affairs – once the nine or ten o'clock curfew bell had sounded no Africans were allowed on the streets. (This was only one of the many restrictions which black townspeople had to suffer – see **Crime and Punishment**.)

The shebeens were places where newcomers to the town could find friends. They were also places where men could find women, for most customers were single men, or else far from home. Prostitution was therefore common. It was also not unusual in these poor communities for some women – especially widows, deserted wives or unmarried mothers – to have 'backdoor' husbands, (**nyatsi**) whom they saw regularly for a fee of R1 or R1,50 a month.

It was also over women that most of the weekend fights took place. After a week's hard work for low pay under harsh conditions, many workers used the drinking parties to release built-up sexual tension and anger. Drunkenness would encourage these feelings, and often a quarrel would turn into a brawl, sometimes also involving the friends of the two who started the fight. Stabbings and severe injuries were not uncommon in the shebeens, so that a weekend party could sometimes end in tragedy.

'These rough sketches show the cunning manner in which the liquor is buried – a method that baffled the police for a long time. A hole is dug 12 feet deep. Into this is placed a big barrel of liquor. A sheet of galvanised iron on top of the barrel supports about 18 inches of soil. Then come paraffin tins full of liquor and then soil. In many previous raids only the tins were found, the presence of the barrels being quite unsuspected. After the tins were removed by the police, the barrel was tapped in the manner shown in the second sketch.'
(Source: S A Pictorial, 24.1.1920)

Extra income

The woman brewer was able to provide extra income for her family, but at the price of hard work, danger and, often, her dignity. The profits varied according to the number of people in employment and workers' wages, as these rose and fell. (Luck in evading the police was also a factor, of course.) In an average week in the 1930s a brewer could make at least R2, which matched a man's weekly wage.

A woman's ability to bring in this much-needed income also gave her independence. Even though the beer profits were usually shared by husband and wife, this extra income enabled the wife to have a say in how money should be spent. And if she was badly treated or deserted by her husband she could choose to stay on in town and continue brewing instead of returning home to her people, who might regard her as an unwanted wife.

Municipal beer halls

The beer brewers took a hard knock, however, when they were made to move to the new locations or municipal townships in the late 1930s (see Chapter 7). In the first place, they lost many of their most valued customers – the domestic workers in the white suburbs and the dwellers in the hostels near the centre of town. They were also hit by the decision of many Rand municipalities to open up legal beer halls in the new townships. Raids and fines increased, for now the brewers were interfering with the profitable municipal monopoly on beer.

But the brewing did not stop. It could not stop. Brewing was a vital source of income for the family. In spite of its dangers and its ugly aspects, brewing was firmly part of black town life. So, while the women brewers had to struggle harder to avoid discovery in the new townships, most were able to continue running their shebeens, with more careful planning and with the help of bribes. There was truth in the African saying:

'If man invents a better mouse-trap, then nature is sure to breed a better mouse'.[25]

From *Down Second Avenue* by Es'kia Mphahlele

'A big terrible light . . . shining steel pokers with sharp points for destroying beer containers . . . heavy footsteps . . . clanging of steel . . . the sound coming faintly . . . I felt sick. The earth was turning and I seemed to hang precariously on the edge. Everything became dark and black before me . . . .

Marabastad continued to brew beer. Police con-

tinued to raid as relentlessly and to destroy. There were Saturday and Sunday mornings when the streets literally flowed with beer. The Chinese and Indian shopkeepers were not prevented from selling corn malt either. Each yard had several holes in which tins of beer were hidden. A house burnt down in Fifth Avenue at one time. When the rubble was being cleared, where there had been a mud floor, a few holes were found. Dokie, the sharp one, swore that tufts of hair had been found in the tins of beer in the holes. 'The things witches can do when they want luck in their beer business!' she said.

Most people feared she was telling the truth. Women brewed some of the most terrifying compounds. 'Its heathen!' grandmother said indignantly. 'My beer's pure and healthy food a man's stomach needs.' And we never had the fighting type of customer. 'But even with that, God'll help me make money to send my children to college.'[26]

Crime and Punishment

'*Factories for the making of criminals*'
(An African opinion of the South African law courts, 1935).[27]

'*During the past thirty years, we have manufactured about 100 000 criminals relative to the contravention of the liquor laws.*'
(Chief Detective of the CID, 1931.)[28]

'*Criminal manufacturing laws.*'
(An African's comment on the pass laws, 1935).

In the towns, black people had to make their way through a thick jungle of laws which could turn anyone into a 'criminal' at any time. The box on pages 212 and 213 shows the extent to which the law of their land discriminated against blacks – pass laws, tax laws, curfews, liquor laws, labour regulations, housing and municipal regulations (not to mention the way they were treated by the police, the law courts and the jails). As a missionary and scholar observed in 1938, this discrimination extended to everyday activities:

'A Native is subject to criminal prosecution for carrying sticks larger than specified; knives longer than specified; for non-payment of rent; for making and selling his tribal drinks, and for being idle in a Native Location. What is the result of this multiplying of crimes on the African's head? The inevitable result: the multiplying of offenders and the bringing of the law into disrepute . . . . As a matter of fact, an African hardly ever overstates the case when he declares: "The urban Native population is a population of lawbreakers".'[30]

What was right for whites was often a crime for blacks.

For black people, the towns were hostile places. In the racist, colonial world of South Africa, many whites saw Africans as a threat. Blacks were tolerated only for their labour, and all other activities in the towns were made as difficult as possible for them by law.

Convictions

In his 1937 report, the manager of Johannesburg's Non-European Housing and Native Affairs Department listed a quarter of the convictions of young blacks for that year. They were:

'creating a disturbance, congregating, begging, hawking, selling newspapers, acting as porters without licences, touting for car attendance, drunkenness, motor vehicles ordinance and wandering without local passes.'[31]

Most of these 'offences' were harmless to society, yet the 'lawbreakers' — often youngsters — would be thrown into jail and exposed to hardened and bitter criminals there. In 1936, the total number of offences against laws which applied to blacks only was 125 032, or 77,9 percent of the year's convictions for Africans. In other words, over three-quarters of black criminals were criminals only because they were black. Yet these people (most of them desperately poor) were arrested, charged in court, and fined or sent to jail.

To make things worse, the *agents* of the law, the police, often behaved in hostile and unfeeling ways. On any night of their lives, blacks could be rudely awakened by pass raids, tax raids, and liquor raids, carried out without any concern for household property or privacy. The police 'pick-up van', a barred truck which could carry more than ten passengers, roamed the streets looking for African passers-by who were not carrying their passes and tax receipts.

A police commission which reported in 1935 was disturbed by the effects on the policemen themselves:

'We have abundant evidence that the enforcement by the police of the present laws is often marked by unnecessary harshness, lack of sympathy and even violence . . . and the very process of constant raiding with its . . . invasion of privacy and use of force, must have a brutalising effect upon the police, apart from the effects on the Natives concerned.'[32]

Attitudes to crime

The result of this constant harassment of black people in the towns was a general hatred of the police. As a congress of 'Native' Advisory Boards reported in 1935:

'The white man regards a policeman as a friend and a protector from danger. The black man regards him as a foreigner and an enemy.'[33]

For most blacks, a jail sentence was generally seen as bad luck and no disgrace. Even 'respectable' people began to reject 'white' justice. As one location resident wrote in the 1930s:

Punishment by lashes at the Fort, then Johannesburg's main prison.

'Police usually come in the night – disturbing people after a hard day's work. Holes are dug through the floor – everything in the house is upset. The householder is enraged. He says next morning to his wife, "What is the good of obeying the law when we are treated as criminals like this?"'[34]

A study made of crime on the Rand concluded:

'There is on the Witwatersrand a sort of undeclared guerilla warfare carried on between the police and the Africans, the [Africans'] hatred of the [police] bringing the law . . . into disrepute and contempt and making it easy to offend against the law with a light heart.'[35]

Crimes

'A stub of candle flickers in a room in Fifteenth Street. A haggard woman and two half-starved kids look at a man sitting at the table with his head buried in his hands.

"I'm hungry, Daddy," the first one whimpers.

"Me too, Daddy," the second one echoes.

The woman stares at him with dull eyes.

"Nothing again?"

He does not move.

"Nothing."

"I'm going out to get something for them."

They look at each other a long time . . . . She goes out.'

. . . .

'Old shrunken Liz is happy tonight. Her man came out of "Big Den" this morning; "Big Den" being jail. They've been boozing the whole day, and now she is very happy.

She and old Japie, her man, walk down Twentieth Street. She jumps about like a young girl to show the world how happy she is. Her old man walks carefully a little way behind her. He tries to walk straight, but his legs are unsteady. In a croaking voice he sings:

"It's a long way to Tipararee,
It's a long way to go.
It's a long way to Tipararee,
Right into Marshall Square."

On the corner of Twentieth Street they meet a group of young fellows. Liz gets carried away by the excitement of her dancing. She jumps into the air. The young fellows are in a happy mood; they clap their hands and encourage her. This excites her more. She dances furiously until she is in a state of frenzy. Then she lifts up her old patched dress and shows her bottom. It is a great joke to everyone, and they all laugh good-humouredly.

A policeman comes down the street and grabs Liz rudely. He walks her down the subway in the direction of the police station. Old Japie shakes his head.

"Fourteen days or a pound, and me just come out this morning."

The young men growl and curse the policeman.'

(From Peter Abrahams's short story, 'Saturday Night'. The writer grew up in Vrededorp in the 1920s and 1930s.)

The crime of poverty

Over half of the crimes brought to court were crimes of theft and robbery. The cause of the great majority of these offences was the very real poverty of the people of the slums and locations. It was poverty, often, that caused people to risk the horrors of arrest and imprisonment by stealing and robbing – either on their own or as members of a gang.

Many young men deliberately chose to avoid wage labour – the wages were miserably low, and there were so many labour, pass and contract regulations that life seemed as hard for legally employed blacks as for those who lived a life of crime. There were many complaints by the municipal authorities that young blacks were lazy and refused to work. In time, the life of the gangster began to appeal to some young men, and a pattern developed in which gangs committed crimes of violence against their own community. But the really big, organised gangs had not yet developed in the 1930s. 'Compared to today's crime', Modikwe Dikobe has written, 'serious crime was very rare in Doornfontein . . . . Murders were due to congregation in beer homes and at Amalaita funs.'[36]

In other words, crimes of violence were not usually planned and organised, but committed in the heat of the moment, often at weekend drinking parties, where men heavily outnumbered women. In Johannesburg in 1938, there were over three thousand convictions for serious assault and murder (culpable homicide).[37] (Compare this with the figure of less than 200 serious crimes of all kinds committed in the Transkei in any year between 1923 and 1938.)[38]

As *Brewers in the Towns* describes, poverty drove people to find other illegal ways of making extra money like brewing and prostitution. Prostitution was a common conviction amongst the white as well as the black poor. Amongst whites, too, there were many convictions for selling 'European liquor' to blacks. Also, overcrowding made 'the streets more attractive and comfortable at night', leading to illegal night-time activities.[39] And in a world of poverty, when children came home with something for the family to share, many parents did not ask where the money or goods came from. They were pleased to accept any contribution to the home.

In the poor, crowded, police-patrolled world of the slums and black locations, criminal activities for many people were a *conscious choice* – crime seemed for them a sensible way of adding much needed income to a super-exploited black working class. In a racist, capitalist world, poverty was the first crime, especially if you were black.

Gambling

'On the corner of Nineteenth Street a group of fellows are playing dice. Dinnie is the scout. He looks out for the police and when he sees them he shouts "Arra-rai!" And when he shouts that they know the police are coming, and run for their lives.

Hakkies, star rugby player for Vrededorp, has the dice. In front of him is a small pile of money. He is on his knees. The dice are between his palms. He rolls them between his palms and speaks to them. He fondles and kisses them. "Come little babies, come baby shoes! Can't you hear your mommy calling? Come now and make the main!"

His voice is coaxing. The others watch his hands silently. One or two plead with the dice to make seven. Hakkies throws them down and they roll a little way. The players hold their breath until the dice stop. It's a six . . . . Someone in the circle throws down a penny.

"Penny you don't."

Hakkies looks at him and shakes his head.

"All or nothing."

There are protests from the whole circle.

"You can't do that, Boeta Hakkies, you break the bank, and you want to say all or nothing. That's not fair."

The fellow who threw down a penny throws down two more.

"All right. Tickey [two and a half cents] you don't."

Hakkies looks at them and laughs.

"Sorry fellows, but when you break me I don't grumble. I said all or nothing. Take it or leave it. Well?"

Hakkies is one of the strong men of Vrededorp, but the crowd is angry. They are broke and he is the cause. There is a lot of growling and grumbling, a fight is just around the corner. Hakkies stands up, puts his money into his pocket, hitches up his belt, and watches them smilingly.

Suddenly Dinnie runs past them. "Arra-rai! Arra-rai! The pick-up!"

They all turn and see a group of policemen jumping out of the moving pick-up van and running towards them.

Hakkies smiles at the others.

"So-long, fellows; all or nothing like I said!'

He streaks up Nineteenth Street with a policeman after him. But Hakkies is fast and the policeman will never get him. He smiles as he runs.'

(From 'Saturday Night', a short story by Peter Abrahams.)

Laws for 'Non-Europeans Only'

Long before the era of apartheid, many laws in South Africa discriminated against blacks.

The pass laws

According to the Urban Areas Acts of 1923 and 1930, Africans in proclaimed areas (that is, the towns) had to get the following passes:

- a pass permitting a person to look for work as soon as he arrived in a town;
- or a pass showing that he did not need to carry a work permit (if he was a registered voter in the Cape, a landowner, a chief, a headman, a teacher with high qualifications, a minister of the church, or an interpreter);
- or a certificate of approval for African women from the municipal authority as well as a certificate from the magistrate of her home district;
- a registered service contract at a cost of 20 cents a month when a worker eventually found a job;
- or a badge for temporary labourers to wear;
- or a pass for visiting a town;
- a night pass or 'special' to be signed by the employer, if an African person wished to be outdoors after curfew hours (9 p.m. or 10 p.m., depending on the town regulations).

If a person failed to produce any of these passes on demand, he or she could be arrested, imprisoned for the night, brought to court or fined or jailed if found guilty.

Between 1930 and 1940, the number of convictions for pass offences in Johannesburg nearly tripled, although the African population had not quite doubled in that time.[40]

Tax laws

Under the Native Taxation and Development Act of 1925, African men had to pay the following taxes:

- a poll tax for everyone between the ages of 1 and 25, of R2 a year;
- a tax of R1 per year for every hut in a rural area, otherwise rent or 'squatting' fees.

These taxes had to be paid, no matter how small a man's income might be. The tax laws clearly discriminated against blacks (by far the poorest section of the population). In 1945 a Social and Economic Planning Council criticised the tax system, saying:

'A Native family generally pays a higher proportion of income in taxation than a European family earning perhaps twice as much.'

But, it continued,

> 'one of the main objectives of Native taxation is, or was, to exert pressure on Natives to seek work in agriculture, mining or manufacture. In this object it is probably very successful.'[41]

An African man in the towns had to be able to produce his tax receipt on demand, otherwise he could be arrested and charged, fined (in addition to paying his tax), or jailed.

Liquor laws against Africans

Since the time before Union in 1910, Africans had been forbidden to drink 'intoxicating liquors', except for traditional beer or **utshwala**, which was subject to different laws in different provinces. Natal, for example, had had a Beer Act since 1908, which reserved the brewing and selling of beer for the Natal municipalities only.

These laws were enforced nationally by the Natives (Urban Areas) Act of 1923. On the Rand, for example, there was a total prohibition on the manufacture, sale and possession of beer or other alcoholic drinks by Africans. Instead, the municipalities took over the monopoly of selling beer to raise money for the cost of black housing. (See Chapter 7.)

The breaking of the liquor laws led to the largest number of convictions. In 1935, for example, 41 451 people on the Rand were fined or jailed for this offence alone.[42]

Municipal regulations

In addition to the central government's special laws for Africans, each municipality drew up its own regulations, which covered such matters as:

> 'the building of out houses; sub-letting rooms or stands; the collection of rentals; the registering of children over 18 as tenants; the keeping of homes clean; the keeping of cattle in locations; the holding of entertainments; the carrying of dangerous weapons; and the creation of disturbances.'[43]

In Johannesburg in the years 1937/38 and 1938/39 there were the following convictions for breaking municipal regulations.[44]

	1937/38	1938/39
'Overcrowding in the locations'	1 937	1 477
'Urinating in unauthorised places'	70	154
'Throwing refuse in unauthorised places'	27	8
'General disturbances'	377	616
'Other offences'	11 016	10 228

In addition, there were the following rent cases:

'Number of persons summoned for not paying the rent'	3 619	5 073
'Number of evictions'	27	8
'Amount made from auction sales of property sold of offenders'	R213,64	R255,85

Labour regulations

As Chapter 6 has shown, a number of labour regulations discriminated against African workers in particular. For example, leaving a job before the end of the contract, or going out on strike, were crimes punishable by jail sentences.

Making Music

Music on the Rand took different expressive forms. It was influenced by European church music as well as dance music from America or by **indigenous music** such as the **vastrap**, born in the Cape and developed by the Boers during their trek northwards. Above all there was the rural music of Africa, with its different scale, rhythm and harmony patterns. All these forms influenced the music of the townships, and led to a rich variety — street music with its portable instruments; church and community choirs; **marabi**, the music of the shebeens and the black workers; the big jazz bands; and the many combinations of these and other forms of music.

A 'Cape boys' band in Johannesburg in the early years of the century.

'The Merry Blackbirds' in the late 1930s. Many players in jazz bands gained their experience playing 'marabi' music in the humbler environment of the shebeens.

Migrant mineworkers making music with traditional instruments.

African music

In rural African societies, music was not a thing apart from the everyday activities of life. It was not seen simply as a form of entertainment to be enjoyed after a day's labour or during one's spare time. It was closely woven into every aspect of the day's activities.

The voice was the most common musical instrument and was used to express every experience — there were work songs like grinding and harvesting songs; there were cradle songs, praise songs, drinking songs, war songs, and songs for the sick; there were songs for the important events in life — initiation songs, wedding songs, farewell and welcome songs, and lamentations for the dead. Music, like language, was learnt by living in the community, and everyone took part in producing it.[45]

It is hardly surprising that music became a very intimate part of town life for blacks. Migrant workers, under contract on the mines and the railways or in the municipalities, quickly adapted portable instruments such as the mouth organ, the recorder, the concertina and especially the guitar – they were able to change the strings of the guitar to play the pentatonic scale of African music. With these instruments they played traditional as well as new forms of music, expressing their longing for home and their strange new experiences as wage labourers and compound dwellers.

The music did not remain inside the hostels – the streets of white suburbs were often filled with the sad or lively sounds made on these instruments by domestic workers on their evenings or days off. It also travelled to the living quarters of the black workers – to the yards, locations and townships.

Marabi music

In the black working-class areas, music developed a close relationship with the *informal sector* of the economy. In a world where everyone was poor – the employed as well as the unemployed – people were always on the look-out for ways of making an extra income. Even parties and celebrations became a means of raising money, with the result that there were parties and concerts in the townships whenever possible. *Brewers in the Towns* shows how beer brought in much-needed income, and how music was a way of attracting compound and domestic workers to the drinking parties of the shebeens.

From these parties, a new kind of music developed. The brewers hired anyone who could play an instrument. Sometimes there was a piano in the room; sometimes a small band was engaged to play; sometimes it was a choir, helped along with home-made instruments – empty tins filled with stones to provide a rhythm backing. If the brewer had no money, she would pay the players with beer. Always there was music – *marabi* music.

What exactly was *marabi* music? Like the 'blues' music developed by blacks in the cities of the United States, 'marabi' was the musical expression of an outcast people. Even many sophisticated blacks rejected it. Certainly most musicians in competition with *marabi* were not very complimentary. For example, one jazz band-leader said disapprovingly:

> 'Marabi music was made from whatever instruments were available, by anyone who could play or make a noise.'[46]

And the editor of the weekly journal, *Umteteli wa Bantu*, complained in 1933 about the '*marabi* menace':

> 'The *"marabi"* dances and concerts, and the terrible "jazz" music banged and wailed out of the doors of foul smelling so-called halls are far from representing real African taste.'[47]

But in spite of its humble beginnings, *marabi* gave to the creative young people of the slums the chance to express themselves and develop a new kind of music and song that was special to the Rand. In the words of one of the well-known *marabi* players, Wilson (King Force) Silgee:

> '*Marabi*: that was the environment. It was either organ but mostly piano. You get there you pay your ten cents you get your share of whatever concoction there is and you dance. It used to start from Friday night right through to Sunday evening. You get tired you go home and sleep, and come back again, bob a time each time you get in. The piano and with the audience making a lot of noise. Trying to make some theme out of what is playing.'[48]

Marabi bands

Marabi was the birthplace of some of South Africa's jazz greats; it was where they learnt their music. By the end of the 1920s, small *marabi* bands were forming, the first being the *Japanese Express*, followed by others such as the *Jazz Maniacs*.

As they became more experienced, these bands blended *marabi* rhythms with American swing, creating a new form of African jazz. This was the music which was to inspire great musicians – like Dollar Brand, Hugh Masekela, Kippie Moeketsi and Johannes Gwanga – in later years. The *marabi* bands grew and were in great demand – so much so that they were able to become full-time musicians:

> 'At *marabi* you would sometimes find that we are three *marabi* players on piano. When you get tired the other takes over and you go and dance . . . the owner of the dance would pay us five shillings [50 cents] a night. Ja, plenty of money that time and free beer too. My father used to get a pound [R2] a week and my mother a pound a month. It was not enough for food . . . there was no extra money unless I go play for *marabi*. My parents [would] see me the following morning when I came with five bob sometimes seven and six [75 cents] and they were satisfied.'[49]

Marabi music was therefore an intimate part of ghetto life. It was born in part out of a people's struggle to survive in the hostile world of industrial capitalism. Music was one of the vital, creative ways in which the black poor combined survival with entertainment, to help them forget for a few hours the hardships and sufferings of everyday life.

Dancing, Sports and Spare Time

In rural homesteads people were able to relax in a number of different ways during their spare time. Children practised their skills in counting, jumping and throwing games, or told stories, sang songs, and recited rhymes. Adults too, liked to listen to a tale well told and acted out at the end of the day's work. Another important entertainment was dancing.

Dancing

When people left home and went to the cities to find work, dancing travelled with them and flourished. Dancing was a popular pastime wherever people came together, because many could take part in it.

Dancing also expressed the different styles and ways of life to be found in chiefdoms from different parts of the country. The courtship, war, hunting, and initiation dances reminded new workers of home. Dancing was popular especially in the mining and municipal compounds.

This kind of dancing was soon noticed by employers, who recognised its value in 'managing' the energies of compound workers after working hours. They encouraged separate 'tribal' dancing competitions, which became a popular form of entertainment for the workers and white tourists alike.

As music changed (see *Making Music*), so dancing began to take on new forms — there was dancing to jazz (the music of black Americans, which was becoming popular world-wide) as well as the more middle-class, respectable dancing to the popular European strains of the waltz, the fox-trot, and the tango. Then there was the wilder *marabi* dancing, which was a combination of jazz and traditional dancing, and which developed in the shebeens on Saturday nights.

Soccer

The 'tribal' dancing of the compound workers, however, was soon competing with a new form of entertainment — soccer, or football. Soccer had spread to Johannesburg from Natal, where, along with stick-fighting, it had become popular amongst workers as early as the 1890s. There was a big influx to Durban of young black men after the rinderpest epidemic of 1896 had diminished the cattle herds. Many of them took up work as domestic servants, and:

> 'to re-establish their manhood after working as servants for white women during the week, would form themselves into bands of amalaitas on Sundays and go stick-fighting.'

The Rev. Sivetye, who had been a school teacher and football coach at the Amanzimtoti Institution at the beginning of the century, commented that stick-fighting 'was like their sport. It wasn't a crime.'[50]

Durban workers formed a number of football teams and were soon playing matches against one another and also against school teams like the Adams College football team. There were a number of Indian teams, too, and not long after Johannesburg was established in 1886, its first soccer club was set up — the 'Prides of India', whose members worked in the hotels and boarding houses of the infant town.

Africans in Johannesburg seem to have begun playing after the Anglo-Boer War, and developed rapidly as keen footballers:

> 'I recalled the days when my uncle, R W Msimang [one of the founders of the ANC] told of the period 1907 to 1918 when, thanks to the keen interest of

Pedi dancers in Western Township on a Sunday afternoon, about 1934.

the Military stationed on the Rand, the game received a strong impetus and made great strides. He spoke enthusiastically of the old Natalians, the Crocodiles, the Olympics and the Ocean Swallows – teams that had to cycle from one end of the Reef to the other for a fixture to be played on roughly shuffled grounds, where one could not follow the game for dust.'[51]

Soccer was also encouraged by the mine managers, for, as Dan Twala observed, 'it helped the mines keep [their workers] busy over the weekends' and 'it helped their recruiting programme'.[52]

Football soon spread to the townships, where it became a street sport. An English football fan and writer has remarked that football is a 'people's game':

Winners of the Ladysmith 'Five-a-Side' soccer tournament, 1917. Natal Indians introduced soccer to the Rand, where it rapidly became a popular working-class sport.

'No other sport lent itself so easily and cheaply to the varying conditions of urban life. It was simple to play, easy to grasp and could be played on any surface under any conditions, by indeterminate numbers of men. It needed no equipment but a ball, and could last from dawn to dusk. Football could be played by anyone, regardless of size, skill and strength.'[53]

From the yards of Doornfontein and the streets of Pimville, Sophiatown, Eastern and Western Native Townships and Alexandra, football teams sprang up and soon matches were organised. Where there was not enough space for a match, the teams would play on the flat tops of the mine dumps. The 'aunties' of each team would collect a small sum of money, and hand it to the referee. The winning team would then collect the jackpot.

In 1925, the Bantu Sports Club was started in Johannesburg. The land had been donated by two sympathetic accountants, Howard Pim (after whom Pimville was later named) and John Hardy. There was enough space for two football fields, tennis courts, a club house and stands for 5 000 people. The sports club was a great success, both with members and with the authorities.

'The organisation of sports among Native men in the municipal hostels has resulted in a seventy-five per cent decrease in drunkenness', a Location Managers' conference was told, while a missionary noted that the Bantu Sports Club

'provides wholesome substitutes for vicious activities – gambling and crime. Through it crime has decreased.'[54]

In the 1930s, the popularity of football grew steadily. The Johannesburg Bantu Football Association was able to claim 153 senior and 282 junior clubs by 1937 – mainly location and municipal compound clubs – while an opposition association, the Johannesburg Africans Football Association, formed in 1933, recruited clubs for workers employed by the mines and by business firms.

A national association was formed, with a cup donated by a business firm and, in 1938, a bigger trophy was donated by two prominent ANC sportsmen, Dr. Moroka and R. G. Baloyi. Around that time, too, the first famous soccer club, Orlando Pirates, was started.

From early on, therefore, sports were organised – in fact, sports clubs were called 'unions'. And although there were many splits, the clubs also brought together many people – migrant workers, clerks, factory workers, people of different language groups and backgrounds – to help form a new culture of the city.

City Deep Football Team, Johannesburg 1937.

White Working-class Culture

There were two kinds of unskilled and semi-skilled white workers on the Rand: Afrikaner workers who had come straight from the *platteland*, and immigrants from Europe, including Britain. Many of the European immigrants were not English-speaking, but were either Jews from eastern Europe, or young Greek and Italian peasants, come to the Rand in search of a living and hoping for a share of the wealth that the gold mines were producing.

Working-class neighbourhoods

Chapters 2 and 3 describe how, in the early years, unskilled and lower-paid workers of all colours and language groups lived in the same areas and experienced the hardships and misery of poverty. In many cases, they actually shared houses, as described in *Memories of a 'Poor White' Childhood* on page 234. They bought from the same shops, walked in the same streets, and often drank at the same places. The shops were usually run by immigrants – Greeks, Chinese, Jews or Indians – and often these small traders lived in the neighbourhood, too. (In 1904, for example, the whites in Vrededorp had petitioned against the removal of Indian traders, who granted them credit.)

In later years, too, workers shared many of the day-to-day experiences of the working-class neighbourhood. One highly politicised Afrikaner woman worker pointed out:

> 'From the Nationalist Party, which has to be an Afrikaner party, I hear that the Englishman despises the Afrikaner and keeps us out of jobs, that the *skelm* [crook] Jew tries to bluff and cheat us. But if this is so, why are there as many desperately poor English and Jews in the backyards as Afrikaners, living in the very same conditions?'[55]

There were of course many differences, too. The new workers spoke different languages, cooked different foods, followed different religions, and had different backgrounds and life styles.

Living among strange people, often feeling lost and confused in new surroundings, workers usually preferred to be near others of their own background. Little 'pockets' of different communities could be found in a working-class neighbourhood. It was not unusual, for instance, to find in the older areas such as Fordsburg and Doornfontein a Christian church, an Indian mosque, and a Jewish synagogue within a two-mile radius.

The strange differences all around them often made people suspicious of other groups. They jealously guarded their own traditions. They warned their children to stay away from the children of other groups. But while the children picked up the prejudices of their parents, they also showed that the world of children is the same all over, and they continued to play and fight together in the streets.

City apartments – a white family on the first floor, blacks below.

Landless in the countryside, jobless in town.

Afrikaner workers

Many Afrikaners could be found in the working-class areas — of the white unskilled and semi-skilled workers, 90 per cent were Afrikaners.[56] As described in Chapter 2, the main flow of Afrikaners to the Rand towns began with the Anglo-Boer War, when 30 000 Boer homesteads were burnt down and millions of cattle and sheep were destroyed. Unable to keep going, thousands of **bywoners** and small farmers were driven off the land into the towns.[57]

For many years after the war, small Boer farmers fortunate enough to remain on the land hoped to recover their losses by sending out the young people as migrant workers to the towns to earn cash wages. But conditions in the countryside only got worse for the small farmers. The depression after World War I, and the droughts and cattle diseases that followed, drove more Afrikaners to the towns. By the 1920s, 12 000 Afrikaners were leaving the land every year, creating a large army of unemployed in the towns.[58]

Often, the daughters went first — possibly because they were not as necessary to the economy of the Boer household as were African women to **their** homesteads. (Amongst Africans, the men usually left their rural homesteads first.) Most Afrikaner workers were total newcomers to the towns but, like African and immigrant workers, many tended to go to areas where

friends had jobs. The urban, industrial, capitalist system came as a deep shock to these young people, suddenly removed from their families, and poor in an uncaring world. As a union organiser, Hester Cornelius, wrote:

> 'What sometimes breaks my heart, is to see little girls of scarcely 16 years old, and sometimes 15, coming from the farms, in possession of a letter from the parents to please look after Aletta; that they had to allow her to be uprooted because there is no other future for their little girl; also a testimonial from the school principal who reports that Aletta cannot continue her education because her parents are in great need, they are only **bywoners** and have another six or seven children to care for.'[59]

Afrikaner workers as overseers

The better-off Afrikaner members of the working class were the miners. We have seen how, especially after the loss of the 1922 strike, white miners were steadily deskilled and increasingly given supervisory tasks. White miners were thus placed in the watchdog role of helping to control the black workers and thus extract more production from them. The mining companies needed these supervisors and therefore helped them to stay. After a short trial period, the white newcomers were encouraged to bring their families to live with

Policemen joking with factory workers. While many Afrikaner policemen were relatives and boyfriends of women workers, these relationships could come under stress in times of strikes and disputes with employers.

them in specially provided houses in villages near the mines. They earned higher salaries than workers in most other industries, and usually their wives did not need to work for wages.

But the life of a miner was not always secure. Chapter 4 described the danger facing a miner every time he went underground. In addition, some 5 per cent of white miners were dismissed with compensation every year because they had contracted miners' phthisis — a lung disease from dust underground.[60] Mining could not be considered a permanent job for everyone. Chapters 4 and 6 have already noted that the insecurity of white workers made them hostile to cheap black labour, and encouraged racism that was inherited from the colonial past. It was this insecurity that kept them militant against the mining companies.

Other Afrikaners were able to find work in the police force, in the army, or as warders in the prisons — by the end of 1931 two thirds of the police force were Afrikaners.[61]

As policemen, it was their task to maintain order, and at times there were conflicts in white working-class families when, 'in the line of duty', the police clashed with fellow-Afrikaner workers on strike, as happened in 1922 and in the Thirties. This tension is illustrated in a workers' play of the period, *Broers*. One of the brothers is a policeman, the other a worker on strike.

The policeman is criticised by a woman worker for being a traitor to his class:

'Only through betrayal can you get rid of your duty towards your class . . . when you allow yourself to be used to break a strike, it's nothing but treachery. That's all!'[62]

Policemen, soldiers, and warders had to carry out functions of control. By the very nature of their work, they were often isolated from other workers, more especially black workers. Their attitudes were affected by the very nature of their jobs.

The white poor

As we have seen in Chapters 5 and 6, thousands of Afrikaner workers fell into the class of 'skilled labourers'. In the case of new workers straight from the platteland, many of the men came to the towns too old to learn a trade. As unskilled or even semi-skilled workers, they could never be sure of steady, permanent jobs. They had to rely on casual labour, which meant that much of the time they were looking for work. In the 1920s, as the economy slowly declined, the income of lower-paid workers dropped.[63]

The fathers of the new urban families could not afford to be the only breadwinners. In the towns, the daughters had to work for wages too, and their income often kept the family from starving, especially when the

An industrial training school. A conscious effort by the state to train the children of the white poor uplifted them in later years when the economy expanded and industrial skills were in demand.

father was out of a job. For instance, in an investigation by the department of Labour in the leanest year of the Depression, 1932, women workers gave evidence such as the following:

> 'Of her weekly wages of R5,00, Maria Johanna du Plessis contributed R10 a month to the family budget. Her father, at a monthly wage of R18, earned less than she did and had to keep a family of eight of whom only four were employed. Nellie Murray's father earned R2 per week, whereas her sister, a dressmaker, earned R12 per week and she earned R5 per week. Together they had to support a family of seven in Brixton. In 1931 Ivy Rebock, an 18 year old machinist, helped her father, a telephone exchange worker, to support their family of 14.'[64]

Women's wages were very important. As Chapter 6 has shown, women's work was a cheap form of labour, and women were therefore able to find jobs more easily than their menfolk. Their meagre wages kept their families going.

By 1932, the number of 'poor whites' reached 300 000 – that is, 20 percent or one fifth of the white population.[65] Chapter 2 has described how Afrikaners not only struggled against poverty but also, in the racially divided society of South Africa, suffered deeply

from what they felt was the 'disgrace' of having the same low living standards as black workers. They saw the comfortable living standards of other whites and they asked themselves why they could not live like them too. In a workers' play written for *Garment Worker/Klerewerker*, a poor mother tells her little boy bitterly,

> 'There is no Father Christmas for the poor. Remember that. He is not on our side.'[66]

Training children

However, poor white children differed from poor black children in an important respect. Since the early years of the century, the state had taken on the task of educating and preparing white children for an urban, industrial life. Industrial schools had been set up for the children of the poor 'to accustom them to the atmosphere and discipline of the workshop'. Compulsory education for all white children was introduced after the Anglo-Boer War. In 1917 a government committee pointed out:

> 'The wholly uneducated person is regarded as a potential danger in that he is likely eventually to become a public nuisance, and further will not be equipped to carry out public duties as a citizen. To avoid this the state lays down a certain standard which must be reached before school attendance becomes voluntary.'[67]

Free education, which included school feeding, helped to discipline and socialise white children into developing regular habits, the right attitudes to work, and the skills suitable to industrial employment. The story told in *Memories of a 'Poor White' Childhood* shows how the white child had to go to school, and how the social worker kept an eye on his progress. It describes the painful adjustments he had to make before he was accepted by white society. Eventually, through state education, he grew up to become a professional man, far removed from the black playmates of his childhood. At the very least, compulsory schooling kept the children of white working mothers off the streets.

Breaking the law

Like the black poor, whites turned to other ways (besides wage earning) of adding to the family income. Two ways to make easier money presented themselves to whites: one was to sell liquor at high prices to blacks (who were forbidden the 'white man's liquor') and the other was prostitution — in the Rand towns, men outnumbered women of all races. In a study of white prostitution in the 1940s, it was found that many of the part-time prostitutes were struggling, underpaid factory workers or waitresses and shop assistants:

> 'After paying her rent, there is very little left over for the bare necessities of life . . . . [Part-time prostitutes] are drawn largely from our army of ill-paid workers in industry and commerce, particularly from the ranks of waitresses, maidservants, probation nurses, shop girls'.[68]

Another study found that young girls were forced into part-time prostitution to pay their rent.[69] The problem already existed at the beginning of the century.[70] And in 1920, a tailors' union pamphlet declared:

> 'We ask you to *imagine your sisters* in this struggle. We ask you to declare that the conditions of labour on the Rand for young girls shall be such as to safeguard them from the *terrors of prostitution*.'[71]

On a smaller scale, shop-lifting was a way of adding to the meagre income:

> 'Hunger compelled us to do what we would never have done before — namely to steal. The four of us would go to a shop; one would buy something for a few pennies, and the other three would take their chances there. When we got home, everybody had something; one would come with potatoes, the other with something else. In that way we kept hunger at bay.'[72]

On the other hand, poverty and exploitation strengthened the resolve of many workers. For

Women workers pose with their manager, owner of a clothing factory, 1939.

instance, as family breadwinners, women workers learned to be more confident and bolder — hard experience taught them that they would have to use new ways of improving their lives, by making demands for better working conditions and wages through organising into trade unions.

Working class culture

For some workers, especially those young women workers who were not living with their families, the unions came as a blessing. Firstly, organisation gave them the hope that there was something they themselves could do to improve their wages and working conditions. The unions also served as a link between country girls and other workers with their own background. (See the extract from 'Ripe Discovery' on page 225.) Just as African workers formed 'home-boy networks', 'union girls' developed their own cultural activities after working hours.

To get away from their cramped and miserable rooms, union members would organise outings such as picnics, parties, dances and sports days. May Day celebrations became an important social event for workers. And the Garment Workers' Union recognised the growing Afrikaner nationalist movement by organising their own celebrations of the hundredth anniversary of the Great Trek — see the picture on the next page.

The organisers of the GWU were also pioneers in creating workers' theatre. For instance, in the late 1930s, the national organiser, Hester Cornelius, wrote a play called *Die Offerhande* — 'The Sacrifice' — which was described by the union magazine:

> '*Die Offerhande* is an Afrikaans working-class drama that deals with the traditions and life of the platteland people of the 20th century. It describes the struggle of the small farmer; how he battles to maintain his farm but nevertheless falls into misfortune and is forced to turn to digging for a living, in

the passionate hope that one day he will be able to cultivate his farm again. The mother and son become the sacrifices to the cruel Capitalist system.'

However, as workers in that capitalist system, they find hope:

'But a new outcome, a message of a free and better life takes hold of the hearts of the diggers. Workers of the towns, who unite into powerful Trade unions, bring these joyful tidings to the diggers.'[73]

A member of the Garment Workers' Union dressed as a 'Kappie Kommando'. The centenary celebrations of the Great Trek stirred up Afrikaner national consciousness throughout South Africa. The GWU took part in the celebrations, trying bravely to show that nationalism and class struggle need not work against one another.

The importance of the church

But for most Afrikaner workers, the central point of their social lives was the church.[74] The Dutch Reformed Church was a strong link connecting the new urban life with the rural life and the families they had left behind. Sunday was not only a day of spiritual renewal, it was also a time when one could meet other Afrikaners in the same circumstances – *plattelanders*, who spoke the same language, shared similar experiences, and as Christians had similar values and views of life.

One worker, remembering the struggle to survive in her first few years in the city, described the hardships of poverty in the towns – the meals of bread and jam, the holes in the shoes and the threadbare clothes. Yet:

'Each one of us had a hat of some sort, and two pairs of stockings that we wore to go to church. Two pairs of stockings for four girls, so we could go to church two at a time. We always had church money, and put aside two shillings every week, which the deacon collected for the community poor.'[75]

Yet the church itself was slow to adapt to urban conditions. The Carnegie Commission of 1932 – an enquiry conducted by Afrikaner intellectuals into the conditions of poor whites – gently criticised the church for failing to understand the needs of modern industrial society. While the NG Kerk in particular (one of the three main Dutch Reformed churches) had been concerned with the rural poor since the beginning of the century, it was only in a congress in 1934 that the church seriously examined the problem of the Afrikaner poor in the cities. The year before, the *Vrouefederasie* (the Afrikaner women's movement) had also held a conference to discuss this question.

Both organisations then accepted that Afrikaners were in the town to stay, and should be helped to become successful townspeople. This could be achieved, they felt, by pushing for a stronger 'civilised labour' policy and encouraging the creation of reserves for Africans. Many Afrikaner clergymen, teachers, university professors, lawyers, and journalists – who were now becoming active in the Broederbond – urged a solution which lay in the upliftment of the Afrikaner people as a *nation*. They therefore called on Afrikaner workers to support the new 'reformed' Nationalist Party, established after Hertzog's party fused with the South African Party to form the United Party.

Class and Nationalism

Chapter 6 described how there was a battle for the hearts and minds of Afrikaner workers during the 1930s and 1940s. It showed how the industrial unions emphasised *class solidarity* regardless of nationality.

On the other hand, Afrikaner nationalism had strong attractions for the platteland newcomers. Afrikaners had come to the Rand to find a capitalist, English-speaking world that placed little value on their rural skills and way of life. Their language was scorned as 'kitchen Dutch', and they themselves were often regarded as ignorant, simple '*plaasjapies*' – country bumpkins. Of course, black newcomers were also experiencing the 'shock of the city'. Without industrial skills both groups had to start from the bottom as the lowest-paid workers in the job market.

But the Afrikaner nationalist movement promised to uplift the Afrikaner poor. An 'Afrikaner consciousness' developed in the 1920s and 1930s – in much the same way as black consciousness grew in the 1970s. This nationalism aimed to promote the Afrikaans language, education, and culture, as well as economic power. And because Afrikaners had the vote, they had more political influence on the state, and Afrikaner nationalist organisations were able to achieve some of their aims. *The Birth of Afrikaner Capitalism* in Chapter 5, and *Afrikaner Nationalism in the Unions* in Chapter 6, have already described this development.

Chapter 5 showed how the PACT and Nationalist governments set up welfare systems for whites only, began to remove the poor from the mixed slum areas (see Chapter 7), introduced special training schools for skills, and cut down white unemployment by the 'civilised labour' policy, which favoured whites instead of blacks for semi-skilled jobs. The story of Margaret Anderson in *Two Women* on page 245 touches on some of these experiences.

The culture of Nationalism

Gradually, with the policy of upliftment by the state, the church, and cultural organisations, the lives of Afrikaner workers began to change. During the economic boom of World War 2, many improved their standard of living. As more blacks became factory workers, thousands of white women left factory employment after the war to become secretaries or clerical workers, while more and more white men moved into supervisory jobs.

Welcoming the trekker wagons, 1938. 1938 was the centenary of the 'Great Trek'. It was celebrated by driving several ox-wagons from Cape Town along different routes taken by Voortrekkers in the last century. The ox-wagons stopped in hundreds of small towns or *dorps* along the way. 'Passionate enthusiasm seized Afrikaans-speaking South Africa. Men grew beards and women donned Voortrekker dress; street after street in hamlet after hamlet was renamed after one or another trek hero; babies were baptized in the shade of the wagons . . . and young couples were married in full trekker regalia on the village green before the wagons. With tearful eyes old men and women climbed onto the wagons – "Lord, now lettest thou thy servant depart in peace," said one old man – and the younger ones jostled with one another in their efforts to rub grease from the wagon-axles onto their handkerchiefs.' (From *The Rise of Afrikanerdom*, by Dunbar Moodie, p.180.)

By 1948, the Afrikaner National Party had secured most of the votes of Afrikaner workers, and was thus able to come into power. In this way, *nationalism* rather than *class* won the battle for the hearts and minds of Afrikaner workers, and became an integral part of their culture.

Hello, Germiston!

DON'T MISS THE

TRADE UNION RALLY
AND PAGEANT

THURSDAY, 14th MARCH, 1940

TOWN HALL, GERMISTON

8 p.m.

MUSIC!
SONGS!
ACTION!

FIGHT FOR A LIVING WAGE!

A worker's story*: extract from 'Ripe Discovery', April/May 1940

'There was a knock on the door. Bettie went to open it. A dark young woman stepped inside with the words, "Do Anna Cloete and Bettie Groenewald live here?"

Shy and wondering, Bettie answered while she looked at their neatly dressed visitor: "Yes, that's us. Sit down." The newcomer introduced herself. She was Dora van der Walt and she had come to visit the garment workers in the neighbourhood. She wanted to recruit them for her organisation, which was trying to combine all garment workers into a strong union.

They sat on the bed and listened attentively to what Dora was saying. Then Anna shook her head and said: "You won't get the two of us to join, because we earn too little to pay dues. Anyway, only this morning I heard one of the girls at the factory say that the union is just out to get workers into trouble, and then they lose their jobs."

"Yes," added Bettie, "and we don't have the time, either; we're sorry to disappoint you, but we don't believe in foreign things like that."

Dora looked at the two of them rather reproachfully. "Is it foreign for us to try and improve your wages and lift you out of the mud — to free you from your dreary lives in dirty back yards? Are your mothers foreign when they worry over the pathetic little room you live in, when you go hungry because you can't afford to eat properly? No, we want a strong union to protect our fellow workers against poverty and misery. I won't preach any further; I know you are tired, but promise me that tomorrow night you will come to the union meeting. You'll soon find out if it's foreign or not." She stood up to go. "See you tomorrow night at the meeting."

Anna and Bettie looked at each other dumbfounded when she was gone. "I like her. She's so friendly. And I admire her because she gives up her free time to help us." That was Anna's verdict.

Bettie nodded. "Right. Let's go to that meeting tomorrow night. I'll ask Willie to come along. We were going to a film, but now I'm curious to hear what the union people are going to say."

* 'Rype Ondervinding', by 'Klerewerker', *Klerewerker* April/May 1940, p.13. (My translation.)

Jewish Workers on the Rand

Jews played a prominent role in the history of the Rand from its earliest days. An early Jewish manufacturer, Nellmapius, exerted an important influence over Paul Kruger, while other Jews were on the other side — mining capitalists like Lionel Phillips, Solly and Woolf Joel, and Barney Barnato sided with the British during the Anglo-Boer War.

However, Jews were often sharply divided, for they were active in all walks of life on the Rand. Besides the few rich and famous capitalists, or the notorious illegal liquor traders, pimps, and prostitutes in the underworld of the early Rand, or the growing numbers of middle-class professionals, there was a less well-remembered class of Jews.[76] These were the Jewish workers — who were often refugees from anti-Jewish riots and laws in western Russia, Lithuania, and Latvia — amongst the poorest parts of eastern Europe. For centuries, Jews had not been allowed to own land there, and they developed either trades or skills to survive.

When they arrived in South Africa more than half took up their trades on the Rand — for example as tailors or shoemakers — or found work as shop assistants to more established Jews in business (usually, in the early years, in 'native eating houses' or mining concession stores).[77]

Zionists and socialists

They also brought with them a tradition of opposition to Russian Czarist rule, either as Zionists who hoped to create an independent Jewish state in Palestine or, in the case of many working-class Jews at that time, as socialists who preferred to work inside South Africa. This socialism was to have a significant influence on the labour movement in South Africa, for a number of Jews joined or started trade unions and supported black unions — people like Solly Sachs, Eli Weinberg, Ray Alexander, Issy Diamond, Benny Weinbren and Fanny Klenerman (to name but a few) were all Jewish immigrants who were important in the trade union movement.

The Jewish Workers' Club

In the 1920s, thousands of Jews arrived from eastern Europe and many settled on the Rand. In Johannesburg a survey in 1935 found that most Jewish workers were living in the very poor districts of Doornfontein, Bertrams, and Jeppe.[78] Like many Greeks and Indians, those who did not have a skill earned low wages and worked long, hard hours in small trading stores owned by wealthier relatives. The Shop Assistants' Union was formed and organised by this group of Jews.

It was this group of newcomers who formed the Jewish Workers' Club in the late 1920s. The club provided a meeting place for immigrant workers — another 'home boy' club where they could find companionship, attend social events such as dances and picnics, and converse in their native Yiddish, the language of the Jewish masses.

The club drew on rich Yiddish cultural and socialist traditions — it reviewed working-class plays, published Yiddish literature, and conducted debates on labour and political issues. It was active in workers' cultural events. At a May Day meeting in 1935, for example, the Labour Party newspaper reported that the Jewish Workers' Club Choir sang 'The International' and 'We are Builders' in Yiddish.[79]

The club also gave financial support to strike funds and worker education. Its members gave practical support to left-wing and labour organisations. The following is a description of the excitement of the young people who rallied to protect their speakers against possible racist attacks during the by-election campaign of the black CPSA candidate, J B Marks, in Germiston in 1932:

We set out early. It was a lovely morning with the brilliant sunshine and high clear sky of the highveld spring. A sympathiser had provided a motor lorry and onto this we piled speakers, interpreters, an assortment of stalwarts from the Jewish Workers' Club, and girls in their bright cotton frocks. On the way we laid our plans. Our supporters were to stand in close rank round our platform facing the audience and were not to leave their places whatever in the way of disturbance might develop among the crowd. In retrospect there seems something of quite splendid absurdity in our journey that morning — some thirty young dreamers, starry-eyed, a lorryload of laughter setting forth to defeat the oppression of the toiling masses.'[80]

A Jewish tailor stitches canvas in a tent factory.

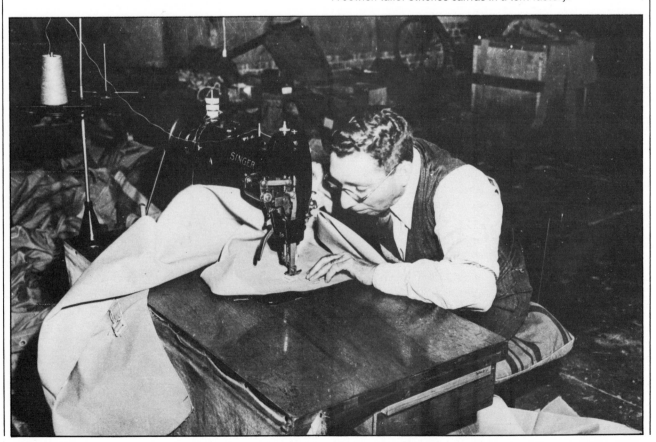

The Jewish Workers' Club became even more directly involved following the rise of anti-Jewish racism, known as anti-semitism, encouraged by the success of the Nazi movement in Germany in the 1930s. Members of the Jewish Workers' Club, along with other Jews, joined Popular Front organisations to fight propaganda against Jews. Anti-semitism found ready followers in South Africa — Jews were blamed for being exploiting capitalists *and* subversive communists. In the mid-thirties, the Nationalist party wanted to limit the number of Jewish immigrants to South Africa. A small but influential organisation calling itself the Ossewa Brandwag was actively anti-semitic, and a group of Nazi supporters called the Greyshirts held rallies at which Jews were attacked in speeches and, at times, physically.

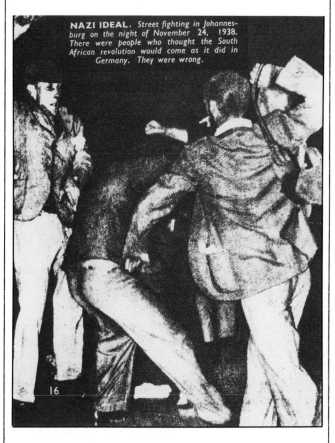

NAZI IDEAL. *Street fighting in Johannesburg on the night of November 24, 1938. There were people who thought the South African revolution would come as it did in Germany. They were wrong.*

16

In 1938 a journalist photographed one of the many clashes between young Jews and the anti-Jewish supporters of Nazism.

Club members, many of them with personal experience of anti-semitism in eastern Europe, felt that they should fight back by holding their own public meetings against Nazism and by trying to break up anti-semitic meetings. There were many fights in the streets and outside the Johannesburg City Hall steps (much to the official disapproval of the Jewish community). A first aid station was even set up in a nearby doctor's rooms so that fighters could be patched up and sent back into the fray. Helping them were volunteers from the Mine Workers' Union, the Furniture Workers'

Union, the Leather Workers' Union, and the Garment Workers' Union.

After World War II thousands of South African Jews learnt of the murder of relatives trapped in concentration camps — Jews, along with gypsies and communists who were too old, too sick, or too young to provide productive slave labour for the Nazi war effort. In all, six million Jews were starved, shot, or gassed to death in these camps — the biggest systematic mass murder in the history of mankind.

The decline of Jewish workers

Like the white working class population of which they were a part, Jewish workers as a group declined with South Africa's rapid economic development during the war. As whites, the children of Jewish workers received free education, and many grew up to become professionals — lawyers, accountants, and doctors — or else went into business. After the slaughter of the Jews in Europe, the struggle for a Jewish state seemed more urgent than ever, and thousands of young Jews became Zionists — some of them in the hope that the new Jewish state would be a socialist one.

Without a working-class base the Jewish Workers' Club lost its influence. The young people were by now fluent in English and integrated into many cultural activities. The cinema, plays, and musical concerts were well patronised by up-and-coming Jews. Yiddish no longer seemed relevant. So when in 1948 the Doornfontein club office burnt down, it seemed a sign that its days had come to an end.

Christianity and the Ancestors

Religion amongst blacks in the towns took three main forms:

1. There were the 'pure' practising Christians, often educated in mission schools, who no longer had any contact with the religion of their ancestors — in many cases, their ties with the land were altogether broken.

2. Then there were those who had never been Christians, or had become disappointed with the Christian faith, and were practising the traditional religion of their ancestors. They still had access to land and considered their homes to be in the rural areas and not in the towns.

3. The majority of townspeople practised a combination of Christianity and ancestor religion.

A procession of members of the separatist Bantu Methodist Church in Pimville.

3. Many belonged in name only to the Christian church. They seldom went to church, but tended to turn to religion mainly in times of trouble — usually to both the Christian and the traditional religions, borrowing from each whatever seemed to have the most meaning under the conditions of town life. Or they joined one of the independent, 'separatist' churches, which drew from both religions[81] and thus reflected the lives of the people of two worlds — migrant workers moving between the new life of the industrial towns, and the more familiar life of the land.

The separatist or independent churches

About a hundred years ago, a movement began for independent black Christian churches, so that they could be free from white supervision. The cause of this move was partly the racial inequality in the church, and partly the fact that many Africans wanted to retain their own customs and ways of life, while still remaining Christian.

The movement also came at a time of great disruption. Through wars and conquest, thousands of people suddenly found themselves dispossessed of land and forced to serve as squatters on Boer farms or as labourers on the mines and in the towns.

And so, in the 1890s, the *Ethiopian* churches were born, so named from a prophecy in the Bible that 'Ethiopia shall soon stretch out her hands to God'.[82] The Ethiopian movement gave birth to a number of churches. One of the first was the American Methodist Episcopal Church. There were also the Bantu Methodist Church, the Zulu Congregation and the Africa Church. These all kept the service and hymn book of the churches they had left behind, but insisted on African leadership. They also held before them the vision of 'Ethiopia' — God's promise of a free, black Africa, ruled by Africans themselves.

Another important family of separatist churches also emerged after a time of upheaval. The Anglo-Boer War uprooted thousands of Africans from their land. Over 100 000 more Africans fled to refugee camps, where a new church, the *Zionist* Church, spread from a small missionary group of Zionists — *'Amaziyoni'* — in Wakkerstroom. Many of the leaders of the Zion churches later recalled that they joined at a time of wandering during the war.[83] The war was followed by the drought of 1903, and famine. Then in Zululand came the rebellion against the poll tax imposed by the British in Natal. Like the Ethiopians, the Zionists had a vision of a God-given land, a society living in freedom, peace, order, and love. They longed for Mount Zion, a sacred place as promised in the Old Testament.

Some independent Christian churches included more African traditions than others. For instance, many churches kept the traditional use of ashes as a symbol of healing and forgiveness, and to appease ancestors. All the separatist churches retained a deep respect for ancestors.

The church services were much freer than western Christian forms. For example, many independent churches scorned prayers written in a book — they felt that the western form of prayer was too stiff and lacking in expression. Instead, they used sacred dance, the singing of hymns to the beat of the drum or clapping, loud rhythmic 'testimonies' or confessions, and 'speaking in tongues'. For their members, the Saviour was a black Christ. In the words of a Nazarite Church hymn of the 1930s:

'Africa rise!
And seek thy Saviour.
Today our sons and daughters are slaves.'[84]

The separatist churches in town

As industrialisation spread and the towns grew, so did the new churches. For many workers, the church was an important way to express their feelings. Out in the open veld, next to the healing waters of streams, away from the eyes of the whites, or in tiny yard or location rooms, people crowded to weekend meetings for prayer and healing. In the words of a missionary in 1930:

'The mine labourer and the kitchen boy and the policeman and the clerk, and the honorable army of Bantu women who have worked hard all week washing and ironing — all these take a pride in their Church which is their very own.'[85]

Baptism in a Johannesburg stream. Water was important in cleansing and healing rituals in many of the black churches.

African Judeo-Christianity. A church prelate with a worshipper, who had arrived in his worker's clothes but changed into traditional dress for the service.

During the week, workers had to live in a harsh world dictated by the employer. The lives of compound and domestic workers were controlled even outside working hours. Thus the free and emotional singing, praying, and dancing of the independent church services provided an outlet for people's pent-up feelings. The church promised to follow them and care for them in times of trouble. Its fellowship brought its members warmth and comfort in the bitter world of strangers and poverty.

The largest separatist church on the Rand was the African Methodist Episcopal Church (AME) which took its form from the black American Episcopal Church. By the late 1930s, it had 7 000 members, with 1 000 waiting to be accepted. The Zionist churches, which were more 'African' than the AME, had been spread to the Rand by migrant workers from Zululand and Natal.

In general, the other separatist churches were small and scattered in the towns during the 1930s. For example, the Nations Church of Christ in Africa had only 53 members in 1938, all in Alexandra township; the Church of God Apostolic Jerusalem in Zion had 50 members across the whole of the Rand; the Christ Apostolic Holy Spirit Church in Zion of South Africa had 230 members.[86]

In the years to come, as more and more black

workers streamed to the towns, the separatist churches took on greater social meaning. Their fellowship and warmth brought comfort to the poorly paid or unemployed black newcomers who were struggling to make sense of the hostile world of capitalist industrial society. In the towns many a humble labourer, cleaner, or 'night-watch boy' served his or her people as a highly respected preacher and spiritual leader after working hours.

Religion as resistance

Many black Christians in the 1920s and 1930s tried hard to live 'respectable' lives and win acceptance from white Christians. On the other hand, many were very critical of white society and joined opposition movements. For instance, during the 1920s many black Christians were also members of the African National Congress. Indeed, many leaders of the ANC, like the Rev. Calata, were also religious leaders.

But the practising Christians were only a small minority of the black population in the towns. Most people belonged to the second and third categories — those who rejected Christianity, or combined Christian and ancestor religions to fit in with their migrant way of life between town and countryside.

For both these groups, the white man's Christianity was at least partly resisted because it seemed to have taken more away than it gave to blacks. For example, A W G Champion, Natal leader of the ICU, related the bitterness of losing land to losing faith in the religion of the white rulers:

> 'As from 1913 [the Land Act] we knew one thing — there is no God with the white man!'[87]

People who had been taught the Christian code of brotherly love arrived in the towns to find the gross inequalities and the heartlessness of a racist, competitive society. Although most whites professed to be Christians, they did not have '*Ubuntu*' — that concern and warmth and fellow-feeling so valued in traditional society.

As the journalist and political leader R. V. Selope Thema wrote in *The Bantu World* in 1936:

> 'There are Africans who, on account of the un-Christian attitude of the majority of Europeans, are beginning to question whether or not it pays to follow the white man in his journey along Christian lines. Some go so far as to say Christianity is an instrument of oppression; it is an institution which has been exploited by Europeans for their own ends; for it tames warlike tribes and thus enables the white man to impose his will upon them. This belief is not general, but that it is gaining ground no man can deny. Christianity is now being weighed in the balance all over Africa where the white

man has come into contact with the black man. Here and there the new African is questioning the sincerity of the white man in so far as Christianity is concerned.'[88]

Church welfare

On the other hand, the churches made an important practical contribution to the lives of black towns-people. They were almost the only bodies to respond with essential services which, as we saw in Chapter 7, the state failed to provide for blacks — the clinics, schools, and advice offices which any community requires.

The Anglican, Catholic and Methodist priests, ministers, and nuns tried to set these up in as many places as possible. But the resources of the churches were limited — they could not hope to cover the needs of all the neglected and exploited communities that were growing ever faster on the Rand in the 1930s, so their services tended to be restricted to a few areas.

At that time, most established church officials were middle-class whites, and many (although not all) were themselves affected by the racist attitudes common in South Africa — some of the most well-meaning and liberal people had paternalistic attitudes towards the poor. The people they helped, some felt, were like children — 'ignorant' and 'morally backward' because they were poor and because they were black. Many of these missionaries confused Christian teachings with middle-class western European culture and customs — behaving as if the two were one and the same thing. Several decades were to pass before black Christians pointed out this confusion and challenged it in the name of black theology.

Nevertheless, the dedication and hard work of the churches had an important effect on many people who were later to become community and national leaders. Their work deserves to be remembered and valued.

Healing

In the township world of low wages, poor feeding and regular child deaths, healing was a very important part of religion, and it was not only the Christian churches that tried to provide bodily as well as spiritual healing.

In traditional society, healing, prophecy, and prayer went together. Healing could not be lasting without prophecy and prayer. In the words of one observer:

> 'The practice of medicine and religious experience spring from a common root.'[89]

On the other hand, European medical treatment looked only at the needs of the body. It did not consider the wholeness of the person. For many black townspeople, uprooted and torn from the land, this approach to healing was incomplete, and they as often turned to the *inyanga* (diviner and herbal doctor) or to the spritual healers and prophets of their church, as they did to the western-trained doctor.

Above: 'Medicine men' in town. Traditionally, healing and religious experience sprang 'from a common root'.

Below: Children in Prospect Township, 1937.

Children of the Ghetto

The first dangerous years

The first point to note about children born in the ghetto is that the majority never lived beyond their first birthday.[90] The first few years of life were highly dangerous for most black town children. Chapter 7 has described the conditions that led to this high death rate — the lack of water, the poor food supply, the absence of a sewerage system and the overcrowding. Town life was

so uncertain for the very young that many anxious parents preferred to send their children to be brought up in the more spacious and cleaner surroundings of the countryside.'

Divided families

In the 1920s and 1930s, more than half of the children born to black women in the towns lived away from their parents — for at least part of their childhood —usually in the charge of rural relatives.[91] But already in the 1930s the rural areas were declining. In the following extract from *Down Second Avenue*, Ezekiel Mphahlele describes these hard times in the life of a child in the country.

'But all in all perhaps I led a life shared by all other country boys. Boys who are aware of only one purpose of living; to be. Often the crops failed us. Mother sent us a few tins of jam and we ate that with corn-meal [mealie meal]. Sometimes she sent us sugar which we ate with the porridge. Other times we ate roasted flying ants or hairy tree worms or wild spinach with porridge. I can never forget how delicious a dish we had by making porridge out of pumpkin and corn meal. The only time we tasted tea and bread was when our mother came to see us at Christmas. On such occasions many other people in the village came to our home to taste these rare things. If hunting was bad we didn't have meat. About the only time we had goat's meat or beef was when the livestock died. A man might have a herd of fifty or more goats, as we had, and slaughter one in six months. I can never forget the stinking carcasses we feasted on. Often we just ate practically dry boiled corn.'[92]

But the growing poverty of the land forced the mother to take her children back to town:

'I never dreamt I should go back to the city, which I couldn't picture in my mind anyhow. We thrilled at the idea of riding a train, my brother and sister and I, when our mother came in the middle of the year to tell us that she had come to fetch us. Three things stick in my mind about those few days . . . . First, my grandmother cried. I had only seen her cry at revival services at the Methodist church house. I knew my mother couldn't just come in the middle of the year like that to move a hard-hearted mother-in-law to tears with a kind of domestic joke. Secondly, mother shook off our lousy rags and scrubbed us clean and wrapped us up in brand new clothes. That couldn't be a joke either. I overheard her say to grandmother: "I can't change my mind, any more than I can change your son. They're my children and I'm taking them away." Thirdly, those bright lights we found on Pietersburg station after travelling many miles of dusty road . . . . The train arrived. I was too dazed to be happy. Too frightened to ask questions. We found ourselves at Pretoria station the next day. In the midst of a winter's morning we were whisked away by a taxi-cab to Marabastad, a black location.'[93]

Learning and education

The education of black children in the towns was left entirely in the hands of the parents. Schooling was neither free nor compulsory, nor was it the responsibility of the state to provide schools or teachers for black children (although it did so for white children). The few black schools in the towns were run by missionaries and church groups, who usually tried to keep the fees as low as possible. The schools were usually grossly overcrowded, though, and all the classes were often held in one large room, the church hall. Most town parents were well aware of the benefits of schooling. They realised that knowledge of reading, writing and arithmetic, as well as the English language, were economically useful to every town worker. So nearly every child who lived near enough attended school at least some of the time. But in the world of poverty children are also needed to help bring in extra money. Absence from school was therefore common. For example:

Pimville children at play. Few children managed to attend school regularly.

'A teacher in the Albert School informed me that the school attendance on Mondays and Fridays is considerably lower than on other days. The following were the reasons for absence from school given by a teacher in the New Doornfontein School by sixteen children: errands for parents, 7; sickness, 3; fetching washing for mother, 3; looking after baby (while mother at work), 2; attending a wedding, 1.'[94]

(See also *A Day in the Life of a Ghetto Child*.)

In the homestead society, education and life ran side by side, and children's everyday tasks were part of their education. In the towns, schooling was not only a way of life imposed on black people by a white ruling class, it was also a means of training black children to become docile workers in an industrial society. The lessons taught in school were not relevant to the everyday life of the ghetto or slum.

The economic activity of children

Industrial life changed the nature of learning for children. They no longer absorbed the skills of the grown-ups just by watching them at work. In the towns, the fathers worked away from home, and their children had no practical knowledge of how they earned their living. In the towns, there could be no task set to the small boy, like the task of herd boy in the countryside.

On the other hand, most little town girls watched and helped their mothers with the washing, ironing, cooking and scrubbing. And as *A Day in the Life of a Ghetto Child* shows, boys were often expected to help with the household chores, too. Besides running errands, older children also had to stay home to look after the younger children on mothers' work days. They also played an important role in the process of beer brewing, acting as *izimbamgothi* – guards – who stood outside to look out for the police. Their warning cry, 'Araraai!' is mentioned in the novels of Modikwe Dikobe and Peter Abrahams.[95]

Township children found many ways to earn money directly themselves. They took part-time and temporary jobs (for very little money) whenever they had the chance. They found jobs in shops and offices as messengers; or in sweeping and cleaning, making tea, or delivering dairy milk; they got domestic work in the kitchens or gardens of houses in the white suburbs; they worked as caddies on the golf courses, sold newspapers in the streets, and delivered them to houses. Often, they were tipped or given food by hawkers for help in getting customers; or they constructed home-made carts from old boxes and wheels to carry the washing for women from the station to the bus terminus.

The children of the poor were constantly on the lookout for ways of making a few cents. Where they could not find jobs, many children turned to begging, pickpocketing, or small-scale stealing. (See *Crime and Punishment*.) They would form themselves into small gangs and go out looking for opportunities to grab whatever they could find, either as a group or separately. When they reported back, the members would pool their money, food, and spoils, and then share them out amongst themselves. Ghetto life thus taught children to be independent and fend for themselves. From an early age they learnt to join in their parents' struggle to survive.

Helping to supplement the family income – child labour at a railway station.

A Day in the Life of a Ghetto Child

I did most of the domestic work, because my sister and brother were still too small. My uncles were considered too big. I woke up at 4.30 in the morning to make fire in a brazier fashioned out of an old lavatory bucket. I washed, made breakfast coffee for the family and tea for grandmother as she did not like coffee . . . .

After morning coffee, which we often had with mealie-meal porridge from the previous night's leftovers, we went to school. Back from school I had to clean the house as Aunt Dora and grandmother did the white people's washing all day. Fire had to be made, meat had to be bought from an Indian butchery in the Asiatic Reserve. We were so many in the family that I had to cook porridge twice in the same big pot. We hardly ever bought more than a pound of mutton. Week-days supper was very simple: just porridge and meat. When there was no money we fried tomatoes. We never ate vegetables except on Sundays. We never had butter except when we had a visitor from Johannesburg. Same with custard . . . .

On Monday mornings, at about four o'clock, I started off for the suburbs to fetch washing for Aunt Dora. Thursday and Friday afternoons I had to take back the washing. If I was lucky enough I borrowed a bicycle from a tenant of ours we called simply 'Oompie' – uncle – when he was not using it on his rounds in the location collecting numbers from gamblers for the Chinaman's fahfee. If I couldn't get the bicycle for the morning or afternoon I carried the bundles on my head and walked – about seven miles' single journey. Like all other tenants, Oompie sometimes quarrelled with grandmother over tidiness. I was sure, then, that I wasn't going to get the bicycle. When I walked I couldn't use the pair of tennis shoes I'd bought for Sunday wear. Winter mornings were most trying when the air penetrated the big cracks round the edges of my feet.

When I came back I went to school. I could never do my homework until about ten o'clock at night when I had washed up and everybody else had gone to bed. We all slept in the same room which had boxes of clothing and a kitchen dresser. My aunt and her husband slept in the room which had a table and chairs.

Because we were so many in the family, there was only one bedstead – a three-quarter institution occupied by grandmother and Aunt Dora's children. The wooden floor of the room we slept in had two large holes. There was always a sharp young draught coming up from underneath the floor. Coupled with this our heads were a playground for mice which also did havoc to food and clothing.[96]

(From *Down Second Avenue*, by Ezekiel Mphahlele.)

Memories of a 'Poor White' Childhood[97]

Living in Denver

As far as I can remember we were the only whites living with blacks – with coloureds and blacks. We lived in a semi-detached house and next door there was a coloured woman who was a shebeen queen. Her name was Mrs Mynhard. She was quite an affluent member of our community, considering our standards of living at that time. She had a car.

We were sharing our rooms. In the front bedroom was a coloured woman living there. The lounge was our bedroom, and the dining room was occupied by an African man and his wife. But you mustn't forget that there were changes. We had actually Europeans living with us in the beginning – Germans, the Stoppels – she was divorced – then they left and then a coloured couple moved in.

At the back of the house was the 'native quarters', a run-down, ramshackle little place and that was occupied by a couple.

Across the road from us there was an Afrikaans family, living on the corner of Crystal and Sanders Streets. Their son was quite a lad, had up for many charges – assault, rape was one of them.

Round the other side, in another portion of the area, which wasn't very far from us, lived a lot of 'neat' Europeans – they were the miners and other similar workers. Some of them lived in houses that belonged to the mines – they were quite wealthy in that they owned motor cars and they had a home of their own. We were the poorest in the community – there were none other poorer than we were.

My father was working. It was the time of the depression . . . he had a job in a butchery as a blockman. He received somewhere about R12 a month at the time. He used to commute to work on a bicycle which had a broken handle. I remember that, and he had a carrier in the front. He used to put me in the carrier and take me for a ride. That was my form of entertainment.

My mother didn't work. She couldn't speak English very well, you know. She wasn't skilled in any form of work.'

Food

'My mother used to economise in many ways. We used to go early in the morning, on Wednesday morning, to Fotheringham's Bakery, which was three or four miles away. She would take one bag and I would take one bag. We would get there as early as possible so that the coloureds and Africans wouldn't take first position in the line. When the bloke opened up the hatch, he would give the less stale bread to the first in the queue, and those at the end of the queue would get the rock hard bread, which was two or three days old.

We would buy about a dozen loaves of bread, and we would go home and she would keep the bread until we needed it for our meals, and she would soak it in a basin of water. By the time it came to the last loaf of bread, which was about a week after we had bought it, it had turned a bit mouldy – then we couldn't eat it, so we had

Magazine cover, 1942.

to make sure we ate as much as possible as soon as possible.

Our meals consisted principally of beans, string beans. This was our staple food — we had that and nothing else, just the bread. Usually the meal would last us two or three days. She would just heat it up — stewed beans, with tomato.

At the weekends, the best time of all, Maud Mynhard — she was very kind to us — would send over a plate of chicken and rice, pumpkin, and potatoes. I remember it to this day. So we would have a plate of potatoes, rice, chicken, and pumpkin — we would have chicken for that week. She was very good to us. My parents when they were alive always remembered her and were grateful to her. She was quite well off, you see.

The perils and rewards of brewing

Maud was related to a woman up the road who was also a shebeen queen. I'll never forget the story she once told me about Detective Smit, who was the terror of the area because he would raid regularly. We used to stand cavey — we used to watch out to see if these blokes were coming, and we would signal. We would be standing up to six blocks away at various points and there would be somebody standing there. And of course then they would get rid of the beer, which they had dug into the ground. They used to dig quite deeply into the grass.

They used to come with long spikes, the police, and they used to dig into the ground and they would hit the drum, you see. So they would dig all over the ground,

trying to find the drum. So what they did, in order to avoid the detection of this beer, they used to dig deeper than what the spike was, the length of the spike, so that they couldn't reach the drum — say twelve feet deep instead of six — and then they would put a pipe connected to the beer and they would suction off the beer. She and Helen, who lived up the road, were very wealthy women — to me at any rate. In my eyes, nearly everyone was wealthier than we were; we were the poorest, and they were exceptionally rich. She had a motor car, and a European boy friend.

The mines were close by. It was not the industrial site it is today. There were hundreds of blacks, pitching up at weekends, coming to drink, and every weekend there was either a death, a murder, or a rape — there was never a weekend when you didn't get one of these things happening. So that is how they made their money. So blacks were involved — Indians, there was an Indian family across the road. They were well off as well.

Friends

We were all well integrated, we all had very few problems with each other. There was a sense of community, a sense of camaraderie, and there was a sense of belonging, too. Our common enemy was the cops, because they were denying them a living.

One of my very good friends was Poona Poon, and his brother. They were blacks. I remember he was a very good piano player — he had a piano at home. He lived around the corner and he used to play the piano very well. He had nine toes. He taught himself and he was very good. He lived in a little *kaya* — a nice house — they were also involved with liquor.

But there was a general sense of happiness, and there was a general sense of belonging. There was the outside world, even in our groups that were formed which involved blacks and Indians — the Python Gang, the Panther Gang, and the Eagles. We fought the Europeans from Rosherville — the mining area. But there wasn't any colour discrimination. We belonged to the Panthers and even I went along to the Good Hope bioscope and the Rio bioscope, because I felt I belonged to them, you see.

My mother, of course, and my father I think, suffered very badly from it all . . . . My father was much too frightened to do anything, he didn't want to get involved. I remember he was bitten by a dog once which belonged to one of the European friends I used to try and fraternise with, and he wouldn't take any action because he was scared of the law. He didn't have any money anyway. He was a frightened man at the time.

They never really felt that they belonged. But I identified myself as a black. I went to bioscope with them, I dressed like them. I wore takkies — if I went to the Rio bioscope I wore black takkies. We went to the mine dumps together. We went to the 'slippery slops' together. I didn't identify with the Europeans. We spoke Afrikaans – it wasn't an English environment. It was a very broken-down Afrikaans that we spoke.

I was actually afraid of Europeans. We used to go to their schools – the very school that I eventually went to – begging for food. I didn't see it as begging at the time, you know. We used to go and stand at the gates and wait for the breaks, and the children would come out. They always gave me the food, you see, because I was obviously European – I never realised it at the time. They always liked taking me, the other kids, because the other children saw me as a European amongst the blacks, you see, and they would hand me the sandwiches, so I would share with my friends. And I remember once when I was looking in the dustbins at the school, for food that had been thrown away by the other school kids, the 'watchboy', the *matshingalane* – we used to call him the *matshingalane* – chased me away. We were always looking out for the *matshingalane* because he was the one who always caused problems with us kids.

School

When I went to the Hellenic School – I was seven or eight when I started – I had a skin disease, I was malnutritioned, and I had tuberculosis. The social welfare department sent a social welfare officer to check up on whether I was being fed properly and

regularly. The Transvaal Helping Hand Society used to hand us food parcels which my mother used to sell in order to clothe me. They wanted to take me away, as a matter of fact – they wanted to put me in an institution and my father fought against it.

When I went to school I was always shy, frightened. I felt I was equal, but I was intimidated, first of all by their wealth and also by their appearance. They looked clean, and I never had a bath. It was maybe once a month I would have a wash. My feet were black. I remember a white boy who came to see us once only. I was very friendly with him at school. I was quite old then, I must have been about eleven or twelve. And I was playing with my friends, and my feet were black. I used to go to bed like that; we never had sheets. We used to sleep between blankets and the place was swarming with bugs. My feet were black and I was so embarrassed because this friend of mine was a nice boy. He left me his bicycle – he died early in life, leukaemia I think. And his mom came to visit us – she was a widow – with this young bloke, and caught me in my natural surroundings. I was very embarrassed about my home. I became conscious of my poverty. You see, I was fairly old at the time . . . .

Then they put me apart in class because I was covered in sores, and because the other mothers protested that their children, their kids, were sitting next to this bloke who had – what was the name of my disease? – *vuilsiekte*, which means filthy disease. Then of course the school doctor who used to come around had to bandage my legs, because my legs were

A social worker talks to undernourished children. White children benefited from welfare programmes promoted by the state.

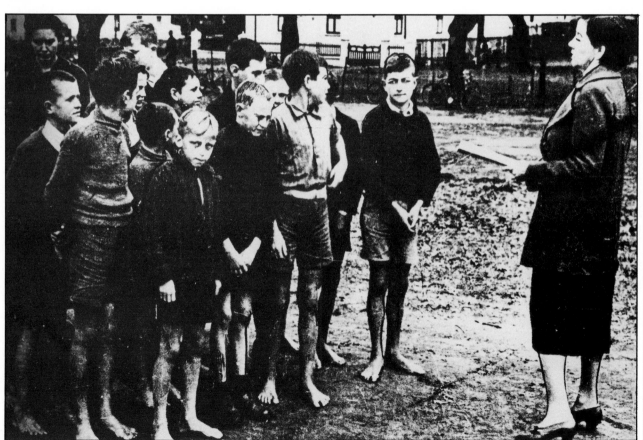

THE WORLD THE WORKERS MADE

never bandaged properly, and these sores were always exposed, especially on the flexors of the arms, the flexors of the legs, behind my ears. Of course this created tremendous emotional trauma in me at the time. I would go out during the break period and I would sit by myself, you see.

I remember I was one of the fastest swimmers. Do you know why I was one of the fastest swimmers in the school, eventually when we did sports? Because I used to swim in Rosherville Dam, you see. And I used to swim across the dam and back. This is how I used to entertain myself with my African friends. And when I went to school I was quite a good swimmer. But I didn't want to go swimming because I couldn't put my trunks on because there I was, covered with sores. And that was the picture.

Moving upwards

We must have stayed in Denver about twelve or fourteen years. Then we moved from there and we stayed next to the railway station. The house was very old and broken down. I think I must have been about fifteen. We had moved out of **Moddergat**. We had moved from Denver into Malvern; we moved into the area of the Europeans, but on the border . . . . And when I look at those houses today, I can't believe that in my child's mind these were magnificent dwelling places.

Our Malvern house was pure corrugated iron — it wasn't brick, it wasn't anything else but corrugated iron . . . . All the windows were barred. You never had a window you could open because of the robberies, and the fights that used to take place. I never knew what it was to have an open window. There were bars, and the windows were tied with wire, and we had no fence because that had been knocked down and people used to walk right past our front door, the Africans, so that they could go to the shebeen that was next door, you see . . . . And it was right on the railway line. You could hear the trains passing right through the night. But it was ours, our own little spot, and it was definitely nobody else's.

Then we moved from there into Jules Street, and that was our first brick house, and the windows could be opened. I'll never forget that, because I could open the windows, and I used to always have my bed next to the window so that I could see the stars. It was quite an experience for me — I had never known that before.

And then I turned eighteen and our conditions improved. My father began to earn more money and he became a partner with a chap by the name of Keele, who took him for a ride — made him work very hard. He had one afternoon off, and that was a Thursday. And he used to work through all the festive holidays. There wasn't a day he had off except on a Thursday afternoon. He would come home, and in the afternoon he would go to the market place, my mother and my father — that was the big occasion, when things had gone better —

and we would buy vegetables and come home and we would have a good meal.

That is how things slowly improved.

Meeting an old friend

'What happened to your other friends? Did you still keep in touch with them?'

Yes. I'll tell you a rather sad story about that. This chap with the nine toes, hey, who was a good piano player? Poona Poon was an African boy, a good friend of mine. It was quite a few years ago, I was outside the Colosseum bioscope — and I think was unmarried at the time. And this African chap came across, he saw me, and approached me. And I looked at him and there was just something about him that triggered off . . . some memory in my mind, of something past, you see. And he said to me:

'Are you . . . Jack?'

So I said, '. . . Yes.'

And he said, 'My name is Poona Poon.'

So I said, 'Poona Poon from Denver?' He said, 'Yes.' So I said, 'My God!' and I threw my arms around him and I hugged him. And he was as stiff as a ramrod — you know, he didn't reciprocate in his affection. I hugged him and I squeezed him and I said, 'Poona Poon, it's so beautiful to see you!' I said, 'What are you doing? What's happened to you?'

And then he said to me, 'Baas,' he said, 'can you give me a job?'

I almost hit him, you know that? I almost hit him I was so cross. Here I was trying to — you know what I mean — I saw him as an equal. I always saw him as an equal. And I thought to myself, 'My God! How can you ask me for a job?' You know what I mean? That was one story. That was the gap that developed after we left.

'I suppose part of the difference was that as a white you were able to rehabilitate yourself?'

Yes! Could you imagine if I wasn't a white, hey? . . . 'Baas, can you give me a job?' And he was a good pianist! He played well. We used to sit and watch him play. He played by ear — he never had any lessons of any sort . . . . Ja, it's a long road we've travelled.

An industrial school for the children of the poor.

Politics and Protest

The vote was a form of political power which divided the workers racially. Most black workers in South Africa did not have the vote, whereas white workers did. Poor as many of them were, they could influence state policies because the Labour and Nationalist parties needed their votes. This was clearly seen when these two parties formed the Pact government and took power in 1924.

In 1930, the racial divisions were widened when the vote was granted to white women, many of whom were workers, while black women, along with black men (except for some property owners in the Cape) remained voteless. (*Labour Laws in the 1920s* on page 152 describes in more detail how the state favoured white workers.) So black political parties had to find ways other than the vote to put pressure on the rulers of South Africa.

Early black politics

Most of the earliest black political parties in the towns were formed after the Anglo-Boer War. For example, the African People's Organisation (APO) was formed in 1903 and based in Cape Town, with a largely coloured membership. A 'Native Vigilance Association' based in the Transkei, a 'South African Native Congress' based in the western Cape and an 'Orange River Colony Native Congress' were formed in 1902 and 1903.

All these organisations were bitterly disappointed by the failure of the British to recognise the rights of blacks after they had won the war. They had hoped that the rights held by blacks in the Cape would be extended to the rest of the country. These were limited rights, but to black leaders at that time they represented the first steps on the road to freedom. Instead, even these rights were disallowed in the rest of South Africa. In 1903 the vote was granted to whites only in the Transvaal; in the same year the Transvaal government announced a policy of racial segregation in housing; and in 1904 a job colour bar became the rule on the mines.

In the rural areas, too, hopes were dashed. Many blacks had hoped that a British victory would bring a return of the land they had lost to Boers in recent years. Asian and coloured people were also disappointed. In the Transvaal and Orange Free State, Asians continued to be prohibited from owning land, and in 1906 the Transvaal governor introduced a regulation to register all Indians by taking their fingerprints.

Black leaders felt that the British had 'sold out' to appease the Boers. In 1908, the white political leaders

A Sunday meeting, mid-1930s.

held a National Convention to discuss how the four provinces of the Transvaal, the Cape, Natal and the Orange Free State might unite. It drew up a blueprint which excluded all blacks from parliament, denied blacks the vote in the Transvaal, the Orange Free State and Natal, and even allowed for the possibility of taking away the black vote in the Cape if more than two thirds of the members of parliament wanted it.

The following year, 60 black leaders held a South African Native Convention to protest against the 'illiberal and short-sighted' views of the white leaders of South Africa.

A family photograph of H I Bud 'Mbelle, taken soon after the founding of the African National Congress. In the early years, most members were professional men, landowners or chieftains.

The birth of the African National Congress

The most significant African political party in later years was the African National Congress, formed in 1912. It was a direct response to the planning of the Land Act, which aimed to remove land ownership from Africans in all but proclaimed 'reserves'. Its focus of resistance was therefore the restoration of land and property rights.

The new Congress considered that its most important task was to unite Africans from all chiefdoms, in order to strengthen the black population as a whole. Its members consisted mainly of professional men, land-owners, and chiefs, and its policy in the early years was to use their educational skills to put pressure on the British and South African governments by petitions and deputations to explain their plight. These were largely ignored.

The African National Congress, Bloemfontein, 1930. *Front row, left to right*: Albert Nzula, Johnny Gomas, next two unidentified, Elliot Tonjeni. *Second row*: first six unidentified, J T Gumede, Chief Mandlesilo Nkosi, Z R Mahabane, Chief Stephen Mini, next two unidentified, Pixley ka I Seme. *Third row*: Edwin Mofutsanyana, next four unidentified, S M Masabalala, Thomas Mpikela, L T Mvabaza, S M Magatho, unidentified, Mazingi, unidentified. *Back row*: P Phatlane, Dave Mark, unidentified, R V Selope Thema, C D Modiakgotla, A W G Champion, Bhulose, Theodore Lujiza, A M Rakaoane, T D Mweli Skota, unidentified, Morris Somtunzi, H S Msimang, unidentified. The activities of a number of these people have already been mentioned in earlier chapters.

A militant period

But rapid changes in the Rand towns forced the leadership into more active politics for a time. Chapter 4 described how blacks continued to stream into the towns looking for jobs, particularly after the 1913 Land Act began to deny the use of white-owned land to black sharecroppers. World War I pushed up the cost of living, while wages remained the same, causing greater hardship for workers and waves of protests which alarmed the government and management. Although the Congress leadership was largely drawn from the educated and professional classes, the racial oppression felt by Africans regardless of class pushed the Transvaal leaders into making common cause with Africans of all groups. They were active in much of the protest at this time.

But after the 1920 black miners' strike was crushed, the ANC leaders seemed to lose their fire. Not long after the strike, ANC leaders met at the Smuts government's first Native Conference to consider the outline of the proposed Urban Areas Act (discussed in Chapter 7). When the Act was passed, the ANC expressed its anger and disappointment, especially at the clauses which did away with African land ownership in the towns. Yet in the end it reluctantly accepted the terms of the law − provided that housing was improved in the black-owned locations and black trading rights were granted.

Yet neither of these demands touched the main problems of workers − the miserably low wages, the control of labour and the total lack of decent living conditions in the slums and yards of the inner city. As the ANC retreated, its popularity as the champion of the black masses was overtaken by that of the ICU (discussed in Chapter 4).

Many of the younger members of the ANC had moved

into more militant activities. For example, two thirds of the delegates to the 1927 annual ICU meeting were, or had been, members of the ANC. Other ANC members joined the Communist Party. The ANC moderates came to be looked down on by the militants as 'the good boys' club' and 'the old brigade'.[98]

During the 1920s, it was the ICU that led the mass of the people. And its greatest rival was not the ANC but the Communist Party. It was the ICU that led demonstrations against the Urban Areas Act in Johannesburg and delayed the removal of blacks from the city's slumyards. The ICU, backed by the Communist Party, voiced the strong feelings of black workers when the Pact Government tried to introduce night passes for women in 1925. The ICU was also active in small towns near the farming areas – for example, there were protest demonstrations by black workers in Middelburg, Rouxville and Kroonstad.[99]

In the late 1920s, however, the President General of the ANC, J T Gumede, became more radical as a result of his travels to Europe (including the Soviet Union – see page 166). Also, a number of Communist Party members joined Congress after they were expelled from the ICU. In 1930 the majority of ANC delegates, threatened by the left-wingers who wanted to push a more militant policy inside the ANC, voted a more conservative president into power: Pixley Ka I. Seme.

A liberal policy

This was not to say that the conservatives did not feel strongly about the injustices in South Africa. The ANC policy was clearly anti-racist, but liberal rather than radical. It emphasised the need for extending the vote, dropping racial discrimination and working towards equal rights for all civilised men.[100] It believed in representations to those in power rather than in the necessity of collective action. Congress members spoke powerfully to the Native Economic Commission (1930 to 1932) about the unjust and unequal treatment of blacks throughout the country. But an important part of Seme's evidence stressed the needs of the middle class, and the importance of building up a black, property-owning and trading class, free of racial restrictions. He said in his evidence:

> 'The good policy to follow is to encourage the Native to own property whenever possible. This would encourage thrift and enterprise among them. There is a great need for developing this class of Native in urban areas in order to counteract the evils of rowdyism . . . . The better class Natives, who are compelled to accommodate themselves uncomfortably in locations, would invest their money in private stands in these townships, and they would continue to work in town, and on their own, wherever possible.'

Concerning greater opportunities for blacks in trade and commerce he advised:

Pixley Ka I Seme, who was elected President of the ANC in 1930.

'The Natives should be given freedom of trade amongst their own people; for instance, the mines are given the exclusive privilege of trading with the Natives; the Natives are excluded from trading with the Natives on the mines.'[101]

It was the concern of the ANC to build up a prosperous black middle class with property and land, to pave the way for an economically vigorous African nation.

The All-African Convention

In 1935, 500 black delegates met in Bloemfontein at the all-African Convention (the AAC). For the first time since 1910 blacks from all racial groups were represented – Africans, coloureds and Indians. The ANC was the largest organisation there.

The convention was brought together to protest against two laws proposed by the Hertzog-Smuts government in 1935. The first law removed the vote from Africans in the Cape. Instead, Africans could elect a Native Representative Council to advise the government on African affairs and they could also elect four whites to parliament. The second law, the Native Trust and Land Bill, added a little more land to the reserves but at the same time took away the right of Cape Africans to buy land outside the reserves.

These laws were clearly racist. As well as removing further rights from the black masses, they also aimed to stunt any growth of the tiny African middle class of the time. The AAC and ANC sent a deputation to the Prime Minister, Hertzog, who was very charming and nearly persuaded them to accept a special compromise for Cape Africans. Hertzog suggested that they be allowed to vote for an extra three *white* members of parliament. He appealed to them to be reasonable.

But two young executives of the AAC, Dr A B Xuma and Dr James Moroka, had heard of the wavering of the older men and rushed to Cape Town. In the discussions with the Prime Minister that followed, Moroka politely rejected the offer saying that indeed,

'I want the vote to be extended from the Cape to the Free State and the Transvaal – to the whole country!'

At that time it still seemed possible to achieve votes for at least middle-class blacks throughout the country, and so change the system through parliamentary means.

The ANC's rival

In the meantime, the Communist Party began to embark on a policy of activism in communities as well as trade unions after its decision to work for a Black Republic, as described in Chapter 6. It was successful

in a number of small town locations, especially after the decline of the ICU. Chapter 7 has described the housing shortages and high rents, the distances from work and expensive transport, and the lack of health and other facilities that most blacks had to suffer in the towns. In addition, black townspeople were subjected to the mass of municipal regulations described in 'Laws for Non-Europeans Only'.

Counting the votes. While white men – and after 1930, white women too – had the vote, all except a few propertied black men in the Cape were denied the right to vote in general elections. After 1936, this right, too, was removed from Africans in the Cape.

In Natal, beer brewers became the militant leaders of resistance to municipal monopolies on liquor in the locations. In Ladysmith, for example, 150 women, armed with sticks, marched to the jail to demand the release of beer brewers who had been arrested. They attacked a force of policemen who tried to stop them. The battle lasted for half an hour, and a number of policemen were injured.

In Durban there were a number of riots in 1929 and 1930 resulting from the municipal monopoly on beer which deprived Durban's black women of a living. During this time, hundreds of Durban blacks joined the campaign of the Communist Party against the pass system. But in Durban the campaign ended in tragedy. During a meeting at which 4 000 passes had been collected for burning, a young communist speaker, Johannes Nkosi, and three other men were killed by the police. The affair ended with the arrest and trial of thirty members of the audience.

The Communist Party also recruited many members in Bloemfontein, Kroonstad, and Vereeniging, and its newspaper, *Umsebenzi*, made large sales. A worried editor of a Bloemfontein newspaper wrote:

'Communism has gained a firm foothold on hundreds of natives in the Bloemfontein location during the year and there is every reason to believe that the movement is spreading, particularly among the younger natives.'[102]

Albert Nzula's Tribute to Johannes Nkosi, 1930

'Comrade Nkosi joined the CPSA in 1926 whilst working as kitchen 'boy' in Johannesburg. His political career, however, began earlier . . . . As early as 1919 he was . . . engaged in the struggle being one of those who took part in the strike against the pass laws in that year. He also took part in the strikes led by the Red Trade Unions in Johannesburg.

At the beginning of 1929 he was appointed CP Organiser for Durban where he has since worked hard in pushing forward the cause of the African workers until he met his death at the hands of the brutal police thugs of Pirow and Hertzog on Dingaan's Day, 16th December 1930.

An uncompromising fighter, he died as he lived, fearless and conscious of the great fight in which he was engaged, as his final message, short but characteristic, shows. The message addressed, in Zulu: "To the Workers of South Africa: Never under the sun has a nation been so shackled with the chains of slavery. We are not even allowed to voice our opinion on the state of affairs of our Motherland. Why not awake and stand on our feet? Men, women and youngwomen, we must support organisations that *fight* for our freedom."

A thousand Africans must take the place of Nkosi. Let his cowardly murderers know that the African Giant is awakening and nothing will stop his progress.

Long live the name of Nkosi!
Long live a Free Africa!'

In the Transvaal towns, too, municipal authorities were resisted if they tried to interfere with people's informal methods of survival. The story of resistance in Potchefstroom on page 190 is an example of how protest could involve the whole community.

Protest against removals

Protest on the Rand became more determined during the removals of people from the slumyards into locations in the late 1930s. Many small local organisations sprang up.

For example, a Tenants' League was formed around 1936 by the coloured and Indian residents of Bertrams to fight eviction. In Ferreirastown, Ophirton, Newclare, and Vrededorp, as well as in Benoni, other tenants' organisations were formed. And in 1939, the Coloured Urban Tenants Association organised a rent strike by 400 people in Vrededorp because of shocking housing conditions there. The strike lasted for nine months. Another 30 families moved out of their homes to squat in the local church until the council provided good houses at reasonable rents.[103] The protests of these organisations received enough publicity to force the Johannesburg council to vote R8 000 to build more houses in Coronationville before they evicted people from Bertrams.

Organised protest

During the 1920s and 1930s, organised protest was uneven — it came and went. But with the sudden growth of the black working class during World War II, and as housing shortages, transport problems, and police harassment increased, protest was to become a way of life — in the towns it seemed as if just to survive was an act of resistance.

In the years that followed, black townspeople began to become more conscious of organised protest. Thousands joined the African National Congress, which was forced to change its nature and become an active, militant, mass organisation.

The ANC labour policy in the 1930s

Essentially, the ANC in the 1930s was liberal and anti-racist. Its means of achieving a non-racial society was to argue for a free market along with civil rights such as freedom of movement and expression for everyone. Its labour policy was explained by H Selby Msimang to the Native Economic Commission in March 1931 in the extract below.

Question: 'Supposing that you set up a furniture factory in the Transkei for the benefit of the Natives and that factory was able to produce for export outside the

Transkei, how would you meet European complaints if the Natives in the Transkei were not being paid the same wages approximately that the European manufacturer has to pay in a European area?'

Mr Msimang: 'The principle should be, sir, that if there is within the Union [of South Africa] a price or standard of wages fixed for factories in one area, it should apply to similar factories in all areas.'

'Has that assumption been discussed by the Congress?'

'Yes. I may say, sir, to be more emphatic, we should have a free labour market where each worker should be free to compete to the best of his ability and not be hampered or handicapped by a certain wage fixed at a standard of living, because we believe the standard of living would depend on his income . . . . If we accept the principle of equal work for equal wages, then I would say that I am against the fixing of wages, because the wages would determine themselves and naturally the employer would look for the best man to give him the best service.'

'What protection would you give to the unskilled worker . . . whose wages remain very low?'

'I would remove the pass laws, sir; . . . you would find that a Native, because he comes under the pass laws, has not got the freedom to bargain as best he can, because his time is limited, under the permit, to look for work; he is bound to accept whatever standard of wages is offered to him; but if the pass laws were removed, Natives would begin to say, "Well, I am not going to accept the standard of wages, and if this district is not going to pay more I will transfer to another district that will pay me a better price.'[104]

Changing Marriage and Family Patterns

Modikwe Dikobe's novel *The Marabi Dance* describes town life and some of the problems of mixed marriages in a Johannesburg yard of the 1930s.[105] The tension arising out of irregular unions is one of the themes in the book. Consider, for instance, the marriage of Mabongo, one of the main characters in the story. When he turned thirteen, Mabongo was initiated and became betrothed to his cousin Sarai:

'He went to work as a farm labourer and gave his first earnings to his aunt with instructions that part of it was to buy dresses for Sarai — "my young wife". But he did not marry Sarai. Anger and frustration struck brother and sister [his father and

aunt] when they heard years later that July, as Mabongo was called in the city, had taken a woman far away in the town and that they had had a child.

'"He has defied the gods of the Mabongos and he shall be rewarded for it!" Mabongo's father, a much feared witchdoctor, assured his sister Masekosana. "My father would have ended his life if he had dared defy his orders."

'"I have loved my nephew as much as my own son and wished him to inherit part of my wealth — cattle, goats, and my art in medicines," said Masekosana. "He has not only disappointed you, and the gods of our forefathers, but the whole tribe of the Ndebeles. Our father was a respected man. You are feared by Chief Thulare, the Great Chief of the Bapedis. They dare never refuse you a woman. But your own son has defied you. If you are my own father's and mother's child you will not allow him to enter your kraal."

'"He will not enter my kraal while I am still alive," the eldest Mabongo swore by the gods of Mathathakanye, the great-great grandfather of his father.'

The marriage of Mabongo thus cut him off from the ties of the land and his homestead, and he had to settle permanently in the town. Yet his breaking of tradition came back to haunt him. Years later he tried to arrange the marriage of his daughter to the nephew of Sarai, but he realised he would have to pay cattle to his aunt for compensation for having deserted Sarai so long ago. His own marriage had thrown away all tradition. His wife protested:

'"Today your people are ready to forgive you because you have a daughter who is old enough to be married. Ah! They think they can save *bogadi* [*lobola*]. Never! You have not paid even a fowl for me. Who are they to claim my daughter's *bogadi*?"'

In the town marriage of Mabongo and his wife, *lobola* had been disregarded, yet Mabongo longed to be accepted by his own people again and wanted a traditional marriage for his daughter.

Mrs Mabongo herself had lost many traditional customs through being a townswoman all her life. When Mabongo instructed his daughter, Martha (or Moipone), on how a woman should behave towards her man, Martha realised that she had not been brought up in the traditional way.

'Martha had [never seen her mother] doing such things as her father had mentioned. The day her father's cousin had paid a visit, she had seen her father blush when her mother pushed a plate in front of the visitor without going down on her knees, and after meals she did not bring water until Ndala began licking the food from his fingers.'

Mabongo himself is worried that Martha will not be able to adjust to a country marriage. Remembering

A wedding group.

how he disappointed his own father, he voices his fears to his cousin and wife:

'"Cousy, we cannot guarantee that our children will respect the wishes of their parents. They agree to parents' suggestions and then fail to carry them out. My daughter was born, and has been brought up, in town. She may well not agree with a man born and bred in the country."

'"Ntate Moipone," interjected his wife, "Moipone is a woman. She knows how to cook and she dresses like a woman. You want to spoil the marriage for my daughter!"

'"My wife, I am speaking of what happens to a girl who has grown up in the town and a young man who has grown up in the country. The town girl wants furniture, fancy dresses, nice shoes. They dislike the rough work which is done by country women and a country man does not understand the life of one who has to buy food, coal, and wood, and pay for the roof which he has to keep over his

family. He does not understand the life of the town man who has to work for the whole of his life without possessing anything: a house, goats, fowl or cattle. He must always be on the run to go and work. If he loses his work, his children will go without food and be chased out of the house. Moipone must understand that my cousin's son will not like to stay in town. He wants to see his cattle and when he has built up his first home he might like to take another wife."'

But the marriage does not come to pass. Visited by the relatives of the young man, Moipone refuses to marry her cousin. Her friend rebukes her:

'"Moipone, you have shocked these people. You say you don't know them. What they mean is: Do you love their boy; do you want to be married by him?"

'"I understand what they are saying. I told my mother that if they like him I can't stop them. But they can give him a woman they like, not me. I have chosen a man I like." Then she paused and lifted her hand to stop her friend from speaking: "Wait, I still want to tell you something. I don't want to put a load on a person who is not the owner."

'"What do you mean?"

'"You are a woman and I am woman. You don't like to say a man is the father of your child when you know that another man is the father. It will eat you and you will get thinner and thinner until everyone says: she has made a sin."

'"Do you mean to say you are in body?"

'"I am a woman. Why should I not get in body? Some girls smaller than me have children. I don't care if I get a child without a father. It is my child. God has willed that I should get it."

'"Moipone, you are a woman. A woman never likes to give someone a thing which does not belong to him. She is proud to say: my child's father, so and so. Who got you in body?"

'"Ag! He is just a Marabi boy. He has got a lot of girls. Plenty children. But I love him. He is clever, he is not a *skapie* like Sephai. I don't like farm boys. They work in the kitchens, take out night chamber pots for the white women and wash their bloomers."

Martha did not return to where the talk was held. She left for an unknown place:

'"Tell us what she said," Ma-Mapena asked the young woman.

'The young woman called her aside: "She is in body."

'Ma-Mapena threw up her hands: "It is finished! It will not help us to talk. She has been eaten by night animals. People of God, go back to your homes." 'They all understood. They felt relief after being kept in suspense. "*Senkganang se nthola morulo* – he who refuses me relieves me of a load." They consoled one another with such phrases as: "The gods have not liked."'

Moipone has disappointed her parents. Her father no longer has any hope of uniting with his family. He leaves to join the army in World War 2. Her mother begins to pine and sicken. One day, the ambulance stops outside the yard to collect Mrs Mabongo:

'Martha looked on as the white man, helped by Ma-Mapena, moved her mother from the bed to the van. Then she wept and wept until her heart felt like bursting: "How shall I live without a mother or a father? My father has gone to fight." She covered her face at the thought of soldiers killing one another. She had seen pictures of soldiers and had read about their killings. She had also sung at the Mendi Memorial Day: "*Ke bana bana ba tseteng metsa a matala, Bashoele bothle, Bashoetse Afrika, Bashoetse tokoloho* – They have crossed the blue sea, They died all, Died for Africa, Died for freedom".

'"My father has gone to fight for white people yet they still ask the people for passes. Look how that missus pays for this washing!" She opened her purse and threw a ten shilling [R1] note on the floor: "Washing and ironing – ten shillings!"

'Ma-Mabongo died in hospital a few days after being admitted. She died poor but she left a legacy for the white people – that her daughter remain a servant to them: a nanny, housekeeper, cook, even to the extent of opening and closing the gates for the master's car. She had cursed the "missus" as *le hulo* – stingy; *chobolo* – cheeky; but all the same she ironed the master's shirts to the best of her ability.

'"Sies, I iron her man's shirt nice. She sleeps and takes money for nothing. I am the wife and I get nothing."'

Two Women

Two South African women, one black, one white; both poor; both in the prime of their lives in the 1930s. They were strangers to one another, and the reader might expect that they had very different lives. Yet there are surprising similarities – as the following extracts from their life stories will show.

Childhood

In both cases their parents' separation changed their lives dramatically at an early age.

Epsie Zondo, born Ndaba in the Ermelo district in 1911, was the child of a farm worker.[106]

'My father worked on a farm. He had a few cattle and ploughed mealies and *mabela*. I never went to school. My eldest brother he go to school and he got lost till today. My father built the house we were living in. Of stones, and an iron roof. I was very small but my eldest sister was working on the farm and my brothers too.'

Then her father and mother were divorced, and her mother moved with her daughters to Pimville. There, Epsie had to help support her family.

Margaret Anderson was born Jennings in Johannesburg in December, 1908.[107] Her mother was the daugher of a German immigrant, her father an English miner, thirty years older than his wife and a heavy drinker. At an early age, her parents separated. Her father then took her to a farm in Sandown outside Johannesburg.

'Terrible big farm. My step-granny had fruit trees, flowers – carnations and all kinds of flowers and that. Once a week they had to pick and take to the market. The old market, the square.

'I was there nearly two years with Uncle Ned. Working there. I was treated like a servant. My Uncle Ned too. He used to help me. Well, he was working on the farm there. He used to go and steal the eggs and come and boil them in a tin [laughs]. For us to eat. We'd only have one meal a day. In the night when my grandfather come home.

'My mother struggled to find out where I was. For a whole year. And then she found out where I was and she said to me she's got work with an elderly couple. The man was pensioned off with phthisis and they were travelling with donkey wagons to Natal. I was about ten, eleven years old. Then she took me down with them.'

After the old man died of phthisis, Margaret's mother found work at Zebediela orange plantation, a government employment project for poor whites. There,

'She met up with my stepfather and he was a good man, and she married him.'

'Then he left there and we all came back to my aunt in Westdene. Then he got work on the mines in Roodepoort. And he got a mine house there and we shifted into the mine house. And that was where my mother died.'

Helping the family

Both took on responsibilities at an early age.

Epsie:

'I started to work in Johannesburg when I was about thirteen years old. My wages was twelve shillings, what you call today R1,20. A month. Some friends took me to the job [in Braamfontein], my mother's friend. I was very frightened. I used to run away and go home and they took me back to work again. I used to cry and run away and go back to Pimville and I came to my mother. I told a lie that the baby I looked after was dead so the madam said I must go home. I was telling a lie because I wanted to go home to my mother [laughs]. One day the madam took me to sleep under the kitchen table because I was frightened to sleep alone in the back room.

'I was looking after the baby and they used to teach me how to clean the house — must scrub and put polish. I didn't understand English, I didn't understand Afrikaans. The madam gave me a roasting fowl, they ate half and they said I must put it away. I sat down and ate it [laughs]. And so when the madam said, 'Epsie, where did you put that fowl?' I didn't know what she was saying. She showed me many ways until I understood and I showed her that I had eaten it. She wasn't cross. She just said "Shame!"'

Margaret:

'I went to standard four at school, in Braamfon-

tein . . . . My mother took me out of school to look after her . . . . I looked after my mother while my brother and sister went to school, you know. I couldn't go and play. It was not happy. I was with my mother and she was so ill. Died of cancer. Ill for nearly two years.

'And then my father came and fetched us back; the three of us. I wasn't full sixteen yet. I was keeping house for him and my sister and my brother. I saw them off to school and I did the cleaning up and the work in the house. And I cooked for him. I didn't stay there very long.'

Her father was living with a woman who ran a boarding house. Margaret was unhappy there and ran away to her mother's sister in Westdene. Mr Jennings applied for a court order to get his daughter back.

'The magistrate, he looked the case through and he said, no this child is right: you're not a fit father . . . . So they sent me to the industrial school in Standerton.

'I was put to work in the kitchen to cook for them, you know, because they found out I could cook and so on. And we went to the laundry and did washing. There was no servants then. And we had to clean our cottages up. But I was mainly in the kitchen; kept the kitchen clean. Three other girls and myself.'

'Then they put me out to work for Dr Timm, there in Modder B. I was happy there. Because I'd take the calls and go out with the doctor to see them. I used to go and help bandage the patients, the miners, when they got hurt. They had a baby two years old. I'd see to him. One pound ten [R3] a month.'

'Then my dad come and tell me that Mrs Miller [the lady with the boarding house] is gone and he wants me home again. Then he went to the lawyer and they got me home again. I was seventeen then.'

Marriage

Both women were disappointed in marriage — both husbands were unable or unwilling to be reliable breadwinners.

Margaret married about a year after her father fetched her back home:

'We were sitting playing cards, my sister, myself, her boyfriend and him, and my father come out and he says, "You're not going to make a knock-shop of my house. You either marry my girls or get out." So he, my old man [her husband] stood up and said, "Mr Jennings, I'll marry your daughter". That's how I got married. Known him six weeks. We were married for 46 years. He's dead now, this year, eleven years.

Boarding school for 'poor white' children.

'We got married on the 22nd December in 1927, and on Christmas Eve we went to town, to all the street things and that, and I didn't see him again until the New Year. He just disappeared in the crowd. Ja. Then my dad said to me, that man's no good to me, and I must leave him alone.

'Oh, he was a ladies' man. He disappears and then he comes back. And especially when I said to him, "You know Phil, I'm pregnant." Phew! Then he packs his bags and he's gone. Then he comes, the baby's eight months, ten months old, then he comes back again.'

So you really supported yourself?

'Ja, I always used to manage.'

Were you in love with him when you got married?

'I'm still in love with the man! He was a ladies' man, he really was a ladies' man. He was a handsome man, too.'

Her husband came and went. When she was pregnant with her sixth child, she was working in the factory.

'I told my old man. I said, "No, I can't go on like this. When I'm pregnant you leave me. You'd better stay away for good." Then he left me for five solid years. I heard every time, his friends come and tell me he's there with this woman, that woman.

I said, "Good luck to him. Just leave me alone." I'm working with all my children. I don't worry.

'He came back to me after the war broke out — 1939. A friend said to me — God rest her soul today, she's dead — "Andy, take him back, because he might go up north and he'll get killed and you'll get a war pension". But he didn't go up north on account of his left hand. He had no fingers, just stumps. He lost it in the mines.

'I had a terrible life with my old man. After the war he was working night shift, painting the roads for the municipality. He was very good to me the last thirty-two years, but it was too late to mend things. He bought me this outfit [kitchen table and chairs]. I don't want nothing to do with it. Don't want it. Then he gave it to my other daughter as a wedding present when she got married. I don't want it. I used my own stuff.'

Epsie:

'I married John Zondo, a Zulu. He used to work in the shop when we get married. He pay *lobola* to my brother.'

After she married she carried on working as a domestic and living in a backyard:

'I used to wash for the room. Madam say you must wash and iron but that means to say you pay for the room.

'The man who married me, I was pulling like an ox; no rest. Till this today, I'm pulling *hard*. I used

Returning the washing to the 'madams', 1937.

to do the washing and ironing for two madams a day to push this four daughters to school . . . . The father couldn't pay a farthing for these four daughters. He was working. He gave me nix.'

Several of Epsie's children died in infancy, but four daughters survived:

'Myself, I'm sick. I've been sick for four years. My husband, when he come from work he used to bath Janet, used to rinse napkins, because I was sick for four years. After that I start to feel better.

'And I was helping the man, he said I must help him. "After you help me, my wife, you'll sit down till this today."

'He used to wake me up in the morning for the bus. "Your bus will leave without you." I used to take a bus to Parkmore. There was only one bus in the morning and one bus five o'clock. If you lost this one, you won't go to work. He used to wake me and he used to stay at home. I must go to work. Oooh, I don't want to think about that man. Ja. [With a deep sigh].'

In the years that followed, Zondo became a builder. Epsie and Zondo bought and paid off a stand in Alexandra township. Together they built a house. After the birth of their third daughter they moved to 19th Avenue and built another house there.

'I used to carry water with my head, fill up four drums to make bricks, to build my house. And we built five rooms in 10th Avenue, five rooms in the back yard. I used to have four rooms for my house. My husband used to build. I used to be the dagha boy. Ja, haai, I used to be dagha boy. And after I've been dagha boy so long time and I didn't get a cent.'

She then described how Zondo secretly sold the property in 10th Avenue and bought a van.

'I said, "Where did you get such a lot of money to buy a little van? Why didn't you ask me, Zondo, so we should go together to town?"

'He said, "You've got nothing to do with it." He said, "My mother didn't ask my father a question, not *one* day."

'He buy a little lorry and he didn't build any more. He used to go and drink somewhere and sit on this lorry. Near the Indian shops here there was another place used to sell drinks — beers, brandy. He used to stay there. I used to do washing, washing, till I'm like this — can you see my hand [shows how her right hand is misshapen]? I've got a big lump here. I used to wash for two madams a day.

'He went up and down with this lorry. The lorry get broken when he was taking a trip to Tzaneen. He couldn't come back with this lorry, it's pieces there . . . . His heart is on the lorry. Went to all these lawyers. They can't lend us money any more. Try to lend money – no, couldn't get money. Got to sell this property again – this last property.

'Ja, if it's heaven, that man must wait for me till I come. Then we going to talk. And we'll talk [laughs]. We going to talk. He going to tell me why did he do this to me.'

Motherhood

Motherhood was a struggle for both women. Each had to give up her first-born to the care of others.

Margaret:

'I was nineteen when I had my first child. I had my three boys and a baby that died in between. He was eleven months old. He had septic enteritis [the cause of this illness, so common in black babies at the time, was probably malnutrition].

'Those days they couldn't cure it, but today they can, you see. I was working in the factory then.

'I had a little girl, the eldest one, but she was brought up by my aunt. It was necessary with the depression – 1932. She was premature. Those days they didn't have an incubator. We had to struggle through with her. Then I had the four boys, and the three after that again. Now six are alive. Two boys are gone.

DESPONDENT MOTHER: A human study from Zeerust.
NEERSLAGTIGE MOEDER: 'n Aandoenlike afbeelding uit Zeerust.

'In the factory, Mr Meyerson let the children sit in the factory there. Play around in the factory. But when I went to other factories I put the children in a crèche.

'I got my daughter back when she turned fifteen, you know. I didn't see much of her [while she was away] because [the aunt] told me she put the child into Pietermaritzburg Convent, which was a lie. She put her in Nazareth Home, because [the daughter] didn't want to listen. All the time she was in Nazareth House, just under my nose. [Then the aunt's] husband died and she couldn't keep her on. Well, when she got back she used to fight with her brothers, that's all I know. Wasn't used to other children, 'cause she'd been the only child there. I wanted to put her to school but they said, no. Then I put her in the factory. She was very good.

'I didn't see much of the children. When they were going to school, they'd come home, do their homework and tidy up a little bit, and then I'd come home. That was before I was catering. You know, when I was at Victoria Shirt I used to run home lunch times, and get the stove going, and then the children would put the meat on, and so on. They were good to me, the children.'

A working mother's struggle

Epsie had an even harder time with her first child:

'I had two babies before I was married. The father he run away. He was Levy Mbatha. Also a Zulu. He promised me that he is going to pay *lobola*, but hide away that he's got a wife, he's a married man. I was working in Malvern, Polly Street. So he leave me there.

'The baby was crying all the time, and the madam couldn't keep me. I can't cover the work, can't finish all my work. So I leave that work. I find the room, also in Malvern. The baby was *crying*. And then that madam also say she couldn't keep me, they can't sleep, the baby's crying the whole night and the room was near the house, you see. I leave that room because the madam couldn't sleep.

'She said, "Epsie my girl, I can't help it because the master's working and he can't sleep. He's going to work in the morning."

'So I try to find another room. The while I try to find another room, just can't find it easy. When the sun set where must I go to sleep with the baby? One day I climb on the tree with the baby, I tie the baby onto me with straps.'

After many hardships, Epsie decided to ask a relative to care for the child:

'I've no friends that time. Then until this baby grow big, I find this baby's auntie, that boy's sister [the

Child deaths

The most heartbreaking difference between the two women was the loss of baby after baby for Epsie — a tragedy common in the lives of so many black mothers in the towns. After Epsie won the court case to recover her child,

'I went to take the baby without nothing — no clothes, no blanket, nothing. I use a big scarf for a blanket. The baby was four years old then. She wasn't sick; a nice baby, fresh, very fresh. I took the baby. The baby stay with me six months then the baby start to be sick for *three months*, day and night. Like the baby was mad; used to torn her clothes and talk and say, "There's a snake! There's an aeroplane!" For three months.

'Till my husband [she was now married to John Zondo] he went to the father, he said, "Will you please come and see your daughter, she might rest after you been there." You see, sometimes it's something like that, she's waiting for her father to see her, or what. We don't know what we're doing. We went to call him and he didn't come. Then a couple of days and the baby passed away. She was five years and two months when she passed away.

'That time I had no money. My husband was sick. The baby was sick. I had a boy that time while Rita is sick. I had a little baby and he live only seven days; a nice, very big boy and he died when he was seven days old and Rita was still sick. And then we buried Rita. After two, three weeks she passed away.

'Before I was married I had two children — two girls. After I was married I had nine. Eleven children — only four alive. They all died. I had five boys and six girls, but seven died.

'I used to have baby and die, baby and die — all this. The time I came to Alexandra five babies died. Sometimes they used to stay two months, three months, they die. Until the one, seven days, my sister said I mustn't feed him with my breast because we want to find out what makes them die. And he died, the same.

'I remember myself with my little baby. If he's dead in my hands I just put him away one side because he's no more alive. No more babies now, he's gone. I had to bury all these babies. I didn't run away because it's my babies, what could I do? I've no mother, no aunties, nothing. I used to wash my baby and put him in the coffin myself. Ja. All my babies. I used to take my machine and sew whatever I want to cover the baby, sew it myself, wiping the tears and doing this job. Sew the nightdresses, that dress they put on the dead somebody.

'Then I take my machine away, I take water, I wash my baby nice, I put him in the coffin. There come the minister. He only come for open the Bible

sister of the father of the baby]. I ask her to take the baby because she wasn't working, she was staying in Germiston location. She take the baby. I start to think if I can get somebody to take the baby I can find work.

'One day I wanted to go and see the baby in Germiston. I find that they've been to church with this baby and baptise this baby with a new name; it's not my name. I cry then and I said, "Why didn't you baptise the baby with my name? You meant to say that you taking that baby, that I did give that baby for a present?" I was going to give her [the name of] Rita Ndaba. Rita was now Josephina, no more Rita. And she tell everybody in Germiston that she's got a baby from a rubbish girl — "she didn't know where to put the baby and she gave the baby to me for a present."

'I cry, I go back to work. She wouldn't give the baby to me. She say, "I won't give it to you. If you're taking this baby you're going to pay a lot of expenses."'

Eventually Epsie managed to recover her child after a court case, paying the lawyer with her sewing machine as a deposit.

. . . . Two babies is buried here in Alexandra, one is in Brixton, the first son; the first daughter is in Pimville; the second one is in Croesus [cemetery] . . . . At Croesus you only pass two graves and you find mine again.

Work

Both women struggled to make ends meet. They took in washing, sold liquor illegally to raise their children, and worked hard all their lives.

Epsie described her work as a domestic servant:

'Start half past six in the morning. We used to work all day. No day off. Lunch you eat it in the kitchen. Just when you finish eating you start the work. Finish at seven o'clock. You do the washing and ironing; there's no washing machine. No polishing machine. You scrub the floors and you come put the polish, rub it off again. Thursdays you do the windows, right around the house.'

After her first employer left Johannesburg, Epsie got a job in Jeppe.

'There I was clever. I was no more *mampara* [laughs]. I work long time there, two or three years for that madam. She was good for me. Afrikaans. Ooh, she's so good! When she's go out to bioscope or something like a party I must stay in. When she come she find me sleeping on the floor, she take a blanket. She says, "You mustn't go to the room, Epsie, you sleep here because you fast asleep. Sleep till tomorrow morning."

'When they were having dinner I used to have the same what they eat. She was paying me R3 a month. [When she was cooking] she used to call me to come and see. "Some time, Epsie, you'll cook — come and see what madam's doing." I used to peel. Whatever you want me to peel, I must peel.

'Once a week, Sunday afternoon, you get off — after they had lunch, wash the dishes, and then you can take the train and go home. Come in the morning, early. You see your mother only two, three hours. And you sleep and in the morning you get up, take the train out.'

After she married the hard work continued:

'Ooh, I was fighting for my four daughters . . . . Ja, I used to have a petticoat, you see, a mealie-meal bag. Ja. And even for my pantie, I cut that mealie-meal bag and make a pantie. Push my four daughters to school.

'In Kensington it was empty that time, no houses. I start to make beer there, African beer. I sell for the boys. One boy was jealous because I was selling a lot, you see. He used to come with other boys when they coming to drink at my home, see. And he get jealous and he call the police.

'And the madam didn't know, master didn't know, because Kensington used to be big houses, your room used to be far away from the big house. They didn't know I'm doing something like that, but the day he call the police then the police tell them.'

'"Did you know your girl is making *skokiaan* at this home?" "No, I didn't know."

'And that day I go away from Mrs de Kok.'

Epsie then became a laundrywoman:

'I used to wash there, at the madam's house. Sometimes *two* madams a day. I used to wash in Rosebank, take a bus to town. I used to have another washing in town.

'I've got no time to pray because I always think of my troubles at my back. At my home there's no mealie-meal. There's no coal to make fire, there's no 35 cents for bread, there's no blanket to cover myself and to cover my sons and daughters. The winter is in but I'm not ready [with] the blankets because I've no money to buy. Ja, I'm only thinking about what can help me. Nothing else. When I think to pray I always disappoint myself because I think, 'Oh, I've no coal at home and it's so cold. I have no mealie meal. What we going to eat and I've got no piece of meat."'

Surviving during the depression

The 1920s and 1930s were hard times for many un-skilled white women, too. Margaret described her working life:

'I used to go out and work. Wash and iron for other people. I'd take [my children] with. Put them in a pram – I had a pram given to me. Put Billy-boy into the pram, and Tommy and Brian used to walk with me. Go looking for washing and ironing . . . . Going from door to door . . . all over Jeppe and Fairview and Belgravia. Yes, I used to work there . . . . They're paying 2s.6d [25 cents] a week for a big bundle of washing like *that*. Washing and ironing. No wash machines; there were no bathrooms. Used to stand and wash in the yard with the bath on two blocks and wash there. Take me the whole day because it's cold water and blue soap. Then I got to go next day and do the ironing. They wouldn't let me into the house. I had to sit outside with the children. They bring me a mug of coffee and two slices of bread. Then I give it to the children – the two boys, because the other one I was breast-feeding.

'When I was washing and ironing during the Depression, I was even washing and ironing for a lady whose baby died. To get those clothes for my child.'

A new job

But after the Depression the manufacturing industry began to develop rapidly, and semi-skilled labour was needed in the growing clothing industry. One day, said Margaret,

'I went and knocked at the door in Hans Street and I heard this terrible noise inside and the man came to the door. He said, "Yes?" I said, "I'm looking for washing and ironing and cleaning the house." He said, "No, I've got a factory. I'm working. Can you sew?" I said, "Yes, I can sew. I make my children's clothes." And he looked at them and he said, "Come in". Then I went in. There were five girls at the machines. And I said, 'But I can't work these machines – electric – I'm used to the treadle." He says, "I'll show you."

'And I worked the double-needle machine while I worked there. Then he closed down and I went to the Union Clothing Factory. And they closed down. For three years I worked there. And then I went to Victorian Shirt here in Jules Street. I worked there for fourteen years . . . . The women working there were all white . . . . The native boys did the pressing.'

Although Margaret became a garment worker, she did not have a clear memory of her union. When asked, 'Did you ever get support or get involved in the unions?' she replied,

'I never worried . . . . They were mostly Afrikaans women . . . . No, I didn't worry with the union people, no.'

But later she said,

'I belonged to a union, the Garment . . . that's right. Solly Sachs was a marvellous man . . . . He used to come round to the factories . . . . We started off with 18 shillings a week. And of course every three months there was a 2s.6d. increase [25 cents].

'For 22 years I worked. Trousers. Ja. I put in the back pockets and made the pants and jackets and shirts. And I went catering at the same time over the weekends. Friday night, Saturdays, Sundays . . . Jewish parties, Jewish weddings, Jewish bar-mitzvahs. I spoke to one woman and she said she caters during the evenings. And then she said she'd take me along but I must say I am an ex-perienced waitress. Then after that I worked for about a year in the catering department. Then Mr Meritsky said, "I'll put you in the kitchen." I had to cook for 700 people. Fry the fish and fry the meat, you know.'

To supplement her income from the factories and catering work, Margaret also sold 'white' liquor to black customers.

'[When] I started [factory work] I had three boys already. Because my old man worked when he felt like it, and I had to jump out . . . . He was a miner . . . . if he felt like working, he worked, and if he didn't, he didn't work. That's how I struggled with my three boys.'

Phthisis

In Margaret's story miners' phthisis weaves itself in and out of her experiences. We have seen how her mother had found a job nursing a phthisis victim until he died. Her own father and her father-in-law both died of phthisis.

'Funny thing: when my old man [her father] was bedridden with phthisis and that, my husband went down to go to clean him, 'cause my step-mother didn't. She wouldn't be bothered with him. My old man went to clean him up three times a week . . . yes.'

Phthisis finished her husband too.

'My dad got him [her husband] a job on the mines, as a learner miner. He worked, off and on, nearly forty years underground. He died of phthisis in the General Hospital.'

Looking back

As old women looking back on their lives, the memories of both women were dominated by the hard, unremitting labour of their lives:

Looking back, when do you think was the happiest time in your life?

Margaret:

'Well, I don't think I had a happy time in my life at all. It was work and work all the time. At night when I came home from the factory I'd sit with the hand machine making extra shirts. My [son] Brian turned the handle and I'd sit and stitch the shirts for extra money. No, I got on all right with my children.'

Epsie:

'I always think I must stay in Church. I might have a rest somewhere because they say there's heaven where you get rest. Because here I didn't get rest. All of my life. No, I didn't have a rest in this country.

As well as the similarities in the lives of these two women, there are, of course, differences. Belonging as they did to different racial groups in South Africa, they did not have the same opportunities. Epsie was a black country girl who moved to town in her early teens, while Margaret was the child of white working-class parents. Epsie did not have the same access to medical attention for her children as a white woman. Her work as a black domestic brought in even lower wages than Margaret's job.

As a white, Margaret had more employment opportunities and eventually she was able to get a steady job as a factory worker by day, as well as a catering job by night and at weekends. Yet her story brings out very clearly the uncertain position of many whites in the 1930s (for Margaret Anderson was not an exceptional case). There was a time when whites, too, suffered from poverty and rejection – before state protection and the changing economy lifted them out of the unskilled working class. This is an aspect of South Africa's history which should not be forgotten or hidden away. The more we know about the working lives of all South Africans in past decades, the better we shall understand the struggle to create a just society which continues in the present.

Notes

1) In this chapter the word *culture* is used to describe a way of life consisting of everyday practices, customs, music, writings, attitudes, and behaviour towards other people.

2) Modikwe Dikobe, 'Class, Community and Conflict' – paper presented to the History Workshop, University of the Witwatersrand, February 1984.

3) T Couzens, 'Nobody's baby', in (ed.) B Bozzoli, *Labour, Townships and Protest* (Ravan Press, 1979), p.83.

4) E Hellman, *Rooiyard* (Johannesburg, 1934), p.13.

5) Cited by E Koch, 'Doornfontein and its African working class, 1914-1945: A study of popular culture in Johannesburg', MA thesis, University of the Witwatersrand, (1983), p.116.

6) As above.

7) Modikwe Dikobe, Unpublished Notes; also quoted by Koch.

8) P Mayer, *Black Villagers in an Industrial Society* (OUP, Cape Town, 1980), p.43.

9) Mayer, as above, p.43.

10) E Koch, as above, p.202.

11) Ed. E Hellman, *Handbook of Race Relations in South Africa* (SAIRR, Johannesburg, 1949).

12) As above, p.270.

13) These figures are drawn from information given in Hellman (ed.), *Handbook*, p.270.

14) E Hellman, *Rooiyard*, p.42.

15) Quoted in R Phillips, *The Bantu in the City* (The Lovedale Press, 1935), p.34.

16) Phillips, as above, pp.35-37.

17) Hellman, *Rooiyard*, p.23.

18) Hellman (ed.), *Handbook*, p.269.

19) E S Sachs, *Rebel's Daughter*(McGibbon and Kie, London, 1957), pp.46.

20) *Rand Daily Mail*, cited by *Garment Worker*, August 1938, p.4.

21) *Garment Worker*, as above.

22) Evidence to the Native Economic Commission by Dr A B Xuma, 1931, p.8.

23) See C van Onselen, 'Randlords and Rotgut', in *Studies in the Social and Economic History of the Witwatersrand 1886 – 1914, Vol I, New Babylon* (Ravan Press, Johannesburg, 1982).

24) Hellman, *Rooiyard*, p.49.

25) Quoted by Jon Qwelane in *The Star*, 18.11.82.

26) E Mphahlele, *Down Second Avenue* (Faber and Faber, London, Boston, 1959), p.43.

27) Quoted by Phillips, as above, p.203.

28) Evidence before the Native Commission, 1932. Quoted by Phillips, as above, p.207.

29) Quoted by Phillips, as above, p.204.

30) Phillips, as above, p.176.

31) Annual Report, Johannesburg City Council, 30 June 1937, p.248.

32) Report of Police Commission of Inquiry, UG No. 50, 1937, Para.275.

33) Memorandum of the National Advisory Board's Congress to the Conference of Reef Superintendents and Native Affairs Officials at Springs, February 1935.
at Springs, February 1935.

34) Quoted by Phillips, as above, p.201.

35) Phillips, as above, p.202.

36) Modikwe Dikobe, unpublished notes on working class life in Doornfontein in the 1920s and 1930s. I am very grateful to Mr Dikobe for permission to quote him and to Eddie Koch for showing me these notes.

37) 1938 Annual Report, Johannesburg City Council, p.237.

38) Hellman, (ed.), as above, pp.93, 306.

39) Quoted by Julian Cohen, 'Growing up in the Ghetto', p.19.

40) Hellman (ed.), as above, p.290.

41) Quoted in Hellman (ed.), p.296.

42) Phillips, as above, p.207.

43) Phillips, as above, p.208.

44) Annual Report of the Manager, Non-European Housing and Native Administration Department, 1939, p.255.

45) These comments are based on Chapter 1 of M Andersson, *Music in the Mix* (Ravan Press, Johannesburg, 1981).

46) Quoted by M Andersson, as above, p.23.

47) Quoted by D Coplan, 'The African performer and the Johannesburg entertainment industry: The struggle for African culture on the Witwatersrand', in ed. B Bozzoli, *Labour, Townships and Protest* (Ravan Press, Johannesburg, 1979).

48) Interviewed by Koch, 11.9.79., as above, p.112.

49) Koch, as above, p.113.

50) Tim Couzens, 'An introduction to the history of football in South Africa', in ed. B Bozzoli, *Town and Countryside in the Transvaal* (Ravan Press, Johannesburg, 1983), p.200. The description of the history of soccer given here is taken from Couzens's paper.

51) Dan Twala, quoted by Couzens, as above, pp.203-4.

52) Couzens, as above, p.204.

53) J Walvin, *The People's Game*, quoted by Couzens, as above, p.205.

54) Couzens, as above, p.207.

55) Petronella van Heerden, 'Waarom ek 'n sosialis is', *Klerewerker* September 1938, p.5. My translation.

56) O'Meara, *Volkskapitalisme* (Ravan Press, Johannesburg, 1983), p.82.

57) O'Meara, as above, p.25.

58) O'Meara, as above, p.26.

59) Hester Cornelius, 'Woon ons werkers in agterbuurtes en waarom?' *Klerewerker*, September 1938, p.3. My translation.

60) Carnegie Commission, *The Poor White Problem in South Africa* Vol. 1 (Pro-Ecclesia Drukkery, Stellenbosch, 1932), p.200.

61) Carnegie Commission, as above, p.194.

62) Cited by Elsabie Brink, 'Plays, poetry and production: The literature of garment workers', *South African Labour Bulletin*, Vol. 9, No. 8, July 1984.

63) Elsabe Brink, 'Maar 'n klomp "factory" meide', paper presented to the History Workshop, University of the Witwatersrand, February 1984, p.8.

64) Brink, as above, p.14.

65) O'Meara, as above, p.26.

66) Cited by Elsabe Brink, 'A passion for poetry: Artists and artisans', unpublished paper, p.12. My translation.

67) The Report of the Committee on Industrial Education (UG 9, 1917), cited by Robert H Davies, *Capital, State and White Labour in South Africa 1900 – 1960* (Humanities Press, 1979), p.237.

68) L Freed, *European Prostitution* (Juta, Johannesburg, 1949), p.52.

69) H Pollak, 'Women in Witwatersrand industries: An economic and sociological study', MA thesis, University of the Witwatersrand, 1932.

70) See Van Onselen, 'Prostitutes and Proletarians' in *Social and Economic History*.

71) Brink, 'Maar 'n klomp "factory" meide', p.21.

72) Hester Cornelius, 'Die lewe van 'n klerewerker', *Klerewerker* (November 1936), p.5. My translation.

73) *Klerewerker*, July/August, 1942. My translation.

74) The three main Dutch Reformed churches were the Nederduits Gereformeerde Kerk, the Gereformeerde Kerk and the Hervormde Kerk.

75) Cornelius, as above.

76) See C van Onselen, *Studies in the Social and Economic History of the Witwatersrand 1886 – 1914* Vols. 1 and 2 (Ravan Press, Johannesburg, 1982) for some discussion of Jews in early Johannesburg.

77) See Riva Krut, 'The making of a South African Jewish Community in Johannesburg 1886-1914' and E A Mantzaris, 'Radical community: The Yiddish speaking branch of the International Socialist League 1918-1920' in ed. B Bozzoli, *Class, Community and Conflict* (Ravan Press, Johannesburg, 1987).

78) Taffy Adler, 'Lithuanian diaspora: The Johannesburg Jewish Workers' Club' *Journal of Southern African Studies* 1 (October 1979),p.70.

79) Adler, as above, p.77.

80) Eddie Roux, *Rebel Pity* (Penguin Books, Harmondsworth, 1970) quoted by Adler, as above, p.85.

81) E Hellman, *Rooiyard*, Chapter 5.

82) Quoted by E Roux, *Time Longer than Rope* (University of Wisconsin Press, Wisconsin, 1964), p. 80.

83) B Sundkler, *Zulu Zion and some Swazi Zionists* (O.U.P., London, 1976), pp.23, 43, 61, 215, 321.

84) B Sundkler, *Bantu Prophets in South Africa* (O.U.P., London, 1961), p.198.

85) R Phillips, *The Bantu are Coming* (S.C.M. Press, London, 1930).

86) See Sundkler, as above, Chapter 1.

87) Cited by Sundkler, as above, p.311.

88) Cited by R Phillips, *The Bantu in the City*, p.267.

89) Sundkler, as above, pp.236-37.

90) J Cohen, 'Growing up in the ghetto: Working class youth in Benoni during the 1930s', paper presented to the Gubbins Society, University of the Witwatersrand, 31.3.1982, p.10.

91) For example, 62% of the children of Rooiyard women were living in the countryside. E Hellman, *Rooiyard*, p.14.

92) E Mphahlele, *Down Second Avenue* (Faber and Faber, London, 1959), pp.23-24.

93) E Mphahlele, as above, pp.23-24.

94) Hellman, *Rooiyard*, p.68.

95) See *The Marabi Dance* by Modikwe Dikobe and *Mine Boy* by Peter Abrahams.

96) E Mphahlele, as above, pp.37-38.

97) Interview with Dr Z Zampetakis, Johannesburg, 4.11.83.

98) H Bradford, 'Leadership, ideology and organisation', unpublished paper.

99) E Koch, as above.

100) See Seme's evidence to the Native Economic Commission, 1930-1932, p.7401.

101) Native Economic Commission, Minutes of the Evidence, Johannesburg, March 1931, pp.7403, 7412.

102) Quoted by E Koch, as above, p.169.

103) Most of the information in this paragraph is taken from E Koch's thesis as above, Chapter 6.

104) Native Economic Commission, as above, pp.7430-31.

105) Modikwe Dikobe, *Marabi Dance*, as above.

106) Interview with Epsie Zondo by Suzanne Gordon. See S Gordon, *A Talent for Tomorrow* (Ravan Press, Johannesburg, 1985).

107) Material taken from a series of interviews by Kathy Kirkwood, Johannesburg, August-December 1984. The interviewee's name has been changed.

Conclusion
Themes to Think About

This book has shown how working life changed for the millions of people who came to live on the Rand between 1886 and 1940. It was a dramatic change, for in only sixty years the Rand witnessed an industrialisation so rapid that it revolutionised the economy, the society and the very way of life of the working people of the Rand.

Sixty years is a short period of time in history — it is not easy to analyse accurately in that space of time the unfolding of events, or the significance of issues which are not yet settled. Nevertheless, this book has offered the following themes for the reader to consider.

The changing nature of work

Firstly, for millions of blacks and whites, the nature of production changed dramatically. Production based on the land, from which the family mainly benefited, changed to paid labour for the profit of others in industry.

This change was a revolutionary event for society in general, and for people's lives in particular; for the nature of production is very significant. Men and women have always had to *produce* in order to live — we have always had to produce food, clothing and shelter for survival and protection, and the way this is done helps to shape the kind of society we live in.

On the Rand, the nature of production affected the kinds of work done by different people. For example, changes in production in the factories altered the composition of the workers — in the earlier years, craftsmen, with control over their own tools, were the most productive workers. In later years, through new labour processes in the factories, goods were produced by semi-skilled women and men — at much lower wages.

The changing nature of production affected many other aspects of life, too. As we saw in Chapter 2, industrial society separated work and home. In fact, the Rand mine owners developed this separation to an extreme degree by establishing the migrant labour system, which separated workers from their families for long periods of time.

On the other hand, the requirements of other industries demanded different living conditions for workers – factories, for example, needed a stable supply of workers who could live cheaply with their families in town. Chapter 7 shows how 'locations' were eventually developed for a black urban working class. So the nature of production on the Rand – whether it was for the mines, for the factories or in the homes of whites, often influenced important factors such as where people worked, where and how they and their families lived, how they worked, for whom – and of course for what wages.

The changing composition of the working class

We have seen how some people arrived on the Rand as experienced workers. These were mostly skilled artisans, or craftsmen from already industrialised countries such as Britain. Most people, however, both black and white, had come straight from the land, with little or no experience of working for cash wages.

But even among inexperienced workers, there were differences. There were those who managed to avoid wage labour at first, and made an independent living. A few of these made enough money to enable their enterprises to grow; but in the end most self-employed workers succumbed to more powerful competition. If they were black, the state often combined with capital to destroy the independent working life they had made – the case of the *Amawasha* laundrymen in Chapter 2 is just one example.

We have also seen how different people entered the labour market at different times – if the land was more prosperous in one region, for example, those people would tend to prefer short migrant labour contracts to bringing their families to town. Not all people came to town at the same time, therefore. The timing of their arrival also affected to some extent their living and working situations.

We have already noted that in the early years on the mines, the few skilled workers were white and the mass of unskilled workers were black. But as trade, construction and manufacturing began to develop, new and different kinds of workers were required by the employers. In Chapter 5 we saw how employers were able to break the craftworkers' power over production by changing the labour process through deskilling. Employers introduced new ways of producing which cut down the need for skilled artisans, and increased the use of semi-skilled workers.

At first, this semi-skilled cheaper labour was drawn from the ranks of white women, mostly young Afrikaners fresh from the land. But gradually, as this book has shown, more and more black men were employed in factories (while most semi-skilled white men enjoyed the protection of the railways or other government industries, or the mines). By 1940, new changes were taking place. By then, more black men had entered the factories and would do so increasingly in the years of World War II, when many white men left to join the army. It was only in the 1950s that black women joined the industrial workforce in large numbers. By the 1960s, the bulk of the productive workers in South Africa were black.

A divided working class

While industrialisation created a class of workers, these workers came to be divided. We saw in Chapters 5 and 6 that divisions developed amongst workers according to how much control they had over production. The balance of power between employers and workers' organisations varied from sector to sector of the economy, and the size of workers' wages varied accordingly. This book has shown how division emerged:

- between the skilled and the unskilled (including the low-paid apprentices);
- between men and women;
- between black and white.

These divisions were exploited by the employers and the state to prevent workers from becoming too strong, expensive and disruptive of the production process.

But the story of exploitation is not always simple and straightforward. Deskilling, which eventually broke the influence of the craft worker, was to give a new kind of power to the new industrial workers – the power of numbers, and the possibility of strength through collective solidarity. The more the industries grew, the more workers were needed. But the greater the number of workers, the more workers were able to combine, to organise, and to unite in struggle against the exploitation of their labour. In the 1930s, the militant traditions of the craft unions and some industrial unions were still strong. While both white women and black men earned low wages doing similar jobs in the same factories, the possibility of united, non-racial worker resistance was real. It was only when the Nationalist Party government placed further restrictions on the trade union movement in the early 1950s that this possibility was finally sabotaged.

The colonial background

The features of the industrial revolution in South Africa can be seen in the histories of many other industrialised countries; how people lost the land for various reasons; how they had to turn to wage labour in order to survive; how badly the new workers were exploited, particularly the weakest (women and children in Britain, blacks and immigrants in the USA); and how, in time, the workers combined to develop their own organisations in order to strengthen their resistance to exploitation.

But the economic forces which triggered off the industrial revolution in *this* country must be seen against the background of colonialism. And to this day it remains an important debate as to what extent the history of colonialism deformed the development of capitalism in this country. To what extent did capitalists benefit from the colonial heritage of racism? Would racism have disappeared if it had interfered with production in the new capitalist society? These are questions which a study of past events can help us to answer.

South Africa's colonial past has also had a bearing on the role of the state. In Chapter 6 for example we saw how, after the shock of the 1922 strike, the state began to co-opt white workers by giving them protection through labour regulations, and also by providing welfare for the white poor. These racially defined privileges reinforced the racial divisions of work which had been established in parts of the country in the colonial, pre-industrial era, and developed with the gold and manufacturing industries. The state supported the system by allowing migrant labour to develop and by expanding the pass laws and other labour restrictions on blacks.

A racial form of capitalism

During the period up to 1940, it is possible to trace the growth of a system based on the ultra-exploitation of black labour. Over the years, a system was developed which enabled both the state and most employers to control this labour and keep it cheap.

- We have observed that the rural areas supplemented wages in the towns by supporting the aged and the sick and raising the children. All this was made possible by the migrant labour system, which kept down the wages and reduced for a while the number of black families settling in town.

- We have observed how the cost of reproduction of black workers in the towns was cut down by segregating black from white workers and providing very few services in the black living quarters. Chapter 7 has shown how cheap housing built by the municipalities was actually financed by black workers themselves through the beer halls. In these ways, both the state and employers saved on costs — cheap housing and the low standard of living meant that wages could be kept down to a minimum.

- But an organised system of control was needed to make sure that black townspeople would accept these harsh conditions. The 'locations' were supervised. Influx control was enforced to stem the labour flow to towns and direct it to areas of 'labour shortage', including the commercial farms. Political rights were denied, so that the state was not directly accountable to blacks for their policies.

- White workers, on the other hand, did have some political influence through the vote, and the Afrikaner nationalist movement did much to further the short-term interests of white workers. Furthermore, after the struggles of the 1920s and 1930s, their unions were recognised by employers, with the help of the state, as described in Chapter 6. Their unions benefited from the experience of craft unions, and immigrants from industrial countries. For white workers, conditions began to improve after the economy recovered from the Depression. The state (at the time of the Nationalist-Labour Pact government described in Chapter 5) also embarked on welfare programmes for whites.

Community responses

We have noted the importance of production in human society. Through production, human beings maintain themselves. Through *reproduction*, human beings renew themselves — they have children, raise them and train them until they are old enough to take care of themselves and perhaps their parents in their old age. Reproduction is as necessary for the survival of the human race as is production.

In industrial society, production takes place at the workplace, while the community is the sphere of reproduction. It is in the community that people live their daily lives, raise their children and develop a culture — that is, a way of life which will make sense of their day-to-day experiences.

The Rand towns were hostile to black settlers, as we have seen. But people had ways of coping with harsh and hostile conditions, and were constantly alert for ways of surviving:

- Chapters 6 and 8 described the development of *collective resistance* through unions, political parties and community action such as stayaways and boycotts. We have also seen how collective self-help through *stokvels* also became an important means of survival. For white workers, it was the collective struggle through the unions that achieved important concessions: for example, safety legislation was improved only after the militant Mineworkers Union went on strike in 1913.

- We have also seen how the *informal sector* activities of brewing, hawking and small trading — and in more desperate circumstances, prostitution and crime — earned people extra money.

Chapter 8 described how, out of all these experiences, an urban popular culture emerged; urban traditions began to form. And although these continued to change, slowly a way of life began to take shape.

Nationalism and class

During the period covered by this book two strong nationalist movements developed. 1912 saw the founding of the African National Congress, followed shortly afterwards by the Afrikaner

National Party. At that time, both Africans and Afrikaners were conquered peoples dispossessed of land, most of them poorly paid because they had had little training for industrial life. While many Afrikaners were resisting the control of British imperialism over the wealth and the political power of South Africa, black leaders were wanting to restore the land to blacks, and to unite them against the crude racial oppression that industrial life was continuing to impose on them. Slowly, industrialisation shifted the sites of struggle for blacks. In this period on the Rand, we see black resistance beginning to move from a struggle over land (see for example the policy of the ICU; the 1913 Land Act was also an important cause of the formation of the ANC) to a struggle for survival in the towns, for better wages, for housing, indeed for the right to remain in the city.

As industries developed, new groups emerged. The experiences of exploitation drew workers together, and we saw in Chapter 6 many examples of class struggle through trade union organisation. We saw, too, how at times class cut across national aspirations — how Afrikaner nationalists were very threatened by the unions of the women workers in the factories. They felt that people should regard themselves as Afrikaners first, workers second. There followed a battle for the hearts and minds of the Afrikaner workers that was to come to a head in 1948, when the Nationalist Party won the general election and was able to draw the bulk of Afrikaners under its sway.

For blacks, nationalism was in its early stages of organisation during the period up to 1940. Nevertheless, the rapid spread of the popular ICU movement which alarmed so many white employers (as described in Chapter 4) was also a foretaste of the excitement and the challenge of the mass movements of the ANC and the Pan Africanist Congress in the 1950s.

Never entirely absent from black national resistance was a consciousness of exploitation in the workplace. Although black industrial workers were too few and too easily replaced in those years, many were slowly establishing the trade union traditions which were to be developed in the 1950s by the South African Congress of Trade Unions (SACTU) and were to become a powerful force in the 1970s and 1980s. The precise relationship between national liberation and the trade union movement continues to remain an issue. How successfully the protagonists of class struggle and black nationalism will be able to combine their organisations remains to be seen.

The making of a working class

We have witnessed the creation of a black townspeople, whose lives changed vastly in both their working and living places. We have seen how this was an *on-going process* — that is, it did not end at any particular point, for it still continues in its formation. This process expressed itself in different political, social and economic movements, according to the experiences of different groups of people, the precise nature of their work, their position in society and the region in which they found themselves.

We have witnessed the birth of a working class on the Rand. During the past century the class of productive workers − that is to say the workers who produced the commodities that could be sold for profit − has changed. It changed from a small, immigrant group of skilled artisans who controlled their knowledge of production, to a much larger class of semi-skilled workers. This class included some white workers, many of whom were women as we have seen, but was increasingly made up of black men and women.

The story has not ended − it continues to unfold. To this day, the working class in South Africa − its needs, its aims, its hopes and its political expression − is still in the making. A study of history will enrich our understanding of a process and a struggle in which each of us has a part to play●

Acknowledgements: Photographs/Illustrations

Afrapix, Sandy Smit, page 9
Africana Museum JPL, pages 16, 25, 27, 33, 37, 38,
39, 40, 41, 43, 45, 49, 53, 60, 63, 65, 67, 68, 69, 74, 76,
82, 84, 91, 93, 94, 95, 96, 99, 122, 127, 169, 171, 175,
177, 178, 186, 187, 143, 147, 148, 152, 196, 201, 204,
210, 216, 217, 226, 244, 251
African Studies Institute Collection, pages 43, 54
Berlin Missionary Society Publications, pages 12, 13
Carnegie Commission, page 20
Church of the Province Archives, University of the
Witwatersrand, pages 83, 86, 113, 151, 164, 166, 205,
214, 238, 240
Mrs Bob Connolly, page 159
Kevin French, pages 20, 163
The Garment Worker/Die Klerewerker, page 147, 148,
150, 161, 193, 220, 222, 223, 225
Lou Haysom, page 99
E Hellman, pages 79, 173, 183, 189, 212, 214, 231,
250, 251
History of the 20th Century, Purnell, pages 106, 131,
132, 134
Industrial Development in South Africa 1904-05, pages
119, 125, 133, 135, 136, 141, 145, 146, 156, 162
Industrial Review, pages 139, 166
Eddie Koch, page 213
Libertas, pages 155, 166, 172, 176, 185, 187, 202, 203,
218, 219, 227, 228, 229, 235, 236, 249
Lovedale Press, pages 115, 238
Luckhart and Wall, *Organise or Starve*, page 151
W M MacMillan, *My South African Years*, pages 72,
173, 181, 182
McGregor Memorial Museum, Kimberley, pages 19,
211
Minutes of the Mayor, 1933-36, pages 43, 104, 178,
184, 186, 198, 205, 217, 229, 248
Beyers Naudé, page 126
SA Stage and Cinema, pages 79, 87, 91, 97
SA Review Pictorial, 1935-36, pages 35, 195, 207
SAR Magazine, 1905-36, pages 15, 17, 18, 19, 24, 29,
34, 40, 41, 45, 46, 48, 50, 51, 52, 61, 67, 73, 87, 88, 99,
100, 101, 102, 104, 108, 114, 118, 120, 121, 122, 123,
128, 129, 130, 132, 137, 140, 146, 154, 157, 170, 174,
193, 194, 195, 196, 199, 201, 231, 233, 237, 241
SAIRR collection, page 92
I Schapera, *Western Civilisation and the Native Tribes
of South Africa*, pages 21, 31, 64, 189
B Shepherd, *African Contrasts*, pages 13, 14, 30, 179
T D Mweli Skota, *The African Who's Who* and
African Yearly Register, pages 90, 112, 167, 190, 239
Star Barnett Collection, pages 41, 46/7, 61, 105
Star Weekly Illustrated, 1903-13, pages 20, 28, 40, 41,
42, 59, 64, 70, 71, 76, 78, 85, 89, 98, 117, 221, 247
Susie Strachan, page 57
Transvaal Weekly Illustrated, page 54
Unisa Photographic Library, pages 108, 109, 110, 111,
115
Walker and Weinbren, *2 000 Casualties*, page 100

The remaining illustrations are from the author's
private collection. Thanks also to Lesley Lawson, who
generously shared some of her photographic 'finds'
with me, and to Stephen Rothenburg for his drawings.